ESSAYS
Old and New

EDITED BY
ROBERT U. JAMESON
The Haverford School
Haverford, Pennsylvania

THIRD EDITION

Harcourt, Brace & World, Inc.
NEW YORK · CHICAGO · ATLANTA
DALLAS   BURLINGAME

COPYRIGHTS AND ACKNOWLEDGMENTS

The author thanks the following publishers and copyright holders for their permission to use the selections reprinted in this book:

The Bobbs Merrill Company, Inc., for " Grandeurs and Miseries of Old **Age** " from *But We Were Born Free*, by Elmer Davis, copyright, 1954.

The Curtis Publishing Company, for permission to reprint " On Discovering **the** United States " by Alistair Cooke, from *Holiday* magazine, copyright, 1953, by the Curtis Publishing Company.

Dodd, Mead & Company, for " On Lying in Bed " from *Tremendous Trifles* by G. K. Chesterton, copyright, 1909, by Dodd, Mead & Company ; renewal copyright, 1936, by Frances Chesterton. Canadian rights granted by A. P. Watt and Son, Methuen and Co., and Miss D. E. Collins, executrix of the author's estate. For " A, B, and C — The Human Element in Mathematics " from *Literary Lapses* by Stephen Leacock.

Doubleday & Company, Inc., for " I Entertain an Agent Unawares " from *Adventures in Contentment*, by David Grayson, copyright, 1907, by Doubleday & Company, Inc.

E. P. Dutton & Co., Inc., for " The Death of an Old Dog " from *Far Away and Long Ago*, by William H. Hudson, copyright, 1918, by E. P. Dutton & Co., Inc. renewed, 1946, by the Royal Society for the Protection of Birds.

Harcourt, Brace and Company. Inc., for " The Fifty-first Dragon " from *Seeing Things at Night*, by Heywood Broun, copyright, 1921, by Harcourt, Brace and Company, Inc. ; renewed, 1949, by Heywood Hale Broun and Constance Broun. For " A Lincoln Preface," copyright, 1953, by Carl Sandburg. For " Tolerance " and " Julius Caesar " from *Two Cheers for Democracy*, copyright, 1951, by E. M. Forster.

Harper and Brothers, for " Walden " from *One Man's Meat* by E. B. White, copyright, 1939, by E. B. White. For " Getting Ready for a Cow " from *One Man's Meat* by E. B. White, copyright, 1942, by E. B. White. For " The Tooth, the Whole Tooth, and Nothing but the Tooth " from *Inside Benchley* by Robert Benchley, copyright, 1922, by Harper Brothers; copyright, 1950, by Gertrude Benchley. For " The Literary Offenses of Fenimore Cooper " from *In Defense of Harriet Shelley* by Mark Twain.

Houghton, Mifflin Company for " Eastern White Oak " from *A Natural History of Trees* by Donald Culross Peattie. For " A Kitten " from *In the Dozy Hours* by Agnes Repplier.

Helen Keller and the *Altantic Monthly* for " Three Days to See."

Alfred A. Knopf, Inc., for " The Noblest Instrument " from *Life with Father* by Clarence Day, copyright, 1924, 1935, by Clarence Day.

J. B. Lippincott Company, for " On Unanswering Letters " from *Mince Pie* by Christopher Morley, copyright. 1919, 1947, by Christopher Morley.

Walter Lippmann and the *Atlantic Monthly*, for " The Rivalry of Nations," copyright, 1948, by Walter Lippmann.

Little, Brown and Company, for " A Garland of Ibids for Van Wyck Brooks " from *A Rock in Every Snowball* by Frank Sullivan, copyright, 1946, by Frank Sullivan.

The Macmillan Company, for " The First Citizens of the Atomic Age " from *Who Speaks for Man* by Norman Cousins, copyright, 1953.

William Morris Agency and the *Atlantic Monthly*, for " Tenants of the House," copyright, 1948, by Josephine W. Johnson.

The *New Yorker* Magazine, for " The Night the Bed Fell " and " The Macbeth Murder Mystery " by James Thurber, copyright, 1933 and 1937, the *New Yorker* Magazine, Inc.

The Oxford University Press, for " The Long Snowfall " from *The Sea Around Us*, by Rachel Carson, copyright, 1950, 1951, by Rachel Carson.

G. P. Putnam's Sons, for " Jungle Sluggard " from *Jungle Days* by William Beebe, copyright, 1925.

Random House, Inc., for " Nobel Prize Acceptance Speech " by William Faulkner.

Charles Scribner's Sons, for " Holiday " from *A Commentary* by John Galsworthy. Canadian rights granted by William Heinemann, Ltd. For " Harrow " from *A Roving Commission* by Sir Winston Churchill, copyright, 1930, by Charles Scribner's Sons. Canadian rights granted by Odhams Press, Ltd. (Publshed in England as *My Early Life*.)

W. L. White for " Mary White " by William Allen White.

CONTENTS

iii

FOREWORD

    This book is a revision of an essay anthology which first appeared in 1926 and was revised in 1934. I have attempted to bring the book up to date by including writers who have made their reputations during the last twenty years. Choice of the material has not always been easy. However, one criterion has been paramount: the high literary quality of the essays. In this, Miss Chamberlain, the original editor of the book, established a wise precedent.

The chronological arrangement of the essays is used for convenience only. I do not suggest that this book be used as the basis for a course in the history of the essay. Indeed, no literary type lends itself less to the historical approach, at least in the secondary school, than this one. On pages 421–25 will be found groupings of the essays according to types and according to main themes for teachers who wish to use the material in these ways. The composition topics given at the end of each essay are by no means to be followed to the letter. I hope that they may be adapted to suit the needs of the students who study the book.

Whenever it has been possible, I have included two or more essays with approximately the same theme or at least with similar points of view. I hope that one of the virtues of the book will be the opportunity it affords for the student to compare two or more related ideas on the same topic.

I should like to state my indebtedness to certain people for their assistance in the organization of this book: to many colleagues in several schools, public and private, who have given me suggestions concerning what to include in the volume; to Mr. Paul Chancellor and Mr. Edwin Bowers, of the Hill School, Pottstown, Pa., for their invaluable aid in the preparation of the manuscript; to Mr. Paul Evans, my colleague at the Haverford School, for reading the book in proof; to Mrs. Elizabeth Hyland, of the Haverford School library, for assembling a large part of the reading list; and to my wife, who has listened very patiently to more problems about the assembling of an anthology than she has cared to — who, like the wedding guest, as Coleridge put it, could not choose but hear.

R. U. J.

Haverford, Pa.
October, 1954

INTRODUCTION

       Proteus was only a minor deity in Greek mythology, but in battle he was a champion. He was a prophet who did not like to prophesy although he knew everything about the past, present, and future. Anyone who wished information from Proteus had to surprise him in his cave and bind him. But getting the better of Proteus was not easy, even though he was old and looked frail, for he had the power to change himself into anything he chose. Just when someone thought he had whipped Proteus, that someone would find himself trying for a toe-hold on a whale, or throwing a roundhouse punch at a raging flood, or confronting a charging bull; and while fleeing the bull, in turn, he might find that the bull had become a lovely, flower-filled meadow under his feet. No one ever succeeded in pinning Proteus's shoulders to the ground. He always slipped safely away in another form.

Anyone who tries to pin down the essay with a definition is tackling a Proteus, and he has no more chance of success than Proteus's opponents had. The essay does not change under one's hands, but it has so many forms that it is impossible to squeeze all of them into a single definition. Its variety is infinite. It is amazingly plastic, and each age has molded it into the form most pleasant or useful to that age.

Just the same, if we are to discuss the essay, we must have some idea of what it is, and though we cannot provide a complete definition, we can generalize about it. Almost anyone can immediately think of exceptions to our generalizations, but for the present they will serve our purpose.

Let us say then that the essay is a short piece of prose, seldom longer than five or six thousand words, devoted to the expression and development of an idea, sometimes formal, sometimes informal, sometimes abstract, sometimes factual, but at its best distinguished by a superior literary style.

In one form or another, the essay is very old. While we do not know how the first essays came to be written or who wrote them, we do know that the essay is as old as civilization. In Biblical times the form of the essay was not established; each writer used the form best suited to his purpose. The Book of Proverbs is a collection of gnomic essays — that is, essays made up of a series of related maxims or wise sayings. Prophets such as Hosea, Amos, Isaiah, and Nehemiah wrote philosophical essays about man's conduct and his relationship to God.

In the New Testament we find essays in other forms. St. Paul's epistles are essays except in name; indeed, some critics speak of them as epistolary essays — essays written as letters. Most of the parables of Jesus are essays too, though again the form is different. He told a story, not for the sake of the story, but to give an idea significance, to dramatize it, and to make it understandable to those of little understanding. The story of the prodigal son is so movingly told that we are not likely to forget the idea it dramatizes.

The ancient Greeks embodied their thoughts in various short prose forms. Plato recorded his philosophical ideas in dialogues, or essays in the form of conversations. Aristotle, a philosopher who tutored Alexander the Great, wrote scientific essays similar to those Tyndall and Huxley were to write in the nineteenth century. Plutarch wrote biographical essays not unlike those we find in the best periodicals and books today. The most famous Roman essayists — Cicero, Seneca, and Lucan — wrote essays on social problems, politics, and philosophy. In one form or another the tradition of the essay continued down through the great revival of learning and culture called the Renaissance; and during this era lived the father of the modern essay, Michel Eyquem Montaigne.

Montaigne (1533–1592) was a lawyer who retired at thirty-eight to his estates, where he could read and think. He wished to get his ideas down on paper, so he began to write *leçons morales* — literally moral lessons, a popular contemporary French prose form. Like the proverbs, they were maxims — wise sayings pithily expressed. Montaigne, however, wished to express himself more fully than the *leçons* would permit, and began writing more lengthy prose pieces.

While Montaigne did not invent the essay, it can be said that he did create the personal essay, because no one before him had written so charmingly or with such intimacy and ease. For obvious reasons the personal essay is also called the informal or familiar essay. Of all essays, it is perhaps the type most loved. The essay acquired its name in 1580 when Montaigne published his short pieces and called them *Essais* — that is, trials or attempts. The *essai*, as Montaigne created it, was a brief, not an exhaustive, treatment of an idea.

Seventeen years after the appearance of Montaigne's book, Francis Bacon, Elizabethan scholar and statesman, published ten gnomic pieces similar to Montaigne's and called them *Essayes*. (We have now dropped the final *e* and almost forgotten the original meaning, but the word is still with us.)

The King James version of the Bible was translated by scholarly contemporaries of Bacon's; passages from the Book of Proverbs bear a remarkable resemblance to Bacon's essays. Here, for example, are two selections; the first is from the Proverbs, and the second from Bacon's essay " Of Studies." The resemblance is at once apparent — in the balanced sentence, in the diction, and in the mode of expression.

Proverbs:

> Happy is the man that findeth wisdom, and the man that getteth understanding. For the merchandise of it is better than the merchandise of silver, and the gain thereof than fine gold. She is more precious than rubies: and all the things thou canst desire are not to be compared unto her. Length of days is in her right hand; and in her left hand riches and honor. Her ways are ways of pleasantness, and all her paths are peace. She is a tree of life to them that lay hold upon her: and happy is everyone that retaineth her.

Bacon's " Of Studies ":

> Studies serve for delight, for ornament, and for ability. Their chief use for delight is in privateness and retiring; for ornament, is in discourse; and for ability, is in the judgment and disposition of business. . . . To spend too much time in studies is sloth; to use them too much for ornament is affectation; to make judgment wholly by their rules is the humor of a scholar. They perfect nature, and are perfected by experience.

Later, Bacon had Montaigne's experience; the gnomic essay no longer answered his needs. Hence, he too turned to the longer essay. To us his later essays seem more " modern," because they are approximately the same length as contemporary essays.

Although Montaigne's and Bacon's essays were collected and published in books, a book was not to remain a home for the essay. The essay needed its own medium just as the drama needed a stage. The proper medium for the essay in the eighteenth century proved to be the newspaper.

At the beginning of the eighteenth century the " journals," as newspapers were then called, began to appear in London. The *Tatler* was founded by Richard Steele in 1709, and when it failed in 1711, Steele joined Joseph Addison and published the *Spectator* (1711–1714). Steele and Addison hold a unique place in the history of the English essay. They perfected the familiar essay, making it light, graceful, and amusing. Not the least of their achievements was giving to English literature one of its most attractive characters, Sir Roger de Coverley.

The eighteenth-century newspapers, or journals, increased the popularity of the essay, but the essay remained relatively brief because space was still limited. The weekly *Tatler* and *Spectator* were only a single sheet printed on both sides, containing one essay and a few advertisements. As a result, Addison's and Steele's essays were but one thousand to fifteen hundred words long, no longer than themes sometimes written by high school students. Essayists needed yet another medium which would provide them with space to express their ideas more fully.

The political magazine, the forerunner of the modern magazine, gave the essayists this additional space. In 1802, the *Edinburgh Review* was founded to advance the fortunes of the Whig political party. Seven years later the Tories founded the *Quarterly Review* for their own political advantage. Both reviews had space for something other than politics, and the essayists rapidly utilized that space for their own ends. They now had two things essential to them: an interested audience and adequate room in which to develop their thoughts.

What is more, toward the end of the eighteenth century a new kind of interest began to develop: interest in man, in nature, and in many subjects which earlier writers had considered trivial. Essayists like Charles Lamb, William Hazlitt, and Thomas De Quincey took up these new interests and led the way in the "Romantic Movement," as this literary age is called. In the middle and latter part of the nineteenth century — the Victorian Age — the essay continued to flourish in the writings of Thomas Carlisle, John Stuart Mill, Matthew Arnold, and Walter Pater, among others.

The twentieth century has added such forms as the story-essay, like " The Fifty-first Dragon," and the journalistic article, but both of these have their roots in the traditions of the past. New methods of writing have not been invented, but old forms have been adapted to fit new ideas and new societies. This is as true in the history of literature as it is in the history of music or painting. Beethoven, for example, built his music on the music of Mozart, as E. B. White built his writings on the writings of Thoreau.

It is difficult to classify all essays narrowly according to type. Nevertheless, a few arbitrary categories may be helpful. The reader must understand, however, that one essay may have the characteristics of more than one type. Professor Henry Beers of Yale is reported to have said, " The essay is everything that any other kind of literature is not." When we take into consideration all the different kinds of essays that have been written, it seems almost as if we had to agree with him.

Broadly, all essays are either formal or informal. Whether an essay is formal or informal depends upon the spirit in which it is written. The informal essay is written in a familiar style, and the author's purpose is primarily to entertain the reader. Robert Benchley's " The Tooth, the Whole Tooth, and Nothing but the Tooth " is an excellent example of the informal essay. The formal essay, on the other hand, appeals primarily to the reader's intelligence. Walter Lippmann's " The Rivalry of Nations " is an outstanding example of the formal essay.

There are other ways of characterizing the essay. The following groups are not intended to be exhaustive, but the reader should be aware of the characteristics of each group.

A *descriptive* essay presents a subject as seen through the eyes of a gifted observer. Essays by Rachel Carson, William Beebe, and Alistair Cooke in this volume are examples of this type.

A *character* sketch defines itself and is represented in this book by William Allen White and Clarence Day, Jr.

A *critical* essay usually deals with a work of art — and, like the character sketch, it too defines itself. Mark Twain's essay on Cooper and Frank Sullivan's piece on Van Wyck Brooks are critical essays. The book, play, movie, or concert review found in everyday magazines and newspapers are also critical essays.

A *reflective* essay is concerned with a moral or philosophical problem. It is generally profound, and, as in the case of Emerson's " Self-Reliance," demands careful reading

Today we may be liberal enough to classify newspaper " columns," even sports columns, as essays. Many editorials and the articles of such writers as the Alsop brothers are essays, sometimes very fine ones. John Kieran a few years ago wrote essays on sports for the New York *Times;* Red Smith now writes them for the New York *Herald Tribune.* Mr. Kieran and Mr. Smith may write about a horse race or a baseball game, but whatever the subject, their style is likely to arouse the admiration of everyone — even literary critics.

But to return again to our original " working definition." " The essay is a short piece of prose, seldom longer than five or six thousand words, usually devoted to the expression and development of an idea, sometimes formal, sometimes informal, sometimes abstract, sometimes factual, and at its best distinguished by a superior literary style."

That definition, as the reader must realize by now, is not wholly sufficient. But one thing can be said with assurance — one thing is completely true: good essays are good reading. The essays in this book are good reading.

MICHEL EYQUEM DE MONTAIGNE,
1533–1592

Montaigne, the Frenchman who is called the "father of the essay," was the son of a wealthy and influential man, a nobleman and the mayor of Bordeaux. A German servant taught him to speak Latin before he learned French, and he was well versed in philosophy, science, and law. He was a courtier in the palace of Henry II and was granted the title of Seigneur (Lord) by the monarch. But at the age of thirty-eight, "weary," as he wrote, "of court employments and public honors," he withdrew "entirely into the converse of the learned virgins where he intended to spend the remaining moiety of the time allotted to him in tranquil seclusion."

Although he emerged from this retirement after ten years and went on to a career in public life, the seclusion made possible the writing of his essays, which appeared in 1580.

It was Montaigne who decided that the essay should be brief. It was he who first showed the enormous range of the essay. A glance at his subjects shows this range: "Of Cannibals," "Of Names," "Of Smells," "Of Sleeping." The last, reprinted here, is somewhat shorter than most of his other writings, but it fits his own description of the way he wrote.

To the modern reader, Montaigne's style is somewhat difficult because it is so full of allusions to Greek and Roman history. But Greece and Rome were probably more familiar to him than the War between the States is to the average American. Thus an essay like "Of Sleeping" was, to Montaigne, informal and conversational in tone. And the ideas are certainly clear enough: a description of great men to whom sleep came easily.

OF SLEEPING

Reason directs that we should always go the same way, but not always at the same pace. And, consequently, though a wise man ought not so much to give the reins to human passions as to let him deviate from the right path, he may, notwithstanding, without prejudice to his duty, leave it to them to hasten or to slacken his speed, and not fix himself like a motionless and insensible Colossus. Could virtue itself put on flesh and blood, I believe the pulse would beat faster going on to an assault than in going to dinner: that is to say, there is a necessity she should heat and be moved upon this account. I have taken notice, as of an extraordinary thing, of some great men, who in the highest enterprises and most important affairs have kept themselves in so settled and serene a calm, as not at all to break their sleep. Alexander the Great, on the day assigned for that furious battle betwixt him and Darius, slept so profoundly and so long in the morning, that Parmenio was forced to enter his chamber, and coming to his bedside, to call him several times by his name, the time to go to fight compelling him so to do. The Emperor Otho, having put on a resolution to kill himself that night, after having settled his domestic affairs, divided his money amongst his servants, and set a good edge upon a sword he had made choice of for the purpose, and now staying only to be satisfied whether all his friends had retired in safety, he fell into so sound a sleep that the gentlemen of his chamber heard him snore. The death of this emperor has in it circumstances parallelling that of the great Cato, and particularly this just related: for Cato being ready to despatch himself, whilst he only stayed his hand in expectation of the return of a messenger he had sent to bring him news whether the senators he had sent away were put out from the port of Utica, he fell into so sound a sleep, that they heard him snore in the next room; and the man, whom he had sent to the port, having awakened him to let him know that the tempestuous weather had hindered the senators from putting to sea, he despatched away another messenger, and composing again himself in the bed, settled to sleep, and slept till by the return of the last messenger he had certain intelligence they were gone. We may here further compare him with Alexander in the great and dangerous storm that threatened him by the sedition of the tribune Metellus who, attempting to publish a decree for the calling in of Pompey with his army into the city, at the time of Catiline's conspiracy, was only and that stoutly opposed by Cato, so that very sharp language and bitter menaces passed betwixt them in the senate about that affair; but it was the next day, in the forenoon, that the controversy was to be decided; where Metellus, besides the favor of the people, and of Caesar — at that time of Pompey's faction — was to appear accompanied with a rabble of slaves and gladiators; and Cato only fortified with his own courage and constancy; so that his relations, domestics, and many virtuous people of his friends were in great apprehensions for him; and to that degree, that some there were who passed over the whole night without sleep, eating, or drinking, for the danger they saw him running into; his wife and sisters did nothing but weep and torment themselves in his house; whereas he, on the contrary, comforted every one, and after having supped after his usual manner, went to bed, and slept profoundly till morning, when one of his fellow-tribunes roused him to go to the encounter. The knowledge we have of the greatness of this man's courage by the rest of his life, may warrant us certainly to judge that his indifference proceeded from a soul so much elevated above such accidents, that he disdained to let it take any more hold of his fancy than any ordinary incident.

In the naval engagement that Augustus won of Sextus Pompeius in Sicily, just as they were to begin the fight, he was so fast asleep that his friends were compelled to wake him to give the signal of battle: and this was it that gave Mark Antony afterwards occasion to reproach him that he had not the courage so much as with open eyes to behold the order of his own squadrons, and not to have dared to present himself before the soldiers, till first Agrippa had brought him news of the victory obtained. But as to the young Marius, who did much worse (for the day of his last battle against Sylla, after he had marshalled his army and given the word and signal of battle, he laid him down under the shade of a tree to repose himself, and fell so fast asleep that the rout and flight of his men could hardly waken him, he having seen nothing of the fight), he is said to have been at that time so extremely spent and worn out with labor and want of sleep, that nature could hold out no longer. Now, upon what has been said, the physicians may determine whether sleep be so necessary that our lives depend upon it: for we read that King Perseus of Macedon, being prisoner at Rome, was killed by being kept from sleep; but Pliny instances such as have lived long without sleep. Herodotus speaks of nations where the men sleep and wake by half-years. And they who write the life of the sage Epimenides, affirm that he slept seven-and-fifty years together.

STUDYING THE ESSAY

1. Discuss the paragraphing in Montaigne's essay.
2. Can you find a single central thought in this essay?
3. Montaigne said that the essay should resemble conversation. Does he practice what he preached?
4. After you have read Bacon's essay " Of Friendship," compare its literary and historical allusions with the ones in this essay.

COMPOSITION TOPICS

1. Of Sleeping in the Study Hall
2. Try to write a short essay, in Montaigne's style, about a similar subject well known to you: dozing in the library, reading comic books, or sitting in a canoe, for example. Use all the history and mythology you can.

FRANCIS BACON, 1561–1626

        The Elizabethan Age in England was the Renaissance — the Rebirth of Learning — in that country. Elizabeth I ascended the throne in 1558 and died in 1603, but the cultural revival which began shortly after she became queen did not slow down until after the death in 1625 of her successor, James I, the first Stuart king. This was an age of geniuses: the age of Shakespeare, Marlowe, Spencer, Raleigh, Drake — and Bacon.

    It was an exciting age. England rose, in a few years, from the position of a third-rate nation, behind Spain and France, to that of the world's greatest sea power. Drake and his "sea dogs," aided by a strong wind and some poor Spanish navigation, wiped out the Spanish Armada, the greatest fleet the world had ever seen. Hudson had established English claims to North America, and Raleigh and then the Pilgrims and Puritans sailed to establish colonies in the New World. In those days men were not content to center their interests on one goal. They tried everything. Sir Walter Raleigh was a soldier, an explorer, and a courtier; but while he was in prison he was also a poet and the author of a history of the world. Shakespeare was an actor, a playright, a poet, and, if we believe some authorities, a successful dealer in real estate. It must have been a fascinating age in which to live.

    In many ways Francis Bacon epitomizes this age. The son of a nobleman, he studied at Cambridge University between the ages of twelve and fourteen, went to France as an aide to the ambassador at the age of fifteen, became a lawyer at twenty-one, and entered Parliament at twenty-three. Later he was Attorney General, Lord Keeper of the Privy Seal, and Lord Chancellor. To his great discredit, he accepted some bribes while he was

Lord Chancellor, confessed his guilt, was fined 40,000 pounds and imprisoned in the Tower of London for a few days.

All of this would seem enough to crowd into one man's life. But it was not so with Bacon. He also wrote books of essays, for which he is best known today, and other important works in philosophy, education, and science. One of these, called *The Advancement of Learning*, is generally considered his greatest book. He is even credited by some people with having written the plays of Shakespeare. He didn't need to do that to gain lasting fame, however.

In his essays Bacon is a close parallel to Montaigne. Both write in the same idiom, that of the classical scholar. Both comment brilliantly on such topics as truth, friendship, learning, and riches. Of the two, Montaigne is the more informal. Bacon's style is severely classical. His sentences have the same balance and the same careful parallel structure that can be found in Latin writers like Cicero.

Bacon's sentences are full of quotable epigrams like " Reading maketh a full man; conference, a ready man; and writing, an exact man." He packs a great deal of meaning into a very small number of words. As in the essays of Emerson, the unit of thought in Bacon is the sentence, not the paragraph. " Of Studies " is only one paragraph, but there are many ideas in it. In fact, all of Bacon's writings are full of ideas worth remembering.

Both of the essays that follow must be read slowly and thoughtfully. In the first essay Bacon discusses books that should be " chewed and digested." This is good advice to follow in reading Bacon's own works.

OF STUDIES

Studies serve for delight, for ornament, and for ability. Their chief use for delight is in privateness and retiring; for ornament, is in discourse; and for ability, is in the judgment and disposition of business. For expert men can execute and perhaps judge of particulars, one by one; but the general counsels, and the plots and marshaling of affairs, come best from those that are learned. To spend too much time in studies is sloth; to use them too much for ornament is affectation; to make judgment wholly by their rules is the humor of a scholar. They perfect nature, and are perfected by experience; for natural abilities are like natural plants, that need proyning by study; and studies themselves do give forth directions too much at large, except they be bounded in by experience. Crafty men contemn studies; simple men admire them; and wise men use them: for they teach not their own use; but that is a wisdom without them and above them, won by observation. Read not to contradict and confute; nor to believe and take for granted; nor to find talk and discourse; but to weigh and consider. Some books are to be tasted, others to be swallowed, and some few to be chewed and digested: that is, some books are to be read only in parts; others to be read, but not curiously; and some few to be read wholly, and with diligence and attention. Some books also may be read by deputy, and extracts made of them by others; but that would be only in the less important arguments, and the meaner sort of books; else distilled books are like common distilled waters, flashy things. Reading maketh a full man; conference a ready man; and writing an exact man. And therefore, if a man write little, he had need have a great memory; if he confer little, he had need have a present wit; and if he read little, he had need have much cunning, to seem to know that he doth not. Histories make men wise; poets witty; the mathematics subtile; natural philosophy deep; moral grave; logic and rhetoric able to contend. *Abeunt studia in mores.* Nay, there is no stond or impediment in the wit, but may be wrought out by fit studies: like as diseases of the body may have appropriate exercises. Bowling is good for the stone and reins; shooting for the lungs and breast; gentle walking for the stomach; riding for the head; and the like. So if a man's wit be wandering, let him study the mathematics; for a demonstration, if his wit be called away never so little, he must begin again: if his wit be not apt to distinguish or find differences, let him study the schoolmen; for they are *cymini sectores:* if he be not apt to beat over matters, and to call one thing to prove and illustrate another, let him study the lawyers' case: so every defect of the mind may have a special receipt.

STUDYING THE ESSAY

1. Discuss Bacon's ability to pack his thought in brief statements. Select any sentence or section and try to express completely in your own words Bacon's thought.
2. Discuss the purposes of your own reading, as you see them.
3. Give examples of books suited to each one of the following purposes of reading: "Studies serve for delight, for ornament, and for ability."
4. What does Bacon mean when he says, "Some books are to be tasted, others to be swallowed, and some few to be chewed and digested"?
5. An *aphorism* is a "terse saying embodying a universal truth."

Find aphorisms in Bacon's essays. Are these aphorisms worth remembering?

6. Why does Bacon put all of this essay into one paragraph?

COMPOSITION TOPICS

1. Studies Serve for Delight
2. Spending Too Much Time in Studies
3. Books to be Tasted
4. Books to be Chewed and Digested
5. When My Wits Went Wandering
6. Books I Don't Care to Chew Any More

OF FRIENDSHIP

It had been hard for him that spake it to have put more truth than untruth together in a few words, than in that speech, *Whosoever is delighted in solitude is either a wild beast or a god*. For it is most true that a natural and secret hatred and aversation towards society, in any man, hath somewhat of the savage beast; but it is most untrue that it should have any character at all of the divine nature; except it proceed, not out of a pleasure in solitude, but out of a love and desire to sequester a man's self for a higher conversation: such as is found to have been falsely and feignedly in some of the heathen; as Epimenides the Candian, Numa the Roman, Empedocles the Sicilian, and Apollonius of Tyana; and truly and realy in divers of the ancient hermits and holy fathers of the church. But little do men perceive what solitude is, and how far it extendeth. For a crowd is not company, and faces are but a gallery of pictures, and talk but a tinkling cymbal, where there is no love. The Latin adage meeteth with it a little. *Magna civitas, magna solitudo;* because in a great town friends are scattered; so that there is not that fellowship, for the most part, which is in less neighborhoods. But we may go farther, and affirm most truly that it is a mere and miserable solitude to want true friends, without which the world is but a wilderness; and even in this sense also of solitude, whosoever in the frame of his nature and affections is unfit for friendship, he taketh it of the beast, and not from humanity.

A principal fruit of friendship is the ease and discharge of the fullness and swellings of the heart, which passions of all kind do cause and induce. We know diseases of stoppings and suffocations are the most dangerous in the body; and it is not much otherwise in the mind; you may take sarza to open the liver, steel to open the spleen, flowers of sulphur for the lungs, castoreum for the brain; but no receipt openeth the heart but a true friend, to whom you may impart griefs, joys, fears, hopes, suspicions, counsels, and whatsoever lieth upon the heart to oppress it, in a kind of civil shrift or confession.

It is a strange thing to observe how high a rate great kings and monarchs do set upon this fruit of friendship whereof we speak: so great, as they purchase it many times at the hazard of their own safety and greatness. For princes, in regard of the distance of their fortune from that of their subjects and servants, cannot gather this fruit, except (to make themselves capable thereof) they raise some persons to be as it were companions and almost equals to themselves, which many times sorteth to inconvenience. The modern languages give unto such persons the name of *favorites,* or *privadoes;* as if it were matter of grace, or conversation. But the Roman name attaineth the true use and cause thereof, naming them *participes curarum;* for it is that which tieth the knot. And we see plainly that this hath been done, not by weak and passionate princes only, but by the wisest and most politic that ever reigned; who have oftentimes joined to themselves some of their servants, whom both themselves have called *friends,* and allowed others likewise to call them in the same manner, using the word which is received between private men.

L. Sylla, when he commanded Rome, raised Pompey (after surnamed the Great) to that height, that Pompey vaunted himself for Sylla's overmatch. For when he had carried the consulship for a friend of his, against the pursuit of Sylla, and that Sylla did a little resent thereat, and began to speak great, Pompey turned upon him again, and in effect bade him be quiet; *for that more men adored the sun rising than the sun setting.* With Julius Caesar, Decimus Brutus had obtained that interest, as he set him down in his testament for heir in remainder after his nephew; and this was the man that had power with him to draw him forth to his death. For when Caesar would have discharged the senate, in regard of some ill presages, and specially a dream of Calpurnia, this man lifted him gently by the arm out of his chair, telling him he hoped he would not dismiss the senate till his wife had dreamt a better dream. And it seemeth his favor was so great, as Antonius, in a letter which is recited *verbatim* in one of Cicero's Philippics, called him *venefica,* "witch"; as if he had enchanted Caesar. Augustus raised Agrippa (though of mean birth) to that height, as, when he consulted with Maecenas about the marriage of his daughter Julia, Maecenas took the liberty to tell him, *that he must either marry his daughter to Agrippa, or take away his life; there was no third way, he had made him so great.* With Tiberius Caesar, Sejanus had ascended to that height, as they two were termed and reckoned as a pair of friends. Tiberius in a letter to him saith, *Hæc pro amicitiâ nostrâ non occultavi;* and the whole senate dedicated an altar to Friendship, as to a goddess, in respect of the great dearness of friendship between them two. The like or more was between Septimius Severus and Plautianus. For he forced his eldest son to marry the daughter of Plautianus; and would often maintain Plautianus in doing affronts to his son; and did write also in a letter to the senate by these words: *I love the man so well, as I wish he may over-live me.* Now if these princes had been as a Trajan, or a Marcus Aurelius, a man might have thought that this had proceeded of an abundant goodness of nature; but being men so wise, of such strength and severity of mind, and so extreme lovers of themselves, as all these were, it proveth most plainly that they found their own felicity (though as great as ever happened to mortal men) but as an half piece, except they might have a friend to make it entire: and yet, which is more, they were princes that had wives, sons, nephews; and yet all these could not supply the comfort of friendship.

It is not to be forgotten, what Comineus observeth of his first master, Duke Charles the Hardy; namely, that he would communicate his secrets with none; and least of all, those secrets which troubled him most. Whereupon he goeth on and saith that towards his latter time *that closeness did impair and a little perish his understanding.* Surely Comineus might have made the same judgment also, if it had pleased him, of his second master, Lewis the Eleventh, whose closeness was indeed his tormentor. The parable of Pythagoras is dark, but true; *Cor ne edito*, " Eat not the heart." Certainly, if a man would give it a hard phrase, those that want friends to open themselves unto are cannibals of their own hearts. But one thing is most admirable (wherewith I will conclude this first fruit of friendship), which is, that this communicating of a man's self to his friends works two contrary effects; for it re-doubleth joys, and cutteth griefs in halves. For there is no man that imparteth his joys to his friend, but he joyeth the more; and no man that imparteth his griefs to his friend, but he grieveth the less. So that it is, in truth of operation upon a man's mind, of like virtue as the alchemists use to attribute to their stone for man's body; that it worketh all contrary effects, but still to the good and benefit of nature. But yet, without praying in aid of alchemists, there is a manifest image of this in the ordinary course of nature. For in bodies, union strengtheneth and cherisheth any natural action; and, on the other side, weakeneth and dulleth any violent impression: and even so is it of minds.

The second fruit of friendship is healthful and sovereign for the understanding, as the first is for the affections. For friendship maketh indeed a fair day in the affections, from storm and tempests; but it maketh daylight in the understanding, out of darkness and confusion of thoughts. Neither is this to be understood only of faithful counsel, which a man receiveth from his friend; but before you come to that, certain it is that whosoever hath his mind fraught with many thoughts, his wits and understanding to clarify and break up, in the communicating and discoursing with another: he tosseth his thoughts more easily; he marshaleth them more orderly; he seeth how they look when they are turned into words; finally, he waxeth wiser than himself; and that more by an hour's discourse than by a day's meditation. It was well said by Themistocles to the king of Persia, *that speech was like cloth of Arras, opened and put abroad; whereby the imagery doth appear in figure; whereas in thoughts they lie but as in packs*. Neither is this second fruit of friendship, in opening the understanding, restrained only to such friends as are able to give a man counsel (they indeed are best); but even without that, a man learneth of himself,

and bringeth his own thoughts to light, and whetteth his
wits as against a stone, which itself cuts not. In a word, a
man were better relate himself to a statua or picture, than
to suffer his thoughts to pass in smother.

Add now, to make this second fruit of friendship complete, that other point, which lieth more open, and falleth
within vulgar observation; which is faithful counsel from a
friend. Heraclitus saith well in one of his enigmas, *Dry light
is ever the best*. And certain it is that the light that a man
receiveth by counsel from another is drier and purer than
that which cometh from his own understanding and judgment; which is ever infused and drenched in his affections
and customs. So as there is as much difference between the
counsel that a friend giveth, and that a man giveth himself,
as there is between the counsel of a friend and of a flatterer
For there is no such flatterer as is a man's self; and there is no
such remedy against flattery of a man's self as the liberty
of a friend. Counsel is of two sorts: the one concerning manners, the other concerning business. For the first; the best
preservative to keep the mind in health is the faithful admonition of a friend. The calling of a man's self to a strict
account is a medicine, sometimes too piercing and corrosive.
Reading good books of morality is a little flat and dead.
Observing our faults in others is sometimes unproper for our
case. But the best receipt (best, I say, to work, and best to
take) is the admonition of a friend. It is a strange thing to
behold what gross errors and extreme absurdities many
(especially of the greater sort) do commit, for want of a
friend to tell them of them, to the great damage both of
fame and fortune. For, as S. James saith, they are as men
*that look sometimes into a glass, and presently forget their
own shape and favor*. As for business, a man may think, if
he will, that two eyes see no more than one; or that a
gamester seeth always more than a looker-on; or that a man

in anger is as wise as he that hath said over the four-and-twenty letters; or that a musket may be shot off as well upon the arm as upon a rest; and such other fond and high imaginations, to think himself all in all. But when all is done, the help of good counsel is that which setteth business straight. And if any man think that he will take counsel, but it shall be by pieces, asking counsel in one business of one man, and in another business of another man; it is well (that is to say, better perhaps than if he asked none at all); but he runneth two dangers. One, that he shall not be faithfully counseled; for it is a rare thing, except it be from a perfect and entire friend, to have counsel given, but such as shall be bowed and crooked to some ends which he hath that giveth it. The other, that he shall have counsel given, hurtful and unsafe (though with good meaning), and mixed partly of mischief and partly of remedy; even as if you would call a physician, that is thought good for the cure of the disease you complain of, but is unacquainted with your body; and therefore may put you in way for a present cure, but overthroweth your health in some other kind; and so cure the disease and kill the patient. But a friend that is wholly acquainted with a man's estate will beware, by furthering any present business, how he dasheth upon other inconvenience. And therefore rest not upon scattered counsels; they will rather distract and mislead than settle and direct.

After these two noble fruits of friendship (peace in the affections, and support of the judgment) followeth the last fruit, which is like the pomegranate, full of many kernels; I mean aid and bearing a part in all actions and occasions. Here the best way to represent to life the manifold use of friendship is to cast and see how many things there are which a man cannot do himself; and then it will appear that it was a sparing speech of the ancients, to say *that a friend is another himself:* for that a friend is far more than himself. Men have their time, and die many times in desire of some things which they principally take to heart; the bestowing of a child, the finishing of a work, or the like. If a man have a true friend, he may rest almost secure that the care of those things will continue after him. So that a man hath as it were two lives in his desires. A man hath a body, and that body is confined to a place; but where friendship is, all offices of life are as it were granted to him and his deputy; for he may exercise them by his friend. How many things are there which a man cannot, with any face or comeliness, say or do himself! A man can scarce allege his own merits with modesty, much less extol them; a man cannot sometimes brook to supplicate or beg; and a number of the like. But all these are graceful in a friend's mouth, which are blushing in a man's own. So again, a man's person hath many proper relations which he cannot put off. A man cannot speak to his son but as a father; to his wife but as a husband; to his enemy but upon terms: whereas a friend may speak as the case requires, and not as it sorteth with the person. But to enumerate these things were endless: I have given the rule, where a man cannot fitly play his own part: if he have not a friend, he may quit the stage.

STUDYING THE ESSAY

1. What estimate does Bacon place upon friendship?
2. What are the "fruits of friendship"?
3. List the qualities you demand in your good friends.
4. Study Bacon's literary and historical references. In what literature was he particularly interested?
5. The sentence, "For a crowd is not company, and faces are but a gallery of pictures, and talk but a tinkling cymbal, where there is no love," should test your knowledge of the Bible.

What is the reference? Why is Bacon's use of this reference apt?

6. Use the dictionary as you read this essay. Words to learn: *adage, felicity, parable, vulgar, supplicate.*

COMPOSITION TOPICS

1. The Responsibilities of Friendship
2. When a Crowd Is Not Company
3. Friendship Redoubles Joy and Cuts Griefs in Half
4. The Difference Between a Friend and an Acquaintance

JOSEPH ADDISON, 1672–1719

In 1688 the "Glorious Revolution" expelled the last of the Stuarts, James II, from the English throne and brought over from Holland William III, Prince of Orange, as king. During his reign (1688–1702) and that of Queen Anne (1702–1714), many changes took place in the structure of English society. In the first place, the nobility lost greatly in wealth and prestige after the 1688 revolution. In the second place, wars on the continent and rapidly expanding trade increased the size of the middle class.

Literary men like Richard Steele, Joseph Addison, Alexander Pope, and Jonathan Swift gathered daily in their favorite coffee houses. Here they found both a source of ideas and a public for their writings. The conversation which went on endlessly in the coffee houses produced the periodical — the newspaper — and the informal essay which Montaigne had characterized a century earlier.

Richard Steele (1672–1729) was the first to capitalize on the people's wide interests. His *Tatler*, to which Addison contributed about forty essays, appeared three times a week from 1709 to 1711. Its articles about news of the world, manners, the position of women, and a hundred other subjects, were immensely popular. *The Spectator*, largely the work of Addison, was published every day from March 1, 1711, to December 6, 1712, and irregularly after that until December, 1714. The essay printed below is Number 112, dated Monday, July 9, 1711.

Joseph Addison (1672–1719) was a school and college friend of Steele. After taking his M.A. at Oxford in 1693 and traveling extensively on the continent for a number of years, he returned to England and created a literary sensation with *The Campaign.*

This was an epic poem celebrating the British victory at the battle of Blenheim in 1704. From 1706 on, Addison was continually in politics, as Under-Secretary of State, as Chief Secretary to the Lord Lieutenant of Ireland, as Member of Parliament from 1708 until his death. He was an expert classicist and wrote several volumes in Latin. He produced a very successful verse tragedy, *Cato*, and best of all, the essays which give him a place in this volume.

The *Spectator* was aptly named. It looked around and commented in an informal, conversational way, upon almost every aspect of life in early eighteenth-century England. Each of the 635 *Spectator* papers was confined to a single theme and was concerned with some aspect of morals or manners. A few characters, invented mostly by Steele, appear to serve as actors in the society which the essayists described: Sir Roger de Coverley, the country squire; Will Honeycomb, a fop; Captain Sentry, a retired army man; Sir Andrew Freeport, a merchant. Some of the papers about these men are close to the short story in form, and the characterizations contributed much to the development of fiction in later years.

Throughout his essays, Addison shows himself to be scholarly but not pedantic, humorous but never sarcastic, and always gently satirical. As he describes the churchly behavior of the " old knight," Sir Roger (actually he is supposed to be fifty-six years old), Addison could easily be scornful of such a man. But he is genial toward his old friend and points out all his good qualities. If you enjoy this essay, you should read further in the *Spectator* and particularly in the so-called " Sir Roger de Coverley Papers."

SIR ROGER DE COVERLEY IN CHURCH

I am always very well pleased with a country Sunday, and think if keeping holy the seventh day were only a human institution, it would be the best method that could have been thought of for the polishing and civilizing of mankind. It is certain the country people would soon degenerate into a kind of savages and barbarians were there not such frequent returns of a stated time, in which the whole village meet together with their best faces and in their cleanliest habits, to converse with one another upon indifferent subjects, hear their duties explained to them, and join together in adoration of the Supreme Being. Sunday clears away the rust of the whole week, not only as it refreshes in their minds the notions of religion, but as it puts both the sexes upon appearing in their most agreeable forms, and exerting all such qualities as are apt to give them a figure in the eye of the village. A country fellow distinguishes himself as much in the churchyard as a citizen does upon the Change, the whole parish politics being generally discussed at that place, either after sermon or before the bell rings.

My friend Sir Roger, being a good churchman, has beautified the inside of his church with several texts of his own choosing; he has likewise given a handsome pulpit cloth, and railed in the communion table at his own expense. He has often told me that, at his coming to his estate, he found his parishioners very irregular; and that in order to make them kneel and join in the responses, he gave every one of them a hassock and a Common Prayer Book, and at the same time employed an itinerant singing-master, who goes about the country for that purpose, to instruct them rightly in the tunes of the Psalms, upon which they now very much value themselves, and indeed outdo most of the country churches that I have ever heard.

As Sir Roger is landlord to the whole congregation, he keeps them in very good order, and will suffer nobody to sleep in it besides himself; for, if by chance he has been surprised into a short nap at sermon, upon recovering out of it he stands up and looks about him, and if he sees any-body else nodding, either wakes them himself or sends his servant to them. Several other of the old knight's particu-larities break out upon these occasions; sometimes he will be lengthening out a verse in the singing Psalms half a minute after the rest of the congregation have done with it; sometimes, when he is pleased with the matter of his de-votion, he pronounces " Amen " three or four times to the same prayer; and sometimes stands up when everybody else is upon their knees, to count the congregation, or see if any of his tenants are missing.

I was yesterday very much surprised to hear my old friend, in the midst of the service, calling out to one John Matthews to mind what he was about, and not disturb the congregation. This John Matthews, it seems, is remarkable for being an idle fellow, and at that time was kicking his heels for his diversion. This authority of the knight, though exerted in that odd manner which accompanies him in all circumstances of life, has a very good effect upon the parish, who are not polite enough to see anything ridiculous in his behavior; besides that, the general good sense and worthiness of his character makes his friends observe these little singularities as foils that rather set off than blemish his good qualities.

As soon as the sermon is finished, nobody presumes to

stir till Sir Roger is gone out of the church. The knight walks down from his seat in the chancel between a double row of his tenants, that stand bowing to him on each side, and every now and then inquires how such an one's wife, or son, or father do, whom he does not see at church — which is understood as a secret reprimand to the person that is absent.

The chaplain has often told me that, upon catechizing day, when Sir Roger had been pleased with a boy that answers well, he has ordered a Bible to be given him next day for his encouragement, and sometimes accompanies it with a flitch of bacon to his mother. Sir Roger has likewise added five pounds a year to the clerk's place; and that he may encourage the young fellows to make themselves perfect in the church service, has promised, upon the death of the present incumbent, who is very old, to bestow it according to merit.

The fair understanding between Sir Roger and his chaplain and their mutual concurrence in doing good, is the more remarkable because the very next village is famous for the differences and contentions that rise between the parson and the squire, who live in a perpetual state of war. The parson is always preaching at the squire, and the squire, to be revenged on the parson, never comes to church. The squire has made all his tenants atheists and tithe stealers; while the parson instructs them every Sunday in the dignity of his order, and insinuates to them in almost every sermon that he is a better man than his patron. In short, matters are come to such an extremity that the squire has not said his prayers either in public or private this half year; and that the parson threatens him, if he does not mend his manners, to pray for him in the face of the whole congregation.

Feuds of this nature, though too frequent in the country, are very fatal to the ordinary people, who are so used to be dazzled with riches that they pay as much deference to the understanding of a man of an estate as of a man of learning, and are very hardly brought to regard any truth, how important soever it may be, that is preached to them, when they know there are several men of five hundred a year who do not believe it.

STUDYING THE ESSAY

1. In what ways has Sir Roger endeared himself to his tenants?
2. In what ways can his behavior in church be called eccentric?
3. Does your church have one member who likes to think of himself as " it " — as the leading light of the congregation?
4. Why does Addison close this essay as he does?
5. What important truth is to be found in the last paragraph?

COMPOSITION TOPICS

1. Read four or five additional essays about Sir Roger de Coverley, and then write a character sketch of the man. The following numbers in the *Spectator* (see your school library) tell more about the knight: 106–10, inclusive; 113, 116, 122, 174, 269, 329. All of these are good reading.
2. Eccentrics in My Church
3. Of Those Who Sing during the Rests

CHARLES LAMB, 1775-1834

The only autobiography which Charles Lamb ever wrote was contained in a short letter to a friend, in 1827. This is what he said of himself:

Charles Lamb, born in the Inner Temple, 10th February, 1775; educated in Christ's Hospital; afterwards a clerk in the Accountant's Office, East India House; pensioned off from that service, 1825, after thirty-three years' service; is now a gentleman at large; can remember few specialties in his life worth noting, except that he once caught a swallow flying. Below the middle stature; cast of face slightly Jewish, with no Judaic tinge in his complexional religion; stammers abominably, and is therefore more apt to discharge his occasional conversation in a quaint aphorism, or a poor quibble, than in set and edifying speeches; has consequently been libelled as a person always aiming at wit; which, as he told a dull fellow that charged him with it, is at least as good as aiming at dullness. A small eater, but not drinker; confesses a partiality for the production of the juniper berry; was a fierce smoker of tobacco, but may be resembled to a volcano burnt out, emitting only now and then a casual puff. Has been guilty of obtruding upon the public a tale, in prose, called " Rosamund Gray "; a dramatic sketch, named " John Woodvil "; a " Farewell Ode to Tobacco," with sundry other poems, and light prose matter, collected in two slight crown octavos, and pomp-

ously christened his works, though in fact they were
his recreations; and his true works may be found on
the shelves of Leadenhall Street, filling some hundred folios. He is also the true Elia, whose Essays
are extant in a little volume, published a year or two
since, and rather better known from that name without a meaning than from anything he has done, or
can hope to do, in his own. He was also the first to
draw the public attention to the old English drama-
tists, in a work called " Specimens of English Dramatic Writers who lived about the Time of Shakespeare," published about fifteen years since.

He died 18   , much lamented.

Witness his hand,

Charles Lamb

It is entirely characteristic of the man that he omitted from
his humorous autobiography all of the tragedy in his very unhappy life. In 1796 his sister Mary went suddenly mad, stabbed
and killed their mother, and seriously wounded their father. She
was put into an insane asylum, but Charles managed to have her
released on the condition that he would be responsible for her.
Thus from the age of 21 to the end of his life he sacrificed himself for his sister, who, ironically, survived him by fourteen
years. He loved children, but he could never marry. He loved
people, but his schedule was so strictly regulated by his sister's
needs that he could never find a normal social life.

The remarkable thing is that Lamb's sadness appeared only
in his letters to his friends, particularly Coleridge, the great
poet, who was perhaps even more unhappy than Lamb. And
even in the letters the sadness is not gloomy or melancholy.
Three weeks after Mary's attack on her parents, for instance,
Lamb tried to cheer up Coleridge, who at that time was deeply
depressed. In his essays Lamb never " takes down his hair," as
one might expect him to do.

In the *Essays of Elia,* which appeared first in 1823, Lamb
shows himself to be the master of the informal reflective essay.

As he says, these works were his recreations. The gentle, sometimes humorous, sometimes satirical style reminds the reader very often of Addison. But Lamb is more intimate, more self-revealing, more fanciful or whimsical, more human than Addison. "A Dissertation upon Roast Pig" is the most popular of these essays. The humor, the amazingly vivid vocabulary, the ease and flow of the style, and the delight in the imagination are all typical of this essayist. Further reading in the essays by Lamb should lead you to "Dream Children," "Mrs. Battle's Opinions on Whist," and "Poor Relations," at the very least. There is no essay by Elia that is not worth reading.

A DISSERTATION UPON ROAST PIG

Mankind, says a Chinese manuscript, which my friend M. was obliging enough to read and explain to me, for the first seventy thousand ages ate their meat raw, clawing or biting it from the living animal, just as they do in Abyssinia to this day. This period is not obscurely hinted at by their great Confucius in the second chapter of his Mundane Mutations, where he designates a kind of golden age by the term Cho-fang, literally the Cook's holiday. The manuscript goes on to say that the art of roasting, or rather broiling (which I take to be the elder brother), was accidentally discovered in the manner following. The swineherd, Ho-ti, having gone out into the woods one morning, as his manner was, to collect mast for his hogs, left his cottage in the care of his eldest son, Bo-bo, a great lubberly boy, who being fond of playing with fire, as younkers of his age commonly are, let some sparks escape into a bundle of straw, which kindling quickly, spread the conflagration over every part of their poor mansion, till it was reduced to ashes. Together with the cottage (a sorry antediluvian makeshift of a building, you may think it), what was of much more importance, a fine litter of new-farrowed pigs, no less than nine in number, perished. China pigs have been esteemed a luxury all over the East from the remotest periods that we read of. Bo-bo was in utmost consternation, as you may think, not so much for the sake of the tenement, which his father and he could easily build up again with a few dry branches, and the labor of an hour or two, at any time, as for the loss of the pigs. While he was thinking what he should say to his father, and wringing his hands over the smoking remnants of one of those untimely sufferers, an odor assailed his nostrils, unlike any scent which he had before experienced. What could it proceed from? — not from the burnt cottage — he had smelt that smell before — indeed this was by no means the first accident of the kind which had occurred through the negligence of this unlucky young firebrand. Much less did it resemble that of any known herb, weed, or flower. A premonitory moistening at the same time overflowed his nether lip. He knew not what to think. He next stooped down to feel the pig, if there were any signs of life in it. He burnt his fingers, and to cool them he applied them in his booby fashion to his mouth. Some of the crumbs of the scorched skin had come away with his fingers, and for the first time in his life (in the world's life indeed, for before him no man had known it) he tasted — *crackling!* Again he felt and fumbled at the pig. It did not burn him so much now, still he licked his fingers from a sort of habit. The truth at length broke into his slow understanding, that it was the pig that smelt so, and the pig that tasted so delicious; and, surrendering himself up to the new-born pleasure, he fell to tearing up whole handfuls of the scorched skin with the flesh next it, and was cramming it down his throat in his beastly fashion, when his sire entered amid the smoking rafters, armed with retributory cudgel, and finding how affairs stood, began to rain blows upon the young rogue's shoulders, as thick as hailstones, which Bo-bo heeded not any more than if they had been flies. The tickling pleasure, which he experienced in his lower regions, had rendered him quite callous to any inconveniences he might feel in those remote quarters. His father might lay on, but he could not beat him from his pig, till he had fairly made an end of it, when, becoming a little more sensible of his situation, something like the following dialogue ensued.

"You graceless whelp, what have you got there devouring? Is it not enough that you have burnt me down three houses with your dog's tricks, and be hanged to you, but you must be eating fire, and I know not what — what have you got there, I say? "

"O, father, the pig, the pig, do come and taste how nice the burnt pig eats."

The ears of Ho-ti tingled with horror. He cursed his son, and he cursed himself that ever he should beget a son that should eat burnt pig.

Bo-bo, whose scent was wonderfully sharpened since morning, soon raked out another pig, and fairly rending it asunder, thrust the lesser half by main force into the fists of Ho-ti, still shouting out, "Eat, eat, eat the burnt pig, father, only taste — O Lord," — with such-like barbarous ejaculations, cramming all the while as if he would choke.

Ho-ti trembled in every joint while he grasped the abominable thing, wavering whether he should not put his son to death for an unnatural young monster, when the crackling scorching his fingers, as it had done his son's, and applying the same remedy to them, he in his turn tasted some of its flavor, which, make what sour mouths he would for a pretense, proved not altogether displeasing to him. In conclusion (for the manuscript here is a little tedious) both father and son fairly sat down to the mess, and never left till they had despatched all that remained of the litter.

Bo-bo was strictly enjoined not to let the secret escape, for the neighbors would certainly have stoned them for a couple of abominable wretches, who could think of improving upon the good meat which God had sent them. Nevertheless strange stories got about. It was observed that Ho-ti's cottage was burnt down now more frequently than ever. Nothing but fires from this time forward. Some would break out in broad day, others in the nighttime. As often as the sow farrowed, so sure was the house of Ho-ti to be in a blaze; and Ho-ti himself, which was the more remarkable, instead of chastising his son, seemed to grow more indulgent to him than ever. At length they were watched, the terrible mystery discovered, and father and son summoned to take their trial at Pekin, then an inconsiderable assize town. Evidence was given, the obnoxious food itself produced in court, and verdict about to be pronounced, when the foreman of the jury begged that some of the burnt pig, of which the culprits stood accused, might be handed into the box. He handled it, and they all handled it, and burning their fingers, as Bo-bo and his father had done before them, and Nature prompting to each of them the same remedy, against the face of all the facts, and the clearest charge which judge had ever given — to the surprise of the whole court, townsfolk, strangers, reporters, and all present — without leaving the box, or any manner of consultation whatever, they brought in a simultaneous verdict of Not Guilty.

The judge, who was a shrewd fellow, winked at the manifest iniquity of the decision; and, when the court was dismissed, went privily, and bought up all the pigs that could be had for love or money. In a few days his Lordship's town house was observed to be on fire. The thing took wing, and now there was nothing to be seen but fires in every direction. Fuel and pigs grew enormously dear all over the district. The insurance offices one and all shut up shop. People built slighter and slighter every day, until it was feared that the very science of architecture would in no long time be lost to the world. Thus this custom of firing houses continued, till in process of time, says my manuscript, a sage arose, like our Locke, who made a discovery, that the flesh of swine, or indeed of any other animal, might be cooked (*burnt*, as they called it) without the necessity of consuming a whole house to dress it. Then first began the rude form of a gridiron. Roasting by the string, or spit, came in a century or two later, I forget in whose dynasty. By such slow degrees, concludes the manuscript, do the most useful, and seemingly the most obvious, arts make their way among mankind.

Without placing too implicit faith in the account above given, it must be agreed that if a worthy pretext for so dangerous an experiment as setting houses on fire (especially in these days) could be assigned in favor of any culinary object, that pretext and excuse might be found in ROAST PIG.

Of all the delicacies in the whole *mundus edibilis*, I will maintain it to be the most delicate — *princeps obsoniorum*.

I speak not of your grown porkers — things between pig and pork — those hobbydehoys — but a young and tender suckling — under a moon old — guiltless as yet of the sty — with no original speck of the *amor immunditiæ*, the hereditary failing of the first parent, yet manifest — his voice as yet not broken, but something between a childish treble, and a grumble — the mild forerunner or *præludium*, of a grunt.

He must be roasted. I am not ignorant that our ancestors ate them seethed, or boiled — but what a sacrifice of the exterior tegument!

There is no flavor comparable, I will contend, to that of
the crisp, tawny, well-watched, not over-roasted, *crackling*,
as it is well called — the very teeth are invited to their share
of the pleasure at this banquet in overcoming the coy, brittle
resistance — with the adhesive oleaginous — O call it not
fat — but an indefinable sweetness growing up to it — the
tender blossoming of fat — fat cropped in the bud — taken
in the shoot — in the first innocence — the cream and quintes-
sence of the child-pig's yet pure food —— the lean, no lean,
but a kind of animal manna — or, rather, fat and lean (if it
must be so) so blended and running into each other, that both
together make but one ambrosian result, or common substance.

Behold him, while he is doing — it seemed rather a refresh-
ing warmth, than a scorching heat, that he is so passive to.
How equably he twirleth round the string! — Now he is
just done. To see the extreme sensibility of that tender age,
he hath wept out his pretty eyes — radiant jellies — shooting
stars —

See him in the dish, his second cradle, how meek he lieth!
— wouldst thou have had this innocent grow up to the
grossness and indocility which too often accompany maturer
swinehood? Ten to one he would have proved a glutton,
a sloven, an obstinate, disagreeable animal — wallowing in
all manner of filthy conversation — from these sins he is
happily snatched away —

> Ere sin could blight, or sorrow fade,
> Death came with timely care —

his memory is odoriferous — no clown curseth, while his
stomach half rejecteth, the rank bacon — no coal-heaver
bolteth him in reeking sausages — he hath a fair sepulchre in
the grateful stomach of the judicious epicure — and for such
a tomb might be content to die.

He is the best of Sapors. Pineapple is great. She is indeed almost too transcendent — a delight, if not sinful, yet so like to sinning, that really a tender-conscienced person would do well to pause — too ravishing for mortal taste, she woundeth and excoriateth the lips that approach her — like lovers' kisses, she biteth — she is a pleasure bordering on pain from the fierceness and insanity of her relish — but she stoppeth at the palate — she meddleth not with the appetite — and the coarsest hunger might barter her consistently for a mutton chop.

Pig — let me speak his praise — is no less provocative of the appetite, than he is satisfactory to the criticalness of the censorious palate. The strong man may batten on him, and the weakling refuseth not his mild juices.

Unlike to mankind's mixed characters, a bundle of virtues and vices, inexplicably intertwisted, and not to be unraveled without hazard, he is — good throughout. No part of him is better or worse than another. He helpeth, as far as his little means extend, all around. He is the least envious of banquets. He is all neighbors' fare.

I am one of those who freely and ungrudgingly impart a share of the good things of this life which fall to their lot (few as mine are in this kind) to a friend. I protest I take as great an interest in my friend's pleasures, his relishes, and proper satisfactions, as in mine own. " Presents," I often say, " endear Absents." Hares, pheasants, partridges, snipes, barn-door chickens (those " tame vilatic fowl "), capons, plovers, brawn, barrels of oysters, I dispense as freely as I receive them. I love to taste them, as it were, upon the tongue of my friend. But a stop must be put somewhere. One would not, like Lear, " give everything." I make my stand upon pig. Methinks it is an ingratitude to the Giver of all good flavors, to extra-domiciliate, or send out of the house slightingly (under pretext of friendship, or I know not what), a blessing so particularly adapted, predestined, I may say, to my individual palate — it argues an insensibility.

I remember a touch of conscience in this kind at school. My good old aunt, who never parted from me at the end of a holiday without stuffing a sweetmeat, or some nice thing, into my pocket, had dismissed me one evening with a smoking plum-cake, fresh from the oven. In my way to school (it was over London Bridge) a gray-headed old beggar saluted me (I have no doubt at this time of day that he was a counterfeit). I had no pence to console him with, and in the vanity of self-denial, and the very coxcombry of charity, schoolboy-like, I made him a present of — the whole cake. I walked on a little, buoyed up, as one is on such occasions, with a sweet soothing of self-satisfaction; but before I had got to the end of the bridge, my better feelings returned, and I burst into tears, thinking how ungrateful I had been to my good aunt, to go and give her good gift away to a stranger, that I had never seen before, and who might be a bad man for aught I knew; and then I thought of the pleasure my aunt would be taking in thinking that I — I myself, and not another — would eat her nice cake. And what should I say to her the next time I saw her? — how naughty I was to part with her pretty present — and the odor of that spicy cake came back upon my recollection, and the pleasure and the curiosity I had taken in seeing her make it, and her joy when she sent it to the oven, and how disappointed she would feel that I had never had a bit of it in my mouth at last — and I blamed my impertinent spirit of alms-giving, and out-of-place hypocrisy of goodness, and above all I wished never to see the face again of that insidious, good-for-nothing, old gray impostor.

Our ancestors were nice in their method of sacrificing these tender victims. We read of pigs whipped to death with something of a shock, as we hear of any other obsolete custom. The age of discipline is gone by, or it would be curious to inquire (in a philosophical light merely) what effect this process might have towards intenerating and dulcifying a substance, naturally so mild and dulcet as the flesh of young pigs. It looks like refining a violet. Yet we should be cautious, while we condemn the inhumanity, how we censure the wisdom of the practice. It might impart a gusto —

I remember an hypothesis, argued upon by the young students, when I was at St. Omer's, and maintained with much learning and pleasantry on both sides, "Whether, supposing that the flavor of a pig who obtained his death by whipping (*per flagellationem extremam*) superadded a pleasure upon the palate of a man more intense than any possible suffering we can conceive in the animal, is man justified in using that method of putting the animal to death? " I forget the decision.

His sauce should be considered. Decidedly, a few bread crumbs, done up with his liver and brains, and a dash of mild sage. But banish, dear Mrs. Cook, I beseech you, the whole onion tribe. Barbecue your whole hogs to your palate, steep them in shallots, stuff them out with plantations of the rank and guilty garlic; you cannot poison them, or make them stronger than they are — but consider, he is a weakling — a flower.

STUDYING THE ESSAY

1. Can you explain why this essay is included in almost every collection of essays for schools?
2. How is Lamb's personality revealed in this essay?
3. One of the wonderful things about this essay is the way in which Lamb uses vivid figures of speech to stimulate the

reader's senses of smell, taste, and touch. Find examples of this kind of language.

4. Why does Lamb use the narrative method to describe the origin of roast pig?

COMPOSITION TOPICS

1. Select any other custom which has become commonplace and make up an explanation of its origin. You can use such customs as putting candles on a birthday cake or driving on the right-hand side of the road. Use your imagination.
2. The Pleasures of Eating
3. The Humor of Charles Lamb
4. Proper Topics of Conversation at the Dinner Table
5. The Importance of Food in Books I Have Read

WASHINGTON IRVING, 1783–1859

Like Montaigne, Bacon, and Addison, Washington Irving was a man of many talents. After a rather spotty education in New York, where he was born, he was admitted to the bar in 1806 and practiced law somewhat negligently until 1810. While he was learning law, he was apparently much more interested in writing and in the history of New York. At any rate, one of his best books, *A History of New York from the Beginning of the World to the End of the Dutch Dynasty*, by Diedrich Knickerbocker, appeared in 1809. This hilarious and by no means accurate " history " of the city is a wonderful burlesque in which people like Peter Stuyvesant move with mock-heroic grandeur.

In 1815 Irving went to Liverpool as manager of his brothers' mercantile firm, and he stayed in Europe for seventeen years. During these years he published, in England, *The Sketch Book*, from which " The Country Church " is taken; a life of Columbus; and two books about Spanish history, one of which, *The Alhambra*, is still widely read. For a short period during this European stay, he was secretary of the United States legation in London.

When Irving returned to the United States in 1832, he was a famous man. He had not led an army or a navy to victory, but he had done something even more important: he had raised the prestige of America in Europe through his writings. A few years later Edgar Allan Poe was to take Europe by storm, but Irving was the first to prove to Europe that Americans were good at things other than shooting Indians and buffalo.

During the later years of his life Irving was Secretary of the Navy under Van Buren and Minister to Spain from 1842 to

1846. But most of his time was occupied in writing a series of biographies and historical works. It is appropriate that his magnum opus was a six-volume life of George Washington, for whom he was named.

Irving's style is modeled closely after the British essayists of the eighteenth century, particularly Addison. His writing is British, rather than American; the real "American English" did not appear until the age of Mark Twain. But in the Knickerbocker *History* and in the stories of the Hudson River Valley, like "The Legend of Sleepy Hollow" and "Rip Van Winkle," Irving brought American legends to life in a completely delightful way. His somewhat humorous, somewhat shocked description of a country church service is like Addison's in some respects, different in others. Irving visited England a hundred years after Addison described Sir Roger de Coverley, but some details had not greatly changed in those years. In an essay like this one, Irving is revealed as America's first good reflective essayist — personal, meditative, intelligent.

THE COUNTRY CHURCH

A gentleman!
What, o' the woolpack? or the sugar chest?
Or lists of velvet? which is't, pound, or yard,
You vend your gentry by?

— BEGGAR's BUSH

There are few places more favorable to the study of character than an English country church. I was once passing a few weeks at the seat of a friend, who resided in the vicinity of one, the appearance of which particularly struck my fancy. It was one of those rich morsels of quaint antiquity which give such a peculiar charm to English landscape. It stood in the midst of a country filled with ancient families, and contained, within its cold and silent aisles, the congregated dust of many noble generations. The interior walls were incrusted with monuments of every age and style. The light streamed through windows dimmed with armorial bearings, richly emblazoned in stained glass. In various parts of the church were tombs of knights, and high-born dames, of gorgeous workmanship, with their effigies in colored marble. On every side the eye was struck with some instance of aspiring mortality; some haughty memorial which human pride had erected over its kindred dust, in this temple of the most humble of all religions.

The congregation was composed of the neighboring people of rank, who sat in pews, sumptuously lined and cushioned, furnished with richly-gilded prayer books, and decorated with their arms upon the pew doors; of the villagers and peasantry, who filled the back seats, and a small gallery beside the organ; and of the poor of the parish, who were ranged on benches in the aisles.

The service was performed by a snuffling well-fed vicar, who had a snug dwelling near the church. He was a privileged guest at all the tables of the neighborhood, and had been the keenest fox-hunter in the country; until age and good living had disabled him from doing anything more than ride to see the hounds throw off, and make one at the hunting dinner.

Under the ministry of such a pastor, I found it impossible to get into the train of thought suitable to the time and place: so, having, like many other feeble Christians, compromised with my conscience, by laying the sin of my own delinquency at another person's threshold, I occupied myself by making observations on my neighbors.

I was as yet a stranger in England, and curious to notice the manners of its fashionable classes. I found, as usual, that there was the least pretension where there was the most acknowledged title to respect. I was particularly struck, for instance, with the family of a nobleman of high rank, consisting of several sons and daughters. Nothing could be more simple and unassuming than their appearance. They generally came to church in the plainest equipage, and often on foot. The young ladies would stop and converse in the kindest manner with the peasantry, caress the children, and listen to the stories of the humble cottagers. Their countenances were open and beautifully fair, with an expression of high refinement, but, at the same time, a frank cheerfulness, and an engaging affability. Their brothers were tall, and elegantly formed. They were dressed fashionably, but simply; with strict neatness and propriety, but without any mannerism or foppishness. Their whole demeanor was easy and natural, with that lofty grace, and noble frankness, which bespeak freeborn souls that have never been checked in their growth by feelings of inferiority. There is a healthful hardiness about real dignity, that never dreads contact and communion with others, however humble. It is only spurious pride that is morbid and sensitive, and shrinks from every touch. I was pleased to see the manner in which they would converse with the peasantry about those rural concerns and field-sports, in which the gentlemen of this country so much delight. In these conversations there was neither haughtiness on the one part, nor servility on the other; and you were only reminded of the difference of rank by the habitual respect of the peasant.

In contrast to these was the family of a wealthy citizen, who had amassed a vast fortune; and, having purchased the estate and mansion of a ruined nobleman in the neighborhood, was endeavoring to assume all the style and dignity of an hereditary lord of the soil. The family always came to church *en prince*. They were rolled majestically along in a carriage emblazoned with arms. The crest glittered in silver radiance from every part of the harness where a crest could possibly be placed. A fat coachman, in a three-cornered hat, richly laced, and a flaxen wig, curling close round his rosy face, was seated on the box, with a sleek Danish dog beside him. Two footmen, in gorgeous liveries, with huge bouquets, and gold-headed canes, lolled behind. The carriage rose and sunk on its long springs with peculiar stateliness of motion. The very horses champed their bits, arched their necks, and glanced their eyes more proudly than common horses; either because they had caught a little of the family feeling, or were reined up more tightly than ordinary.

I could not but admire the style with which this splendid pageant was brought up to the gate of the churchyard. There was a vast effect produced at the turning of an angle of the wall -- a great smacking of the whip, straining and scrambling of horses, glistening of harness, and flashing of wheels through gravel. This was the moment of triumph and vainglory to the coachman. The horses were urged and checked until they were fretted into a foam. They threw out their feet in a prancing trot, dashing about pebbles at every step. The crowd of villagers sauntering quietly to church, opened precipitately to the right and left, gaping in vacant admiration. On reaching the gate, the horses were pulled up with a suddenness that produced an immediate stop, and almost threw them on their haunches.

There was an extraordinary hurry of the footman to alight, pull down the steps, and prepare everything for the descent on earth of this august family: The old citizen first emerged his round red face from out the door, looking about him with the pompous air of a man accus-

tomed to rule on 'Change, and shake the Stock Market
with a nod. His consort, a fine, fleshy, comfortable dame,
followed him. There seemed, I must confess, but little pride
in her composition. She was the picture of broad, honest,
vulgar enjoyment. The world went well with her; and she
liked the world. She had fine clothes, a fine house, a fine
carriage, fine children, everything was fine about her: it
was nothing but driving about, and visiting and feasting.
Life was to her a perpetual revel; it was one long Lord
Mayor's day.

Two daughters succeeded to this goodly couple. They
certainly were handsome; but had a supercilious air, that
chilled admiration, and disposed the spectator to be critical. They were ultra-fashionable in dress; and, though no
one could deny the richness of their decorations, yet their
appropriateness might be questioned amidst the simplicity
of a country church. They descended loftily from the
carriage, and moved up the line of peasantry with a step
that seemed dainty of the soil it trod on. They cast an ex-
cursive glance around, that passed coldly over the burly
faces of the peasantry, until they met the eyes of the nobleman's family, when their countenances immediately brightened into smiles, and they made the most profound and
elegant courtesies, which were returned in a manner that
showed they were but slight acquaintances.

I must not forget the two sons of this aspiring citizen,
who came to church in a dashing curricle, with outriders.
They were arrayed in the extremity of the mode, with all
that pedantry of dress which marks the man of question-
able pretensions to style. They kept entirely by themselves, eying everyone askance that came near them, as
if measuring his claims to respectability; yet they were
without conversation, except the exchange of an occasional
cant phrase. They even moved artificially; for their bodies, in

compliance with the caprice of the day, had been disciplined into the absence of all ease and freedom. Art had done everything to accomplish them as men of fashion, but nature had denied them the nameless grace. They were vulgarly shaped, like men formed for the common purposes of life, and had that air of supercilious assumption which is never seen in the true gentleman.

I have been rather minute in drawing the pictures of these two families, because I considered them specimens of what is often to be met with in this country — the unpretending great, and the arrogant little. I have no respect for titled rank, unless it be accompanied with true nobility of soul; but I have remarked in all countries where artificial distinctions exist, that the very highest classes are always the most courteous and unassuming. Those who are well assured of their own standing are least apt to trespass on that of others: whereas nothing is so offensive as the aspirings of vulgarity, which thinks to elevate itself by humiliating its neighbor.

As I have brought these families into contrast, I must notice their behavior in church. That of the nobleman's family was quiet, serious, and attentive. Not that they appeared to have any fervor of devotion, but rather a respect for sacred things, and sacred places, inseparable from good breeding. The others, on the contrary, were in a perpetual flutter and whisper; they betrayed a continual consciousness of finery, and a sorry ambition of being the wonders of a rural congregation.

The old gentleman was the only one really attentive to the service. He took the whole burden of family devotion upon himself, standing bolt upright, and uttering the responses with a loud voice that might be heard all over the church. It was evident that he was one of those thorough church and king men, who connect the idea of devotion and loyalty; who consider the Deity, somehow or other, of the government party, and religion "a very excellent sort of thing, that ought to be countenanced and kept up."

When he joined so loudly in the service, it seemed more by way of example to the lower orders, to show them that, though so great and wealthy, he was not above being religious; as I have seen a turtle-fed alderman swallow publicly a basin of charity soup, smacking his lips at every mouthful, and pronouncing it "excellent food for the poor."

When the service was at an end, I was curious to witness the several exits of my groups. The young noblemen and their sisters, as the day was fine, preferred strolling home across the fields, chatting with the country people as they went. The others departed as they came, in grand parade. Again were the equipages wheeled up to the gate. There was again the smacking of whips, the clattering of hoofs, and the glittering of harness. The horses started off almost at a bound; the villagers again hurried to right and left; the wheels threw up a cloud of dust; and the aspiring family was rapt out of sight in a whirlwind.

STUDYING THE ESSAY

1. Compare the nobleman in this essay with Sir Roger de Coverley in Addison's essay.
2. Compare the rich man in this essay with Sir Roger.
3. How does Irving's style resemble Addison's?
4. What sort of man is the vicar in this church?
5. Is there a member of your congregation who drives to church in his high-powered car and makes a grand entrance just in time for the service? What sort of person is he?
6. Why does the nobleman act as he does?
7. Why does the wealthy citizen act as he does?

8. Does Irving find anything good about the wealthy man's display?
9. How do the rich parents in the essay differ from their children?

COMPOSITION TOPICS

1. The Unpretending Great
2. The Arrogant Little

RALPH WALDO EMERSON, 1803–1882

"Whoso would be a man must be a noncon-formist," wrote Emerson in "Self-Reliance." If this sentence is a key to the meaning of the essay, it is also a significant state-ment about Emerson's own life. During the first thirty years of his life he was a conformist, and got nowhere. Then he broke with his past and established the reputation which he deserved.

The son of a Unitarian minister, a graduate of Harvard at the age of seventeen, a schoolteacher for a short time, Emerson at first followed his father and in 1829 was made pastor of a Unitarian church in Boston. Three years later he broke away from the church, because of an argument over the significance of communion, and went to Europe for two years. There he met most of the important literary men of the time. One of these men, Thomas Carlyle, said this of Emerson: "When he came to Europe, he was a lonely, wayfaring man." That was quite true, but when he returned to the United States and set-tled in Concord, Massachusetts, in 1834, he had his philosophy of life well in hand.

While he was in Europe, he had come into contact with sev-eral philosophies which influenced him deeply. The most im-portant of these were Hinduism and transcendentalism. Both believed that the world should be reformed from the inside out and that man was a creature who could be perfected through himself alone, and could thereby improve the world. The two most important parts of this philosophy Emerson put into his best-known essays, "Self-Reliance" and "Compensation." In "Self-Reliance" Emerson says that man is his own guide and that independence of mind is his best trait. In "Compensation" he advises moderation in all things, which, as Emerson learned from Hindu religion, will lead to right thoughts in man.

After Emerson returned to the United States and became the center of a distinguished literary group in Concord, he earned his living mainly by lecturing to large audiences all over the country. He never made more than $600 a year from his writings. As he grew older, he became more conservative, but he was a violent abolitionist before the War between the States. Toward the end of his life he lost his memory. But by that time he was to the entire nation " The Sage of Concord," and many honors, from many countries, had come to him.

Emerson's best writing is found in his *Essays,* published in two series in 1841 and 1844; in *Representative Men* (1850), studies of some of the great men of history; in some of his lectures; and in his *Journal,* published forty years after his death. " Self-Reliance," the first part of which is printed here, is from the first series of the essays.

Emerson is probably the most often quoted American writer. Many of his sentences have become epigrams; you will find several in " Self-Reliance." In his prose, one thought is piled on another, with little consideration for formal paragraph organization. Reading Emerson is something like reading Bacon; the reader must get the ideas in the sentences.

" The purpose of life seems to be to acquaint man with himself . . . Nothing can bring you peace but yourself . . ." wrote Emerson in his *Journal.* " Self-Reliance " states this philosophy clearly to a generation of young Americans who need the self-reliance of which the Sage of Concord speaks.

SELF-RELIANCE

I read the other day some verses written by an eminent painter which were original and not conventional. The soul always hears an admonition in such lines, let the subject be what it may. The sentiment they instill is of more value than any thought they may contain. To believe your own thought, to believe that what is true for you in your private heart is true for all men — that is genius. Speak your latent conviction, and it shall be the universal sense; for the inmost in due time becomes the outmost — and our first thought is rendered back to us by trumpets of the Last Judgment. Familiar as the voice of the mind is to each, the highest merit we ascribe to Moses, Plato, and Milton is, that they set at naught books and traditions, and spoke not what men, but what they thought. A man should learn to detect and watch that gleam of light which flashes across his mind from within, more than the luster of the firmament of bards and sages. Yet he dismisses without notice his thought, because it is his. In every work of genius we recognize our rejected thoughts; they come back to us with a certain alienated majesty. Great works of art have no more affecting lesson for us than this. They teach us to abide by our spontaneous impression with good-humored inflexibility then most when the whole cry of voices is on the other side. Else, tomorrow a stranger will say with masterly good sense precisely what we have thought and felt all the time, and we shall be forced to take with shame our own opinion from another.

There is a time in every man's education when he arrives at the conviction that envy is ignorance; that imitation is suicide; that he must take himself for better, for worse, as his portion; that, though the wide universe is full of good, no kernel of nourishing corn can come to him but through his toil bestowed on that plot of ground which is given to him to till. The power which resides in him is new in nature, and none but he knows what that is which he can do, nor does he know until he has tried. Not for nothing one face, one character, one fact, makes much impression on him, and another none. This sculpture in the memory is not without pre-established harmony. The eye was placed where one ray should fall, that it might testify of that particular ray. We but half express ourselves, and are ashamed of that divine idea which each of us represents. It may be safely trusted as proportionate and of good issues, so it be faithfully imparted, but God will not have his work made manifest by cowards. A man is relieved and gay when he has put his heart into his work and done his best; but what he has said or done otherwise shall give him no peace. It is a deliverance which does not deliver. In the attempt his genius deserts him; no muse befriends; no invention, no hope.

Trust thyself: every heart vibrates to that iron string. Accept the place the divine providence has found for you, the society of your contemporaries, the connection of events. Great men have always done so, and confided themselves childlike to the genius of their age, betraying their perception that the absolutely trustworthy was seated at their heart, working through their hands, predominating in all their being. And we are now men, and must accept in the highest mind the same transcendent destiny; and not minors and invalids in a protected corner, not cowards fleeing before a revolution, but guides, redeemers, and benefactors, obeying the Almighty effort, and advancing on Chaos and the Dark.

What pretty oracles nature yields us on this text in the

face and behavior of children, babes, and even brutes! That divided and rebel mind, that distrust of a sentiment because our arithmetic has computed the strength and means opposed to our purpose, these have not. Their mind being whole, their eye is as yet unconquered, and when we look in their faces, we are disconcerted. Infancy conforms to nobody: all conform to it, so that one babe commonly makes four or five out of the adults who prattle and play to it. So God has armed youth and puberty and manhood no less with its own piquancy and charm, and made it enviable and gracious and its claims not to be put by, if it will stand by itself. Do not think the youth has no force, because he cannot speak to you and me. Hark! in the next room his voice is sufficiently clear and emphatic. It seems he knows how to speak to his contemporaries. Bashful or bold, then, he will know how to make us seniors very unnecessary.

The nonchalance of boys who are sure of a dinner, and would disdain as much as a lord to do or say aught to conciliate one, is the healthy attitude of human nature. A boy is in the parlor what the pit is in the playhouse; independent, irresponsible, looking out from his corner on such people and facts as pass by, he tries and sentences them on their merits, in the swift, summary way of boys, as good, bad, interesting, silly, eloquent, troublesome. He cumbers himself never about consequences, about interests; he gives an independent, genuine verdict. You must court him: he does not court you. But the man is, as it were, clapped into jail by his consciousness. As soon as he has once acted or spoken with éclat, he is a committed person, watched by the sympathy or the hatred of hundreds, whose affections must now enter into his account. There is no Lethe for this. Ah, that he could pass again into his neutrality! Who can thus avoid all pledges and, having observed, observe again from the

same unaffected, unbiased, unbribable, unaffrighted innocence, must always be formidable. He would utter opinion
on all passing affairs, which being seen to be not private
but necessary, would sink like darts into the ear of men, and
put them in fear.

These are the voices which we hear in solitude, but they
grow faint and inaudible as we enter into the world. Society
everywhere is in conspiracy against the manhood of every
one of its members. Society is a joint-stock company, in
which the members agree, for the better securing of his
bread to each shareholder, to surrender the liberty and culture of the eater. The virtue in most request is conformity.
Self-reliance is its aversion. It loves not realities and creators,
but names and customs.

Whoso would be a man must be a nonconformist. He
who would gather immortal palms must not be hindered by
the name of goodness, but must explore if it be goodness.
Nothing is at last sacred but the integrity of your own
mind. Absolve you to yourself, and you shall have the
suffrage of the world. I remember an answer which when
quite young I was prompted to make to a valued adviser,
who was wont to importune me with the dear old doctrines
of the church. On my saying, " What have I to do with the
sacredness of traditions, if I live wholly from within? " my
friend suggested: " But these impulses may be from below,
not from above." I replied: " They do not seem to me to be
such; but if I am the Devil's child, I will live then from the
Devil." No law can be sacred to me but that of my nature.
Good and bad are but names very readily transferable to
that or this; the only right is what is after my constitution,
the only wrong is against it. A man is to carry himself in
the presence of all opposition, as if everything were titular
and ephemeral but he. I am ashamed to think how easily
we capitulate to badges and names, to large societies and

dead institutions. Every decent and well-spoken individual affects and sways me more than is right. I ought to go upright and vital, and speak the rude truth in all ways. If malice and vanity wear the coat of philanthropy, shall that pass? If an angry bigot assumes this bountiful cause of Abolition, and comes to me with his last news from Barbados, why should I not say to him: " Go love thy infant; love thy woodchopper; be good-natured and modest; have that grace, and never varnish your hard, uncharitable ambition with this incredible tenderness for black folk a thousand miles off. Thy love afar is spite at home." Rough and graceless would be such greeting, but truth is handsomer than the affectation of love. Your goodness must have some edge to it — else it is none. The doctrine of hatred must be preached as the counteraction of the doctrine of love when that pules and whines. I shun father and mother and wife and brother, when my genius calls me. I would write on the lintels of the doorpost, *Whim.* I hope it is somewhat better than whim at last, but we cannot spend the day in explanation. Expect me not to show cause why I seek or why I exclude company. Then, again, do not tell me, as a good man did today, of my obligation to put all poor men in good situations. Are they *my* poor? I tell thee, thou foolish philanthropist, that I grudge the dollar, the dime, the cent I give to such men as do not belong to me and to whom I do not belong. There is a class of persons to whom by all spiritual affinity I am bought and sold; for them I will go to prison, if need be; but your miscellaneous populai charities; the education at college of fools; the building of meeting-houses to the vain end to which many now stand; alms to sots, and the thousandfold relief societies — though I confess with shame I sometimes succumb and give the dollar, it is a wicked dollar which by and by I shall have the manhood to withhold.

Virtues are, in the popular estimate, rather the exception than the rule. There is the man *and* his virtues. Men do what is called a good action, as some piece of courage or charity, much as they would pay a fine in expiation of daily nonappearance on parade. Their works are done as an apology or extenuation of their living in the world — as invalids and the insane pay a high board. Their virtues are penances. I do not wish to expiate, but to live. My life is not an apology, but a life. My life is for itself and not for a spectacle. I much prefer that it should be of a lower strain, so it be genuine and equal, than that it should be glittering and unsteady. I wish it to be sound and sweet, and not to need diet and bleeding. I ask primary evidence that you are a man, and refuse this appeal from the man to his actions. I know that for myself it makes no difference whether I do or forbear those actions which are reckoned excellent. I cannot consent to pay for a privilege where I have intrinsic right. Few and mean as my gifts may be, I actually am, and do not need for my own assurance or the assurance of my fellows any secondary testimony.

What I must do is all that concerns me, not what the people think. This rule, equally arduous in actual and in intellectual life, may serve for the whole distinction between greatness and meanness. It is the harder, because you will always find those who think they know what is your duty better than you know it. It is easy in the world to live after the world's opinion; it is easy in solitude to live after our own; but the great man is he who in the midst of the crowd keeps with perfect sweetness the independence of solitude.

The objection to conforming to usages that have become dead to you is that it scatters your force. It loses your time and blurs the impression of your character. If you maintain a dead church, contribute to a dead Bible society, vote with

a great party either for the government or against it, spread
your table like base housekeepers — under all these screens
I have difficulty to detect the precise man you are. And, of
course, so much force is withdrawn from your proper life.
But do your work, and I shall know you. Do your work,
and you shall reinforce yourself. A man must consider what
a blindman's-bluff is this game of conformity. If I know
your sect, I anticipate your argument. I hear a preacher
announce for his text and topic the expediency of one of the
institutions of his church. Do I not know beforehand that
not possibly can he say a new and spontaneous world? Do I
not know that, with all this ostentation of examining the
grounds of the institution, he will do no such thing? Do I
not know that he is pledged to himself not to look but at
one side — the permitted side, not as a man, but as a parish
minister? He is a retained attorney, and these airs of the
bench are the emptiest affectation. Well, most men have
bound their eyes with one or another handkerchief, and attached themselves to some one of these communities of
opinion. This conformity makes them not false in a few
particulars, authors of a few lies, but false in all particulars.
Their every truth is not quite true. Their two is not the real
two, their four not the real four; so that every word they
say chagrins us, and we know not where to begin to set
them right. Meantime nature is not slow to equip us in the
prison uniform of the party to which we adhere. We come
to wear one cut of face and figure, and acquire by degrees
the gentlest asinine expression. There is a mortifying experience in particular, which does not fail to wreak itself
also in the general history; I mean " the foolish face of
praise," the forced smile which we put on in company
where we do not feel at ease in answer to conversation
which does not interest us. The muscles, not spontaneously
moved, but moved by a low usurping wilfulness, grow

tight about the outline of the face with the most disagreeable sensation.

For nonconformity the world whips you with its displeasure. And therefore a man must know how to estimate a sour face. The bystanders look askance on him in the public street or in the friend's parlor. If this aversion had its origin in contempt and resistance like his own, he might well go home with a sad countenance; but the sour faces of the multitude, like their sweet faces, have no deep cause, but are put on and off as the wind blows and a newspaper directs. Yet is the discontent of the multitude more formidable than that of the senate and the college. It is easy enough for a firm man who knows the world to brook the rage of the cultivated classes. Their rage is decorous and prudent, for they are timid as being very vulnerable themselves. But when to their feminine rage the indignation of the people is added, when the ignorant and the poor are aroused, when the unintelligent brute force that lies at the bottom of society is made to growl and mow, it needs the habit of magnanimity and religion to treat it godlike as a trifle of no concernment.

The other terror that scares us from self-trust is our consistency, a reverence for our past act or word, because the eyes of others have no other data for computing our orbit than our past acts, and we are loath to disappoint them.

But why should you keep your head over your shoulder? Why drag about this corpse of your memory, lest you contradict somewhat you have stated in this or that public place? Suppose you should contradict yourself; what then? It seems to be a rule of wisdom never to rely on your memory alone, scarcely even in acts of pure memory, but to bring the past for judgment into the thousand-eyed present, and live ever in a new day. In your metaphysics you have denied personality to the Deity: yet when the devout motions of the soul come, yield to them heart and life, though they should clothe God with shape and color. Leave your theory, as Joseph his coat in the hand of the harlot, and flee.

A foolish consistency is the hobgoblin of little minds, adored by little statesmen and philosophers and divines. With consistency a great soul has simply nothing to do. He may as well concern himself with the shadow on the wall. Speak what you think now in hard words, and tomorrow speak what tomorrow thinks in hard words again, though it contradict everything you said today. " Ah, so you shall be sure to be misunderstood." Is it so bad, then, to be misunderstood? Pythagoras was misunderstood, and Socrates, and Jesus, and Luther, and Copernicus, and Galileo, and Newton, and every pure and wise spirit that ever took flesh. To be great is to be misunderstood.

I suppose no man can violate his nature. All the sallies of his will are rounded in by the law of his being, as the inequalities of Andes and Himmaleh are insignificant in the curve of the sphere. Nor does it matter how you gauge and try him. A character is like an acrostic or Alexandrian stanza — read it forward, backward, or across, it still spells the same thing. In this pleasing contrite wood-life, which God allows me, let me record day by day my honest thought without prospect or retrospect, and, I cannot doubt, it will be found symmetrical, though I mean it not and see it not. My book should smell of pines and resound with the hum of insects. The swallow over my window should interweave that thread or straw he carries in his bill into my web also. We pass for what we are. Character teaches above our wills. Men imagine that they communicate their virtue or vice only by overt actions, and do not see that virtue or vice emits a breath every moment.

There will be an agreement in whatever variety of actions, so they be each honest and natural in their hour. For of one will, the actions will be harmonious, however unlike they seem. These varieties are lost sight of at a little distance, at a little height of thought. One tendency unites them all. The voyage of the best ship is a zigzag line of a hundred tacks. See the line from a sufficient distance, and it straightens itself to the average tendency. Your genuine action will explain itself, and will explain your other genuine actions. Your conformity explains nothing. Act singly, and what you have already done singly will justify you now. Greatness appeals to the future. If I can be firm enough today to do right, and scorn eyes, I must have done so much right before as to defend me now. Be it how it will, do right now. Always scorn appearances, and you always may. The force of character is cumulative. All the foregone days of virtue work their health into this. What makes the majesty of the heroes of the senate and the field, which so fills the imagination? The consciousness of a train of great days and victories behind. They shed a united light on the advancing actor. He is attended as by a visible escort of angels. That is it which throws thunder into Chatham's voice, and dignity into Washington's port, and America into Adams's eye. Honor is venerable to us because it is no ephemeris. It is always ancient virtue. We worship it today because it is not of today. We love it and pay it homage, because it is not a trap for our love and homage, but is self-dependent, self-derived, and therefore of an old immaculate pedigree, even if shown in a young person.

I hope in these days we have heard the last of conformity and consistency. Let the words be gazetted and ridiculous henceforward. Instead of the gong for dinner, let us hear a whistle from the Spartan fife. Let us never bow and apologize more. A great man is coming to eat at my house. I do not wish to please him; I wish that he should wish to please me. I will stand here for humanity, and though I would make it kind, I would make it true. Let us affront and reprimand the smooth mediocrity and squalid contentment of the times, and hurl in the face of custom and trade and office, the fact which is the upshot of all history, that there is a great responsible Thinker and Actor working wherever a man works; that a true man belongs to no other time or place, but is the center of things. Where he is, there is nature. He measures you and all men and all events. Ordinarily, everybody in society reminds us of somewhat else, or of some other person. Character, reality, reminds you of nothing else; it takes place of the whole creation. The man must be so much, that he must make all circumstances indifferent. Every true man is a cause, a country, and an age; requires infinite spaces and numbers and time fully to accomplish his design — and posterity seems to follow his steps as a train of clients. A man Caesar is born, and for ages after we have a Roman Empire. Christ is born, and millions of minds so grow and cleave to his genius, that he is confounded with virtue and the possible of man. An institution is the lengthened shadow of one man; as Monachism, of the Hermit Antony; the Reformation, of Luther; Quakerism, of Fox; Methodism, of Wesley; Abolition, of Clarkson. Scipio, Milton called " the height of Rome "; and all history resolves itself very easily into the biography of a few stout and earnest persons.

Let a man then know his worth, and keep things under his feet. Let him not peep or steal, or skulk up and down with the air of a charity-boy, a bastard, or an interloper in the world which exists for him. But the man in the street, finding no worth in himself which corresponds to the force which built a tower or sculptured a marble god, feels poor when he looks on these. To him a palace, a statue, or a costly book has an alien and forbidding air, much like a gay equipage, and seems to say like that, " Who are you, sir? " Yet they all are his suitors for his notice, petitioners to his faculties that they will come out and take possession. The picture waits for my verdict: it is not to command me, but I am to settle its claims to praise. That popular fable of the sot who was picked up dead drunk in the street, carried to the duke's house, washed and dressed and laid in the duke's bed, and, on his waking, treated with all obsequious ceremony like the duke, and assured that he had been insane, owes its popularity to the fact that it symbolizes so well the state of man, who is in the world a sort of sot, but now and then wakes up, exercises his reason, and finds himself a true prince.

Our reading is mendicant and sycophantic. In history our imagination plays us false. Kingdom and lordship, power and estate, are a gaudier vocabulary than private John and Edward in a small house and common day's work; but the things of life are the same to both; the sum total of both is the same. Why all this deference to Alfred and Scanderbeg and Gustavus? Suppose they were virtuous; did they wear out virtue? As great a stake depends on your private act today, as followed their public and renowned steps. When private men shall act with original views, the luster will be transferred from the actions of kings to those of gentlemen.

The world has been instructed by its kings, who have so magnetized the eyes of nations. It has been taught by this colossal symbol the mutual reverence that is due from man to man. The joyful loyalty with which men have every-where suffered the king, the noble, or the great proprietor to walk among them by a law of his own, make his own scale of men and things and reverse theirs, pay for benefits not with money but with honor, and represent the law in his person, was the hieroglyphic by which they obscurely signified their consciousness of their own right and comeli-ness, the right of every man.

STUDYING THE ESSAY

1. Give examples from the essay of what Emerson means by self-reliance.
2. From your own experience give examples of self-reliance.
3. Independence of mind, or self-reliance, can be troublesome. What is the difference between self-reliance (or liberty, or freedom) and license?
4. What does Emerson mean when he says, " Whoso would be a man must be a nonconformist "?
5. What does Emerson mean by " consistency "? Why does he consider consistency an undesirable trait?
6. This essay is full of epigrams. Find five or more.
7. Do you agree with most of what Emerson said? If you do not agree, explain the reasons for your disagreement.
8. Words to learn: *oracles, nonchalance, integrity, bigot, prudent, affront, mediocrity.*
9. Who were these men: Pythagoras, Socrates, Luther, Newton, Galileo, Copernicus?

COMPOSITION TOPICS

1. Emerson and Modern Politics
2. " What I must do is all that concerns me, not what the people think."
3. " Trust thyself."

HENRY DAVID THOREAU, 1817–1862

Thoreau was one of the original masters in nineteenth-century American literature. Two others, Melville and Whitman, were not essayists. A fourth, Mark Twain, is represented in this book. In many ways Thoreau was the most original of the lot. As the cowboys say of a steer that won't be caught, he was a maverick.

He was born in Concord, Massachusetts, and, except for an unhappy season as a tutor on Long Island, lived there all his life. He graduated from Harvard but refused to take his diploma because he thought he could use the five dollars — the price of the sheepskin — to better advantage elsewhere. He loved children, but when, as a teacher in a private school run by his brother, he was reprimanded for not whipping the boys, he grabbed a half dozen youngsters, beat them severely, and resigned from his job. He hated conformity so much that he went to jail rather than pay his poll tax to a government which allowed slavery. And he was disgusted when his aunt paid his tax and got him out of jail. A story has it that Emerson visited him in the Concord lockup and said, " Henry, why are you here? " " Waldo, why are you *not* here? " was Henry's reply.

In Concord he lived with Emerson for two years and became, like Emerson, a transcendentalist. But he was hard to get along with. He was a natural rebel, often surly and unapproachable, a complete individualist. He was an even stronger supporter of abolition than Emerson. He openly defended John Brown and cared little that his views could be dangerous to him. He hated war. One of his essays, " Civil Disobedience," is such a powerful defense of the non-violent resistance to authority that it became, much later, one of the great inspirations of another pacifist,

Mohandas Gandhi, as he studied ways to free his people in India from the rule of the British.

But for American readers the most famous thing Thoreau did was to spend $28 to build a cabin on the shore of Walden Pond, near Concord, and "retire" for a year and a half to live with nature. Actually he was no hermit. He went to town nearly every day, and he had scores of visitors. Rather, he was trying to show that man can live without society if he so chooses. What is remarkable about his life at Walden is, for us, that he wrote a book about it. The essay reprinted here is from that book.

Thoreau was a born naturalist. He knew wild life by instinct: wild birds would sit on his shoulder; he had the rare ability to catch fish bare-handed. *Walden* is a marvelous description of nature and an equally marvelous description of Thoreau. The essay in this book is only a sample of the riches to be found in it. The entire book repays reading and rereading.

One critic says this about Thoreau's prose: "In its directness, in its curt, vigorous rhythms, its delight in racy words, its wit, it is the best American prose ever written, and as American as it is good." It will be clear to you that something about this essay is very different from the writings of Irving and Emerson. The difference lies in the complete originality of Thoreau.

WHERE I LIVED,
AND WHAT I LIVED FOR

At a certain season of our life we are accustomed to consider every spot as the possible site of a house. I have thus surveyed the country on every side within a dozen miles of where I live. In imagination I have bought all the farms in succession, for all were to be bought, and I knew their price. I walked over each farmer's premises, tasted his wild apples, discoursed on husbandry with him, took his farm at his price, at any price, mortgaging it to him in my mind — even put a higher price on it; took everything but a deed of it; took his word for his deed, for I dearly love to talk; cultivated it, and him to some extent, I trust, and withdrew when I had enjoyed it long enough, leaving him to carry it on. This experience entitled me to be regarded as a sort of real estate broker by my friends. Wherever I sat, there I might live, and the landscape radiated from me accordingly. What is a house but a *sedes*, a seat? — better if a country seat. I discovered many a site for a house not likely to be soon improved, which some might have thought too far from the village, but to my eyes the village was too far from it. Well, there I might live, I said; and there I did live, for an hour, a summer and a winter life; saw how I could let the years run off, buffet the winter through, and see the spring come in. The future inhabitants of this region, wherever they may place their houses, may be sure that they have been anticipated. An afternoon sufficed to lay out the land into orchard, woodlot, and pasture, and to decide what fine oaks or pines should be left to stand before the door, and whence each blasted tree could be seen to the best advantage; and then I let it lie, fallow perchance, for a man is rich in proportion to the number of things which he can afford to let alone.

My imagination carried me so far that I even had the refusal of several farms — the refusal was all I wanted — but I never got my fingers burned by actual possession. The nearest that I came to actual possession was when I bought the Hollowell place, and had begun to sort my seeds, and collected materials with which to make a wheelbarrow to carry it on or off with; but before the owner gave me a deed of it, his wife — every man has such a wife — changed her mind and wished to keep it, and he offered me ten dollars to release him. Now, to speak the truth, I had but ten cents in the world, and it surpassed my arithmetic to tell, if I was that man who had ten cents, or who had a farm, or ten dollars, or all together. However, I let him keep the ten dollars and the farm too, for I had carried it far enough; or rather, to be generous, I sold him the farm for just what I gave for it, and, as he was not a rich man, made him a present of ten dollars, and still had my ten cents, and seeds, and materials for a wheelbarrow left. I found thus that I had been a rich man without any damage to my poverty. But I retained the landscape, and I have since annually carried off what it yielded without a wheelbarrow. With respect to landscapes,

> I am monarch of all I *survey*,
> My right there is none to dispute.

I have frequently seen a poet withdraw, having enjoyed the most valuable part of a farm, while the crusty farmer supposed that he had got a few wild apples only. Why, the owner does not know it for many years when a poet has put his farm in rhyme, the most admirable kind of invisible fence, has fairly impounded it, milked it, skimmed it, and got all the cream, and left the farmer only the skimmed milk.

The real attractions of the Hollowell farm, to me, were: its complete retirement, being about two miles from the village, half a mile from the nearest neighbor, and separated from the highway by a broad field; its bounding on the river, which the owner said protected it by its fogs and frosts in the spring, though that was nothing to me; the gray color and ruinous state of the house and barn, and the dilapidated fences, which put such an interval between me and the last occupant; the hollow and lichen-covered apple trees, gnawed by rabbits, showing what kind of neighbors I should have; but above all, the recollection I had of it from my earliest voyages up the river, when the house was concealed behind a dense grove of red maples, through which I heard the house dog bark. I was in haste to buy it, before the proprietor finished getting out some rocks, cutting down the hollow apple trees, and grubbing up some young birches which had sprung up in the pasture, or, in short, had made any more of his improvements. To enjoy these advantages I was ready to carry it on, like Atlas, to take the world on my shoulders — I never heard what compensation he received for that — and do all those things which had no other motive or excuse but that I might pay for it and be unmolested in my possession of it; for I knew all the while that it would yield the most abundant crop of the kind I wanted if I could only afford to let it alone. But it turned out as I have said.

All that I could say, then, with respect to farming on a large scale (I have always cultivated a garden) was that I had had my seeds ready. Many think that seeds improve with age. I have no doubt that time discriminates between the good and the bad; and when at last I shall plant, I shall be less likely to be disappointed. But I would say to my fellows, once for all: as long as possible live free and uncommitted. It makes but little difference whether you are committed to a farm or the county jail.

Old Cato, whose "De Re Rustica" is my "Cultivator," says, and the only translation I have seen makes sheer nonsense of the passage, "When you think of getting a farm, turn it thus in your mind, not to buy greedily; nor spare your pains to look at it, and do not think it enough to go around it once. The oftener you go there the more it will please you, if it is good." I think I shall not buy greedily, but go round and round it as long as I live, and be buried in it first, that it may please me the more at last.

The present was my next experiment of this kind, which I purpose to describe more at length, for convenience putting the experience of two years into one. As I have said, I do not propose to write an ode to dejection, but to brag as lustily as chanticleer in the morning standing on his roost, if only to wake my neighbors up.

When first I took up my abode in the woods, that is, began to spend my nights as well as days there, which, by accident, was on Independence Day, or the Fourth of July, 1845, my house was not finished for winter, but was merely a defense against the rain, without plastering or chimney, the walls being of rough weather-stained boards, with wide chinks, which made it cool at night. The upright white hewn studs and freshly planed door and window casings gave it a clean and airy look, especially in the morning, when its timbers were saturated with dew, so that I fancied that by noon some sweet gum would exude from them. To my imagination it retained throughout the day more or less of this auroral character, reminding me of a certain house on a mountain which I had visited the year before. This was an airy and unplastered cabin, fit to entertain a traveling god, and where a goddess might trail her garments. The winds which passed over my dwelling were such as sweep over the ridges of mountains, bearing the broken strains, or celestial parts only, of terrestrial music. The morning wind forever blows, the poem of creation is uninterrupted; but few are the ears that hear it. Olympus is but the outside of the earth everywhere.

The only house I had been the owner of before, if I except a boat, was a tent, which I used occasionally when making excursions in the summer, and this is still rolled up in my garret; but the boat, after passing from hand to hand, has gone down the stream of time. With this more substantial shelter about me, I had made some progress toward settling in the world. This frame, so slightly clad, was a sort of crystallization around me, and reacted on the builder. It was suggested somewhat as a picture in outlines. I did not need to go outdoors to take the air, for the atmosphere within had lost none of its freshness. It was not so much within doors as behind a door where I sat, even in the rainiest weather. The Harivansha says, " An abode without birds is like a meat without seasoning." Such was not my abode, for I found myself suddenly neighbor to the birds, not by having imprisoned one, but having caged myself near them. I was not only nearer to some of those which commonly frequent the garden and the orchard, but to those wilder and more thrilling songsters of the forest which never, or rarely, serenade a villager: the woodthrush, the veery, the scarlet tanager, the field-sparrow, the whippoorwill, and many others.

I was seated by the shore of a small pond, about a mile and a half south of the village of Concord and somewhat higher than it, in the midst of an extensive wood between that town and Lincoln, and about two miles south of that our only field known to fame, Concord Battle Ground; but I was so low in the woods that the opposite shore, half a mile off, like the rest, covered with wood, was my most distant horizon. For the first week, whenever I looked out on the pond, it impressed me like a tarn high up on the side of a mountain, its bottom far above the surface of other lakes, and as the sun arose, I saw it throwing off its nightly clothing of mist, and here and there, by degrees, its soft ripples or its smooth reflecting surface was revealed, while the mists, like ghosts, were stealthily withdrawing in every direction into the woods, as at the breaking up of some nocturnal conventicle. The very dew seemed to hang upon the trees later into the day than usual, as on the sides of mountains.

This small lake was of most value as a neighbor in the intervals of a gentle rain storm in August, when, both air and water being perfectly still, but the sky overcast, mid-afternoon had all the serenity of evening, and the wood-thrush sang around, and was heard from shore to shore. A lake like this is never smoother than at such a time; and, the clear portion of the air above it being shallow and darkened by clouds, the water, full of light and reflections, becomes a lower heaven itself so much the more important. From a hilltop near by, where the wood had been recently cut off, there was a pleasing vista southward across the pond, through a wide indentation in the hills which form the shore there, where their opposite sides sloping toward each other suggested a stream flowing out in that direction through a wooded valley, but stream there was none. That way I looked between and over the near green hills to some distant and higher ones in the horizon, tinged with blue. Indeed, by standing on tiptoe I could catch a glimpse of some of the peaks of the still bluer and more distant mountain ranges in the northwest, those true-blue coins from heaven's own mint, and also of some portion of the village. But in other directions, even from this point, I could not see over or beyond the woods which surrounded me. It is well to have some water in your neighborhood to give buoyancy to and float the earth. One value even of the smallest well is that when you look into it you see that earth is not continent but insular. This is as important as that it keeps butter cool. When I looked across the pond from this peak toward the Sudbury meadows, which in time of flood I distinguished elevated perhaps by a mirage in their seething valley, like a coin in a basin, all the earth beyond the pond appeared like a thin crust insulated and floated even by this small sheet of intervening water, and I was reminded that this on which I dwelt was but dry land.

Though the view from my door was still more contracted, I did not feel crowded or confined in the least. There was pasture enough for my imagination. The low shrub-oak plateau to which the opposite shore arose stretched away toward the prairies of the West and the steppes of Tartary, affording ample room for all the roving families of men. " There are none happy in the world but beings who enjoy freely a vast horizon," said Damodara, when his herds required new and larger pastures.

Both place and time were changed, and I dwelt nearer to those parts of the universe and to those eras in history which had most attracted me. Where I lived was as far off as many a region viewed nightly by astronomers. We are wont to imagine rare and delectable places in some remote and more celestial corner of the system, behind the constellation of Cassiopeia's Chair, far from noise and disturbance. I discovered that my house actually had its site in such a withdrawn, but forever new and unprofaned, part of the universe. If it were worth the while to settle in those parts near to the Pleiades or the Hyades, to Aldebaran or Altair, then I was really there, or at an equal remoteness from the life which I had left behind, dwindled and twinkling with as fine a ray to my nearest neighbor, and to be seen only in moonless nights by him. Such was that part of creation where I had squatted:

> There was a shepherd that did live,
>   And held his thoughts as high
> As were the mounts whereon his flocks
>   Did hourly feed him by.

What should we think of the shepherd's life if his flocks always wandered to higher pastures than his thoughts?

Every morning was a cheerful invitation to make my life of equal simplicity, and I may say innocence, with Nature herself. I have been as sincere a worshiper of Aurora as the Greeks. I got up early and bathed in the pond; that was a religious exercise, and one of the best things which I did. They say that characters were engraven on the bathing tub of King Tchingthang to this effect: " Renew thyself completely each day; do it again and again, and forever again." I can understand that. Morning brings back the heroic ages. I was as much affected by the faint hum of a mosquito making its invisible and unimaginable tour through my apartments at earliest dawn, when I was sitting with door and windows open, as I could be by any trumpet that ever sang of fame. It was Homer's requiem; itself an Iliad and Odyssey in the air, singing its own wrath and wanderings. There was something cosmical about it, a standing advertisement, till forbidden, of the everlasting vigor and fertility of the world. The morning, which is the most memorable season of the day, is the awakening hour. Then there is least somnolence in us; and for an hour, at least, some part of us awakes which slumbers all the rest of the day and night. Little is to be expected of that day, if it can be called a day, to which we are not awakened by our Genius, but by the mechanical nudgings of some servitor, are not awakened by our own newly acquired force and aspirations from within, accompanied by the undulations of celestial music, instead of factory bells, and a fragrance filling the air — to a higher life than we fell asleep from; and thus the darkness bears its fruit, and proves itself to be good, no less than the light. That man who does not believe that each day contains an earlier, more sacred, and auroral hour than he has yet profaned has despaired of life, and is pursuing a descending and darkening way. After a partial cessation of his sensuous life, the soul of man, or its organs rather, are reinvigorated each day, and his Genius tries again what noble life it can make. All memorable events, I should say, transpire in morning time and in a morning atmosphere. The Vedas say, "All intelligences awake with the morning." Poetry and art and the fairest and most memorable of the actions of men date from such an hour. All poets and heroes, like Memnon, are the children of Aurora and emit their music at sunrise. To him whose elastic and vigorous thought keeps pace with the sun the day is a perpetual morning. It matters not what the clocks say or the attitudes and labors of men. Morning is when I am awake and there is a dawn in me. Moral reform is the effort to throw off sleep. Why is it that men give so poor an account of their day if they have not been slumbering? They are not such poor calculators. If they had not been overcome with drowsiness, they would have performed something. The millions are awake enough for physical labor; but only one in a million is awake enough for effective intellectual exertion, only one in a hundred millions to a poetic or divine life. To be awake is to be alive. I have never yet met a man who was quite awake. How could I have looked him in the face?

We must learn to reawaken and keep ourselves awake, not by mechanical aids, but by an infinite expectation of the dawn, which does not forsake us in our soundest sleep. I know of no more encouraging fact than the unquestionable ability of man to elevate his life by a conscious endeavor. It is something to be able to paint a particular picture, or to carve a statue, and so to make a few objects beautiful; but it is far more glorious to carve and paint the very atmosphere and medium through which we look, which morally we can do. To affect the quality of the day, that is the highest of arts. Every man is tasked to make his life, even in its details, worthy of the contemplation of his most elevated and critical hour. If we refused, or rather used up, such paltry information as we get, the oracles would distinctly inform us how this might be done.

I went to the woods because I wished to live deliberately, to front only the essential facts of life, and see if I could not learn what it had to teach, and not, when I came to die, discover that I had not lived. I did not wish to live what was not life, living is so dear; nor did I wish to practice resignation, unless it was quite necessary. I wanted to live deep and suck out all the marrow of life, to live so sturdily and Spartan-like as to put to rout all that was not life, to cut a broad swath and shave close, to drive life into a corner, and reduce it to its lowest terms, and, if it proved to be mean, why then to get the whole and genuine meanness of it, and publish its meanness to the world; or if it were sublime, to know it by experience, and be able to give a true account of it in my next excursion. For most men, it appears to me, are in a strange uncertainty about it, whether it is of the devil or of God, and have somewhat hastily concluded that it is the chief end of man here to " glorify God and enjoy him forever."

Still we live meanly, like ants, though the fable tells us that we were long ago changed into men; like pygmies we fight with cranes; it is error upon error, and clout upon clout, and our best virtue has for its occasion a superfluous and evitable wretchedness. Our life is frittered away by detail. An honest man has hardly need to count more than his ten fingers, or in extreme cases he may add his ten toes, and lump the rest. Simplicity, simplicity, simplicity! I say, let your affairs be as two or three, and not a hundred or a thousand; instead of a million count half a dozen, and keep your accounts on your thumb nail. In the midst of this chopping sea of civilized life, such are the clouds and storms and quicksands and thousand-and-one items to be allowed for, that a man has to live, if he would not founder and go to the bottom and not make his port at all, by dead reckoning, and he must be a great calculator indeed who succeeds. Simplify, simplify. Instead of three meals a day, if it be necessary eat but one; instead of a hundred dishes, five; and reduce other things in proportion. Our life is like a German Confederacy, made up of petty states, with its boundary forever fluctuating so that even a German cannot tell you how it is bounded at any moment. The nation itself, with all its so-called internal improvements, which, by the way, are all external and superficial, is just such an unwieldy and overgrown establishment, cluttered with furniture and tripped up by its own traps, ruined by luxury and heedless expense, by want of calculation and a worthy aim, as the million households in the land; and the only cure for it, as for them, is in a rigid economy, a stern and more than Spartan simplicity of life and elevation of purpose. It lives too fast. Men think that it is essential that the nation have commerce, and export ice, and talk through a telegraph, and ride thirty miles an hour, without a doubt, whether they do or not; but whether we should live like baboons or like men is a little uncertain. If we do not get out sleepers, and forge rails, and devote days and nights to the work, but go to tinkering upon our lives to improve them, who will build railroads? And if railroads are not built, how shall we get to heaven in season? But if we stay at home and mind our business, who will want railroads? We do not ride on the railroad; it rides upon us. Did you ever think what those sleepers are that underlie the railroad? Each one is a man, an Irishman, or a Yankee man. The rails are laid on them, and they are covered with sand, and the cars run smoothly over them. They are sound sleepers, I assure you. And every few years a new lot is laid down and run over; so that, if some have the pleasure of riding on a rail, others have the misfortune to be ridden upon. And when they run over a man that is walking in his sleep, a supernumerary sleeper in the wrong position, and wake him up, they suddenly stop the cars and make a hue and cry about it, as if this were an exception. I am glad to know that it takes a gang of men for every five miles to keep the sleepers down and level in their beds as it is, for this is a sign that they may sometime get up again.

Why should we live with such hurry and waste of life? We are determined to be starved before we are hungry. Men say that a stitch in time saves nine, and so they take a thousand stitches today to save nine tomorrow. As for work, we haven't any of any consequence. We have the Saint Vitus's dance, and cannot possibly keep our heads still. If I should only give a few pulls at the parish bell-rope, as for a fire, that is, without setting the bell, there is hardly a man on his farm in the outskirts of Concord, notwithstanding that press of engagements which was his excuse so many times this morning, nor a boy, nor a woman, I might almost say, but would forsake all and follow that sound, not mainly to save property from the flames, but, if we will confess the truth, much more to see it burn, since burn it must, and we, be it known, did not set it on fire — or to see it put out, and have a hand in it, if that is done as handsomely; yes, even if it were the parish church itself. Hardly a man takes a half hour's nap after dinner but when he wakes he holds up his head and asks, " What's the news? " as if the rest of mankind had stood his sentinels. Some give directions to be waked every half hour, doubtless for no other purpose; and then, to pay for it, they tell what they have dreamed. After a night's sleep the news is as indispensable as the breakfast. " Pray tell me anything new that has happened to a man anywhere on this globe," and he reads it over his coffee and rolls that a man has had his eyes gouged out this morning on the Wachito River, never dreaming the while that he lives in the dark unfathomed mammoth cave of this world and has but the rudiment of an eye himself.

For my part, I could easily do without the post office. I think that there are very few important communications made through it. To speak critically, I never received more than one or two letters in my life — I wrote this some years ago — that were worth the postage. The pennypost is, commonly, an institution through which you seriously offer a man that penny for his thoughts which is too often safely offered in jest. And I am sure that I never read any memorable news in a newspaper. If we read of one man robbed, or murdered, or killed by accident, or one house burned, or one vessel wrecked, or one steamboat blown up, or one cow run over on the Western Railroad, or one mad dog killed, or one lot of grasshoppers in the winter, we never need read of another. One is enough. If you are acquainted with the principle, what do you care for a myriad instances and applications? To a philosopher all *news*, as it is called, is gossip, and they who edit and read it are old women over their tea. Yet not a few are greedy after this gossip. There was such a rush, as I hear, the other day at one of the offices to learn the foreign news by the last arrival that several large squares of plate glass belonging to the establishment were broken by the pressure, news which I seriously think a ready wit might write a twelvemonth, or twelve years, beforehand with sufficient accuracy. As for Spain, for instance, if you know how to throw in Don Carlos and the Infanta, and Don Pedro and Seville and Granada, from time to time in the right proportions — they may have changed the names a little since I saw the papers — and serve up a bull-fight when other entertainments fail, it will be true to the letter, and give us as good an idea of the exact state or ruin of things in Spain as the most succinct and lucid reports under this head in the newspapers; and as for England, almost the last significant scraps of news from that quarter was the revolution of 1649; and if you have learned the history of her crops for an average year, you never need attend to that thing again, unless your speculations are of a merely pecuniary character. If one may judge who rarely looks into the newspapers, nothing new does ever happen in foreign parts, a French revolution not excepted.

What news! how much more important to know what that is which was never old! Kieou-he-yu (great dignitary of the state of Wei) sent a man to Khoung-tseu to know his news. Khoung-tseu caused the messenger to be seated near him, and questioned him in these terms: " What is your master doing? " The messenger answered with respect: " My master desires to diminish the number of his faults, but he cannot come to the end of them." The messenger being gone, the philosopher remarked: " What a worthy messenger! What a worthy messenger! " The preacher, instead of vexing the ears of drowsy farmers on their day of rest at the end of the week — for Sunday is the fit conclusion of an ill-spent week, and not the fresh and brave beginning of a new one — with this one other draggletail of a sermon, should shout with thundering voice, " Pause! Avast! Why so seeming fast, but deadly slow? "

Shams and delusions are esteemed for soundest truths, while reality is fabulous. If men would steadily observe realities only and not allow themselves to be deluded, life, to compare it with such things as we know, would be like a fairy tale and the Arabian Nights' Entertainments. If we respected only what is inevitable and has a right to be, music and poetry would resound along the streets. When we are unhurried and wise, we perceive that only great and worthy things have any permanent and absolute existence, that petty fears and petty pleasures are but the shadow of the reality. This is always exhilarating and sublime. By closing the eyes and slumbering, and consenting to be deceived by shows, men establish and confirm their daily life of routine and habit everywhere, which still is built on purely illusory foundations. Children, who play life, discern its true law and relations more clearly than men, who fail to live it worthily, but who think that they are wiser by experience, that is, by failure. I have read in a Hindoo book, that " there was a king's son, who, being expelled in infancy from his native city, was brought up by a forester, and, growing up to maturity in that state, imagined himself to belong to the barbarous race with which he lived. One of his father's ministers, having discovered him, revealed to him what he was, and the misconception of his character was removed, and he knew himself to be a prince." " So the soul," continues the Hindoo philosopher, " from the circumstances in which it is placed, mistakes its own character, until the truth is revealed to it by some holy teacher, and then it knows itself to be *Brahm*." I perceive that we inhabitants of New England live this mean life that we do because our vision does not penetrate the surface of things. (We think that that *is* which *appears* to be.) If a man should walk through this town and see only the reality, where, think you, would the " Mill-dam " go to? If he should give us an account of the realities he beheld there, we should not recognize the place in his description. Look at a meeting-house, or a court-house, or a jail, or a shop, or a dwelling-house, and say what that thing really is before a true gaze, and they would all go to pieces in your account of them. Men esteem truth remote, in the outskirts of the system, behind the farthest star, before Adam and after the last man. In eternity there is indeed something true and sublime. But all these times and places and occasions are now and here. God himself culminates in the present moment, and will never be more divine in the lapse of all the ages. And we are enabled to apprehend at all what is sublime and noble only by the perpetual instilling and drenching of the reality that surrounds us. The universe constantly and obediently answers to our conceptions; whether we travel fast or slow, the track is laid for us. Let us spend our lives in conceiving them. The poet or the artist never yet had so fair and noble a design but some of his posterity at least could accomplish it.

Let us spend one day as deliberately as Nature, and not be thrown off the track by every nutshell and mosquito's wing that falls on the rails. Let us rise early and fast, or breakfast gently and without perturbation; let company come and let company go, let the bells ring and the children cry — determined to make a day of it. Why should we knock under and go with the stream? Let us not be upset and overwhelmed in that terrible rapid and whirlpool called a dinner, situated in the meridian shallows. Weather this danger and you are safe, for the rest of the way is down hill. With unrelaxed nerves, with morning vigor, sail by it, looking another way, tied to the mast like Ulysses. If the engine whistles, let it whistle till it is hoarse for its pains. If the bell rings, why should we run? We will consider what kind of music they are like. Let us settle ourselves and work and wedge our feet downward through the mud and slush of opinion and prejudice, and tradition, and delusion and appearance, that allusion which covers the globe, through Paris and London, through New York and Boston and Concord, through church and state, through poetry and philosophy and religion, till we come to a hard bottom and rocks in place, which we can call reality, and say, This is, and no mistake; and then begin, having a *point d'appui*, below freshet and frost and fire, a place where you might found a wall or a state, or set a lamp-post safely, or perhaps a gauge, not a Nilometer, but a Realometer, that future ages might know how deep a freshet of shams and appearances had gathered from time to time. If you stand right fronting and face to face to a fact, you will see the sun glimmer on both its surfaces, as if it were a cimeter, and feel its sweet edge dividing you through the heart and marrow, and so you will happily conclude your mortal career. Be it life or death, we crave only reality. If we are really dying, let us hear the rattle in our throats and feel cold in the extremities; if we are alive, let us go about our business.

Time is but the stream I go a-fishing in. I drink at it; but while I drink I see the sandy bottom and detect how shallow it is. Its thin current slides away, but eternity remains. I would drink deeper; fish in the sky, whose bottom is pebbly with stars. I cannot count one. I know not the first letter of the alphabet. I have always been regretting that I was not as wise as the day I was born. The intellect is a cleaver; it discerns and rifts its way into the secret of things. I do not wish to be any more busy with my hands than is necessary. My head is hands and feet. I feel all my best faculties concentrated in it. My instinct tells me that my head is an organ for burrowing, as some creatures use their snout and forepaws, and with it I would mine and burrow my way through these hills. I think that the richest vein is somewhere hereabouts; so by the divining rod and thin rising vapors I judge; and here I will begin to mine.

STUDYING THE ESSAY

1. Thoreau's *Walden* is one of the most deeply personal books in our literature. Find places in this essay which show what kind of man Thoreau was.
2. "I went to the woods because I wished to live deliberately." Explain what Thoreau means by this.
3. Find examples of Thoreau's feeling for nature.

4. Explain Thoreau's ideas about the post office.
5. What kinds of reading had Thoreau done?
6. In a collection of English poetry find William Wordsworth's sonnet beginning " The world is too much with us." Compare this poem with Thoreau's essay.
7. Explain: " We do not ride on the railroad; it rides upon us."
8. How does Thoreau in this essay agree with Emerson in " Self-Reliance "?

COMPOSITION TOPICS

1. " Why should we live with such hurry and waste of life? "
2. The Pleasures of Fishing
3. On Getting Off by One's Self
4. The Pioneer
5. Things I Cannot Live Without

MARK TWAIN (SAMUEL LANGHORNE CLEMENS)   1835–1910

Many readers of *Tom Sawyer* and *Huckleberry Finn* have never heard of Samuel L. Clemens. But Sam Clemens, of Hannibal, Missouri, never used the pen name " Mark Twain " until he was almost thirty years old. Readers of Clemens, or Twain, should know about both.

Sam Clemens was born in Florida, Missouri, in 1835 and stopped school when he was twelve because his father died and he had to go to work. For twenty years he was, at various times, a newspaper writer, a journeyman printer, a Mississippi River pilot, a soldier (for two weeks; he hated it), and a prospector for gold. His experience as a river pilot gave him his pen name, Mark Twain. The expression was used by the man measuring the depth of the river from the bow of the boat. If he called " Mark twain " to the bridge, he meant that the boat was in two fathoms of water. This same river experience also gave the world *Life on the Mississippi*, one of his unforgettable books.

He made no impression on the literary world until he wrote " The Celebrated Jumping Frog of Calaveras County " for a San Francisco newspaper in 1865. This story brought him some prominence — enough to get him an assignment to write a series of travel sketches for a Sacramento newspaper. These sketches eventually were published as his first book, *Innocents Abroad*, in 1869.

In the same year he became editor of the Buffalo *Express*, which he ran for twelve years. Later he and his family (he had married in 1870) moved to Hartford, Connecticut. In New England he was an investor in a publishing house which went bankrupt. He lost every penny he had, but he paid off the firm's debts by going on a grueling lecture tour of the world from 1895 to 1896. His last years were outwardly a triumph. He was given honorary degrees by Yale and Oxford, and his books were best sellers. Inwardly his later life was as unhappy as Charles Lamb's. The death of his wife and his own feeling that he was a failure made him, privately, a tortured man. This sense of frustration appears in some of his works, but not in the books that America remembers best: those mentioned already, plus *Roughing It*, *The Prince and the Pauper*, and *A Connecticut Yankee at the Court of King Arthur*.

Mark Twain was at his best as a storyteller. But he was a man of violent personal likes and dislikes, and these positive feelings produced a number of essays. A few, like " Saint Joan of Arc," are unexpectedly tender. Others, like " The Killing of Julius Caesar Localized," are satires — in this case on the sensational reporting of crime in the American press. The essay on Cooper's *Deerslayer*, which is reprinted below, has several qualities to recommend it. In the first place, it is funny. Mark Twain delighted in the humor of exaggeration, and this essay proves it. In the second place, it is a very intelligent, if very prejudiced, piece of literary criticism. Readers of the essay may have to reread *The Deerslayer* to realize how intelligent and how prejudiced the essay is. In the third place, the essay is a good example of Mark Twain's originality. He was one of the few really original writers whom nineteenth-century America produced. While this essay is not his best writing (his novels are his best work), it is a stimulating example of what happens when a highly original, creative, and humorous mind is applied to the criticism of a book which the essayist could have written better than the author wrote it.

FENIMORE COOPER'S
LITERARY OFFENSES

The Pathfinder and *The Deerslayer* stand at the head of Cooper's novels as artistic creations. There are others of his works which contain parts as perfect as are to be found in these, and scenes even more thrilling. Not one can be compared with either of them as a finished whole.

The defects in both of these tales are comparatively slight. They were pure works of art. — PROF. LOUNSBURY.

The five tales reveal an extraordinary fullness of invention.

. . . one of the very greatest characters in fiction, Natty Bumppo . . .

The craft of the woodsman, the tricks of the trapper, all the delicate art of the forest, were familiar to Cooper from his youth up. — PROF. BRANDER MATTHEWS.

Cooper is the greatest artist in the domain of romantic fiction yet produced by America. — WILKIE COLLINS.

                It seems to me that it was far from right for the Professor of English Literature in Yale, the Professor of English Literature in Columbia, and Wilkie Collins to deliver opinions on Cooper's literature without having read some of it. It would have been much more decorous to keep silent and let persons talk who have read Cooper.

Cooper's art has some defects. In one place in *Deerslayer*, and in the restricted space of two-thirds of a page, Cooper has scored 114 offenses against literary art out of a possible 115. It breaks the record.

There are nineteen rules governing literary art in the domain of romantic fiction — some say twenty-two. In *Deerslayer* Cooper violated eighteen of them. These eighteen require:

1. That a tale shall accomplish something and arrive somewhere. But the *Deerslayer* tale accomplishes nothing and arrives in the air.

2. They require that the episodes of a tale shall be necessary parts of the tale, and shall help to develop it. But as the *Deerslayer* tale is not a tale, and accomplishes nothing and arrives nowhere, the episodes have no rightful place in the work, since there was nothing for them to develop.

3. They require that the personages in a tale shall be alive, except in the case of corpses, and that always the reader shall be able to tell the corpses from the others. But this detail has often been overlooked in the *Deerslayer* tale.

4. They require that the personages in a tale, both dead and alive, shall exhibit a sufficient excuse for being there. But this detail also has been overlooked in the *Deerslayer* tale.

5. They require that when the personages of a tale deal in conversation, the talk shall sound like human talk, and be talk such as human beings would be likely to talk in the given circumstances, and have a discoverable meaning, also a discoverable purpose, and a show of relevancy, and remain in the neighborhood of the subject in hand, and be interesting to the reader, and help out the tale, and stop when the people cannot think of anything more to say. But this requirement has been ignored from the beginning of the *Deerslayer* tale to the end of it.

6. They require that when the author describes the character of a personage in his tale, the conduct and conversation of that personage shall justify said description. But this

law gets little or no attention in the *Deerslayer* tale, as Natty Bumppo's case will amply prove.

7. They require that when a personage talks like an illustrated, gilt-edged, tree-calf, hand-tooled, seven-dollar Friendship's Offering in the beginning of a paragraph, he shall not talk like a Negro minstrel in the end of it. But this rule is flung down and danced upon in the *Deerslayer* tale.

8. They require that crass stupidities shall not be played upon the reader as " the craft of the woodsman, the delicate art of the forest," by either the author or the people in the tale. But this rule is persistently violated in the *Deerslayer* tale.

9. They require that the personages of a tale shall confine themselves to possibilities and let miracles alone; or, if they venture a miracle, the author must so plausibly set it forth as to make it look possible and reasonable. But these rules are not respected in the *Deerslayer* tale.

10. They require that the author shall make the reader feel a deep interest in the personages of his tale and in their fate; and that he shall make the reader love the good people in the tale and hate the bad ones. But the reader of the *Deerslayer* tale dislikes the good people in it, is indifferent to the others, and wishes they would all get drowned together.

11. They require that the characters in a tale shall be so clearly defined that the reader can tell beforehand what each will do in a given emergency. But in the *Deerslayer* tale this rule is vacated.

In addition to these large rules there are some little ones. These require that the author shall

12. *Say* what he is proposing to say, not merely come near it.

13. Use the right word, not its second cousin.

14. Eschew surplusage.

15. Not omit necessary details.
16. Avoid slovenliness of form.
17. Use good grammar.
18. Employ a simple and straightforward style.

Even these seven are coldly and persistently violated in the *Deerslayer* tale.

Cooper's gift in the way of invention was not a rich endowment; but such as it was he liked to work it, he was pleased with the effects, and indeed he did some quite sweet things with it. In his little box of stage properties he kept six or eight cunning devices, tricks, artifices for his savages and woodsmen to deceive and circumvent each other with, and he was never so happy as when he was working these innocent things and seeing them go. A favorite one was to make a moccasined person tread in the tracks of the moccasined enemy, and thus hide his own trail. Cooper wore out barrels and barrels of moccasins in working that trick. Another stage property that he pulled out of his box pretty frequently was his broken twig. He prized his broken twig above all the rest of his effects, and worked it the hardest. It is a restful chapter in any book of his when somebody doesn't step on a dry twig and alarm all the reds and whites for two hundred yards around. Every time a Cooper person is in peril, and absolute silence is worth four dollars a minute, he is sure to step on a dry twig. There may be a hundred handier things to step on, but that wouldn't satisfy Cooper. Cooper requires him to turn out and find a dry twig; and if he can't do it, go and borrow one. In fact, the Leatherstocking Series ought to have been called the Broken Twig Series.

I am sorry there is not room to put in a few dozen instances of the delicate art of the forest, as practiced by Natty Bumppo and some of the other Cooperian experts. Perhaps we may venture two or three samples. Cooper was a sailor — a naval officer; yet he gravely tells us how a vessel, driving toward a lee shore in a gale, is steered for a particular spot by her skipper because he knows of an *undertow* there which will hold her back against the gale and save her. For just pure woodcraft, or sailorcraft, or whatever it is, isn't that neat? For several years Cooper was daily in the society of artillery, and he ought to have noticed that when a cannon ball strikes the ground it either buries itself or skips a hundred feet or so; skips again a hundred feet or so — and so on, till finally it gets tired and rolls. Now in one place he loses some " females " — as he always calls women — in the edge of a wood near a plain at night in a fog, on purpose to give Bumppo a chance to show off the delicate art of the forest before the reader. These mislaid people are hunting for a fort. They hear a cannon blast, and a cannon ball presently comes rolling into the wood and stops at their feet. To the females this suggests nothing. The case is very different with the admirable Bumppo. I wish I may never know peace again if he doesn't strike out promptly and *follow the track* of that cannon ball across the plain through the dense fog and find the fort. Isn't it a daisy? If Cooper had any real knowledge of Nature's way of doing things, he had a most delicate art in concealing the fact. For instance: one of his acute Indian experts, Chingachgook (pronounced Chicago, I think), has lost the trail of a person he is tracking through the forest. Apparently that trail is hopelessly lost. Neither you nor I could ever have guessed out the way to find it. It was very different with Chicago. Chicago was not stumped for long. He turned a running stream out of its course, and there, in the slush in its old bed, were that person's moccasin tracks. The current did not wash them away, as it would have done in all other cases — no, even the eternal laws of Nature have to vacate when Cooper wants to put up a delicate job of woodcraft on the reader.

We must be a little wary when Brander Matthews tells us

that Cooper's books "reveal an extraordinary fullness of invention." As a rule, I am quite willing to accept Brander Matthews's literary judgments and applaud his lucid and graceful phrasing of them; but that particular statement needs to be taken with a few tons of salt. Bless your heart, Cooper hadn't any more invention than a horse; and I don't mean a high-class horse, either; I mean a clothes-horse. It would be very difficult to find a really clever "situation" in Cooper's books, and still more difficult to find one of any kind which he has failed to render absurd by his handling of it. Look at the episodes of "the caves"; and at the celebrated scuffle between Maqua and those others on the table-land a few days later; and at Hurry Harry's queer water-transit from the castle to the ark; and at Deerslayer's half hour with his first corpse; and at the quarrel between Hurry Harry and Deerslayer later; and at — but choose for yourself; you can't go amiss.

If Cooper had been an observer, his inventive faculty would have worked better; not more interestingly, but more rationally, more plausibly. Cooper's proudest creations in the way of "situations" suffer noticeably from the absence of the observer's protecting gift. Cooper's eye was splendidly inaccurate. Cooper seldom saw anything correctly. He saw nearly all things as through a glass eye, darkly. Of course a man who cannot see the commonest little everyday matters accurately is working at a disadvantage when he is constructing a "situation." In the *Deerslayer* tale Cooper has a stream which is fifty feet wide where it flows out of a lake; it presently narrows to twenty as it meanders along for no given reason, and yet when a stream acts like that it ought to be required to explain itself. Fourteen pages later the width of the brook's outlet from the lake has suddenly shrunk thirty feet, and become "the narrowest part of the stream." This shrinkage is not accounted for. The stream has bends in it, a sure indication that it has alluvial banks and cuts them; yet these bends are only thirty and fifty feet long. If Cooper had been a nice and punctilious observer, he would have noticed that the bends were oftener nine hundred feet long than short of it.

Cooper made the exit of that stream fifty feet wide, in the first place, for no particular reason; in the second place, he narrowed it to less than twenty to accommodate some Indians. He bends a " sapling " to the form of an arch over this narrow passage, and conceals six Indians in its foliage. They are "laying" for a settler's scow or ark which is coming up the stream on its way to the lake; it is being hauled against the stiff current by a rope whose stationary end is anchored in the lake; its rate of progress cannot be more than a mile an hour. Cooper describes the ark, but pretty obscurely. In the matter of dimensions " it was little more than a modern canalboat." Let us guess, then, that it was about one hundred and forty feet long. It was of " greater breadth than common." Let us guess, then, that it was about sixteen feet wide. This leviathan had been prowling down bends which were but a third as long as itself, and scraping between banks where it had only two feet of space to spare on each side. We cannot too much admire this miracle. A low-roofed log dwelling occupies " two-thirds of the ark's length " — a dwelling ninety feet long and sixteen feet wide, let us say — a kind of vestibule train. The dwelling has two rooms — each forty-five feet long and sixteen feet wide, let us guess. One of them is the bedroom of the Hutter girls, Judith and Hetty; the other is the parlor in the daytime, at night it is papa's bedchamber. The ark is arriving at the stream's exit now, whose width has been reduced to less than twenty feet to accommodate the Indians — say to eighteen. There is a foot to spare on each side of the boat. Did the Indians notice that there was going to

be a tight squeeze there? Did they notice that they could
make money by climbing out of that arched sapling and
just stepping aboard when the ark scraped by? No, other
Indians would have noticed these things, but Cooper's Indians never notice anything. Cooper thinks they are marvelous
creatures for noticing, but he was almost always in error
about his Indians. There was seldom a sane one among them.

The ark is one hundred and forty feet long; the dwelling
is ninety feet long. The idea of the Indians is to drop softly
and secretly from the arched sapling to the dwelling as the
ark creeps along under it at the rate of a mile an hour, and
butcher the family. It will take the ark a minute and a half
to pass under. It will take the ninety-foot dwelling a minute
to pass under. Now, then, what did the six Indians do? It
would take you thirty years to guess, and even then you
would have to give it up, I believe. Therefore, I will tell you
what the Indians did. Their chief, a person of quite extraordinary intellect for a Cooper Indian, warily watched
the canalboat as it squeezed along under him, and when he
had got his calculations fined down to exactly the right
shade, as he judged, he let go and dropped. And *missed the
house!* That is actually what he did. He missed the house,
and landed in the stern of the scow. It was not much of a
fall, yet it knocked him silly. He lay there unconscious.
If the house had been ninety-seven feet long he would have
made the trip. The fault was Cooper's, not his. The error
lay in the construction of the house. Cooper was no archi-
tect.

There still remained in the roost five Indians. The boat
has passed under and is now out of their reach. Let me explain what the five did — you would not be able to reason
it out for yourself. No. 1 jumped for the boat, but fell in
the water astern of it. Then No. 2 jumped for the boat, but
fell in the water still farther astern of it. Then No. 3 jumped

for the boat, and fell a good way astern of it. Then No. 4 jumped for the boat, and fell in the water *away* astern. Then even No. 5 made a jump for the boat — for he was a Cooper Indian. In the matter of intellect, the difference between a Cooper Indian and the Indian that stands in front of the cigar shop is not spacious. The scow episode is really a sublime burst of invention; but it does not thrill, because the inaccuracy of the details throws a sort of air of fictitiousness and general improbability over it. This comes of Cooper's inadequacy as an observer.

The reader will find some examples of Cooper's high talent for inaccurate observation in the account of the shooting-match in *The Pathfinder*.

A common wrought nail was driven lightly into the target, its head having been first touched with paint.

The color of the paint is not stated — an important omission, but Cooper deals freely in important omissions. No, after all, it was not an important omission; for this nailhead is *a hundred yards from* the marksmen, and could not be seen by them at that distance, no matter what its color might be. How far can the best eye see a common housefly? A hundred yards? It is quite impossible. Very well; eyes that cannot see a housefly that is a hundred yards away cannot see an ordinary nailhead at that distance, for the size of the two objects is the same. It takes a keen eye to see a fly or a nailhead at fifty yards — one hundred and fifty feet. Can the reader do it?

The nail was lightly driven, its head painted, and game called. Then the Cooper miracles began. The bullet of the first marksman chipped an edge of the nailhead; the next man's bullet drove the nail a little way into the target — and removed all the paint. Haven't the miracles gone far enough now? Not to suit Cooper; for the purpose of this whole scheme is to show off his prodigy, Deerslayer-Hawk-eye-Long-Rifle-Leatherstocking-Pathfinder-Bumppo before the ladies.

" Be all ready to clench it, boys! " cried out Pathfinder, stepping into his friend's tracks the instant they were vacant. " Never mind a new nail; I can see that, though the paint is gone, and what I can see I can hit at a hundred yards, though it were only a mosquito's eye. Be ready to clench! "

The rifle cracked, the bullet sped its way, and the head of the nail was buried in the wood, covered by the piece of flattened lead.

There, you see, is a man who could hunt flies with a rifle, and command a ducal salary in a Wild West show today if we had him back with us.

The recorded feat is certainly surprising just as it stands; but it is not surprising enough for Cooper. Cooper adds a touch. He has made Pathfinder do this miracle with another man's rifle; and not only that, but Pathfinder did not have even the advantage of loading it himself. He had everything against him, and yet he made that impossible shot; and not only made it, but did it with absolute confidence, saying, " Be ready to clench." Now a person like that would have undertaken that same feat with a brickbat, and with Cooper to help he would have achieved it, too.

Pathfinder showed off handsomely that day before the ladies. His very first feat was a thing which no Wild West show can touch. He was standing with the group of marksmen, observing — a hundred yards from the target, mind; one Jasper raised his rifle and drove the center of the bull's-eye. Then the Quartermaster fired. The target exhibited no result this time. There was a laugh. " It's a dead miss," said Major Lundie. Pathfinder waited an impressive moment or two; then said, in that calm, indifferent, know-it-all way of his, "No, Major, he has covered Jasper's bullet, as will be seen if any one will take the trouble to examine the target."

Wasn't it remarkable! How *could* he see that little pellet fly through the air and enter that distant bullet hole? Yet that is what he did; for nothing is impossible to a Cooper person. Did any of those people have any deep-seated doubts about this thing? No; for that would imply sanity, and these were all Cooper people.

The respect for Pathfinder's skill and for his *quickness and accuracy of sight* [the italics are mine] was so profound and general, that the instant he made this declaration the spectators began to distrust their own opinions, and a dozen rushed to the target in order to ascertain the fact. There, sure enough, it was found that the Quartermaster's bullet had gone through the hole made by Jasper's, and that, too, so accurately as to require a minute examination to be certain of the circumstance, which, however, was soon clearly established by discovering one bullet over the other in the stump against which the target was placed.

They made a "minute" examination; but never mind, how could they know that there were two bullets in that hole without digging the latest one out? for neither probe nor eyesight could prove the presence of any more than one bullet. Did they dig? No; as we shall see. It is the Pathfinder's turn now; he steps out before the ladies, takes aim, and fires.

But, alas! here is a disappointment; an incredible, an unimaginable disappointment — for the target's aspect is unchanged; there is nothing there but that same old bullet hole!

"If one dared to hint at such a thing," cried Major Duncan, "I should say that the Pathfinder has also missed the target!"

As nobody had missed it yet, the " also " was not necessary; but never mind about that, for the Pathfinder is going
to speak.

" No, no, Major," said he, confidently, " that *would* be a risky
declaration. I didn't load the piece, and can't say what was in
it; but if it was lead, you will find the bullet driving down those
of the Quartermaster and Jasper, else is not my name Pathfinder."
A shout from the target announced the truth of this assertion.

Is the miracle sufficient as it stands? Not for Cooper. The
Pathfinder speaks again, as he " now slowly advances toward
the stage occupied by the females ":

" That's not all, boys, that's not all; if you find the target
touched at all, I'll own to a miss. The Quartermaster cut the
wood, but you'll find no wood cut by that last messenger."

The miracle is at last complete. He knew — doubtless *saw*
— at the distance of a hundred yards — that his bullet had
passed into the hole *without fraying the edges*. There were
now three bullets in that one hole — three bullets embedded
processionally in the body of the stump back of the target.
Everybody knew this — somehow or other — and yet nobody
had dug any of them out to make sure. Cooper is not a close
observer, but he is interesting. He is certainly always that,
no matter what happens. And he is more interesting when
he is not noticing what he is about than when he is. This
is a considerable merit.
The conversations in the Cooper books have a curious
sound in our modern ears. To believe that such talk really
ever came out of people's mouths would be to believe that
there was a time when time was of no value to a person
who thought he had something to say; when it was the

custom to spread a two-minute remark out to ten; when a man's mouth was a rolling-mill, and busied itself all day long in turning four-foot pigs of thought into thirty-foot bars of conversational railroad iron by attenuation; when subjects were seldom faithfully stuck to, but the talk wandered all around and arrived nowhere; when conversations consisted mainly of irrelevancies, with here and there a relevancy, a relevancy with an embarrassed look, as not being able to express how it got there.

Cooper was certainly not a master in the construction of dialogue. Inaccurate observation defeated him here as it defeated him in so many other enterprises of his. He even failed to notice that the man who talks corrupt English six days in the week must and will talk it on the seventh, and can't help himself. In the *Deerslayer* story he lets Deerslayer talk the showiest kind of book-talk sometimes, and at other times the basest of base dialects. For instance, when someone asks him if he has a sweetheart, and if so, where she abides, this is his majestic answer:

" She's in the forest — hanging from the boughs of the trees, in a soft rain — in the dew on the open grass — the clouds that float about in the blue heavens — the birds that sing in the woods — the sweet springs where I slake my thirst — and in all the other glorious gifts that come from God's Providence! "

And he preceded that, a little before, with this:

" It consarns me as all things that touches a fri'nd consarns a fri'nd."

And this is another of his remarks:

" If I was Injin born, now, I might tell of this, or carry in the scalp and boast of the expl'ite afore the whole tribe; or if my inimy had only been a bear " — [and so on].

We cannot imagine such a thing as a veteran Scotch
Commander-in-Chief comporting himself in the field like
a windy melodramatic actor, but Cooper could. On one occasion Alice and Cora were being chased by the French
through a fog in the neighborhood of their father's fort:

"*Point de quartier aux coquins!* " cried an eager pursuer, who
seemed to direct the operations of the enemy.

"Stand firm and be ready, my gallant 6oths! " suddenly exclaimed a voice above them; "wait to see the enemy; fire low,
and sweep the glacis."

"Father, father! " exclaimed a piercing cry from out of the
mist; "it is I! Alice! thy own Elsie! spare, O! save your daughters! "

"Hold! " shouted the former speaker, in the awful tones of
parental agony, the sound reaching even to the woods, and rolling back in solemn echo. " 'Tis she! God has restored me my
children! Throw open the sally-port; to the field, 6oths, to the
field! pull not a trigger, lest ye kill my lambs! Drive off these
dogs of France with your steel! "

Cooper's word-sense was singularly dull. When a person
has a poor ear for music, he will flat and sharp right along
without knowing it. He keeps near the tune, but it is *not* the
tune. When a person has a poor ear for words, the result is a
literary flatting and sharping; you perceive what he is intending to say, but you also perceive that he doesn't *say* it.
This is Cooper. He was not a word-musician. His ear was
satisfied with the *approximate* word. I will furnish some cir-
cumstantial evidence in support of this charge. My instances
are gathered from half a dozen pages of the tale called
Deerslayer. He uses " verbal " for " oral "; " precision " for
" facility "; " phenomena " for " marvels "; " necessary " for
" predetermined "; " unsophisticated " for " primitive ";
" preparation " for " expectancy "; " rebuked " for " sub-

dued "; " dependent on " for " resulting from "; " fact " for " condition "; " fact " for " conjecture "; " precaution " for " caution "; " explain " for " determine "; " mortified " for " disappointed "; " meretricious " for " factitious "; " materially " for " considerably "; " decreasing " for " deepening "; " increasing " for " disappearing "; " embedded " for " inclosed "; " treacherous " for " hostile "; " stood " for " stooped "; " softened " for " replaced "; " rejoined " for " remarked "; " situation " for " condition "; " different " for " differing "; " insensible " for " unsentient "; " brevity " for " celerity "; " distrusted " for " suspicious "; " mental imbecility " for " imbecility "; " eyes " for " sight "; " counteracting " for " opposing "; " funeral obsequies " for " obsequies."

There have been daring people in the world who claimed that Cooper could write English, but they are all dead now — all dead but Lounsbury. I don't remember that Lounsbury makes the claim in so many words, still he makes it, for he says that *Deerslayer* is a " pure work of art." Pure, in that connection, means faultless — faultless in all details — and language is a detail. If Mr. Lounsbury had only compared Cooper's English with the English which he writes himself — but it is plain that he didn't; and so it is likely that he imagines until this day that Cooper's is as clean and compact as his own. Now I feel sure, deep down in my heart, that Cooper wrote about the poorest English that exists in our language, and that the English of *Deerslayer* is the very worst that even Cooper ever wrote.

I may be mistaken, but it does seem to me that *Deerslayer* is not a work of art in any sense; it does seem to me that it is destitute of every detail that goes to the making of a work of art; in truth, it seems to me that *Deerslayer* is just simply a literary *delirium tremens*.

A work of art? It has no invention; it has no order, system, sequence, or result; it has no lifelikeness, no thrill, no stir, no seeming of reality; its characters are confusedly drawn, and by their acts and words they prove that they are not the sort of people the author claims that they are; its humor is pathetic; its pathos is funny; its conversations are — oh! indescribable; its love scenes odious; its English a crime against the language.

Counting these out, what is left is Art. I think we must all admit that.

STUDYING THE ESSAY

1. Have you read *The Deerslayer*? If you have not, ask someone who has read it to tell you the story.
2. Whether or not you have read the book, do you think Mark Twain exaggerates his charges against Cooper in the eighteen numbered criticisms?
3. What passages in the essay are particularly funny? Try to explain *why* they are funny.
4. If you have read Cooper, do you think Twain is fair or unfair in his criticism?
5. Discuss a few of what Twain calls Cooper's " approximate " words. Why is accuracy in the use of words important? Give some examples of your own " approximate " or loose use of vocabulary.
6. What is the purpose of literary criticism?

COMPOSITION TOPICS

1. Write an unfavorable review of a book you like.
2. Write a favorable review of a book you dislike.

WILLIAM HENRY HUDSON, 1841–1922

William Henry Hudson was born of American parents in the Argentine, where his father was in business. His boyhood was spent on the pampas of La Plata. Educated by tutors and by his mother, the boy had long hours alone, and he developed for himself the marvelous observation which made him a great naturalist. His studies were of the wild life all around him both in South America and later in England, where he spent the last fifty years of his life. He cared little or nothing about museums and the problems of scientific research. But he saw animals, birds, trees, and flowers clearly in their natural locations, and he had the power to describe them accurately in his books. Sincere, exact, original, he ranks with Thoreau as a man of letters in the field of nature. He has a fitting memorial in the bird sanctuary in Hyde Park, London.

Ill health, brought on by an attack of rheumatic fever when he was fifteen, and poverty marred most of his life. Having failed to make a living from his works on natural history in South America, he went to England in 1870 and eventually — in 1900 — became a British citizen. The first of his books to gain him any fame was *Green Mansions* (1904), whose success called attention to his earlier works. His poignant story of his youth, *Far Away and Long Ago* (1924), from which the following selection is taken, is considered by many critics to be his best book, although this judgment may be disputed by those who feel the enchantment of the beauty to be found in *Green Mansions*.

Although his writings were slow to win recognition, his audience has grown steadily as readers have come to appreciate the perfect naturalness of his style and the charm of his material.

John Galsworthy has said: "He puts down what he sees and feels, out of sheer love of the thing seen and the emotion felt; the smell of the lamp has not touched a single page that he ever wrote. . . . To use words so true and simple that they oppose no obstacle to the flow of thought and feeling from mind to mind, and yet by juxtaposition of word sounds set up in the recipient continuing emotion or gratification — this is the essence of style." Joseph Conrad, one of his best friends, said of him: "Hudson writes as the grass grows." This simplicity and his deep feeling for life are clear throughout the following essay.

THE DEATH OF AN OLD DOG

When recalling the impressions and experiences of that most eventful sixth year, the one incident which looks biggest in memory, at all events in the last half of that year, is the death of Caesar. There is nothing in the past I can remember so well: it was indeed the most important event of my childhood — the first thing in a young life which brought the eternal note of sadness in.

It was in the early spring, about the middle of August, and I can even remember that it was windy weather and bitterly cold for the time of the year, when the old dog was approaching his end.

Caesar was an old valued dog, although of no superior breed: he was just an ordinary dog of the country, short-haired, with long legs and a blunt muzzle. The ordinary dog or native cur was about the size of a Scotch collie; Caesar was quite a third larger, and it was said of him that he was as much above all other dogs of the house, numbering about twelve or fourteen, in intelligence and courage as in size. Naturally, he was the leader and master of the whole pack, and when he got up with an awful growl, baring his big teeth, and hurled himself on the others to chastise them for quarreling or any other infringement of dog law, they took it lying down. He was a black dog, now in his old age sprinkled with white hairs all over his body, the face and legs having gone quite gray. Caesar in a rage, or on guard at night, or when driving cattle in from the plains, was a terrible being; with us children he was mild-tempered and patient, allowing us to ride on his back, just like old Pechicho the sheep-dog, described in the first chapter. Now, in his decline, he grew irritable and surly, and ceased to be our playmate. The last two or three months of his life were very sad, and when it troubled us to see him so gaunt, with his big ribs protruding from his sides, to watch his twitchings when he dozed, groaning and wheezing the while, and marked, too, how painfully he struggled to get up on his feet, we wanted to know why it was so — why we could not give him something to make him well. For answer they would open his great mouth to show us his teeth — the big blunt canines and old molars worn down to stumps. Old age was what ailed him — he was thirteen years old, and that did verily seem to me a great age, for I was not half that, yet it seemed to me that I had been a very, very long time in the world.

No one dreamed of such a thing as putting an end to him — no hint of such a thing was ever spoken. It was not the custom in that country to shoot an old dog because he was past work. I remember his last day, and how often we came to look at him and tried to comfort him with warm rugs and the offer of food and drink where he was lying in a sheltered place, no longer able to stand up. And that night he died: we knew it as soon as we were up in the morning.

Then, after breakfast, during which we had been very solemn and quiet, our schoolmaster said: "We must bury him today — at twelve o'clock, when I am free, will be the best time; the boys can come with me, and old John can bring his spade." This announcement greatly excited us, for we had never seen a dog buried, and had never even heard of such a thing having ever been done.

About noon that day old Caesar, dead and stiff, was taken by one of the workmen to a green open spot among the old peach trees, where his grave had already been dug. We followed our schoolmaster and watched while the body was lowered and the red earth shoveled in. The grave was deep, and Mr. Trigg assisted in filling it, puffing very much over the task and stopping at intervals to mop his face with his colored cotton handkerchief.

Then, when all was done, while we were still standing silently around, it came into Mr. Trigg's mind to improve the occasion. Assuming his schoolroom expression he looked round at us and said solemnly: "That's the end. Every dog has his day and so has every man; and the end is the same for both. We die like old Caesar, and are put into the ground and have the earth shoveled over us."

Now these simple, common words affected me more than any other words I have heard in my life. They pierced me to the heart. I had heard something terrible — too terrible to think of, incredible — and yet — and yet if it was not so, why had he said it? Was it because he hated us, just because we were children and he had to teach us our lessons, and wanted to torture us? Alas! no, I could not believe that! Was this, then, the horrible fate that awaited us all? I had heard of death — I knew there was such a thing; I knew that all animals had to die, also that some men died. For how could anyone, even a child in its sixth year, overlook such a fact, especially in the country of my birth — a land of battle, murder, and sudden death? I had not forgotten the young man tied to the post in the barn who had killed someone, and would perhaps, I had been told, be killed himself as a punishment. I knew, in fact, that there was good and evil in the world, good and bad men, and the bad men — murderers, thieves, and liars — would all have to die, just like animals; but that there was any life after death I did not know. All the others, myself and my own people included, were good and would never taste death. How it came about that I had got no further in my system or philosophy of life I cannot say; I can only suppose that my mother had not yet begun to give me instruction in such matters on account of my tender years, or else that she had done so and that I had understood it in my own way. Yet, as I discovered later, she was a religious woman, and from infancy I had been taught to kneel and say a little prayer each evening: " Now I lay me down to sleep, I pray the Lord my soul to keep "; but who the Lord was or what my soul was I had no idea. It was just a pretty little way of saying in rhyme that I was going to bed. My world was a purely material one, and a most wonderful world it was, but how I came to be in it I didn't know; I only knew (or imagined) that I would be in it always, seeing new and strange things every day, and never, never get tired of it. In literature it is only in Vaughan, Traherne, and other mystics, that I find any adequate expression of that perpetual rapturous delight in nature and my own existence which I experienced at that period.

And now these never-to-be-forgotten words spoken over the grave of our old dog had come to awaken me from that beautiful dream of perpetual joy!

When I recall this event I am less astonished at my ignorance than at the intensity of the feeling I experienced, the terrible darkness it brought on so young a mind. The child's mind we think, and in fact know, is like that of the lower animals; or if higher than the animal mind, it is not so high as that of the simplest savage. He cannot concentrate his thought — he cannot think at all; his consciousness is in its dawn; he revels in colors, in odors, is thrilled by touch and taste and sound, and is like a well-nourished pup or kitten at play on a green turf in the sunshine. This being so, one would have thought that the pain of the revelation I had received would have quickly vanished — that the vivid impressions of external things would have blotted it out and restored the harmony. But it was not so; the pain continued and increased until it was no longer to be borne; then I sought my mother, first watching until she was alone in her room. Yet when with her I feared to speak lest with a word she should confirm the dreadful tidings. Looking down, she all at once became alarmed at the sight of my face, and began to question me. Then, struggling against my tears, I told her of the words which had been spoken at the old dog's burial, and asked her if it was true, if I — if she — if all of us had to die and be buried in the ground? She replied that it was not wholly true; it was only true in a way, since our bodies had to die and be buried in the earth, but we had an immortal part which could not die. It was true that old Caesar had been a good, faithful dog, and felt and understood things almost like a human being, and most persons believed that when a dog died he died wholly and had no after-life. We could not know that; some very great, good men had thought differently; they believed that the animals, like us, would live again. That was also her belief — her strong hope; but we could not know for certain, because it had been hidden from us. For ourselves, we knew that we could not really die, because God Himself, who made us and all things, had told us so, and His promise of eternal life had been handed down to us in His Book — in the Bible.

To all this and much more I listened trembling, with a

fearful interest, and when I had once grasped the idea that death when it came to me, as it must, would leave me alive after all — that, as she explained, the part of me that really mattered, the myself, the I am I, which knew and considered things, would never perish, I experienced a sudden immense relief. When I went out from her side again I wanted to run and jump for joy and cleave the air like a bird. For I had been in prison and had suffered torture, and was now free again — death would not destroy me!

There was another result of my having unburdened my heart to my mother. She had been startled at the poignancy of the feeling I had displayed, and, greatly blaming herself for having left me too long in that ignorant state, began to give me religious instruction. It was too early, since at that age it was not possible for me to rise to the conception of an immaterial world. That power, I imagine, comes later to the normal child at the age of ten or twelve. To tell him when he is five or six or seven that God is in all places at once and sees all things, only produces the idea of a wonderfully active and quick-sighted person, with eyes like a bird's, able to see what is going on all round. A short time ago I read an anecdote of a little girl who, on being put to bed by her mother, was told not to be afraid in the dark, since God would be there to watch and guard her while she slept. Then, taking the candle, the mother went down stairs; but presently her little girl came down too, in her nightdress, and, when questioned, replied, " I'm going to stay down here in the light, mummy, and you can go up to my room and sit with God." My own idea of God at that time was no higher. I would lie awake thinking of him there in the room, puzzling over the question as to how he could attend to all his numerous affairs and spend so much time looking after me. Lying with my eyes open, I could see nothing in the dark; still, I knew he was there, because I had been told so, and this troubled me. But no sooner would I close my eyes than his image would appear standing at a distance of three or four feet from the head of the bed, in the form of a column five feet high or so and about four feet in circumference. The color was blue, but varied in depth and intensity; on some nights it was sky-blue, but usually of a deeper shade, a pure, soft, beautiful blue like that of the morning-glory or wild geranium.

It would not surprise me to find that many persons have some such material image or presentment of the spiritual entities they are taught to believe in at too tender an age. Recently, in comparing childish memories with a friend, he told me that he too always saw God as a blue object, but of no definite shape.

That blue column haunted me at night for many months; I don't think it quite vanished, ceasing to be anything but a memory, until I was seven — a date far ahead of where we are now.

STUDYING THE ESSAY

1. Can you select an important event of your childhood, as Hudson has done, and recall the very weather associated with it?
2. Select some concrete details in the description of Caesar which help to make him a personality.
3. Discuss: "My world was a purely material one, and a most wonderful world it was."

COMPOSITION TOPICS

1. Describe the burial of a pet.
2. Seeing New and Strange Things
3. Comment on Hudson's power of close observation.

ROBERT LOUIS STEVENSON,
1850–1894

Robert Louis Stevenson was an enormously gifted man whose life was blighted by tuberculosis and who actually crammed into fifteen years of feverish literary activity the many works by which he is remembered.

Born in Scotland of a well-to-do family, he was frail from birth and was coddled as a child by a nurse who loved to tell him ghost stories, which he remembered and later used in books like *Dr. Jekyll and Mr. Hyde* and *Weir of Hermiston*. He had little formal education, and he disliked his father's profession, engineering; he did study law and passed the bar examinations, but he never practiced as a lawyer. About 1875 he began to write essays for various magazines. Although some of these essays were well received, Stevenson attained little or no fame from this early work.

In 1880, in the course of a tour of France and Belgium, he met and fell in love with Mrs. Fannie Osborn, an American woman whom he married in San Francisco after her husband died. After their marriage he and his wife spent fourteen futile years seeking a climate in which Stevenson might regain his health. They tried New England and other parts of the United States; finally, in 1890, they found the right place, in Samoa. But 1890 was too late. He died four years later and was buried on that South Sea island.

The years 1880–1894 were tragic years for Stevenson and his bride, but they were the years during which he published an amazing list of books: *Travels with a Donkey* (1880), *Treasure Island* (1883), *A Child's Garden of Verses* (1885), *Kidnapped* and *Dr. Jekyll and Mr. Hyde* (1886), and *The Black Arrow* (1888).

Like Mark Twain, Stevenson appeals to most readers as a storyteller. Certainly no one should get past the eighth grade without having listened, with Jim Hawkins in the apple barrel, to the plotting of Long John Silver and his piratical friends. But in some respects Stevenson as a person is best revealed in his essays. He was a frail person, living a doomed life — like that of Lamb — without much hope. And his essays, like Lamb's, reveal a man whose personality is full of humor, whose appreciation of life is complete.

" On Falling in Love " is perhaps a one-sided opinion about this very important subject, but it is a delightful revelation of a man who, at the age of about twenty-five, could look with quiet humor at the people who disintegrate when romance hits them for the first time. And " Aes Triplex," while it is an essay about death — a subject which could never have been far from Stevenson's mind — is no more gloomy than something a healthy man might have written.

Stevenson's essays repay careful reading. His organization is sometimes haphazard, his paragraphs sometimes confusing. But his main ideas will be clear to the reader who looks for them. And his style is one of the smoothest, most carefully worked out styles in the whole history of the English essay.

AES TRIPLEX

The changes wrought by death are in themselves so sharp and final, and so terrible and melancholy in their consequences, that the thing stands alone in man's experience and has no parallel upon earth. It outdoes all other accidents because it is the last of them. Sometimes it leaps suddenly upon its victims, like a Thug; sometimes it lays a regular siege and creeps upon their citadel during a score of years. And when the business is done, there is sore havoc made in other people's lives, and a pin knocked out by which many subsidiary friendships hung together. There are empty chairs, solitary walks, and single beds at night. Again, in taking away our friends, death does not take them away utterly, but leaves behind a mocking, tragical, and soon intolerable residue, which must be hurriedly concealed. Hence a whole chapter of sights and customs striking to the mind, from the pyramids of Egypt to the gibbets and dule trees of medieval Europe. The poorest persons have a bit of pageant going towards the tomb; memorial stones are set up over the least memorable; and, in order to preserve some show of respect for what remains of our old loves and friendships, we must accompany it with much grimly ludicrous ceremonial, and the hired undertaker parades before the door. All this, and much more of the same sort, accompanied by the eloquence of poets, has gone a great way to put humanity in error; in many philosophies the error has been embodied and laid down with every circumstance of logic; although in real life the bustle and swiftness, in leaving people little time to think, have not left them time enough to go dangerously wrong in practice.

As a matter of fact, although few things are spoken of with more fearful whisperings than this prospect of death, few have less influence on conduct under healthy circumstances. We have all heard of cities of South America built upon the side of fiery mountains, and how, even in this tremendous neighborhood, the inhabitants are not a jot more impressed by the solemnity of mortal conditions than if they were delving gardens in the greenest corner of England. There are serenades and suppers and much gallantry among the myrtles overhead; and meanwhile the foundation shudders underfoot, the bowels of the mountain growl, and at any moment living ruin may leap sky-high into the moonlight, and tumble man and his merry-making in the dust. In the eyes of very young people, and very dull old ones, there is something indescribably reckless and desperate in such a picture. It seems not credible that respectable married people, with umbrellas, should find appetite for a bit of supper within quite a long distance of a fiery mountain; ordinary life begins to smell of high-handed debauch when it is carried on so close to a catastrophe; and even cheese and salad, it seems, could hardly be relished in such circumstances without something like a defiance of the Creator. It should be a place for nobody but hermits dwelling in prayer and maceration, or mere born-devils drowning care in a perpetual carouse.

And yet, when one comes to think upon it calmly, the situation of these South American citizens forms only a very pale figure for the state of ordinary mankind. This world itself, traveling blindly and swiftly in overcrowded space, among a million other worlds traveling blindly and swiftly in contrary directions, may very well come by a knock that would set it into explosion like a penny squib. And what, pathologically looked at, is the human body with all its organs, but a mere bagful of petards? The least of these is as dangerous to the whole economy as the ship's powder-magazine to the ship; and with every breath we breathe, and every meal we eat, we are putting one more of them in peril. If we clung as devotedly as some philosophers pretend we do to the abstract idea of life, or were half as frightened as they make out we are, for the subversive accident that ends it all, the trumpets might sound by the hour and no one would follow them into battle — the blue-peter might fly at the truck, but who would climb into a sea-going ship? Think (if these philosophers were right) with what a preparation of spirit we should affront the daily peril of the dinner table: a deadlier spot than any battlefield in history, where the far greater proportion of our ancestors have miserably left their bones! What woman would ever be lured into marriage, so much more dangerous than the wildest sea? And what would it be to grow old? For, after a certain distance, every step we take in life we find the ice growing thinner below our feet, and all around us and behind us we see our contemporaries going through. By the time a man gets well into the seventies, his continued existence is a mere miracle; and when he lays his old bones in bed for the night, there is an overwhelming probability that he will never see the day. Do the old men mind it, as a matter of fact? Why, no. They were never merrier; they have their grog at night, and tell the raciest stories; they hear of the death of people about their own age, or even younger, not as if it was a grisly warning, but with a simple childlike pleasure at having outlived someone else; and when a draft might puff them out like a guttering candle, or a bit of a stumble shatter them like so much glass, their old hearts keep sound and unaffrighted, and they go on, bubbling with laughter, through years of man's age compared to which the valley at Balaklava was as safe and peaceful as a village cricket-green on Sunday. It may fairly be questioned (if we look at the peril only) whether it was a much more daring feat for Curtius to plunge into the gulf than for any old gentleman of ninety to doff his clothes and clamber into bed.

Indeed, it is a memorable subject for consideration, with what unconcern and gaiety mankind pricks on along the Valley of the Shadow of Death. The whole way is one wilderness of snares; and the end of it, for those who fear the last pinch, is irrevocable ruin. And yet we go spinning through it all, like a party for the Derby. Perhaps the reader remembers one of the humorous devices of the deified Caligula: how he encouraged a vast concourse of holiday-makers on to his bridge over Baiae bay, and, when they were in the height of their enjoyment, turned loose the Pretorian guards among the company, and had them tossed into the sea. This is no bad miniature of the dealings of nature with the transitory race of man. Only, what a checkered picnic we have of it, even while it lasts! and into what great waters, not to be crossed by any swimmer, God's pale Pretorian throws us over in the end!

We live the time that a match flickers; we pop the cork of a ginger-beer bottle, and the earthquake swallows us on the instant. Is it not odd, is it not incongruous, is it not, in the highest sense of human speech, incredible that we should think so highly of the ginger-beer and regard so little the devouring earthquake? The love of Life and the fear of Death are two famous phrases that grow harder to understand the more we think about them. It is a well-known fact that an immense proportion of boat accidents would never happen if people held the sheet in their hands instead of making it fast; and yet, unless it be some martinet of a professional mariner or some landsman with shattered nerves, every one of God's creatures makes it fast. A strange instance of man's unconcern and brazen boldness in the face of death!

We confound ourselves with metaphysical phrases, which we import into daily talk with noble inappropriateness. We have no idea of what death is, apart from its circumstances and some of its consequences to others; and although we have some experience of living, there is not a man on earth who has flown so high into abstraction as to have any practical guess at the meaning of the word *life*. All literature, from Job and Omar Khayyàm to Thomas Carlyle or Walt Whitman, is but an attempt to look upon the human state with such largeness of view as shall enable us to rise from the consideration of living to the Definition of Life. And our sages give us about the best satisfaction in their power when they say that it is a vapor, or a show, or made out of the same stuff with dreams. Philosophy, in its more rigid sense, has been at the same work for ages; and after a myriad bald heads have wagged over the problem, and piles of words have been heaped one upon another into dry and cloudy volumes without end, philosophy has the honor of laying before us, with modest pride, her contribution towards the subject: that life is a Permanent Possibility of Sensation. Truly a fine result! A man may very well love beef, or hunting, or a woman; but surely, surely, not a Permanent Possibility of Sensation! He may be afraid of a precipice, or a dentist, or a large enemy with a club, or even an undertaker's man; but not certainly of abstract death. We may trick with the word *life* in its dozen senses until we are weary of tricking; we may argue in terms of all the philosophies on earth; but one fact remains true throughout — that we do not love life, in the sense that we are greatly preoccupied about its conservation; that we do not, properly speaking, love life at all, but living. Into the views of the least careful there will enter some degree of providence; no man's eyes are fixed entirely on the passing hour; but although we have some anticipation of good health, good weather, wine, active employment, love, and self-approval, the sum of these anticipations does not amount to anything like a general view of life's possibilities and issues; nor are those who cherish them most vividly at all the most scrupulous of their personal safety. To be deeply interested in the accidents of our existence, to enjoy keenly the mixed texture of human experience, rather leads a man to disregard precautions, and risk his neck against a straw. For surely the love of living is stronger in an Alpine climber roping over a peril, or a hunter riding merrily at a stiff fence, than in a creature who lives upon a diet and walks a measured distance in the interest of his constitution.

There is a great deal of very vile nonsense talked upon both sides of the matter; tearing divines reducing life to the dimensions of a mere funeral procession, so short as to be hardly decent; and melancholy unbelievers yearning for the tomb as if it were a world too far away. Both sides must feel a little ashamed of their performances now and again, when they draw in their chairs to dinner. Indeed, a good meal and a bottle of wine is an answer to most standard works upon the question. When a man's heart warms to his viands, he forgets a great deal of sophistry, and soars into a rosy zone of contemplation. Death may be knocking at the door, like the Commander's statue; we have something else in hand, thank God, and let him knock. Passing bells are ringing the world over. All the world over, and every hour, some one is parting company with all his aches and ecstasies. For us also the trap is laid. But we are so fond of life that we have no leisure to entertain the terror of death. It is a honeymoon with us all through, and none of the longest. Small blame to us if we give our whole hearts to this glowing bride of ours — to the appetites, to honor, to the hungry curiosity of the mind, to the pleasure of the eyes in nature, and the pride of our own nimble bodies.

We all of us appreciate the sensations; but as for caring about the Permanence of the Possibility, a man's head is generally very bald, and his senses very dull, before he comes to that. Whether we regard life as a lane leading to a dead wall — a mere bag's end, as the French say — or whether we think of it as a vestibule or gymnasium, where we wait our turn and prepare our faculties for some more noble destiny; whether we thunder in a pulpit, or pule in little atheistic poetry books, about its vanity and brevity; whether we look justly for years of health and vigor, or are about to mount into a bath-chair, as a step towards the hearse; in each and all of these views and situations there is but one conclusion possible: that a man should stop his ears against paralyzing terror, and run the race that is set before him with a single mind. No one surely could have recoiled with more heart-ache and terror from the thought of death than our respected lexicographer;[1] and yet we know how little it affected his conduct, how wisely and boldly he walked, and in what a fresh and lively vein he spoke of life. Already an old man, he ventured on his Highland tour; and his heart, bound with triple brass,[2] did not recoil before twenty-seven individual cups of tea. As courage and intelligence are the two qualities best worth a good man's cultivation, so it is the first part of intelligence to recognize our precarious estate in life, and the first part of courage to be not at all abashed before the fact. A frank and somewhat headlong carriage, not looking too anxiously before, not dallying in maudlin regret over the past, stamps the man who is well armored for this world.

And not only well armored for himself, but a good friend and a good citizen to boot. We do not go to cowards for tender dealing; there is nothing so cruel as panic; the man who has least fear for his own carcass has most time to consider others. That eminent chemist who took his walks abroad in tin shoes, and subsisted wholly upon tepid milk, had all his work cut out for him in considerate dealings with his own digestion. So soon as prudence has begun to grow up in the brain, like a dismal fungus, it finds its first expression in a paralysis of generous acts. The victim begins to shrink spiritually; he develops a fancy for parlors with a regulated temperature, and takes his morality on the principle of tin shoes and tepid milk. The care of one important body or soul becomes so engrossing that all the noises of the outer

[1] Samuel Johnson.   [2] *Aes triplex* means triple brass.

world begin to come thin and faint into the parlor with the regulated temperature; and the tin shoes go equably forward over blood and rain. To be otherwise is to ossify; and the scruple-monger ends by standing stock still. Now the man who has his heart on his sleeve, and a good whirling weather-cock of a brain, who reckons his life as a thing to be dash-ingly used and cheerfully hazarded, makes a very different acquaintance of the world, keeps all his pulses going true and fast, and gathers impetus as he runs, until, if he be run-ning toward anything better than wildfire, he may shoot up and become a constellation in the end. Lord look after his health, Lord have a care of his soul, says he; and he has at the key of the position, and swashes through incongruity and peril towards his aim. Death is on all sides of him with pointed batteries, as he is on all sides of all of us; unfortu-nate surprises gird him round; mim-mouthed friends and re-lations hold up their hands in quite a little elegiacal synod about his path: and what cares he for all this? Being a true lover of living, a fellow with something pushing and spon-taneous in his inside, he must, like any other soldier, in any other stirring, deadly warfare, push on at his best pace until he touch the goal. "A peerage or Westminster Abbey!" cried Nelson in his bright, boyish, heroic manner. These are great incentives; not for any of these, but for the plain satis-faction of living, of being about their business in some sort or other, do the brave, serviceable men of every nation tread down the nettle danger, and pass flying over all the stum-bling-blocks of prudence. Think of the heroism of Johnson, think of that superb indifference to mortal limitation that set him upon his dictionary, and carried him through trium-phantly until the end! Who, if he were wisely considerate of things at large, would ever embark upon any work much more considerable than a halfpenny postcard? Who would project a serial novel, after Thackeray and Dickens had each fallen in mid-course? Who would find heart enough to begin to live, if he dallied with the consideration of death?

And, after all, what sorry and pitiful quibbling all this is! To forgo all the issues of living, in a parlor with a regulated temperature — as if that were not to die a hundred times over, and for ten years at a stretch! As if it were not to die in one's own lifetime, and without even the sad immunities of death! As if it were not to die, and yet to be the patient spectators of our own pitiable change! The Permanent Possibility is preserved, but the sensations carefully held at arm's length, as if one kept a photographic plate in a dark chamber. It is better to lose health like a spendthrift than to waste it like a miser. It is better to live and be done with it, than to die daily in the sick room. By all means begin your folio; even if the doctor does not give you a year, even if he hesitates about a month, make one brave push and see what can be accomplished in a week. It is not only in finished undertakings that we ought to honor useful labor. A spirit goes out of the man who means execution, which outlives the most untimely ending. All who have meant good work with their whole hearts, have done good work, although they may die before they have the time to sign it. Every heart that has beat strong and cheerfully has left a hopeful impulse behind it in the world, and bettered the tradition of mankind. And even if death catch people, like an open pitfall, and in mid-career, laying out vast projects, and planning monstrous foundations, flushed with hope, and their mouths full of boastful language, they should be at once tripped up and silenced: is there not something brave and spirited in such a termination? and does not life go down with a better grace, foaming in full body over a precipice, than miserably straggling to an end in sandy deltas? When the Greeks made their fine saying that those whom the gods love die young, I cannot help believing they had this sort of death also in their eye. For surely, at whatever age it overtake the man, this is to die young. Death has not been suffered to take so much as an illusion from his heart. In the hot-fit of life, a-tiptoe on the highest point of being, he passes at a bound on to the other side. The noise of the mallet and chisel is scarcely quenched, the trumpets are hardly done blowing, when, trailing with him clouds of glory, this happy-starred, full-blooded spirit shoots into the spiritual land.

STUDYING THE ESSAY

1. What are the circumstances of Stevenson's life which make this essay significant?
2. How does the author show that we are little influenced by the fear of death? What things do people do today which reveal that they have no fear of death?
3. What is the attitude of old people toward death? Do all old people have the same attitude?
4. List the historical and literary allusions found in the essay. Comment on their effectiveness. Do you enjoy the ones which you understand? Watch for " literary echoing " in all your reading for a week.
5. Point out the places in the essay which reveal the deeper qualities of Stevenson's nature.
6. What distinction does Stevenson make between the " love of life " and the " love of living "?
7. The last paragraph is one of the finest passages in all literature. Why?
8. Read John Donne's sonnet called " Death, Be Not Proud " and William Cullen Bryant's poem " Thanatopsis " for two poetic approaches to the same topic.
9. Is this essay gloomy or morbid? Explain your answer.

1. On Courage and Intelligence
2. Too Much Caution Is Bad for Mankind

ON FALLING IN LOVE

Lord, what fools these mortals be!

There is only one event in life which really astonishes a man and startles him out of his prepared opinions. Everything else befalls him very much as he expected. Event succeeds to event, with an agreeable variety indeed, but with little that is either startling or intense; they form together no more than a sort of background, or running accompaniment to the man's own reflections; and he falls naturally into a cool, curious, and smiling habit of mind, and builds himself up in a conception of life which expects tomorrow to be after the pattern of today and yesterday. He may be accustomed to the vagaries of his friends and acquaintances under the influence of love. He may sometimes look forward to it for himself with an incomprehensible expectation. But it is a subject in which neither intuition nor the behavior of others will help the philosopher to the truth. There is probably nothing rightly thought or rightly written on this matter of love that is not a piece of the person's experience. I remember an anecdote of a well-known French theorist, who was debating a point eagerly in his *cénacle*. It was objected against him that he had never experienced love. Whereupon he arose, left the society, and made it a point not to return to it until he considered that he had supplied the defect. " Now," he remarked, on entering, " now I am in a position to continue the discussion." Perhaps he had not penetrated very deeply into the subject after all; but the story indicates right thinking, and may serve as an apologue to readers of this essay.

When at last the scales fall from his eyes, it is not without something of the nature of dismay that the man finds himself in such changed conditions. He has to deal with commanding emotions instead of the easy dislikes and preferences in which he has hitherto passed his days; and he recognizes capabilities for pain and pleasure of which he had not yet suspected the existence. Falling in love is the one illogical adventure, the one thing of which we are tempted to think as supernatural, in our trite and reasonable world. The effect is out of all proportion with the cause. Two persons, neither of them, it may be, very amiable or very beautiful, meet, speak a little, and look a little into each other's eyes. That has been done a dozen or so of times in the experience of either with no great result. But on this occasion all is different. They fall at once into that state in which another person becomes to us the very gist and center-point of God's creation, and demolishes our laborious theories with a smile; in which our ideas are so bound up with the one master-thought that even the trivial cares of our own person become so many acts of devotion, and the love of life itself is translated into a wish to remain in the same world with so precious and desirable a fellow creature. And all the while their acquaintances look on in stupor, and ask each other, with almost passionate emphasis, what so-and-so can see in that woman, or such-a-one in that man? I am sure, gentlemen, I cannot tell you. For my part, I cannot think what the women mean. It might be very well, if the Apollo Belvedere should suddenly glow all over into life, and step forward from the pedestal with that godlike air of his. But of the misbegotten changelings who call themselves men, and prate intolerably over dinner table, I never saw one who seemed worthy to inspire love — no, nor read of any, except Leonardo da Vinci, and perhaps Goethe in his youth. About women I entertain a somewhat different opinion; but there, I have the misfortune to be a man.

There are many matters in which you may waylay Destiny, and bid him stand and deliver. Hard work, high thinking, adventurous excitement, and a great deal more that forms a part of this or the other person's spiritual bill of fare, are within the reach of almost anyone who can dare a little and be patient. But it is by no means in the way of everyone to fall in love. You know the difficulty Shakespeare was put into when Queen Elizabeth asked him to show Falstaff in love. I do not believe that Henry Fielding was ever in love. Scott, if it were not for a passage or two in *Rob Roy*, would give me very much the same effect. These are great names and (what is more to the purpose) strong, healthy, high-strung, and generous natures, of whom the reverse might have been expected. As for the innumerable army of anemic and tailorish persons who occupy the face of this planet with so much propriety, it is palpably absurd to imagine them in any such situation as a love affair. A wet rag goes safely by the fire; and if a man is blind, he cannot expect to be much impressed by romantic scenery. Apart from all this many lovable people miss each other in the world, or meet under some unfavorable star. There is the nice and critical moment of declaration to be got over. From timidity or lack of opportunity a good half of possible love cases never get so far, and at least another quarter do there cease and determine. A very adroit person, to be sure,

manages to prepare the way and out with his declaration in
the nick of time. And then there is a fine solid sort of man,
who goes on from snub to snub; and if he has to declare
forty times, will continue imperturbably declaring, amid
the astonished consideration of men and angels, until he
has a favorable answer. I daresay, if one were a woman,
one would like to marry a man who was capable of doing
this, but not quite one who had done so. It is just a little
bit abject, and somehow just a little bit gross; and mar-
riages in which one of the parties has been thus battered
into consent scarcely form agreeable subjects for meditation. Love should run out to meet love with open arms. Indeed, the ideal story is that of two people who go into love
step for step, with a fluttered consciousness, like a pair of
children venturing together into a dark room. From the first
moment when they see each other, with a pang of curiosity,
through stage after stage of growing pleasure and embarrassment, they can read the expression of their own trouble
in each other's eyes. There is here no declaration properly
so called; the feeling is so plainly shared, that as soon as the
man knows what it is in his own heart, he is sure of what
it is in the woman's.

This simple accident of falling in love is as beneficial as
it is astonishing. It arrests the petrifying influence of years,
disproves cold-blooded and cynical conclusions, and awakens dormant sensibilities. Hitherto the man had found it a
good policy to disbelieve the existence of any enjoyment
which was out of his reach; and thus he turned his back
upon the strong sunny parts of nature, and accustomed himself to look exclusively on what was common and dull. He
accepted a prose ideal, let himself go blind of many sympa-
thies by disuse; and if he were young and witty, or beautiful,
wilfully forwent these advantages. He joined himself to the
following of what, in the old mythology of love, was prettily

called *nonchaloir;* and in an odd mixture of feelings, a fling of self-respect, a preference for selfish liberty, and a great dash of that fear with which honest people regard serious interests, kept himself back from the straightforward course of life among certain selected activities. And now, all of a sudden, he is unhorsed, like St. Paul, from his infidel affectation. His heart, which has been ticking accurate seconds for the last year, gives a bound and begins to beat high and irregularly in his breast. It seems as if he had never heard or felt or seen until that moment; and by the report of his memory, he must have lived his past life between sleep and waking, or with the preoccupied attention of a brown study. He is practically incommoded by the generosity of his feelings, smiles much when he is alone, and develops a habit of looking rather blankly upon the moon and stars. But it is not at all within the province of a prose essayist to give a picture of this hyperbolical frame of mind; and the thing has been done already, and that to admiration. In *Adelaide*, in Tennyson's *Maud*, and in some of Heine's songs, you get the absolute expression of this midsummer spirit. Romeo and Juliet were very much in love; although they tell me some German critics are of a different opinion, probably the same who would have us think Mercutio a dull fellow. Poor Antony was in love, and no mistake. That lay figure Marius, in *Les Misérables*, is also a genuine case in his own way, and worth observation. A good many of George Sand's people are thoroughly in love; and so are a good many of George Meredith's. Altogether, there is plenty to read on the subject. If the root of the matter be in him, and if he has the requisite chords to set in vibration, a young man may occasionally enter, with the key of art, into that land of Beulah which is upon the borders of Heaven and within sight of the City of Love. There let him sit awhile to hatch delightful hopes and perilous illusions.

One thing that accompanies the passion in its first blush is certainly difficult to explain. It comes (I do not quite see how) that from having a very supreme sense of pleasure in all parts of life — in lying down to sleep, in waking, in motion, in breathing, in continuing to be — the lover begins to regard his happiness as beneficial for the rest of the world and highly meritorious in himself. Our race has never been able contentedly to suppose that the noise of its wars, conducted by a few young gentlemen in a corner of an inconsiderable star, does not re-echo among the courts of Heaven with quite a formidable effect. In much the same taste, when people find a great to-do in their own breasts, they imagine it must have some influence in their neighborhood. The presence of the two lovers is so enchanting to each other that it seems as if it must be the best thing possible for everybody else. They are half inclined to fancy it is because of them and their love that the sky is blue and the sun shines. And certainly the weather is usually fine while people are courting. . . . In point of fact, although the happy man feels very kindly toward others of his own sex, there is apt to be something too much of the magnifico in his demeanor. If people grow presuming and self-important over such matters as a dukedom or the Holy See, they will scarcely support the dizziest elevation in life without some suspicion of a strut; and the dizziest elevation is to love and be loved in return. Consequently, accepted lovers are a trifle condescending in their address to other men. An overweening sense of the passion and importance of life hardly conduces to simplicity of manner. To women, they feel very nobly, very purely, and very generously, as if they were so many Joan-of-Arcs; but this does not come out in their behavior; and they treat them to Grandisonian airs marked with a suspicion of fatuity. I am not quite certain that women do not like this sort of thing; but really, after having bemused myself over *Daniel Deronda,* I have given up trying to understand what they like.

If it did nothing else, this sublime and ridiculous superstition, that the pleasure of the pair is somehow blessed to others, and everybody is made happier in their happiness, would serve at least to keep love generous and great-hearted. Nor is it quite a baseless superstition after all. Other lovers are hugely interested. They strike the nicest balance between pity and approval, when they see people aping the greatness of their own sentiments. It is an understood thing in the play, that while the young gentlefolk are courting on the terrace, a rough flirtation is being carried on and a light, trivial sort of love is growing up, between the footman and the singing chambermaid. As people are generally cast for the leading parts in their own imaginations, the reader can apply the parallel to real life without much chance of going wrong. In short, they are quite sure this other love affair is not so deep seated as their own, but they like dearly to see it going forward. And love, considered as a spectacle, must have attractions for many who are not of the confraternity. The sentimental old maid is a commonplace of the novelists; and he must be rather a poor sort of human being, to be sure, who can look on at this pretty madness without indulgence and sympathy. For nature commends itself to people with a most insinuating art; the busiest is now and again arrested by a great sunset; and you may be as pacific or as cold-blooded as you will, but you cannot help some emotion when you read of well-disputed battles, or meet a pair of lovers in the lane.

Certainly, whatever it may be with regard to the world at large, this idea of beneficent pleasure is true as between the sweethearts. To do good and communicate is the lover's grand intention. It is the happiness of the other that makes his own most intense gratification. It is not possible to disentangle the different emotions, the pride, humility, pity and passion, which are excited by a look of happy love or an unexpected caress. To make one's self beautiful, to dress the hair, to excel in talk, to do anything and all things that puff out the character and attributes and make them imposing in the eyes of others, is not only to magnify one's self, but to offer the most delicate homage at the same time. And it is in this latter intention that they are done by lovers; for the essence of love is kindness; and indeed it may be best defined as passionate kindness: kindness, so to speak, run mad and become importunate and violent. Vanity in a merely personal sense exists no longer. The lover takes a perilous pleasure in privately displaying his weak points and having them, one after another, accepted and condoned. He wishes to be assured that he is not loved for this or that good quality, but for himself, or something as like himself as he can contrive to set forward. For, although it may have been a very difficult thing to paint the marriage of Cana, or write the fourth act of *Antony and Cleopatra*, there is a more difficult piece of art before every one in this world who cares to set about explaining his own character to others. Words and acts are easily wrenched from their true significance; and they are all the language we have to come and go upon. A pitiful job we make of it, as a rule. For better or worse, people mistake our meaning and take our emotions at a wrong valuation. And generally we rest pretty content with our failures; we are content to be misapprehended by crackling flirts; but when once a man is moonstruck with this affection of love, he makes it a point of honor to clear such dubieties away. He cannot have the Best of Her Sex misled upon a point of this importance; and his pride revolts at being loved in a mistake.

He discovers a great reluctance to return on former periods of his life. To all that has not been shared with her, rights and duties, bygone fortunes and dispositions, he can look back only by a difficult and repugnant effort of the will. That he should have wasted some years in ignorance of what alone was really important, that he may have entertained the thought of other women with any show of complacency, is a burthen almost too heavy for his self-respect. But it is the thought of another past that rankles in his spirit like a poisoned wound. That he himself made a fashion of being alive in the bald, beggarly days before a certain meeting, is deplorable enough in all good conscience. But that She should have permitted herself the same liberty seems inconsistent with a Divine providence.

A great many people run down jealousy, on the score that it is an artificial feeling, as well as practically inconvenient. This is scarcely fair; for the feeling on which it merely attends, like an ill-humored courtier, is itself artificial in exactly the same sense and to the same degree. I suppose what is meant by that objection is that jealousy has not always been a character of man; formed no part of that very modest kit of sentiments with which he is supposed to have begun the world: but waited to make its appearance in better days and among richer natures. And this is equally true of love, and friendship, and love of country, and delight in what they call the beauties of nature, and most other things worth having. Love, in particular, will not endure any historical scrutiny: to all who have fallen across it, it is one of the most incontestable facts in the world; but if you begin to ask what it was in other periods and countries, in Greece for instance, the strangest doubts begin to spring up, and everything seems so vague and changing that a dream is logical in comparison. Jealousy, at any rate, is one of the consequences of love; you may like it or not, at pleasure; but there it is.

It is not exactly jealousy, however, that we feel when we

reflect on the past of those we love. A bundle of letters found after years of happy union creates no sense of insecurity in the present; and yet it will pain a man sharply. The two people entertain no vulgar doubt of each other: but this pre-existence of both occurs to the mind as something indelicate. To be altogether right, they should have had twin birth together, at the same moment with the feeling that unites them. Then indeed it would be simple and perfect and without reserve or afterthought. Then they would understand each other with a fullness impossible otherwise. There would be no barrier between them of associations that cannot be imparted. They would be led into none of those comparisons that send the blood back to the heart. And they would know that there had been no time lost, and they had been together as much as was possible. For besides terror for the separation that must follow some time or other in the future, men feel anger, and something like remorse, when they think of that other separation which endured until they met. Some one has written that love makes people believe in immortality, because there seems not to be room enough in life for so great a tenderness, and it is inconceivable that the most masterful of our emotions should have no more than the spare moments of a few years. Indeed, it seems strange; but if we call to mind analogies, we can hardly regard it as impossible.

" The blind bow-boy," who smiles upon us from the end of terraces in old Dutch gardens, laughingly hails his bird-bolts among a fleeting generation. But for as fast as ever he shoots, the game dissolves and disappears into eternity from under his falling arrows; this one is gone ere he is struck; the other has but time to make one gesture and give one passionate cry; and they are all the things of a moment. When the generation is gone, when the play is over, when the thirty years' panorama has been withdrawn in tatters from the stage of the world, we may ask what has become of these great, weighty, and undying loves, and the sweethearts who despised mortal conditions in a fine credulity; and they can only show us a few songs in a bygone taste, a few actions worth remembering, and a few children who have retained some happy stamp from the disposition of their parents.

STUDYING THE ESSAY

1. Discuss the second paragraph of the essay. Is Stevenson exaggerating?
2. What are some of the benefits of falling in love?
3. Look up some of the literary allusions in this essay.
4. Why are "accepted lovers a trifle condescending in their address to other men"?
5. What do two lovers think of other people? Why?
6. How does love change a person?
7. Discuss Stevenson's ideas of jealousy.
8. Discuss the general truth of this essay.
9. Words to learn: *vagaries, adroit, infidel, homage, dormant.*

COMPOSITION TOPICS

1. On Falling Out of Love
2. If you know a couple who are in love, write a description of their behavior in public.

AGNES REPPLIER, 1858–1950

To a request for a sketch of her life Agnes Repplier wrote: " Biographical material there is none. My life affords no salient feature for narration. I have been badly injured by an accident, but half the world has been injured by accidents. I have been robbed by burglars; but all Philadelphians are robbed sooner or later by burglars. I am going to Europe in the spring, but who isn't going to Europe in the spring? In these incidents there is no shadow of distinction."

However, during her " uneventful " life Miss Repplier wrote fourteen volumes of essays, two biographies, and several other books. Her life of Father Marquette (1929) and her essays place her in the front rank of American woman writers; her writings won her many honors, including the Gold Medal of the American Academy of Arts and Letters.

Miss Repplier's first literary attempts were short stories, most of them unsuccessful. When she was advised by the editor of the *Catholic World*, to whom she had sent some stories, that her real talent was the essay, she turned to the essay and found it good. In her personal life she was something of a recluse. In Philadelphia, where she made her home, she kept largely to herself. But she spent a great deal of time in Europe, particularly France, and thus her point of view was broad. To her essays she brings the wisdom of a scholar, tempered by the humanity of a well-traveled, cosmopolitan woman of letters. Her essays, with their polished style, their wit, and their depth, stand in the main stream of the English personal essay. She is a literary descendant of Lamb and Stevenson.

Volumes of essays which will be of interest to the reader are *To Think of Tea* (1932) and *The Fireside Sphinx* (1939).

A KITTEN

If
> The child is father of the man,

why is not the kitten father of the cat? If in the little boy there lurks the infant likeness of all that manhood will complete, why does not the kitten betray some of the attributes common to the adult puss? A puppy is but a dog, plus high spirits, and minus common sense. We never hear our friends say they love puppies, but cannot bear dogs. A kitten is a thing apart; and many people who lack the discriminating enthusiasm for cats, who regard these beautiful beasts with aversion and mistrust, are won over easily, and cajoled out of their prejudices by the deceitful wiles of kittenhood.

> The little actor cons another part,

and is the most irresistible comedian in the world. Its wide-open eyes gleam with wonder and mirth. It darts madly at nothing at all, and then, as though suddenly checked in the pursuit, prances sideways on its hind legs with ridiculous agility and zeal. It makes a vast pretense of climbing the rounds of a chair, and swings by the curtain like an acrobat. It scrambles up a table leg, and is seized with comic horror at finding itself full two feet from the floor. If you hasten to its rescue, it clutches you nervously, its little heart thumping against its furry sides, while its soft paws expand and contract with agitation and relief;

> And all their harmless claws disclose,
> Like prickles of an early rose.

Yet the instant it is back on the carpet it feigns to be suspicious of your interference, peers at you out of " the tail o' its ee," and scampers for protection under the sofa, from which asylum it presently emerges with cautious trailing steps, as though encompassed by fearful dangers and alarms. Its baby innocence is yet unseared. The evil knowledge of uncanny things which is the dark inheritance of cathood has not yet shadowed its round infant eyes. Where did witches find the mysterious beasts that sat motionless by their fires, and watched unblinkingly the waxen manikins dwindling in the flame? They never reared these companions of their solitude, for no witch could have endured to see a kitten gamboling on her hearthstone. A witch's kitten! That one preposterous thought proves how wide, how unfathomed, is the gap between feline infancy and age.

So it happens that the kitten is loved and cherished and caressed as long as it preserves the beguiling mirthfulness of youth. Richelieu, we know, was wont to keep a family of kittens in his cabinet, that their grace and gayety might divert him from the cares of state, and from black moods of melancholy. Yet, with short-sighted selfishness, he banished these little friends when but a few months old, and gave their places to younger pets. The first faint dawn of reason, the first indication of soberness and worldly wisdom, the first charming and coquettish pretenses to maturity, were followed by immediate dismissal. Richelieu desired to be amused. He had no conception of the finer joy which springs from mutual companionship and esteem. Even humbler and more sincere admirers, like Joanna Baillie, in whom we wish to believe Puss found a friend and champion, appear to take it for granted that the kitten should be the spoiled darling of the household, and the cat a social outcast, degraded into usefulness, and expected to work for her living. What else can be understood from such lines as these?

> Ah! many a lightly sportive child,
> Who hath, like thee, our wits beguiled,
> To dull and sober manhood grown,
> With strange recoil our hearts disown.
> Even so, poor Kit! must thou endure,
> When thou becomest a cat demure,
> Full many a cuff and angry word,
> Chid roughly from the tempting board.
> And yet, for that thou hast, I ween,
> So oft our favored playmate been,
> Soft be the change which thou shalt prove,
> *When time hath spoiled thee of our love;*
> Still be thou deemed, by housewife fat,
> A comely, careful, mousing cat,
> Whose dish is, for the public good,
> Replenished oft with savory food.

Here is a plain exposition of the utilitarian theory which Shakespeare is supposed to have countenanced because Shylock speaks of the "harmless, necessary cat." Shylock, forsooth! As if he, of all men in Christendom or Jewry, knew anything about cats! Small wonder that he was outwitted by Portia and Jessica, when an adroit little animal could so easily beguile him. But Joanna Baillie should never have been guilty of those smug commonplaces concerning the

> comely, careful, mousing cat,

remembering her own valiant Tabby who won Scott's respectful admiration by worrying and killing a dog. It ill became the possessor of an Amazonian cat, distinguished by

Sir Walter's regard, to speak with such patronizing kindness
of the race.

We can make no more stupid blunder than to look upon
our pets from the standpoint of utility. Puss, as a rule, is
another Nimrod, eager for the chase, and unwearyingly patient in pursuit of her prey. But she hunts for her own pleasure, not for our convenience; and when a life of luxury has
relaxed her zeal, she often declines to hunt at all. I knew
intimately two Maryland cats, well born and of great personal attractions. The sleek, black Tom was named Onyx,
and his snow-white companion Lilian. Both were idle, urbane, fastidious, and self-indulgent as Lucullus. Now, into
the house honored, but not served, by these charming creatures came a rat, which secured permanent lodgings in the
kitchen, and speedily evicted the maidservants. A reign of
terror followed, and after a few days of hopeless anarchy it
occurred to the cook that the cats might be brought from
their comfortable cushions upstairs and shut in at night with
their hereditary foe. This was done, and the next morning,
on opening the kitchen door, a tableau rivaling the peaceful
scenes of Eden was presented to the view. On one side of the
hearth lay Onyx, on the other, Lilian; and ten feet away, upright upon the kitchen table, sat the rat, contemplating them
both with tranquil humor and content. It was apparent to
him, as well as to the rest of the household, that he was an
object of absolute, contemptuous indifference to those two
lordly cats.

There is none of this superb unconcern in the joyous
eagerness of infancy. A kitten will dart in pursuit of everything that is small enough to be chased with safety. Not a
fly on the windowpane, not a moth in the air, not a tiny
crawling insect on the carpet, escapes its unwelcome atten-
tions. It begins to " take notice " as soon as its eyes are open,
and its vivacity, outstripping its dawning intelligence, leads

it into infantile perils and wrongdoing. I own that when
Agrippina brought her first-born son — aged two days —
and established him in my bedroom closet, the plan struck
me at the start as inconvenient. I had prepared another nurs-
ery for the little Claudius Nero, and I endeavored for a
while to convince his mother that my arrangements were
best. But Agrippina was inflexible. The closet suited her in
every respect; and, with charming and irresistible flattery,
she gave me to understand, in the mute language I knew so
well, that she wished her baby boy to be under my immediate protection. " I bring him to you because I trust you,"
she said as plainly as looks can speak. "Downstairs they
handle him all the time, and it is not good for kittens to be
handled. Here he is safe from harm, and here he shall remain." After a few weak remonstrances, the futility of
which I too clearly understood, her persistence carried the
day. I removed my clothing from the closet, spread a shawl
upon the floor, had the door taken from its hinges, and resigned myself, for the first time in my life, to the daily and
hourly companionship of an infant.

I was amply rewarded. People who require the household
cat to rear her offspring in some remote attic, or dark corner
of the cellar, have no idea of all the diversion and pleasure
that they lose. It is delightful to watch the little blind,
sprawling, feeble, helpless things develop swiftly into the
grace and agility of kittenhood. It is delightful to see the
mingled pride and anxiety of the mother, whose parental
love increases with every hour of care, and who exhibits her
young family as if they were infant Gracchi, the hope of all
their race. During Nero's extreme youth, there were times,
I admit, when Agrippina wearied both of his companionship
and of her own maternal duties. Once or twice she abandoned him at night for the greater luxury of my bed, where
she slept tranquilly by my side, unmindful of the little wail-

ing cries with which Nero lamented her desertion. Once or
twice the heat of early summer tempted her to spend the
evening on the porch roof which lay beneath my windows,
and I have passed some anxious hours awaiting her return,
and wondering what would happen if she never came
back, and I were left to bring up the baby by hand.

But as the days sped on, and Nero grew rapidly in beauty
and intelligence, Agrippina's affection for him knew no
bounds. She could hardly bear to leave him even for a little
while, and always came hurrying back to him with a loud
frightened mew, as if fearing he might have been stolen in
her absence. At night she purred over him for hours, or
made little gurgling noises expressive of ineffable content.
She resented the careless curiosity of strangers, and was a
trifle supercilious when the cook stole softly in to give vent
to her fervent admiration. But from first to last she shared
with me her pride and pleasure; and the joy in her beautiful
eyes, as she raised them to mine, was frankly confiding and
sympathetic. When the infant Claudius rolled for the first
time over the ledge of the closet, and lay sprawling on the
bedroom floor, it would have been hard to say which of us
was the more elated at his prowess. A narrow pink ribbon of
honor was at once tied around the small adventurer's neck,
and he was pronounced the most daring and agile of kittens.
From that day his brief career was a series of brilliant tri-
umphs. He was a kitten of parts. Like one of Miss Austen's
heroes, he had air and countenance. Less beautiful than his
mother, whom he closely resembled, he easily eclipsed her
in vivacity and the specious arts of fascination. Never were
mother and son more unlike in character and disposition, and
the inevitable contrast between kittenhood and cathood was
enhanced in this case by a strong natural dissimilarity which
no length of years could have utterly effaced.

Agrippina had always been a cat of manifest reserves. She

was only six weeks old when she came to me, and had already acquired that gravity of demeanor, that air of gentle disdain, that dignified and somewhat supercilious composure, which won the respectful admiration of those whom she permitted to enjoy her acquaintance. Even in moments of self-forgetfulness and mirth her recreations resembled those of the little Spanish Infanta, who, not being permitted to play with her inferiors, and having no equals, diverted herself as best she could with sedate and solitary sport. Always chary of her favors, Agrippina cared little for the admiration of her chosen circle; and, with a single exception, she made no friends beyond it.

Claudius Nero, on the contrary, thirsted for applause. Affable, debonair, and democratic to the core, the caresses and commendations of a chance visitor or of a housemaid were as valuable to him as were my own. I never looked at him "showing off," as children say — jumping from chair to chair, balancing himself on the bedpost, or scrambling rapturously up the forbidden curtains — without thinking of the young Emperor who contended in the amphitheater for the worthless plaudits of the crowd. He was impulsive and affectionate — so, I believe, was the Emperor for a time — and as masterful as if born to the purple. His mother struggled hard to maintain her rightful authority, but it was in vain. He woke her from her sweetest naps; he darted at her tail, and leaped down on her from sofas and tables with the grace of a diminutive panther. Every time she attempted to punish him for these misdemeanors he cried piteously for help, and was promptly and unwisely rescued by some kind-hearted member of the family. After a while Agrippina took to sitting on her tail, in order to keep it out of his reach, and I have seen her many times carefully tucking it out of sight. She had never been a cat of active habits or of showy accomplishments, and the daring agility of the little Nero amazed and bewildered her. "A Spaniard," observes that pleasant gossip, James Howell, "walks as if he marched, and seldom looks upon the ground, as if he contemned it. I was told of a Spaniard who, having got a fall by a stumble, and broke his nose, rose up, and in a disdainful manner said, 'This comes of walking on the earth.'"

Now Nero seldom walked on the earth. At least, he never, if he could help it, walked on the floor; but traversed a room in a series of flying leaps from chair to table, from table to lounge, from lounge to desk, with an occasional dash at the mantelpiece, just to show what he could do. It was curious to watch Agrippina during the performance of these acrobatic feats. Pride, pleasure, the anxiety of a mother, and the faint resentment of conscious inferiority struggled for mastership in her little breast. Sometimes, when Nero's radiant self-sat-isfaction grew almost insufferable, I have seen her eyelids narrow sullenly, and have wondered whether the Roman Empress ever looked in that way at her brilliant and beauti-ful son, when material love was withering slowly under the shadow of coming evil. Sometimes, when Nero had been prancing and paddling about with absurd and irresistible glee, attracting and compelling the attention of everybody in the room, Agrippina would jump up on my lap, and look in my face with an expression I thought I understood. She had never before valued my affection in all her little petted, pampered life. She had been sufficient for herself, and had merely tolerated me as a devoted and useful companion. But now that another had usurped so many of her privileges, I fancied there were moments when it pleased her to know that one subject, at least, was not to be beguiled from al-legiance; that to one friend, at least, she always was and al-ways would be the dearest cat in the world.

I am glad to remember that love triumphed over jealousy, and that Agrippina's devotion to Nero increased with every day of his short life. The altruism of a cat seldom reaches beyond her kittens; but she is capable of heroic unselfishness where they are concerned. I knew of a London beast, a homeless, forlorn vagrant, who constituted herself an outdoor pensioner at the house of a friendly man of letters. This cat had a kitten, whose youthful vivacity won the hearts of a neighboring family. They adopted it willingly, but refused to harbor the mother, who still came for her daily dole to her only benefactor. Whenever a bit of fish or some other especial dainty was given her, this poor mendicant scaled the wall, and watched her chance to share it with her kitten, her little wealthy, greedy son, who gobbled it up as remorselessly as if he were not living on the fat of the land.

Agrippina would have been swift to follow such an example of devotion. At dinner time she always yielded the precedence to Nero, and it became one of our daily tasks to compel the little lad to respect his mother's privileges. He scorned his saucer of milk, and from tenderest infancy aspired to adult food, making predatory incursions upon Agrippina's plate, and obliging us finally to feed them in separate apartments. I have seen him, when a very young kitten, rear himself upon his baby legs, and with his soft and wicked little paw strike his mother in the face until she dropped the piece of meat she had been eating, when he tranquilly devoured it. It was to prevent the recurrence of such scandalous scenes that two dining rooms became a necessity in the family. Yet he was so loving and so lovable, poor little Claudius Nero! Why do I dwell on his faults, remembering, as I do, his winning sweetness and affability? Day after day, in the narrow city garden, the two cats played together, happy in each other's society, and never a yard apart. Night after night they retired at the same time, and slept upon the same cushion, curled up inextricably into one soft, furry ball. Many times I have knelt by their chair to bid them both good-night; and always, when I did so, Agrippina would lift her charming head, purr drowsily for a few seconds, and then nestle closer still to her first-born, with sighs of supreme satisfaction. The zenith of her life had been reached. Her cup of contentment was full.

It is a rude world, even for little cats, and evil chances lie in wait for the petted creatures we strive to shield from harm. Remembering the pangs of separation, the possibilities of unkindness or neglect, the troubles that hide in ambush on every unturned page, I am sometimes glad that the same cruel and selfish blow struck both mother and son, and that they lie together, safe from hurt or hazard, sleeping tranquilly and always, under the shadow of the friendly pines.

STUDYING THE ESSAY

1. Point out descriptive passages which prove that Miss Repplier loved cats and kittens.
2. Comment upon the distinction drawn between the kitten and the cat. Do you agree with the author on this point?
3. Why is it a " stupid blunder to look upon pets from the standpoint of utility "?
4. How was the author " amply rewarded " for giving up her closet to her pets?
5. Point out passages where the essay has gained by the use of literary and historical allusions.
6. Where did Miss Repplier get the names for her cats?
7. Criticize this essay as a " personal " essay. What characteristics of the author are apparent in her writing?
8. Have you read *The Yearling*, by Marjorie Rawlings? Try it.
9. Compare this essay with Hudson's " The Death of an Old Dog."

10. Words to learn: *aversion, feign, urbane, fastidious, anarchy, agile, debonair, altruism.*

COMPOSITION TOPICS

1. I Love Kittens until They Turn into Cats
2. How to Name a Pet
3. The Harmless, Necessary Cat
4. My Cat and My Dog — A Comparison
5. The Relative Intelligence of Animals

JOHN GALSWORTHY, 1867–1933

            John Galsworthy was born into a well-to-do English family. He attended Harrow, where he was a good captain of the football team but a poor student, and Oxford, where he received honors in law. But he was not very much interested in law and, because of a private income, did not have to work for a living. In 1894 he set out on a series of long trips around the world. On a trip to Australia he met Joseph Conrad, who was first officer of the ship on which Galsworthy was traveling. After they had become friends, Galsworthy encouraged Conrad to finish his first novel. The two men, exactly the same age, were lifelong friends as well as two of the finest novelists of their time. In 1905 Galsworthy married, and, with his wife's encouragement, he began to direct his thoughts toward literature.

       The books which won Galsworthy the Nobel Prize for literature in 1932 are his novels, *The Forsyte Saga* and *A Modern Comedy*, and his plays, *The Silver Box*, *Strife*, and *Justice*. He also wrote eight volumes of essays, including *A Commentary*, from which the following selection is taken.

       Galsworthy's point of view as a writer is rather unexpected. He was a patrician, but he was not smug. He was acutely aware of flaws in English society, and his plays and essays are the clearest indication of his state of mind. In this essay he notes with both scorn and sadness the way the average man spends his vacation. He is disturbed by the emptiness in such a vacation and in such a man.

       Further reading in Galsworthy is rewarding. *The Forsyte Saga* is one of the best fictional portraits of the upper-class Englishman; and *Strife*, his play about capital and labor, is as timely today as it was when it was written.

142

HOLIDAY

The curtain whose color changes from dawn to noon, from night to dawn — the curtain which never lifts, is fastened to the dark horizon.

On the black beach, beneath a black sky with its few stars, the sea wind blows a troubling savor from the west, as it did when man was not yet on the earth. It sings the same troubling song as when the first man heard it. And by this black beach man is collected in his hundreds, trying with all his might to take his holiday. Here he has built a theater within the theater of the night, and hung a canvas curtain to draw up and down, and round about lit lights to show him as many as may be of himself, and nothing of the encircling dark. Here he has brought singers, and put a band, armed with pipes of noise, to drown the troubling murmur of the wind. And behind his theater he has made a fire whose smoke has qualified the troubling savor of the sea.

Male and female, from all the houses where he sleeps, he has herded to this music as close as he can herd. The lights fall on his faces, attentive, white, and still — as wonderfully blank as bits of wood cut out in round, with pencil marks for eyes. And every time the noises cease, he claps his hands as though to say: " Begin again, you noises; do not leave me lonely to the silence and the sighing of the night."

Round the ring he circles, and each small group of him seems saying: " Talk — laugh — this is my holiday! "

This is his holiday, his rest from the incessant round of toil that fills his hours; to this he has looked forward all the

year; to this he will look back until it comes again. He walks
and talks and laughs around this pavilion by the beach; he
casts no glances at the pavilion of the night, where Nature is
playing her wind-music for the stars to dance. Long ago he
found he could not bear his mother Nature's inscrutable,
ironic face, bending above him in the dark, and with a moan
he drew the clothes over his head. In Her who gave him being he has perceived the only thing he cannot brave. And
since there is courage and pride in the feeblest of his hearts,
he has made a compact with himself: " Nature! There is no
Nature! For what I cannot understand I cannot face, and
what I cannot face I will not think of, and what I will not
think of does not exist for me; thus, there is nothing that I
cannot face. And — deny it as I may — this is why I herd in
my pavilion under my lights, and make these noises against
the sighing and the silence and the blackness of the night."

Back from the dark sea, across a grassy space, is his row
of houses with lighted windows; and behind it, stretching inland, a thousand more, huddled, closer and closer, round the
lighter railway shed, where, like spider's threads, the rails
run in from the expanse of sleeping fields and marshes and
dim hills; of dark trees and moonpale water fringed with
reeds. All over the land these rails have run, chaining his
houses into one great web so that he need never be alone.

For nothing is so dreadful to this man as solitude. In solitude he hears the voice of Her he cannot understand: " Ah!
the baby that you are, my baby man! " And he sees Her
smile, the ironic smile of evening over land and sea. In solitude he feels so small, so very small; for solitude is silence
and silence irony, and irony he cannot bear, not even that of
Her who gave him birth.

And so he is neither careful of his beauty nor of his
strength; not careful to be clean or to be fine; his only care

is not to be alone. To all his young, from the first day, he teaches the same lesson: Dread Her! Avoid Her! Look not on Her! Towns! more towns! There you can talk and listen to your fellows' talk! Crowd into the towns; the eyes in your whitened faces need never see Her there! Fill every cranny of your houses so that no moment of silence or of solitude can come to any one of you. And if, by unhappy chance, in their parks you find yourself alone, lie neither on your back, for then you will see the quiet sunlight on the leaves, the quiet clouds, and birds with solitude within their wings; nor on your face, or you will catch the savor of the earth, and a faint hum, and for a minute live the life of tiny things that straddle in the trodden grasses. Fly from such sights and scents and sounds, for fear lest terror for your fate should visit you; fly to the streets; fly to your neighbors' houses; talk, and be brave! Or if, and such times will come, your feet and brain and tongue are tired, then sleep! For, next to the drug of fellowship is the anodyne of slumber! And when it is your holiday, and time is all your own, be warned! The lot of those few left among you who are forced to live alone — on the sea, with the sleep of the green hills, guarding the trim wildness of your wood, turning the lonely soil, may for a moment seem desirable. Be sure it is not; the thought has come to you from books! Go to the spot where, though the nights are clear and the sun burns hot, the sea wind smells of salt, and the land wind smells of hay, you can avoid Her, huddled in your throngs! Dread Her! Fly from Her! Hide from Her smile, that seems to say: " Once, when you lived with me, you were a little gentleman. You looked in my eyes and learned a measure of repose, learned not to whimper at the dark, giggle, and jeer, and chatter through your nose, learned to hold yourself up, to think your own thoughts, and be content. And now you have gone from me to be a little cockney man. But for all your airs of courage and your fear of me — I shall get you back! " Dread Her! Avoid Her! Towns, more towns!

Such is the lesson man teaches, from the very birth, to every child of his unstinted breeding. And well he teaches it. Of all his thousands here tonight, drawn from his crowded, evil-smelling towns, not one has gone apart on this black beach to spend a single minute with his shadow and the wind and stars. His laughter fills the air, his ceaseless chatter, songs, and fiddling, the clapping of his hands; so will it be throughout his holiday.

And who so foolish as to say it is not good that man should talk and laugh and clap his hands; who so blind as not to see that these are antidotes to evils that his one great fear has brought to him? This ring of him with vacant faces and staring eyes round that anemic singer with the worn-out voice, or the stout singer with the voice of brass, is but an instance of Her irony: " This, then, is the medicine you have mixed, my little man, to cure the pain of your fevered souls. Well done! But if you had not left me you would have had no fever! There is none in the wind and the stars and the rhythm of the sea; there is none in green growth or fallen leaves; in my million courses it is not found. Fever is fear — to you alone, my restless manikin, has fever come, and this is why, even in your holiday, you stand in your sick crowds gulping down your little homeopathic draughts! "

The show is over. The pipes of noise are still, the lights fall dark, the man is left by the black beach with nothing to look on but the sky, or hear but the beat of wave-wings flighting on the sea. And suddenly in threes and fours he scurries home, lest for one second he should see Her face whose smile he cannot bear.

STUDYING THE ESSAY

1. Compare the point of view here with that expressed by Bacon in the first part of " Of Friendship."
2. Contrast Galsworthy's ideas with those of Thoreau.
3. What do you think of the logic in the fifth paragraph?
4. Why is solitude dreadful to some people?
5. According to Galsworthy, what does the typical person miss on a holiday?
6. Explain " the ironic smile " on page 144.
7. According to ideas expressed in the essay, criticize resorts you have seen. Do you think that Galsworthy is right or wrong in his opinions?

COMPOSITION TOPICS

1. A Holiday Alone
2. Describe the people you have seen at a summer resort. How do they make use of their time?
3. " I want to get away from it all," a tired person says. Prescribe a good holiday for him.

WILLIAM ALLEN WHITE, 1868–1944

        With the exception of nine years of the seventy-six years of his life, William Allen White lived and worked in Emporia, Kansas, a town with a present population of about 16,000. Even those nine years were spent in Kansas: four at Kansas State College, two as business manager of a paper in El Dorado, and three as editorial writer for the Kansas City *Star*. For fifty busy and, according to White, happy years he published the Emporia *Gazette*, a small-town newspaper. He had two children, a daughter who died at the age of seventeen and a son who took over the *Gazette* when his father died. Why should such a man be famous? Probably the main reason is that White, to a great many people, symbolizes America in much the same way that Mark Twain does. He was the independent, common-sense philosopher whose articles about all sorts of topics were straightforward, wise, humane, and simple. His life, far from being hampered by a small-town background, was really national. He was not a Kansan, but an American, and a greatly beloved American.

White's books include *The Court of Boyville* (1899), in which he catches perfectly the spirit of the small town; *A Certain Rich Man* (1909); and a number of biographies, the best of which is *Puritan in Babylon* (1938), a brilliant study of another small-town man, Calvin Coolidge. His best book, however, is probably his *Autobiography*, published two years after his death. It is the story of his life up to 1923, with a sketch of his last twenty years added by his son, William Lindsay White, who is also a writer of note. The autobiography is one of the most sincere, heart-warming, enjoyable books ever written.

Little need be said about "Mary White" except that it is

his most famous editorial, written on the day of his daughter's funeral. To understand how exceptional the essay is, put yourself in White's place and try to imagine how you would write the same thing. Perhaps an appropriate comment on both Mary White and her father is this excerpt from a review of the *Autobiography*, by R. L. Duffus in the New York *Times:* " William Allen White did not die. He was too young to die, too full of life. In 1946 his newspaper goes on, his town goes on, and there is a little of him in all the people who were his neighbors. . . . And now he lives in his final book, which will be read just as long as anyone is interested in what happened in Kansas and in the United States between the year 1868 and the year 1923."

MARY WHITE

The Associated Press reports carrying the news of Mary White's death declared that it came as the result of a fall from a horse. How she would have hooted at that! She never fell from a horse in her life. Horses have fallen on her and with her — " I'm always trying to hold 'em in my lap," she used to say. But she was proud of few things, and one was that she could ride anything that had four legs and hair. Her death resulted not from a fall, but from a blow on the head which fractured her skull, and the blow came from the limb of an overhanging tree on the parking.

The last hour of her life was typical of its happiness. She came home from a day's work at school, topped off by a hard grind with the copy on the High School Annual, and felt that a ride would refresh her. She climbed into her khakis, chattering to her mother about the work she was doing, and hurried to get her horse and be out on the dirt roads for the country air and the radiant green fields of the spring. As she rode through the town on an easy gallop she kept waving at passers-by. She knew every one in town For a decade the little figure with the long pigtail and the red hair ribbon has been familiar on the streets of Emporia, and she got in the way of speaking to those who nodded at her. She passed the Kerrs, walking the horse, in front of the Normal Library, and waved at them; passed another friend a few hundred feet farther on, and waved at her. The horse was walking and as she turned into North Merchant Street she took off her cowboy hat, and the horse swung into a lope. She passed the Tripletts and waved her cowboy hat at them, still moving gaily north on Merchant Street. A *Gazette* carrier passed — a high school boy friend — and she waved at him, but with her bridle hand; the horse veered quickly, plunged into the parking where the low-hanging limb faced her, and, while she still looked back waving, the blow came. But she did not fall from the horse; she slipped off, dazed a bit, staggered, and fell in a faint. She never quite recovered consciousness.

But she did not fall from the horse, neither was she riding fast. A year or so ago she used to go like the wind. But that habit was broken, and she used the horse to get into the open to get fresh, hard exercise, and to work off a certain surplus energy that welled up in her and needed a physical outlet. That need has been in her heart for years. It was back of the impulse that kept the dauntless, little brown-clad figure on the streets and country roads of this community and built into a strong, muscular body what had been a frail and sickly frame during the first years of her life. But the riding gave her more than a body. It released a gay and hardy soul. She was the happiest thing in the world. And she was happy because she was enlarging her horizon.

She came to know all sorts and conditions of men. Charley O'Brien, the traffic cop, was one of her best friends. W. L. Holtz, the Latin teacher, was another. Tom O'Connor, farmer-politician, and Rev. J. H. J. Rice, preacher and police judge, and Frank Beach, music master, were her special friends, and all the girls, black and white, above the track and below the track, in Pepville and Stringtown, were among her acquaintances. And she brought home riotous stories of her adventures. She loved to rollick; persiflage was her natural expression at home. Her humor was a continual bubble of joy. She seemed to think in hyperbole and metaphor. She was mischievous without malice, as full of faults as an old shoe. No angel was Mary White, but an easy girl to live with, for she never nursed a grouch five minutes in her life.

With all her eagerness for the out-of-doors, she loved books. On her table when she left her room were a book by Conrad, one by Galsworthy, *Creative Chemistry* by E. E. Slosson, and a Kipling book. She read Mark Twain, Dickens, and Kipling before she was ten — all of their writings. Wells and Arnold Bennett particularly amused and diverted her. She was entered as a student in Wellesley in 1922; was assistant editor of the High School Annual this year, and in line for election to the editorship of the Annual next year. She was a member of the executive committee of the High School Y. W. C. A.

Within the last two years she had begun to be moved by an ambition to draw. She began as most children do by scribbling in her school books, funny pictures. She bought cartoon magazines and took a course — rather casually, naturally, for she was, after all, a child, with no strong purposes — and this year she tasted the first fruits of success by having her pictures accepted by the High School Annual. But the thrill of delight she got when Mr. Ecord, of the

Normal Annual, asked her to do the cartooning for that book this spring was too beautiful for words. She fell to her work with all her enthusiastic heart. Her drawings were accepted, and her pride — always repressed by a lively sense of the ridiculousness of the figure she was cutting — was a really gorgeous thing to see. No successful artist ever drank a deeper draft of satisfaction than she took from the little fame her work was getting among her schoolfellows. In her glory, she almost forgot her horse — but never her car.

For she used the car as a jitney bus. It was her social life. She never had a " party " in all her nearly seventeen years — wouldn't have one; but she never drove a block in the car in her life that she didn't begin to fill the car with pick-ups! Everybody rode with Mary White — white and black, old and young, rich and poor, men and women. She liked nothing better than to fill the car full of long-legged high school boys and an occasional girl, and parade the town. She never had a " date," nor went to a dance, except once with her brother, Bill, and the " boy proposition " didn't interest her — yet. But young people — great, spring-breaking, varnish-cracking, fender-bending, door-sagging carloads of " kids " — gave her great pleasure. Her zests were keen. But the most fun she ever had in her life was acting as chairman of the committee that got up the big turkey dinner for the poor folks at the county home; scores of pies, gallons of slaw, jam, cakes, preserves, oranges, and a wilderness of turkey were loaded in the car and taken to the county home. And, being of a practical turn of mind, she risked her own Christmas dinner by staying to see that the poor folks actually got it all. Not that she was a cynic; she just disliked to tempt folks. While there she found a blind colored uncle, very old, who could do nothing but make rag rugs, and she rustled up from her school friends rags enough to keep him busy for a season. The last engagement she tried to make was to take the guests at the county home out for a car ride. And the last endeavor of her life was to try to get a rest room for colored girls in the high school. She found one girl reading in the toilet, because there was no better place for a colored girl to loaf, and it inflamed her sense of injustice and she became a nagging harpy to those who she thought could remedy the evil.

The poor she had always with her, and was glad of it. She hungered and thirsted for righteousness; and was the most impious creature in the world. She joined the Congregational Church without consulting her parents; not particularly for her soul's good. She never had a thrill of piety in her life, and would have hooted at a " testimony." But even as a little child she felt the church was an agency for helping people to more of life's abundance, and she wanted to help. She never wanted help for herself. Clothes meant little to her. It was a fight to get a new rig on her; but eventually a harder fight to get it off. She never wore a jewel and had no ring but her high school class ring, and never asked for anything but a wrist watch. She refused to have her hair up, though she was nearly seventeen. " Mother," she protested, " you don't know how much I get by with, in my braided pigtails, that I could not with my hair up." Above every other passion of her life was her passion not to grow up, to be a child. The tomboy in her, which was big, seemed to loathe to be put away forever in skirts. She was a Peter Pan, who refused to grow up.

Her funeral yesterday at the Congregational Church was as she would have wished it; no singing, no flowers save the big bunch of red roses from her Brother Bill's Harvard classmen — Heavens, how proud that would have made her! and the red roses from the *Gazette* force — in vases at her head and feet. A short prayer, Paul's beautiful essay on " Love," from the thirteenth chapter of First Corinthians, some remarks about her democratic spirit by her friend, John H. J. Rice, pastor and police judge, which she would have deprecated if she could, a prayer sent down for her by her friend, Carl Nau, and opening the service the slow, poignant movement from Beethoven's Moonlight Sonata, which she loved, and closing the service a cutting from the joyously melancholy first movement of Tschaikowsky's *Symphonie Pathétique*, which she liked to hear in certain moods on the phonograph; then the Lord's Prayer by her friends in the high school.

That was all.

For her pallbearers only her friends were chosen: her Latin teacher, W. L. Holtz; her high school principal, Rice Brown; her doctor, Frank Foncannon; her friend, W. W. Finney; her pal at the *Gazette* office, Walter Hughes; and her brother Bill. It would have made her smile to know that her friend, Charley O'Brien, the traffic cop, had been transferred from Sixth and Commercial to the corner near the church to direct her friends who came to bid her good-by.

A rift in the clouds in a gray day threw a shaft of sunlight upon her coffin as her nervous, energetic little body sank to its last sleep. But the soul of her, the glowing, gorgeous, fervent soul of her, surely was flaming in eager joy upon some other dawn.

STUDYING THE ESSAY

1. In what ways is Mary White representative of the best type of high school girl?
2. Point out instances which reveal her democratic spirit.
3. How would you rate Mary White on service, leadership, and character if she were a candidate for a commencement prize?
4. Discuss her tastes in reading. How do her tastes and yours agree?

5. What in the essay indicates that William Allen White understood young people?
6. In what ways is this essay a remarkable literary feat?
7. Compare this essay with others in the book which also deal with death — Hudson's "The Death of an Old Dog" and Stevenson's "Aes Triplex."

COMPOSITION TOPICS

1. Pretend someone you know well has just died. Write an essay about this person.
2. Imagine that a friend of yours has died unexpectedly. Write a letter of sympathy to his parents.

STEPHEN LEACOCK, 1869–1944

        Stephen Butler Leacock is another essayist who
had more than one career. He was a success in business, as a
teacher of economics, and in the world of letters. He is best
known as a brilliant essayist and humorist.

Leacock was born in England, but his family moved to Canada when he was eight years old. He was educated at Upper
Canada College, the University of Toronto, and the University
of Chicago, where he received his Ph.D. in 1903. After that he
spent forty years as a professor of economics and political science at McGill University in Montreal and wrote the books
one would expect him to write: *Elements of Political Science,
The Unsolved Riddle of Social Justice,* and others.

But he once said that he would rather have written *Alice in
Wonderland* than the entire *Encyclopædia Britannica.* In a statement like that can be seen a reflection of the kind of whimsical
humor which has delighted the readers of his other books —
the volumes of essays which have made him one of the most
widely read humorists of this century.

Literary Lapses (1910), from which the following essay is
reprinted, is typical of his thirty-odd books in the light vein.
These essays were first given to the publisher of his textbook
on economics, and the publisher thought that Leacock had gone
crazy. But another publisher thought differently, so his career
as a humorist got off to a successful start.

Leacock disliked mere wit, or cleverness, because he felt that
wit was usually sarcastic and would always hurt someone. His
idea of humor was that it should smile openly rather than
sneer. Thus his touch is always light, friendly, and pleasant,
even though he feels very deeply about a subject. There is a

great deal of learning behind many of his essays, but all of them are easy reading — the kind of writing which a reader can enjoy without labor.

As you read the essay about A, B, and C, you may find yourself growling about your algebra course, or you may find yourself laughing about those work problems which didn't mean very much to anybody, anyway. Leacock would have enjoyed your laughter.

A, B, AND C — THE HUMAN ELEMENT IN MATHEMATICS

The student of arithmetic who has mastered the first four rules of his art and successfully striven with money sums and fractions finds himself confronted by an unbroken expanse of questions known as problems. These are short stories of adventure and industry with the end omitted, and though betraying a strong family resemblance, are not without a certain element of romance.

The characters in the plot of a problem are three people called A, B, and C; the form of the question is generally of this sort:

"A, B, and C do a certain piece of work. A can do as much work in one hour as B in two, or C in four. Find how long they work at it."

Or thus: "A, B, and C are employed to dig a ditch. A can dig as much in one hour as B can dig in two, and B can dig twice as fast as C. Find how long, etc., etc."

Or after this wise: "A lays a wager that he can walk

faster than B or C. A can walk half as fast again as B, and C is only an indifferent walker. Find how far, and so forth."

The occupations of A, B, and C are many and varied. In the older arithmetics they contented themselves with doing a " certain piece of work." This statement of the case, however, was found too sly and mysterious, or possibly lacking in romantic charm. It became the fashion to define the job more clearly and to set them at walking matches, ditch-digging, regattas, and piling cordwood. At times, they became commercial and entered into partnership, having, with their old mystery, a " certain " capital. Above all they revel in motion. When they tire of walking matches, A rides on horseback, or borrows a bicycle and competes with his weaker-minded associates on foot. Now they race on loco-motives; now they row; or again they become historical and engage stagecoaches; or at times they are aquatic and swim. If their occupation is actual work, they prefer to pump water into cisterns, two of which leak through holes in the bottom and one of which is watertight. A, of course, has the good one; he also takes the bicycle, and the best locomotive, and the right of swimming with the current. Whatever they do they put money on it, being all three sports. A always wins.

In the early chapters of the arithmetic, their identity is concealed under the names of John, William, and Henry, and they wrangle over the division of marbles. In algebra they are often called X, Y, Z. But these are only their Christian names, and they are really the same people.

Now to one who has followed the history of these men through countless pages of problems, watched them in their leisure hours dallying with cordwood, and seen their panting sides heave in the full frenzy of filling a cistern with a leak in it, they become something more than mere symbols. They appear as creatures of flesh and blood, living men with their own passions, ambitions, and aspirations like the rest of us.

A is full-blooded, hot-headed, and strong-willed. It is he who proposes everything, challenges B to work, makes the bets, and bends the others to his will. He is a man of great physical strength and phenomenal endurance. He has been known to walk forty-eight hours at a stretch, and to pump ninety-six. His life is arduous and full of peril. A mistake in the working of a sum may keep him digging a fortnight without sleep. A repeating decimal in the answer might kill him.

B is a quiet, easy-going fellow, afraid of A and bullied by him, but very gentle and brotherly to little C, the weakling. He is quite in A's power, having lost all his money in bets.

Poor C is an undersized, frail man, with a plaintive face. Constant walking, digging, and pumping have broken his health and ruined his nervous system. His joyless life has driven him to drink and smoke more than is good for him, and his hand often shakes as he digs ditches. He has not the strength to work as the others do; in fact, as Hamlin Smith has said, " A can do more work in one hour than C in four."

The first time that ever I saw these men was one evening after a regatta. They had all been rowing in it, and it had transpired that A could row as much in one hour as B in two, or C in four. B and C had come in dead fagged and C was coughing badly. " Never mind, old fellow," I heard B say, " I'll fix you up on the sofa and get you some hot tea." Just then A came blustering in and shouted, " I say, you fellows, Hamlin Smith has shown me three cisterns in his garden and he says we can pump them until tomorrow night. I bet I can beat you both. Come on. You can pump in your rowing things, you know. Your cistern leaks a little, I think, C." I heard B growl that it was a dirty shame and that C was used up now, but they went, and presently I could tell from the sound of the water that A was pumping four times as fast as C.

For years after that I used to see them constantly about the town and always busy. I never heard of any of them eating or sleeping. After that, owing to a long absence from home, I lost sight of them. On my return I was surprised to find A, B, and C no longer at their old tasks; on inquiry I heard that work in this line was now done by N, M, and O, and that some people were employing for algebraical jobs four foreigners called Alpha, Beta, Gamma, and Delta.

Now it chanced one day that I stumbled upon old D, in the little garden in front of his cottage, hoeing in the sun. D is an aged laboring man who used occasionally to be called in to help A, B, and C. " Did I know 'em, sir? " he answered. " Why I knowed 'em ever since they was little fellows in brackets. Master A, he were a fine-hearted lad, sir, though I always said, give me Master B for kind-heartedness-like. Many's the job as we've been on together, sir, though I never did no racing nor aught of that, but just the plain labor, as you might say. I'm getting a bit too old and stiff for it nowadays, sir — just scratch about in the garden here and grow a bit of a logarithm, or raise a common denominator or two. But Mr. Euclid he uses me still for propositions, he do."

From the garrulous old man I learned the melancholy end of my former acquaintances. Soon after I left town, he told me, C had been ill. It seems that A and B had been rowing on the river for a wager, and C had been running on the bank and then sat in a draught. Of course the bank had refused the draught and C was taken ill. A and B came home and found C lying helpless in bed. A shook him roughly and said, " Get up, C, we're going to pile wood." C looked so worn and pitiful that B said, " Look here, A, I won't stand this, he isn't fit to pile wood tonight." C smiled feebly and said, "Perhaps I might pile a little if I sat up in bed." Then B, thoroughly alarmed, said, "See here, A, I'm going to fetch a doctor; he's dying." A flared up and answered, "You've got no money to fetch a doctor." "I'll reduce him to his lowest terms," B said firmly, "that'll fetch him." C's life might even then have been saved but they made a mistake about the medicine. It stood at the head of the bed on a bracket, and the nurse accidentally removed it from the bracket without changing the sign. After the fatal blunder C seems to have sunk rapidly. On the evening of the next day, it was clear, as the shadows deepened, that the end was near. I think that even A was affected at the last as he stood with bowed head, aimlessly offering to bet with the doctor on C's labored breathing. "A," whispered C, "I think I'm going fast." "How fast do you think you'll go, old man?" murmured A. "I don't know," said C, "but I'm going at any rate." The end came soon after that. C rallied for a moment and asked for a certain piece of work that he had left downstairs. A put it in his arms and he expired. As his soul sped heavenward, A watched its flight with melancholy admiration. B burst into a passionate flood of tears and sobbed, "Put away his little cistern and the rowing clothes he used to wear, I feel as if I could hardly ever dig again." — The funeral was plain and unostentatious. It differed in nothing from the ordinary, except that out of deference to sporting men, and mathematicians, A engaged two hearses. Both vehicles started at the same time, B driving the one which bore the sable parallelopiped containing the last remains of his ill-fated friend. A on the box of the empty hearse generously consented to a handicap of a hundred years, but arrived first at the cemetery by driving four times as fast as B. (Find the distance to the cemetery.) As the sarcophagus was lowered, the grave was surrounded by the broken figures of the first book of Euclid.

It was noticed that after the death of C, A became a changed man. He lost interest in racing with B, and dug but languidly. He finally gave up his work and settled down to live on the interest of his bets. — B never recovered from the shock of C's death; his grief preyed upon his intellect and it became deranged. He grew moody and spoke only in monosyllables. His disease became rapidly aggravated, and he presently spoke in words whose spelling was regular and which presented no difficulty to the beginner. Realizing his precarious condition, he voluntarily submitted to be incarcerated in an asylum, where he abjured mathematics and devoted himself to writing the History of the Swiss Family Robinson in words of one syllable.

STUDYING THE ESSAY

1. Can you find in your mathematics book some " short stories of adventure and industry with the end omitted "?
2. Do A, B, and C still engage in their hard jobs? Or have your texts called them by other names?
3. Characterize A, B, and C as people.
4. Do you know anyone like A, B, or C?
5. From this essay can you deduce anything about the personality of Stephen Leacock?
6. Does this essay have a point? If so, what is it?
7. Words to learn: *frenzy, arduous, garrulous.*

COMPOSITION TOPICS

1. Rewrite a paragraph in one of your textbooks, other than English, in one-syllable words.
2. The Atomic Theory as I See It
3. Physics Problems: Exercises in a Vacuum
4. I explain history to my seven-year-old nephew.

DAVID GRAYSON
(RAY STANNARD BAKER)   1870–1946

        Ray Stannard Baker was born in Lansing, Michigan, and was graduated from Michigan State College in 1889 at the age of nineteen. He had a varied career as newspaper reporter, as a contributor to various magazines, and as an associate editor of *McClure's* magazine (1898–1904) and of the *American* magazine (1906–1915). In 1910 he met Woodrow Wilson, then governor of New Jersey, and was later given the job of editing the Wilson papers. *Woodrow Wilson: Life and Letters* appeared, in eight volumes, between 1927 and 1939 and won the Pulitzer Prize for Baker in 1940.

      "David Grayson" was born in about 1906, when Baker went to the *American* magazine. *Adventures in Contentment*, from which this essay is taken, appeared in 1907, and not even the illustrator knew who the writer was. Grayson wrote four more books of essays before he decided to tell the public that he and Ray Stannard Baker were the same man. He revealed his identity because so many people had been claiming to be Grayson and had even been giving lectures as Grayson.

      The Grayson essays, collected in *The Adventures of David Grayson*, are another example of the essays which a busy man writes for fun. They bear the same relation to the Wilson biography that *Literary Lapses* bears to Leacock's *Elements of Political Economy*. The *Adventures* are drawn from personal recollections of Grayson's walking trips in Michigan. The gentle satirical humor of these essays reminds the reader of Stevenson and Lamb. The essay printed here has a profound thought beneath its quiet humor. Who does own a book, anyway? The author's point of view is important for a student to understand.

I ENTERTAIN AN AGENT UNAWARES

With the coming of winter I thought the life of a farmer might lose something of its charm. So much interest lies in the growth not only of crops but of trees, vines, flowers, sentiments, and emotions. In the summer the world is busy, concerned with many things and full of gossip: in the winter I anticipated a cessation of many active interests and enthusiasms. I looked forward to having time for my books and for the quiet contemplation of the life around me. Summer indeed is for activity, winter for reflection. But when winter really came, every day discovered some new work to do or some new adventure to enjoy. It is surprising how many things happen on a small farm. Examining the book which accounts for that winter, I find the history of part of a forenoon, which will illustrate one of the curious adventures of a farmer's life. It is dated January 5.

I went out this morning with my ax and hammer to mend the fence along the public road. A heavy frost fell last night and the brown grass and the dry ruts of the roads were powdered white. Even the air, which was perfectly still, seemed full of frost crystals, so that when the sun came up one seemed to walk in a magic world. I drew in a long breath and looked out across the wonderful shining country and I said to myself:

" Surely, there is nowhere I would rather be than here " For I could have traveled nowhere to find greater beauty or a better enjoyment of it than I had here at home.

As I worked with my ax and hammer, I heard a light wagon come rattling up the road. Across the valley a man had begun to chop a tree. I could see the ax steel flash brilliantly in the sunshine before I heard the sound of the blow.

The man in the wagon had a round face and a sharp blue eye. I thought he seemed a businesslike young man.

" Say, there," he shouted, drawing up at my gate, " would you mind holding my horse a minute? It's a cold morning and he's restless."

" Certainly not," I said, and I put down my tools and held his horse.

He walked up to my door with a brisk step and a certain jaunty poise of the head.

" He is well contented with himself," I said. " It is a great blessing for any man to be satisfied with what he has got."

I heard Harriet open the door — how every sound rang through the still morning air!

The young man asked some question and I distinctly heard Harriet's answer:

" He's down there."

The young man came back: his hat was tipped up, his quick eye darted over my grounds as though in a single instant he had appraised everything and passed judgment upon the cash value of the inhabitants. He whistled a lively little tune.

" Say," he said, when he reached the gate, not at all disconcerted, " I thought you was the hired man. Your name's Grayson, ain't it? Well, I want to talk with you."

After tying and blanketing his horse and taking a black satchel from his buggy, he led me up to my house. I had a pleasurable sense of excitement and adventure. Here was a new character come to my farm. Who knows, I thought, what he may bring with him: who knows what I may send away by him? Here in the country we must set our little ships afloat on small streams, hoping that somehow, some day, they will reach the sea.

It was interesting to see the busy young man sit down so confidently in our best chair. He said his name was Dixon, and he took out from his satchel a book with a fine showy cover. He said it was called *Living Selections from Poet, Sage and Humourist.*

"This," he told me, "is only the first of the series. We publish six volumes full of literchoor. You see what a heavy book this is?"

I tested it in my hand: it was a heavy book.

"The entire set," he said, "weighs over ten pounds. There are 1,162 pages, enough paper if laid down flat, end to end, to reach half a mile."

I cannot quote his exact language: there was too much of it, but he made an impressive showing of the amount of literature that could be had at a very low price per pound. Mr. Dixon was a hypnotist. He fixed me with his glittering eye, and he talked so fast, and his ideas upon the subject were so original that he held me spellbound. At first I was inclined to be provoked: one does not like to be forcibly hypnotized, but gradually the situation began to amuse me, the more so when Harriet came in.

"Did you ever see a more beautiful binding?" asked the agent, holding his book admiringly at arm's length. "This up here," he said, pointing to the illuminated cover, "is the Muse of Poetry. She is scattering flowers — poems, you know. Fine idea, ain't it? Coloring fine, too."

He jumped up quickly and laid the book on my table, to the evident distress of Harriet.

"Trims up the room, don't it?" he exclaimed, turning his head a little to one side and observing the effect with an expression of affectionate admiration.

"How much," I asked, "will you sell the covers for without the insides?"

"Without the insides?"

" Yes," I said, " the binding will trim up my table just as well without the insides."

I thought he looked at me a little suspiciously, but he was evidently satisfied by my expression of countenance, for he answered promptly:

" Oh, but you want the insides. That's what the books are for. The bindings are never sold alone."

He then went on to tell me the prices and terms of payment, until it really seemed that it would be cheaper to buy the books than to let him carry them away again. Harriet stood in the doorway behind him frowning and evidently trying to catch my eye. But I kept my face turned aside so that I could not see her signal of distress and my eyes fixed on the young man Dixon. It was as good as a play. Harriet there, serious-minded, thinking I was being befooled, and the agent thinking he was befooling me, and I, thinking I was befooling both of them — and all of us wrong. It was very like life wherever you find it.

Finally, I took the book which he had been urging upon me, at which Harriet coughed meaningly to attract my attention. She knew the danger when I really got my hands on a book. But I made up as innocent as a child. I opened the book almost at random — and it was as though, walking down a strange road, I had come upon an old tried friend not seen before in years. For there on the page before me I read:

> The world is too much with us; late and soon,
> Getting and spending, we lay waste our powers:
> Little we see in Nature that is ours;
> We have given our hearts away, a sordid boon!
> The sea that bares her bosom to the moon;
> The wind that will be howling at all hours,
> But are up-gathered now like sleeping flowers;
> For this, for everything, we are out of tune;

And as I read, it came back to me -- a scene like a picture
-- the place, the time, the very feel of the hour when I first
saw those lines. Who shall say that the past does not live!
An odor will sometimes set the blood coursing in an old emotion, and a line of poetry is the resurrection and the life.
For a moment I forgot Harriet and the agent, I forgot myself, I even forgot the book on my knee — everything but
that hour in the past — a view of shimmering hot housetops,
the heat and dust and noise of an August evening in the
city, the dumb weariness of it all, the loneliness, the longing
for green fields; and then these great lines of Wordsworth,
read for the first time, flooding in upon me:

> Great God! I'd rather be
> A pagan suckled in a creed outworn:
> So might I, standing on this pleasant lea,
> Have glimpses that would make me less forlorn;
> Have sight of Proteus rising from the sea;
> Or hear old Triton blow his wreathèd horn.

When I had finished I found myself standing in my own
room with one arm raised, and, I suspect, a trace of tears in
my eyes — there before the agent and Harriet. I saw Harriet
lift one hand and drop it hopelessly. She thought I was captured at last. I was past saving. And as I looked at the agent
I saw " grim conquest glowing in his eye! " So I sat down not
a little embarrassed by my exhibition -- when I had intended
to be self-poised.

" You like it, don't you? " said Mr. Dixon unctuously.

" I don't see," I said earnestly, " how you can afford to
sell such things as this so cheap."

" They *are* cheap," he admitted regretfully. I suppose he
wished he had tried me with the half-morocco.

" They are priceless," I said, " absolutely priceless. If you were the only man in the world who had that poem, I think I would deed you my farm for it."

Mr. Dixon proceeded, as though it were all settled, to get out his black order book and open it briskly for business. He drew his fountain pen, capped it, and looked up at me expectantly. My feet actually seemed slipping into some irresistible whirlpool. How well he understood practical psychology! I struggled within myself, fearing engulfment: I was all but lost.

" Shall I deliver the set at once," he said, " or can you wait until the first of February? "

At that critical moment a floating spar of an idea swept my way and I seized upon it as the last hope of the lost.

" I don't understand," I said, as though I had not heard his last question, " how you dare go about with all this treasure upon you. Are you not afraid of being stopped in the road and robbed? Why, I've seen the time when, if I had known you carried such things as these, such cures for sick hearts, I think I should have stopped you myself! "

" Say, you *are* an odd one," said Mr. Dixon.

" Why do you sell such priceless things as these? " I asked, looking at him sharply.

" Why do I sell them? " and he looked still more perplexed. " To make money, of course; same reason you raise corn."

" But here is wealth," I said, pursuing my advantage. " If you have these you have something more valuable than money."

Mr. Dixon politely said nothing. Like a wise angler, having failed to land me at the first rush, he let me have line. Then I thought of Ruskin's words, " Nor can any noble thing be wealth except to a noble person." And that prompted me to say to Mr. Dixon:

"These things are not yours; they are mine. You never owned them; but I will sell them to you."

He looked at me in amazement, and then glanced around — evidently to discover if there were a convenient way of escape.

"You're all straight, are you?" he asked, tapping his forehead; "didn't anybody ever try to take you up?"

"The covers are yours," I continued as though I had not heard him; "the insides are mine and have been for a long time: that is why I proposed buying the covers separately."

I opened his book again. I thought I would see what had been chosen for its pages. And I found there many fine and great things.

"Let me read you this," I said to Mr. Dixon; "it has been mine for a long time. I will not sell it to you. I will give it to you outright. The best things are always given."

Having some gift in imitating the Scotch dialect, I read:

> November chill blaws loud wi' angry sugh;
>   The short'ning winter day is near a close;
> The miry beasts retreating frae the pleugh;
>   The black'ning trains o' craws to their repose:
> The toil-worn Cotter frae his labour goes,
>   This night his weakly moil is at an end,
> Collects his spades, his mattocks and his hoes,
>   Hoping the morn in ease and rest to spend,
> And weary, o'er the moor, his course does
>   Hameward bend.

So I read "The Cotter's Saturday Night." I love the poem very much myself, sometimes reading it aloud, not so much for the tenderness of its message, though I prize that, too, as for the wonder of its music.

> Compar'd with these, Italian trills are tame;
>   The tickl'd ear no heart-felt raptures raise.

I suppose I showed my feeling in my voice. As I glanced up from time to time I saw the agent's face change, and his look deepen, and the lips, usually so energetically tense, loosen with emotion. Surely no poem in all the language conveys so perfectly the simple love of the home, the quiet joys, hopes, pathos of those who live close to the soil.

When I had finished — I stopped with the stanza beginning:

> Then homeward all take off their sev'ral way;

the agent turned away his head trying to brave out his emotion. Most of us, Anglo-Saxons, tremble before a tear when we might fearlessly beard a tiger.

I moved up nearer to the agent and put my hand on his knee; then I read two or three of the other things I found in his wonderful book. And once I had him laughing and once again I had the tears in his eyes. Oh, a simple young man, a little crusty without, but soft inside — like the rest of us.

Well, it was amazing, once we began talking not of books but of life, how really eloquent and human he became. From being a distant and uncomfortable person, he became at once like a near neighbor and friend. It was strange to me — as I have thought since — how he conveyed to us in few words the essential emotional note of his life. It was no violin tone, beautifully complex with harmonics, but the clear simple voice of the flute. It spoke of his wife and his baby girl and his home. The very incongruity of detail — he told us how he grew onions in his back yard — added somehow to the homely glamour of the vision which he gave us. The number of his house, the fact that he had a new cottage organ, and that the baby ran away and lost herself in Seventeenth Street — were all, curiously, fabrics of his emotion.

It was beautiful to see commonplace facts grow phosphorescent in the heat of true feeling. How little we may come to know Romance by the cloak she wears and how humble must be he who would surprise the heart of her!

It was, indeed, with an indescribable thrill that I heard him add the details, one by one — the mortgage on his place, now rapidly being paid off, the brother who was a plumber, the mother-in-law who was not a mother-in-law of the comic papers. And finally he showed us the picture of the wife and baby that he had in the cover of his watch; a fat baby with its head resting on its mother's shoulder.

"Mister," he said, "p'r'aps you think it's fun to ride around the country like I do, and be away from home most of the time. But it ain't. When I think of Minnie and the kid —"

He broke off sharply, as if he had suddenly remembered the shame of such confidences.

"Say," he asked, "what page is that poem on?"

I told him.

"One forty-six," he said. "When I get home I'm going to read that to Minnie. She likes poetry and all such things. And where's that other piece that tells how a man feels when he's lonesome? Say, that fellow knew!"

We had a genuinely good time, the agent and I, and when he finally rose to go, I said:

"Well, I've sold you a new book."

"I see now, mister, what you mean."

I went down the path with him and began to unhitch his horse.

"Let me, let me," he said eagerly.

Then he shook hands, paused a moment awkwardly as if about to say something, then sprang into his buggy without saying it.

When he had taken up his reins he remarked:

"Say! but you'd make an agent! You'd hynotize 'em."

I recognized it as the greatest compliment he could pay me: the craft compliment.

Then he drove off, but pulled up before he had gone five yards. He turned in his seat, one hand on the back of it, his whip raised.

"Say!" he shouted, and when I walked up he looked at me with fine embarrassment.

"Mister, perhaps you'd accept one of these sets from Dixon free gratis, for nothing."

"I understand," I said, "but you know I'm giving the books to you — and I couldn't take them back again."

"Well," he said, "you're a good one, anyhow. Good-by again," and then, suddenly, business naturally coming uppermost, he remarked with great enthusiasm:

"You've given me a new idea. *Say*, I'll sell 'em."

"Carry them carefully, man," I called after him; "they are precious."

So I went back to my work, thinking how many fine people there are in this world — if you scratch 'em deep enough.

STUDYING THE ESSAY

1. How does David Grayson make the life of a farmer seem attractive?
2. What do you like or dislike in the agent when he is first introduced? Is his attitude toward "literchoor" overdrawn?
3. Have you ever been faced with a magazine or book salesman? What did he have to say?
4. In what sense were the books "owned" by David Grayson?
5. Name some of the books you "own" in that sense of the word. Name some you have been made to read and do not "own."
6. What fine qualities did David Grayson discover in the agent when he had "scratched deep enough"?
7. What sort of person is David Grayson?

COMPOSITION TOPICS

1. The Life of a Salesman Is Not a Happy One
2. Great Books I Have Read
3. Write a speech advertising a product you believe in. You must convince everybody that your product is worth buying.
4. All I Want Is a Shelf Full of Beautiful Bindings

GILBERT KEITH CHESTERTON, 1874–1936

Gilbert Keith Chesterton was the heavyweight among famous English authors. His girth made his friend, Bernard Shaw, who had just produced *Fanny's First Play*, describe Chesterton's own maiden dramatic effort, *Magic*, as " Fatty's First Play." Chesterton was a great talker; he was always ready with a witty answer and an arresting and entertaining phrase. He delighted in making ideas turn somersaults, and it was this which made people eager to read him.

Chesterton was born in London. At St. Paul's School he won no distinction at all because he was lazy. He did have a strong interest in drawing, however, and finally left the school to study art at University College, London. He soon turned to literature, but his art training is reflected in many excellent cartoons, which decorate some of his books. When he was given a job as a reviewer for the *Bookman*, he turned to writing as a career. He was a regular contributor to many magazines, including the London *Illustrated News*, and he produced between sixty and seventy books of essays, verse, fiction, drama, criticism, and philosophy. The range of his writing was so immense that it is difficult to single out particular works for a student to read. His novels of crime featuring Father Brown, a Roman Catholic priest, as the amateur detective have always had a devoted following.

The brilliance and the gaiety of Chesterton's conversation are reflected in many of his essays. All of these essays are incomplete treatments of the subject, and they ramble as the informal speaker rambles. His wit and his deep understanding of humanity are clearly evident in " On Lying in Bed."

ON LYING IN BED

Lying in bed would be an altogether perfect and supreme experience if only one had a colored pencil long enough to draw on the ceiling. This, however, is not generally a part of the domestic apparatus on the premises. I think myself that the thing might be managed with several pails of Aspinall and a broom. Only if one worked in a really sweeping and masterly way, and laid on the color in great washes, it might drip down again on one's face in floods of rich and mingled color like some strange fairy rain; and that would have its disadvantages. I am afraid it would be necessary to stick to black and white in this form of artistic composition. To that purpose, indeed, the white ceiling would be of the greatest possible use; in fact, it is the only use I think of a white ceiling being put to.

But for the beautiful experiment of lying in bed I might never have discovered it. For years I have been looking for some blank spaces in a modern house to draw on. Paper is much too small for any really allegorical design; as Cyrano de Bergerac says, " Il me faut des géants." But when I tried to find these fine clear spaces in the modern rooms such as we all live in I was continually disappointed. I found an endless pattern and complication of small objects hung like a curtain of fine links between me and my desire. I examined the walls; I found them to my surprise to be already covered with wallpaper, and I found the wallpaper to be already covered with very uninteresting images, all bearing a ridiculous resemblance to each other. I could not understand why one arbitrary symbol (a symbol apparently entirely devoid of any religious or philosophical significance) should thus be sprinkled all over my nice walls like a sort of smallpox. The Bible must be referring to wallpapers, I think, when it says, "Use not vain repetitions, as the Gentiles do." I found the Turkey carpet a mass of unmeaning colors, rather like the Turkish Empire, or like the sweetmeat called Turkish Delight. I do not exactly know what Turkish Delight really is; but I suppose it is Macedonian Massacres. Everywhere that I went forlornly, with my pencil or my paint brush, I found that others had unaccountably been before me, spoiling the walls, the curtains, and the furniture with their childish and barbaric designs.

Nowhere did I find a really clear space for sketching until this occasion when I prolonged beyond the proper limit the process of lying on my back in bed. Then the light of that white heaven broke upon my vision, that breadth of mere white which is indeed almost the definition of Paradise, since it means purity and also means freedom. But alas! like all heavens, now that it is seen it is found to be unattainable; it looks more austere and more distant than the blue sky outside the window. For my proposal to paint on it with the bristly end of a broom has been discouraged — never mind by whom; by a person debarred from all political rights — and even my minor proposal to put the other end of the broom into the kitchen fire and turn it into charcoal has not been conceded. Yet I am certain that it was from persons in my position that all the original inspiration came for covering the ceilings of palaces and cathedrals with a riot of fallen angels or victorious gods. I am sure that it was only because Michelangelo was engaged in the ancient and honorable occupation of lying in bed that he ever realized how the roof of the Sistine Chapel might be made into an awful imitation of a divine drama that could only be acted in the heavens.

The tone now commonly taken toward the practice of lying in bed is hypocritical and unhealthy. Of all the marks of modernity that seem to mean a kind of decadence, there is none more menacing and dangerous than the exaltation of very small and secondary matters of conduct at the expense of very great and primary ones, at the expense of eternal ties and tragic human morality. If there is one thing worse than the modern weakening of major morals, it is the modern strengthening of minor morals. Thus it is considered more withering to accuse a man of bad taste than of bad ethics. Cleanliness is not next to godliness nowadays, for cleanliness is made an essential and godliness is regarded as an offence. A playwright can attack the institution of marriage so long as he does not misrepresent the manners of society, and I have met Ibsenite pessimists who thought it wrong to take beer but right to take prussic acid. Especially this is so in matters of hygiene; notably such matters as lying in bed. Instead of being regarded, as it ought to be, as a matter of personal convenience and adjustment, it has come to be regarded by many as if it were a part of essential morals to get up early in the morning. It is upon the whole part of practical wisdom; but there is nothing good about it or bad about its opposite.

Misers get up early in the morning; and burglars, I am informed, get up the night before. It is the great peril of our society that all its mechanism may grow more fixed while its spirit grows more fickle. A man's minor actions and arrangements ought to be free, flexible, creative; the things that should be unchangeable are his principles, his ideals. But with us the reverse is true; our views change constantly; but our lunch does not change. Now, I should like men to have strong and rooted conceptions, but as for their lunch, let them have it sometimes in the garden, sometimes in bed, sometimes on the roof, sometimes in the top of a tree. Let them argue from the same first principles, but let them do it in a bed, or a boat, or a balloon. This alarming growth of good habits really means a too great emphasis on those virtues which mere custom can ensure, it means too little emphasis on those virtues which custom can never quite ensure, sudden and splendid virtues of inspired pity or of inspired candor. If ever that abrupt appeal is made to us we may fail. A man can get used to getting up at five o'clock in the morning. A man cannot very well get used to being burnt for his opinions; the first experiment is commonly fatal. Let us pay a little more attention to these possibilities of the heroic and the unexpected. I dare say that when I get out of this bed I shall do some deed of an almost terrible virtue.

For those who study the great art of lying in bed there is one emphatic caution to be added. Even for those who can do their work in bed (like journalists), still more for those whose work cannot be done in bed (as, for example, the professional harpooners of whales), it is obvious that the indulgence must be very occasional. But that is not the caution I mean. The caution is this: if you do lie in bed, be sure you do it without any reason or justification at all. I do not speak, of course, of the seriously sick. But if a healthy man lies in bed, let him do it without a rag of excuse; then he will get up a healthy man. If he does it for some secondary hygienic reason, if he has some scientific explanation, he may get up a hypochondriac.

STUDYING THE ESSAY

1. Montaigne said that the essay should be like conversation. Does this essay follow Montaigne's rule? Explain carefully.
2. "On Lying in Bed" contains many brilliant sentences. Locate and explain some of them.

3. Can you identify Cyrano de Bergerac, Michelangelo, Sistine Chapel, Ibsen?

4. In what ways is " On Lying in Bed " a " personal " essay?

5. Words to learn: *masterly, arbitrary, awful, hypocritical, hypochondriac, allegorical.*

COMPOSITION TOPIC

Use the first sentence of this essay as a topic sentence and develop it into a short o iginal composition of your own.

WINSTON CHURCHILL, 1874–

It is utterly impossible in this short introduction even to hint at the many-sided greatness of Winston Leonard Spencer Churchill. His career includes enough for many men: wartime Prime Minister of England in her most desperate hours; a superb stylist in the art of writing who won the Nobel Prize for literature in 1953; perhaps the best orator of the century. It is certainly important for American young people to know something more about Churchill than the fact that he has twice been Prime Minister. Many Prime Ministers have been relatively dull men. Not Churchill.

Churchill is a direct descendant of the Duke of Marlborough, who won the Battle of Blenheim in 1704. His father was one of the leading peers of England; his mother was born in Brooklyn. His first twenty-five years were relatively unproductive. At Harrow he was at the bottom of his class; his record was so poor that he had no chance of gaining admission to Oxford or Cambridge. After graduating from the Royal Military Academy at Sandhurst — he did better there — he went into the army just in time to go to South Africa to cover the Boer War as a correspondent for the London *Morning Post*. From that point on, his life was full of excitement. He was captured by the Boers, escaped, had a price on his head, and lived to write the whole story very entertainingly in *A Roving Commission* (1930) from which the selection below is reprinted.

Since 1900, except for two years, he has been a member of Parliament. He has held the Cabinet posts of Home Secretary, First Lord of the Admiralty, Minister of Munitions, Under-Secretary for the Colonies, Minister for War and Air, Chancellor of the Exchequer, and Prime Minister — perhaps an all-time record. Defeated in a general election in 1945, he led the opposition until his party again came into power in 1951. In 1953 he was knighted, and now, at 80, he is to most Americans as much the living symbol of Great Britain as anyone else, even the young Queen.

How in the world does a man like this have time to write books? Evidently Churchill has been able to plan his time amazingly well, and obviously he has the energy of several men. The list of his works is long: twelve volumes about the two World Wars, plus several other books of history, biography, and autobiography. (Incidentally, he has also had time to become a first-rate painter.) Churchill's prose has many things to recommend it. The style is polished and flowing. It is full of pungent and memorable phrases. His choice of words is impeccable, as the selection here shows. There is humor in his work. And there is, when necessary, some of the most effective irony, or even sarcasm, of modern times.

The selection in this book is noteworthy, first, because of the light touch with which Churchill describes his own trials in school and, second, because of the elegant style in which the story is told.

HARROW

I had scarcely passed my twelfth birthday when I entered the inhospitable regions of examinations, through which for the next seven years I was destined to journey. These examinations were a great trial to me. The subjects which were dearest to the examiners were almost invariably those I fancied least. I would have liked to have been examined in history, poetry, and writing essays. The examiners, on the other hand, were partial to Latin and mathematics. And their will prevailed. Moreover, the questions which they asked on both these subjects were almost invariably those to which I was unable to suggest a satisfactory answer. I should have liked to be asked to say what I knew. They always tried to ask what I did not know. When I would have willingly displayed my knowledge, they sought to expose my ignorance. This sort of treatment had only one result: I did not do well in examinations.

This was especially true of my entrance examination to Harrow. The headmaster, Dr. Welldon, however, took a broad-minded view of my Latin prose: he showed discernment in judging my general ability. This was the more remarkable, because I was found unable to answer a single question in the Latin paper. I wrote my name at the top of the page. I wrote down the number of the question " I." After much reflection I put a bracket round it thus " (I)." But thereafter I could not think of anything connected with it that was either relevant or true. Incidentally there arrived from nowhere in particular a blot and several smudges. I gazed for two whole hours at this sad spectacle: and then merciful ushers collected my piece of foolscap with all the others and carried it up to the headmaster's table. It was from these slender indications of scholarship that Dr. Welldon drew the conclusion that I was worthy to pass into Harrow. It is very much to his credit. It showed that he was a man capable of looking beneath the surface of things: a man not dependent upon paper manifestations. I have always had the greatest regard for him.

In consequence of his decision, I was in due course placed in the third, or lowest, division of the Fourth, or bottom, Form. The names of the new boys were printed in the school list in alphabetical order; and as my correct name, Spencer-Churchill, began with an " S," I gained no more advantage from the alphabet than from the wider sphere of letters. I was in fact only two from the bottom of the whole school; and these two, I regret to say, disappeared almost immediately through illness or some other cause.

The Harrow custom of calling the roll is different from that of Eton. At Eton the boys stand in a cluster and lift their hats when their names are called. At Harrow they file past a master in the school yard and answer one by one. My position was therefore revealed in its somewhat invidious humility. It was the year 1887. Lord Randolph Churchill had only just resigned his position as Leader of the House of Commons and Chancellor of the Exchequer, and he still towered in the forefront of politics. In consequence large numbers of visitors of both sexes used to wait on the school steps, in order to see me march by; and I frequently heard the irreverent comment, " Why, he's last of all! "

I continued in this unpretentious situation for nearly a year. However, by being so long in the lowest form I gained an immense advantage over the cleverer boys. They all went on to learn Latin and Greek and splendid things like that. But I was taught English. We were considered such dunces that we could learn only English. Mr. Somervell — a most delightful man, to whom my debt is great — was charged with the duty of teaching the stupidest boys the most disregarded thing — namely, to write mere English. He knew how to do it. He taught it as no one else has ever taught it. Not only did we learn English parsing thoroughly, but we also practiced continually English analysis. Mr. Somervell had a system of his own. He took a fairly long sentence and broke it up into its components by means of black, red, blue, and green inks. Subject, verb, object: relative clauses, conditional clauses, conjunctive and disjunctive clauses! Each had its color and its bracket. It was a kind of drill. We did it almost daily. As I remained in the Third Fourth three times as long as anyone else, I had three times as much of it.

I learned it thoroughly. Thus I got into my bones the essential structure of the ordinary British sentence — which is a noble thing. And when in after years my schoolfellows who had won prizes and distinction for writing such beautiful Latin poetry and pithy Greek epigrams had to come down again to common English, to earn their living or make their way, I did not feel myself at any disadvantage. Naturally I am biased in favor of boys learning English. I would make them all learn English: and then I would let the clever ones learn Latin as an honor, and Greek as a treat. But the only thing I would whip them for would be for not knowing English. I would whip them hard for that.

I first went to Harrow in the summer term. The school possessed the biggest swimming-bath I had ever seen. It was more like the bend of a river than a bath, and it had two bridges across it. Thither we used to repair for hours at a time and bask between our dips eating enormous buns on the hot asphalt margin. Naturally it was a good joke to come up behind some naked friend, or even enemy, and push him in. I made quite a habit of this with boys of my own size or less. One day when I had been no more than a month in the school, I saw a boy standing in a meditative posture wrapped in a towel on the very brink. He was no bigger than I was, so I thought him fair game. Coming stealthily behind I pushed him in, holding on to his towel out of humanity, so that it should not get wet. I was startled to see a furious face emerge from the foam, and a being evidently of enormous strength making its way by fierce strokes to the shore. I fled, but in vain. Swift as the wind my pursuer overtook me, seized me in a ferocious grip, and hurled me into the deepest part of the pool. I soon scrambled out on the other side, and found myself surrounded by an agitated crowd of younger boys. "You're in for it," they said. "Do you know what you have done? It's Amery, he's in the

Sixth Form. He is head of his House; he is champion at gym; he has got his football colors." They continued to recount his many titles to fame and reverence and to dilate upon the awful retribution that would fall upon me. I was convulsed not only with terror, but with the guilt of sacrilege. How could I tell his rank when he was in a bath towel and so small? I determined to apologize immediately. I approached the potentate in lively trepidation. "I am very sorry," I said. "I mistook you for a Fourth Form boy. You are so small." He did not seem at all placated by this; so I added in a most brilliant recovery, "My father, who is a great man, is also small." At this he laughed, and after some general remarks about my "cheek" and how I had better be careful in the future, signified that the incident was closed.

I have been fortunate to see a good deal more of him, in times when three years' difference in age is not so important as it is at school. We were afterwards to be Cabinet colleagues for a good many years.

It was thought incongruous that while I apparently stagnated in the lowest form, I should gain a prize open to the whole school for reciting to the headmaster twelve hundred lines of Macaulay's "Lays of Ancient Rome" without making a single mistake. I also succeeded in passing the preliminary examination for the army while still almost at the bottom of the school. This examination seemed to have called forth a very special effort on my part, for many boys far above me in the school failed in it. I also had a piece of good luck. We knew that among other questions we should be asked to draw from memory a map of some country or other. The night before by way of final preparation I put the names of all the maps in the atlas into a hat and drew out New Zealand. I applied my good memory to the geography of that dominion. Sure enough, the first question in the paper was: "Draw a map of New Zealand." This was what is called at Monte Carlo an *en plein,* and I ought to have been paid thirty-five times my stake. However, I certainly got paid very high marks for my paper.

I was now embarked on a military career. This orientation was entirely due to my collection of soldiers. I had ultimately nearly fifteen hundred. They were all of one size, all British, and organized as an infantry division with a cavalry brigade. My brother Jack commanded the hostile army. But by a Treaty for the Limitation of Armaments he was only allowed to have colored troops, and they were not allowed to have artillery. Very important! I could muster myself only eighteen field guns — besides fortress pieces. But all the other services were complete — except one. It is what every army is always short of — transport. My father's old friend, Sir Henry Drummond Wolff, admiring my array, noticed this deficiency and provided a fund from which it was to some extent supplied.

The day came when my father himself paid a formal visit of inspection. All the troops were arranged in the correct formation of attack. He spent twenty minutes studying the scene — which was really impressive — with a keen eye and captivating smile. At the end he asked me if I would like to go into the army. I thought it would be splendid to command an army, so I said " Yes " at once: and immediately I was taken at my word. For years I thought my father with his experience and flair had discerned in me the qualities of military genius. But I was told later that he had only come to the conclusion that I was not clever enough to go to the bar. However that may be, the toy soldiers turned the current of my life. Henceforward all my education was directed to passing into Sandhurst, and afterwards to the technical details of the profession of arms. Anything else I had to pick up for myself.

I spent nearly four and a half years at Harrow, of which

three were in the army class. To this I was admitted in consequence of having passed the preliminary examination. It
consisted of boys of the middle and higher forms of the
school and of very different ages, all of whom were being
prepared either for the Sandhurst or the Woolwich examination. We were withdrawn from the ordinary movement
of the school from form to form. In consequence I got no
promotion or very little and remained quite low down upon
the school list, though working alongside of boys nearly all
in the Fifth Form. Officially I never got out of the Lower
School, so I never had the privilege of having a fag of my
own. When in the passage of time I became what was called
" a three-yearer," I ceased to have to fag myself, and as I
was older than other boys of my standing, I was appointed
in my House to the position of Head of the Fags. This was
my first responsible office, and the duties, which were honorary, consisted in keeping the roster of all the fags, making
out the lists of their duties and dates, and placing copies of
these lists in the rooms of the monitors, football and cricket
champions, and other members of our aristocracy. I discharged these functions for upwards of a year, and on the
whole I was resigned to my lot.

Meanwhile I found an admirable method of learning my
Latin translations. I was always very slow at using a dictionary: it was just like using a telephone directory. It is
easy to open it more or less at the right letter, but then you
have to turn backwards and forwards and peer up and down
the columns and very often find yourself three or four pages
the wrong side of the word you want. In short I found it
most laborious, while to other boys it seemed no trouble.
But now I formed an alliance with a boy in the Sixth Form.
He was very clever and could read Latin as easily as English. Caesar, Ovid, Virgil, Horace, and even Martial's epigrams were all the same to him. My daily task was perhaps

ten or fifteen lines. This would ordinarily have taken me an hour or an hour and a half to decipher, and then it would probably have been wrong. But my friend could in five minutes construe it for me word by word, and once I had seen it exposed, I remembered it firmly. My Sixth Form friend for his part was almost as much troubled by the English essays he had to write for the headmaster as I was by these Latin crossword puzzles. We agreed together that he should tell me my Latin translations and that I should do his essays. The arrangement worked admirably. The Latin master seemed quite satisfied with my work, and I had more time to myself in the morning. On the other hand, once a week or so I had to compose the essays of my Sixth Form friend. I used to walk up and down the room dictating — just as I do now — and he sat in the corner and wrote it down in longhand. For several months no difficulty arose; but once we were nearly caught out. One of these essays was thought to have merit. It was " sent up " to the headmaster, who summoned my friend, commended him on his work, and proceeded to discuss the topic with him in a lively spirit. " I was interested in this point you make here. You might I think have gone further. Tell me exactly what you had in your mind." Dr. Welldon in spite of very chilling responses continued in this way for some time to the deep consternation of my confederate. However the headmaster, not wishing to turn an occasion of praise into one of caviling, finally let him go with the remark, " You seem to be better at written than at oral work." He came back to me like a man who has had a very narrow squeak, and I was most careful ever afterwards to keep to the beaten track in essay writing.

Dr. Welldon took a friendly interest in me, and knowing that I was weak in the classics, determined to help me himself. His daily routine was heavy; but he added three times a week a quarter of an hour before evening prayers in which to give me personal tuition. This was a great condescension for the headmaster, who of course never taught anyone but the monitors and the highest scholars. I was proud of the honor; I shrank from the ordeal. If the reader has ever learned any Latin prose, he will know that at quite an early stage one comes across the ablative absolute with its apparently somewhat despised alternative " Quum with the pluperfect subjunctive." I always preferred " Quum." True, he was a little longer to write, thus lacking the much admired terseness and pith of the Latin language. On the other hand he avoided a number of pitfalls. I was often uncertain whether the ablative absolute should end in " e " or " i " or " o " or " is " or " ibus," to the correct selection of which great importance was attached. Dr. Welldon seemed to be physically pained by a mistake being made in any of these letters. I remember that later on Mr. Asquith used to have just the same sort of look on his face when I sometimes adorned a Cabinet discussion by bringing out one of my few but faithful Latin quotations. It was more than annoyance, it was a pang. Moreover, headmasters have powers at their disposal with which Prime Ministers have never yet been invested. So these evening quarters of an hour with Dr. Welldon added considerably to the anxieties of my life. I was much relieved when after nearly a whole term of patient endeavor he desisted from his well-meant but unavailing efforts.

I will here make some general observations about Latin which probably have their application to Greek as well. In a sensible language like English important words are connected and related to one another by other little words. The Romans in that stern antiquity considered such a method weak and unworthy. Nothing would satisfy them but that the structure of every word should be reacted on by its neighbors in accordance with elaborate rules to meet the different conditions in which it might be used. There is no doubt that this method both sounds and looks more impressive than our own. The sentence fits together like a piece of polished machinery. Every phrase can be tensely charged with meaning. It must have been very laborious, even if you were brought up to it; but no doubt it gave the Romans, and the Greeks too, a fine and easy way of establishing their posthumous fame. They were the first comers in the fields of thought and literature. When they arrived at fairly obvious reflections upon life and love, upon war, fate or manners, they coined them into the slogans or epigrams for which their language was so well adapted, and thus preserved the patent rights for all time. Hence their reputation. Nobody ever told me this at school. I have thought it all out in later life.

But even as a schoolboy I questioned the aptness of the classics for the prime structure of our education. So they told me how Mr. Gladstone read Homer for fun, which I thought served him right; and that it would be a great pleasure to me in after life. When I seemed incredulous, they added that classics would be a help in writing or speaking English. They then pointed out the number of our modern words which are derived from the Latin or Greek. Apparently one could use these words much better, if one knew the exact source from which they had sprung. I was fain to admit a practical value. But now even this has been swept away. The foreigners and the Scotch have joined together to introduce a pronunciation of Latin which divorces it finally from the English tongue. They tell us to pronounce "audience" "owdience"; and "civil" "keyweel." They have distorted one of my most serviceable and impressive quotations into the ridiculous booby "Wainy, Weedy, Weeky." Punishment should be reserved for those who have spread this evil.

We shall see another instance of perverted pedantry when we reach the Indian chapters of this book. When I was a boy everyone wrote and said " Punjaub," " pundit," " Umbala," etc. But then some learned notables came along saying, " No, you must spell them correctly." So the Englishman now refers to the " Panjab," to the " pandit so and so," or to " the troubles at Ambla and Amritsar." When Indians hear him, they are astonished at his outlandish speech: and that is the sole reward of his superior erudition. I am very conservative in all these things. I always spell the Czar, " Czar." As for the revised version of the Bible and the alterations in the Prayer Book and especially the marriage service, they are grievous.

STUDYING THE ESSAY

1. What has Churchill to say about " mere English "?
2. Did Churchill profit from the study of his own language?
3. Can you find indications in Churchill's prose that he *did* learn Latin, either at school or later?
4. Do any details in this essay parallel your own experience?
5. Harrow is one of the great English public (meaning, to an American, private) schools. How does its curriculum differ from that in your school?
6. Can you see anything good about the studies in which Churchill had so much trouble? In other words, does the study of Latin have any value?

COMPOSITION TOPICS

1. Your troubles with foreign languages, mathematics, or English can give you all sorts of ideas for informal essays.
2. What inspiration can you gain from studying about a great man's scholastic problems? Discuss the point in a short theme.

CLARENCE DAY, 1874–1935

Clarence Day, Jr. — to distinguish him from his father, whom he immortalized in essays like the following one — was born in New York City and educated at St. Paul's School and Yale. After graduation from college he entered his father's brokerage office, but left to join the navy in the Spanish-American War. During the war he contracted arthritis, which made him a bed-ridden cripple for the last years of his life. Although he received a sizable inheritance from his father, his illness used up the money, and until he made a success of his writing, he was in serious financial trouble. He wrote most of his books on immense sheets of paper with a crayon because his hands were too crippled to handle a small pencil or pen. Though few in number, his books bear the stamp of one of the most original writers of the century.

Life with Father, a collection of essays about the Day household, first appeared in magazines, principally the *New Yorker*. When some of these sketches were dramatized by Russell Crouse and Howard Lindsay, the six red-headed Days became the most famous family in America. The play ran in New York for ten years and is still performed on many stages. "The Noblest Instrument" describes an episode which did not appear in the play.

While the "Father" essays are his best-known works, many readers believe that *This Simian World*, his first book, is Day's masterpiece. In this unusual little book he discusses the apelike characteristics of the human race and considers what man would be like had he been descended from some other kind of animal — the cat, the elephant, or the dog, for instance. Still other readers of Clarence Day like *Scenes from the Mezozoic*, a book of queer sketches which are not just fantastic shapes but which, like the drawings of James Thurber, have a great deal of wisdom and depth.

Day's humor is never, as one might expect from a cripple, sarcastic. It is always, as in this essay, sympathetic and warmhearted, based upon a deep understanding of himself and of men in general. His style, simple and full of the evidences of painstaking care, fits his subject perfectly.

THE NOBLEST INSTRUMENT

Father had been away, reorganizing some old upstate railroad. He returned in an executive mood and proceeded to shake up our home. In spite of my failure as a singer, he was still bound to have us taught music. We boys were summoned before him and informed that we must at once learn to play on something. We might not appreciate it now, he said, but we should later on. " You, Clarence, will learn the violin. George, you the piano. Julian — well, Julian is too young yet. But you older boys must have lessons."

I was appalled at this order. At the age of ten it seemed a disaster to lose any more of my freedom. The days were already too short for our games after school; and now here was a chunk to come out of playtime three days every week. A chunk every day, we found afterward, because we had to practice.

George sat at the piano in the parlor, and faithfully learned to pound out his exercises. He had all the luck. He was not an inspired player, but at least he had some ear for music. He also had the advantage of playing on a good robust instrument, which he didn't have to be careful not to drop, and was in no danger of breaking. Furthermore, he did not have to tune it. A piano had some good points.

But I had to go through a blacker and more gruesome experience. It was bad enough to have to come in from the street and the sunlight and go down into our dark little basement where I took my lessons. But that was only the opening chill of the struggle that followed.

The whole thing was uncanny. The violin itself was a queer, fragile, cigar-boxy thing, that had to be handled most gingerly. Nothing sturdy about it. Why, a fellow was liable to crack it putting it into its case. And then my teacher, he was queer too. He had a queer pickled smell.

I dare say he wasn't queer at all really, but he seemed so to me, because he was different from the people I generally met. He was probably worth a dozen of some of them, but I didn't know it. He was one of the violins in the Philharmonic, and an excellent player, a grave, middle-aged little man — who was obliged to give lessons.

He wore a black, wrinkled frock coat, and a discolored gold watchchain. He had small, black-rimmed glasses; not tortoise-shell, but thin rims of metal. His violin was dark, rich, and polished, and would do anything for him.

Mine was balky and awkward, brand new, and of a light, common color.

The violin is intended for persons with a passion for music. I wasn't that kind of person. I liked to hear a band play a tune that we could march up and down to, but try as I would, I could seldom whistle such a tune afterward. My teacher didn't know this. He greeted me as a possible genius.

He taught me how to hold the contraption, tucked under my chin. I learned how to move my fingers here and there on its handle or stem. I learned how to draw the bow across the strings, and thus produce sounds. . . .

Does a mother recall the first cry of her baby, I wonder? I still remember the strange cry at birth of that new violin.

My teacher, Herr M., looked as though he had suddenly taken a large glass of vinegar. He sucked in his breath. His lips were drawn back from his teeth, and his eyes tightly shut. Of course, he hadn't expected my notes to be sweet at the start; but still, there was something unearthly about that first cry. He snatched the violin from me, examined it, readjusted its pegs, and comforted it gently, by drawing his own bow across it. It was only a new and not especially fine violin, but the sounds it made for him were more natural — they were classifiable sounds. They were not richly musical, but at least they had been heard before on this earth.

He handed the instrument back to me with careful directions. I tucked it up under my chin again and grasped the end tight. I held my bow exactly as ordered. I looked up at him, waiting.

" Now," he said, nervously.

I slowly raised the bow, drew it downward. . . .

This time there were *two* dreadful cries in our little front basement. One came from my new violin and one from the heart of Herr M.

Herr M. presently came to, and smiled bravely at me, and said if I wanted to rest a moment he would permit it. He seemed to think I might wish to lie down awhile and recover. I didn't feel any need of lying down. All I wanted was to get through the lesson. But Herr M. was shaken. He was by no means ready to let me proceed. He looked around desperately, saw the music book, and said he would now show me that. We sat down side by side on the window seat, with the book in his lap, while he pointed out the notes to me with his finger, and told me their names.

After a bit, when he felt better, he took up his own violin, and instructed me to watch him and note how he handled the strings. And then at last, he nerved himself to let me take my violin up again. "Softly, my child, softly," he begged me, and stood facing the wall. . . .

We got through the afternoon somehow, but it was a ghastly experience. Part of the time he was maddened by the mistakes I kept making, and part of the time he was plain wretched. He covered his eyes. He seemed ill. He looked often at his watch, even shook it as though it had stopped; but he stayed the full hour.

That was Wednesday. What struggles he had with himself before Friday, when my second lesson was due, I can only dimly imagine, and of course I never even gave them a thought at the time. He came back to recommence teaching me, but he had changed — he had hardened. Instead of being cross, he was stern; and instead of sad, bitter. He wasn't unkind to me, but we were no longer companions. He talked to himself, under his breath; and sometimes he took bits of paper, and did little sums on them, gloomily, and then tore them up.

During my third lesson I saw the tears come to his eyes. He went up to Father and said he was sorry but he honestly felt sure I'd never be able to play.

Father didn't like this at all. He said he felt sure I would. He dismissed Herr M. briefly — the poor man came stumbling back down in two minutes. In that short space of time he had gallantly gone upstairs in a glow, resolved upon sacrificing his earnings for the sake of telling the truth. He returned with his earnings still running, but with the look of a lost soul about him, as though he felt that his nerves and his sanity were doomed to destruction. He was low in his mind, and he talked to himself more than ever. Sometimes he spoke harshly of America, sometimes of fate.

But he no longer struggled. He accepted this thing as his

destiny. He regarded me as an unfortunate something out-side the human species, whom he must simply try to labor with as well as he could. It was a grotesque, indeed a hellish experience, but he felt he must bear it.

He wasn't the only one — he was at least not alone in his sufferings. Mother, though expecting the worst, had tried to be hopeful about it, but at the end of a week or two I heard her and Margaret talking it over. I was slaughtering a scale in the front basement, when Mother came down and stood outside the door in the kitchen hall and whispered, "Oh, Margaret!"

I watched them. Margaret was baking a cake. She screwed up her face, raised her arms, and brought them down with hands clenched.

"I don't know what we shall do, Margaret."

"The poor little feller," Margaret whispered. "He can't make the thing go."

This made me indignant. They were making me look like a lubber. I wished to feel always that I could make any-thing go. . . .

I now began to feel a determination to master this thing. History shows us many examples of the misplaced deter-minations of men — they are one of the darkest aspects of human life, they spread so much needless pain: but I knew little history. And I viewed what little I did know roman-tically — I should have seen in such episodes their heroism, not their futility. Any role that seemed heroic attracted me, no matter how senseless.

Not that I saw any chance for heroism in our front base-ment, of course. You had to have a battlefield or something. I saw only that I was appearing ridiculous. But that stung my pride. I hadn't wanted to learn anything whatever about fiddles or music; but since I was in for it, I'd do it, and show them I could. A boy will often put in enormous amounts of his time trying to prove he isn't as ridiculous as he thinks people think him.

Meanwhile Herr M. and I had discovered that I was near-sighted. On account of the violin's being an instrument that sticks out in front of one, I couldn't stand close enough to the music book to see the notes clearly. He didn't at first realize that I often made mistakes from that cause. When he and I finally comprehended that I had this defect, he had a sudden new hope that this might have been the whole trouble, and that when it was corrected I might play like a human being at last.

Neither of us ventured to take up this matter with Father. We knew that it would have been hard to convince him that my eyes were not perfect, I being a son of his and presumably made in his image; and we knew that he immediately would have felt we were trying to make trouble for him, and would have shown an amount of resentment which it was best to avoid. So Herr M. instead lent me his glasses. These did fairly well. They turned the dim grayness of the notes into a queer bright distortion, but the main thing was they did make them brighter, so that I now saw more of them. How well I remember those little glasses. Poor, dingy old things. Herr M. was nervous about lending them to me; he feared that I'd drop them. It would have been safer if they had been spectacles: but no, they were pince-nez; and I had to learn to balance them across my nose as well as I could. I couldn't wear them up near my eyes because my nose was too thin there; I had to put them about halfway down where there was enough flesh to hold them. I also had to tilt my head back, for the music stand was a little too tall for me. Herr M. sometimes mounted me on a stool, warning me not to step off. Then when I was all set, and when he without his glasses was blind, I would smash my way into the scales again.

All during the long winter months I worked away at this job. I gave no thought, of course, to the family. But they did to me. Our house was heated by a furnace, which had big warm air pipes; these ran up through the walls with wide outlets into each room, and sound traveled easily and ringingly through their roomy, tin passages. My violin could be heard in every part of the house. No one could settle down to anything while I was practicing. If visitors came they soon left. Mother couldn't even sing to the baby. She would wait, watching the clock, until my long hour of scale-work was over, and then come downstairs and shriek at me that my time was up. She would find me sawing away with my forehead wet, and my hair wet and stringy, and even my clothes slowly getting damp from my exertions. She would feel my collar, which was done for, and say I must change it. "Oh, Mother! Please!" — for I was in a hurry now to run out and play. But she wasn't being fussy about my collar, I can see, looking back; she was using it merely as a barometer or gauge of my pores. She thought I had better dry myself before going out in the snow.

It was a hard winter for Mother. I believe she also had fears for the baby. She sometimes pleaded with Father; but no one could ever tell Father anything. He continued to stand like a rock against stopping my lessons.

Schopenhauer, in his rules for debating, shows how to win a weak case by insidiously transferring an argument from its right field, and discussing it instead from some irrelevant but impregnable angle. Father knew nothing of Schopenhauer, and was never insidious, but, nevertheless, he had certain natural gifts for debate. In the first place his voice was powerful and stormy, and he let it out at full strength, and kept on letting it out with a vigor that stunned his opponents. As a second gift, he was convinced at all times that his opponents were wrong. Hence, even if they did win a point or two, it did them no good, for he dragged the issue to some other ground then, where he and Truth could prevail. When Mother said it surely was plain enough that I had no ear, what was his reply? Why, he said that the violin was the noblest instrument invented by man. Having silenced her with this solid premise, he declared that it followed that any boy was lucky to be given the privilege of learning to play it. No boy should expect to learn it immediately. It required persistence. Everything, he had found, required persistence. The motto was, Never give up.

All his life, he declared, he had persevered in spite of discouragement, and he meant to keep on persevering, and he meant me to, too. He said that none of us realized what he had had to go through. If he had been the kind that gave up at the very first obstacle, where would he have been now — where would any of the family have been? The answer was, apparently, that we'd either have been in a very bad way, poking round for crusts in the gutter, or else nonexistent. We might never even have been born if Father had not persevered.

Placed beside this record of Father's vast trials overcome, the little difficulty of my learning to play the violin seemed a trifle. I faithfully spurred myself on again, to work at the puzzle. Even my teacher seemed impressed with these views on persistence. Though older than Father, he had certainly not made as much money, and he bowed to the experience of a practical man who was a success. If he, Herr M., had been a success, he would not have had to teach boys; and sitting in this black pit in which his need of money had placed him, he saw more than ever that he must learn the ways of this world. He listened with all his heart, as to a god, when Father shook his forefinger, and told him how to climb **to** the heights where financial rewards were achieved. The idea he got was that perseverance was sure to lead to great wealth.

Consequently our front basement continued to be the home of lost causes.

Of course, I kept begging Herr M. to let me learn just one tune. Even though I seldom could whistle them, still I liked tunes; and I knew that, in my hours of practicing, a tune would be a comfort. That is, for myself. Here again I never gave a thought to the effect upon others.

Herr M., after many misgivings, to which I respectfully listened — though they were not spoken to me, they were muttered to himself, pessimistically — hunted through a worn old book of selections, and after much doubtful fumbling chose as simple a thing as he could find for me — for me and the neighbors.

It was spring now, and windows were open. That tune became famous.

What would the musician who had tenderly composed this air, years before, have felt if he had foreseen what an end it would have, on Madison Avenue; and how, before death, it would be execrated by that once peaceful neighborhood. I engraved it on their hearts; not in its true form but in my own eerie versions. It was the only tune I knew. Consequently I played and replayed it.

Even horrors when repeated grow old and lose part of their sting. But those I produced were, unluckily, never the same. To be sure, this tune kept its general structure the same, even in my sweating hands. There was always the place where I climbed unsteadily up to its peak, and that difficult spot where it wavered, or staggered, and stuck; and then a sudden jerk of resumption — I came out strong on that. Every afternoon when I got to that difficult spot, the neighbors dropped whatever they were doing to wait for that jerk, shrinking from the moment, and yet feverishly impatient for it to come.

But what made the tune and their anguish so different each day? I'll explain. The strings of a violin are wound at the end around pegs, and each peg must be screwed in and tightened till the string sounds just right. Herr M. left my violin properly tuned when he went. But suppose a string broke, or that somehow I jarred a peg loose. Its string then became slack and soundless. I had to re-tighten it. Not having an ear, I was highly uncertain about this.

Our neighbors never knew at what degree of tautness I'd put such a string. I didn't myself. I just screwed her up tight enough to make a strong reliable sound. Neither they nor I could tell which string would thus appear in a new role each day, nor foresee the profound transformations this would produce in that tune.

All that spring this unhappy and ill-destined melody floated out through my window, and writhed in the air for one hour daily, in sunshine or storm. All that spring our neighbors and I daily toiled to its peak, and staggered over its hump, so to speak, and fell wailing through space.

Things now began to be said to Mother which drove her to act. She explained to Father that the end had come at last. Absolutely. "This awful nightmare cannot go on," she said.

Father pooh-poohed her.

She cried. She told him what it was doing to her. He said that she was excited, and that her descriptions of the sounds I made were exaggerated and hysterical — must be. She was always too vehement, he shouted. She must learn to be calm.

"But you're downtown, *you* don't have to hear it! "

Father remained wholly skeptical.

She endeavored to shame him. She told him what awful

things the neighbors were saying about him, because of the noise I was making, for which he was responsible.

He couldn't be made to look at it that way. If there really were any unpleasantness, then I was responsible. He had provided me with a good teacher and a good violin — so he reasoned. In short, he had done his best, and no father could have done more. If I made hideous sounds after all that, the fault must be mine. He said that Mother should be stricter with me, if necessary, and make me try harder.

This was the last straw. I couldn't try harder. When Mother told me his verdict I said nothing, but my body rebelled. Self-discipline had its limits — and I wanted to be out: it was spring. I skimped my hours of practice when I heard the fellows playing outside. I came home late for lessons — even forgot them. Little by little they stopped.

Father was outraged. His final argument, I remember, was that my violin had cost twenty-five dollars; if I didn't learn it the money would be wasted, and he couldn't afford it. But it was put to him that my younger brother, Julian, could learn it instead, later on. Then summer came, anyhow, and we went for three months to the seashore; and in the confusion of this Father was defeated and I was set free.

In the autumn little Julian was led away one afternoon, and imprisoned in the front basement in my place. I don't remember how long they kept him down there, but it was several years. He had an ear, however, and I believe he learned to play fairly well. This would have made a happy ending for Herr M. after all; but it was some other teacher, a younger man, who was engaged to teach Julian. Father said Herr M. was a failure.

STUDYING THE ESSAY

1. One of the great charms of Clarence Day is his delight in the descriptive phrase, such as " He had a queer pickled smell." Find other apt phrases and discuss their effectiveness.

2. Do you sympathize with Clarence? Why?

3. Do you feel sorry for the teacher? Why?

4. Do you sympathize with Father? Why?

5. Find statements in this essay which you have heard in your own home.

6. What have you learned about Father?

COMPOSITION TOPICS

1. If you have ever taken music lessons, whether successfully or not, you have a world of material for compositions. Try to pick out a particularly pleasant or particularly unpleasant experience in your own musical training and describe your emotional reaction to it.

2. The Fate of the Tone Deaf

3. No Classics for Me! Give Me Bebop!

4. I Like Music, But I Hate to Practice

WILLIAM BEEBE, 1877–

Charles William Beebe has probably done
more than any other man to make the literature of natural science interesting to the non-scientific reader. Beginning in the
early 1920's his books have delighted thousands of readers. The
main reasons for this public reception of his works are two:
Beebe's literary style and his enormous enthusiasm for his subject. His style is often poetic, it is often witty, it is always
clearly descriptive and accurate. There is no "scientific coldness" about it. Thus very often Beebe's books give the reader
the kind of pleasure which comes from reading fiction. But
Beebe is a careful scientist; his truth in many instances is more
interesting than fiction.

The principal virtue of Beebe's books, as in those of Donald Peattie and Rachel Carson, is the writer's obvious love of his
subject. The reader finds this enthusiasm contagious. After looking through Beebe's eyes at the wonders of undersea life in the
West Indies, he can agree that Beebe is right to say, "Don't die
without having borrowed, stolen, purchased, or made a helmet,
to glimpse for yourself this new world." The man who almost
falls overboard with excitement when a new kind of sea snake
appears astern, the man who has a coral snake (behind glass) as
a table centerpiece, the man who "on September twelfth met a
Great Blue Shark in the prime of life" — this man can fortunately convey all of his own fun to the reader because he can
also write very vivid prose. The sloth, says Beebe in "The Jungle Sluggard," has "an enthusiasm for life excelled by a healthy
sunflower." The ability to turn phrases like this is one of Beebe's
great assets in his essays.

206

Beebe was born in Brooklyn and was graduated from Columbia University. Since 1899 he has been Curator of Ornithology and director of the Department of Tropical Research of the New York Zoological Society. His writings include large numbers of technical articles for scientific magazines in addition to the twenty-odd books in which he has taken the ordinary reader to exotic places. Some of his most widely read books are *Jungle Days* (1925), from which "The Jungle Sluggard" is taken; *Galapagos* (1923), the story of an expedition to the Pacific island home of giant tortoises; *Half Mile Down* (1934), a description of his descent in the "bathysphere" to more than 3,000 feet in the ocean; and *High Jungle* (1949), concerning birds, butterflies, and other creatures in the Andes mountains.

THE JUNGLE SLUGGARD

Sloths have no right to be living on the earth today; they would be fitting inhabitants of Mars, where a year is over six hundred days long. In fact they would exist more appropriately on a still more distant planet where time — as we know it — creeps and crawls instead of flies from dawn to dusk. Years ago I wrote that sloths reminded me of nothing so much as the wonderful Rath Brother athletes or of a slowed-up moving picture, and I can still think of no better similes.

Sloths live altogether in trees, but so do monkeys, and the chief difference between them would seem to be that the latter spend their time pushing against gravitation while the sloths pull against it. Botanically the two groups of animals are comparable to the flower which holds its head up to the sun, swaying on its long stem, and, on the other hand, the overripe fruit dangling heavily from its base. We ourselves are physically far removed from sloths — for while we can point with pride to the daily achievement of those ambulatory athletes, floorwalkers and policemen, yet no human being can cling with his hands to a branch for more than a comparatively short time.

Like a rainbow before breakfast, a sloth is a surprise, an unexpected fellow breather of the air of our planet. No one could prophesy a sloth. If you have an imaginative friend who has never seen a sloth and ask him to describe what he thinks it ought to be like, his uncontrolled phrases will fall far short of reality. If there were no sloths, Dunsany would hesitate to put such a creature in the forests of Mluna, Marco Polo would deny having seen one, and Munchausen would whistle as he listened to a friend's description.

A scientist — even a taxonomist himself — falters when he mentions the group to which a sloth belongs. A taxonomist is the most terribly accurate person in the world, dealing with unvarying facts, and his names and descriptions of animals defy discretion, murder, imagination. Nevertheless, when next you see a taxonomist disengaged, approach him boldly and ask in a tone of quarrelsome interest to what order of the Mammalia sloths belong. If an honest conservative he will say, " Edentata," which, as any ancient Greek will tell you, means a toothless one. Then if you wish to enrage and nonplus the taxonomist, which I think no one should, as I am one myself, then ask him " Why? " or, if he has ever been bitten by any of the eighteen teeth of a sloth.

The great savant Buffon, in spite of all his genius, fell into most grievous error in his estimation of a sloth. He says, " The inertia of this animal is not so much due to laziness as to wretchedness; it is the consequence of its faulty structure. Inactivity, stupidity, and even habitual suffering result from its strange and ill-constructed conformation. Having no weapons for attack or defense, no mode of refuge even by burrowing, its only safety is in flight. . . . Everything about it shows its wretchedness and proclaims it to be one of those defective monsters, those imperfect sketches, which Nature has sometimes formed, and which, having scarcely the faculty of existence, could only continue for a short time and have since been removed from the catalogue of living beings. They are the last possible term amongst creatures of flesh and blood, and any further defect would have made their existence impossible."

If we imagine the dignified French savant himself naked, and dangling from a lofty jungle branch in the full heat of the tropic sun, without water and with the prospect of nothing but coarse leaves for breakfast, dinner, and all future meals, an impartial onlooker who was ignorant of man's normal haunts and life could very truthfully apply, to the unhappy scientist, Buffon's own comments. All of his terms of opprobrium would come home to roost with him.

A bridge out of place would be an absolutely inexplicable thing, as would a sloth in Paris, or a Buffon in the trees. As a matter of fact it was only when I became a temporary cripple myself that I began to appreciate the astonishing lives which sloths lead. With one of my feet injured and out of commission I found an abundance of time in six weeks to study the individuals which we caught in the jungle nearby. Not until we invent a superlative of which the word *deliberate* is the positive can we define a sloth with sufficient adequateness and briefness. I dimly remember certain volumes by an authoress whose style pictured the hero walking from the door to the front gate, placing first the right, then the left foot before him as he went. With such detail and speed of action might one write the biography of a sloth.

Ever since man has ventured into this wilderness, sloths have aroused astonishment and comment. Four hundred years ago Gonzalo de Oviedo sat him down and penned a most delectable account of these creatures. He says, in part, " There is another strange beast the Spaniards call the Light Dogge, which is one of the slowest beasts, and so heavie and dull in mooving that it can scarsely goe fiftie pases in a whole day. Their neckes are high and streight, and all equall like the pestle of a mortar, without making any proportion of similitude of a head, or any difference except in the noddle, and in the tops of their neckes. They have little mouthes, and moove their neckes from one side to another, as though they were astonished; their chiefe desire and delight is to cleave and sticke fast unto trees, whereunto cleaving fast, they mount up little by little, staying themselves by their long claws. Their voice is much differing from other beasts, for they sing only in the night, and that continually from time to time, singing ever six notes one higher than another. Sometimes the Christian men find these beasts and bring them home to their houses, where also they creepe all about with their natural slownesse. I could never perceive other but that they live onely of Aire; because they ever turne their heads and mouthes toward that part where the wind bloweth most, whereby may be considered that they take most pleasure in the Aire. They bite not, nor yet can bite, having very little mouthes; they are not venemous or noyous any way, but altogether brutish, and utterly unprofitable and without commoditie yet known to men."

It is difficult to find adequate comparisons for a topsy-turvy creature like a sloth, but if I had already had synthetic experience with a Golem, I would take for a formula the general appearance of an English sheep dog, giving it a face with barely distinguishable features and no expression, an inexhaustible appetite for a single kind of coarse leaf, a gamut of emotions well below the animal kingdom, and an enthusiasm of life excelled by a healthy sunflower. Suspend this from a jungle limb by a dozen strong hooks, and — you would still have to see a live sloth to appreciate its appearance.

At rest, curled up into an arboreal ball, a sloth is indistinguishable from a cluster of leaves; in action, the second hand of a watch often covers more distance. At first sight of the shapeless ball of hay, moving with hopeless inadequacy, astonishment shifts to pity, then to impatience, and finally, as we sense a life of years spent thus, we feel almost disgust. At which moment the sloth reaches blindly in our direction, thinking us a barren, leafless, but perhaps climbable tree, and our emotions change again, this time to sheer delight as a tiny infant sloth raises its indescribably funny face from its mother's breast and sends forth the single tone, the high, whistling squeak, which in sloth intercourse is song, shout, converse, whisper, argument, and chant. Separating him from his mother is like plucking a bur from one's hair, but when freed, he contentedly hooks his small self to our clothing and creeps slowly about.

Instead of reviewing all the observations and experiments which I perpetrated upon sloths, I will touch at once the heart of their mysterious psychology, giving in a few words a conception of their strange, uncanny minds. A bird will give up its life in defending its young; an alligator will not often desert its nest in the face of danger; a male stickleback fish will intrepidly face any intruder that threatens its eggs. In fact, at the time when the young of all animals are at the age of helplessness, the senses of the parents are doubly keen, their activities and weapons are at greatest efficiency for the guarding of the young and the consequent certainty of the continuance of their race.

The resistance made by a mother sloth to the abstraction of its offspring is chiefly the mechanical tangling of the young animal's tiny claws in the long maternal fur. I have taken away a young sloth and hooked it to a branch five feet away. Being hungry, it began at once to utter its high, penetrating penny whistle. To no other sound, high or low, with even a half-tone's difference does the sloth pay any heed, but its dim hearing is attuned to just this vibration. Slowly the mother starts off in what she thinks is the direction of the sound. It is the moment of moments in the life of the young animal. Yet I have seen her again and again on different occasions pass within two feet of the little chap, and never look to right or left, but keep straight on, stolidly and unvaryingly to the high jungle, while her baby, a few inches out of her path, called in vain. No kidnapped child hidden in mountain fastness or urban underworld was ever more completely lost to its parent than this infant, in full view and separated by only a sloth's length of space.

A gun fired close to the ear of a sloth will usually arouse not the slightest tremor; no scent of flower or acid or carrion causes any reaction; a sleeping sloth may be shaken violently without awakening; the waving of a scarlet rag, or a climbing serpent a few feet away brings no gleam of curiosity or fear to the dull eyes; an astonishingly long immersion in water produces discomfort but not death. When we think what a constant struggle life is to most creatures, even when they are equipped with the keenest of senses and powerful means of offense, it seems incredible that a sloth can hold its own in this overcrowded tropical jungle.

From birth to death it climbs slowly about the great trees, leisurely feeding, languidly loving, and almost mechanically caring for its young. On the ground a host of enemies await it, but among the higher branches it fears chiefly occasional great boas, climbing jaguars, and, worst of all, the mighty talons of harpy eagles. Its means of offense is a joke — a slow, ineffective reaching forward with open jaws, a lethargic stroke of arm and claws which anything but another sloth can avoid. Yet the race of sloths persists and thrives, and in past years I have had as many as eighteen under observation at one time.

A sloth makes no nest or shelter; it even disdains the protection of dense foilage. But for all its apparent helplessness it has a *cheval-de-frise* of protection which many animals far above it in intelligence might well envy. Its outer line of defense is invisibility — and there is none better, for until you have seen your intended prey you can neither attack nor devour him. No hedgehog or armadillo ever rolled a more perfect ball of itself than does a sloth, sitting in a lofty, swaying crotch with head and feet and legs all gathered close together inside. This posture, to an onlooker, destroys all thought of a living animal, but presents a very satisfactory white ants' nest or bunch of dead leaves. If we look at the hair of a sloth we shall see small, gray patches along the length of the hairs — at first sight bits of bark and débris of wood. But these minute, scattered particles are of the utmost aid to this invisibility. They are a peculiar species of alga or lichen-like growth, which is found only in this peculiar haunt, and when the rain begins and all the jungle turns a deep, glowing emerald, these tiny plants also react to the welcome moisture and become verdant — thus growing over the sloth a protecting, misty veil of green.

Even we dull-sensed humans require neither sight nor hearing to detect the presence of an animal like the skunk; in the absolute quiet and blackness of midnight we can tell when a porcupine has crossed our path, or when there are mice in the bureau drawers. But a dozen sloths may be hanging to the trees near at hand and never the slightest whiff of odor comes from them. A baby sloth has not even a baby smell, and all this is part of the cloak of invisibility. The voice, raised so very seldom, is so ventriloquial, and possesses such a strange, unanimal-like quality, that it can never be a guide to the location, much less to the identity of the author. Here we have three senses — sight, hearing, smell — all operating at a distance, two of them by vibrations, and all leagued together to shelter the sloth from attack.

But in spite of this dramatic guard of invisibility, the keen eyes of an eagle, the lapping tongue of a giant boa, and the amazing delicacy of a jaguar's sense of smell break through at times. The jaguar scents sign under the tree of the sloth, climbs eagerly as far as he dares, and finds ready to his paw the ball of animal unconsciousness; a harpy eagle half a mile above the jungle sees a bunch of leaves reach out a sleepy arm and scratch itself — something clumps of leaves should not do. Down spirals the great bird, slowly, majestically, knowing there is no need of haste, and alights close by the mammalian sphere. Still the sloth does not move, apparently waiting for what fate may bring — waiting with that patience and resignation which comes only to those of our fellow creatures who cannot say, " I am I! " It seems as if Nature had deserted her jungle changeling, stripped now of its protecting cloak.

The sloth, however, has never been given credit for its powers of passive resistance, and now, with its enemy within striking distance, its death or even injury is far from a certainty. The crotch which the sloth chooses for its favorite outdoor sport, sleep, is unusually high up or far out among the lesser branches, where the eight claws of the eagle or the eighteen of a jaguar find but precarious hold. If the victim were a feathery bush turkey or a soft-bodied squirrel, one stroke would be sufficient, but this strange creature is something far different. In the first place, it is only to be plucked from its perch by the exertion of enormous strength. No

man can seize a sloth by the long hair of the back and pull
it off. So strong are its muscles, so vise-like the grip of its
dozen talons, that either the crotch must be cut or broken
off or the long claws unfastened one by one. Neither of
these alternatives is possible to the attacking cat or eagle.
They must depend upon crushing or penetrating power of
stroke or grasp.

Here is where the sloth's second line of defense becomes
operative. First, as I have mentioned, the swaying branch and
dizzy height are in his favor, as well as his immovable grip.
To begin with the innermost defenses, while his jungle fellows, the ring-tailed and red howling monkeys, have thirteen
ribs, the sloth may have as many as twenty; in the latter animals they are, in addition, unusually broad and flat, slats
rather than rods. Next comes the skin, which is so thick and
tough that many an Indian's arrow falls back without even
scratching the hide. The skin of the unborn sloth is as tough
and strong as that of a full-grown monkey. Finally we have
the fur — two distinct coats, the under one fine, short, and
matted, the outer long, harsh, and coarse. Is it any wonder
that, teetering on a swaying branch, many a jaguar has had
to give up, after frantic attempts to strike his claws through
the felted hair, the tough skin, and the bony latticework
which protects the vitals of this edentate bur!

Having rescued our sloth from his most immediate peril,
let us watch him solve some of the very few problems which
life presents to him. Although the Cecropia tree, on the
leaves of which he feeds, is scattered far and wide through
the jungle, yet sloths are found almost exclusively along river
banks, and, most amazingly, they not infrequently take to the
water. I have caught a dozen sloths swimming rivers a mile
or more in width. Judging from the speed of short distances,
a sloth can swim a mile in three hours and twenty minutes.
Their thick skin and fur must be a protection against croco-

diles, electric eels, and perai fish, as well as jaguars. Why they should ever wish to swim across these wide expanses of water is as inexplicable as the migration of butterflies. One side of the river has as many comfortable crotches, as many millions of Cecropia leaves, and as many eligible lady sloths as the other! In this unreasonable desire for anything which is out of reach, sloths come very close to a characteristic of human beings.

Even in the jungle, sloths are not always the static creatures which their vegetable-like life would lead us to believe, as I was able to prove many years ago. A young male was brought in by Indians, and after keeping it a few days I shaved off two patches of hair from the center of the back, and labeling it with a metal tag, I turned it loose. Forty-eight days later it was captured near a small settlement of Bovianders several miles farther up and across the river. During this time it must have traversed four miles of jungle and one of river.

The principal difference between the male and the female three-toed sloths is the presence on the back of the male of a large, oval spot of orange-colored fur. To any creature of more active mentality such a minor distinction must often be embarrassing. In an approaching sloth, walking upside down as usual, this mark is quite invisible, and hence every meeting of two sloths must contain much of delightful uncertainty, of ignorance whether the encounter presages courtship or merely gossip. But color or markings have no meaning in the dull eyes of these animals. Until they have sniffed and almost touched noses they show no recognition or reaction whatever.

I once invented a sloth island — a large circle of ground surrounded by a deep ditch, where sloths climbed about some saplings and ate, but principally slept, and lived for months at a time. This was within sight of my laboratory table; so I could watch what was taking place by merely raising my head. Some of the occurrences were almost too strange for creatures of this earth. I watched two courtships, each resulting in nothing more serious than my own amusement. A female was asleep in a low crotch, curled up into a perfect ball deep within which was ensconced a month-old baby. Two yards overhead was a male who had slept for nine hours without interruption. Moved by what, to a sloth, must have been a burst of uncontrollable emotion, he slowly unwound himself and clambered downward. When close to the sleeping beauty, he reached out a claw and tentatively touched a shoulder. Ever more deliberately she excavated her head and long neck and peered in every direction but the right one. At last she perceived her suitor and looked away as if the sight was too much for her. Again he touched her post-like neck, and now there arose all the flaming fury of a mother at the flirtatious advances of this stranger. With incredible slowness and effort she freed an arm, deliberately drew it back, and then began a slow forward stroke with arm and claws. Meanwhile her gentleman friend had changed his position; so the blow swept, or more correctly, passed, through empty air, the lack of impact almost throwing her out of the crotch. The disdained one left with slowness and dignity — or had he already forgotten why he had descended? — and returned to his perch and slumber, where, I am sure, not even such active things as dreams came to disturb his peace.

The second courtship advanced to the stage where the Gallant actually got his claws tangled in the lady's back hair before she awoke. When she grasped the situation, she left at once and clambered to the highest branch tip, followed by the male. Then she turned and climbed down and across her annoyer, leaving him stranded on the lofty branch looking eagerly about and reaching out hopefully toward a big green iguana asleep on the next limb in mistake for his fair companion. For an hour he wandered languidly after her, then gave it up and went to sleep. Throughout these and other emotional crises no sound is ever uttered, no feature altered from its stolid repose. The head moves mechanically and the dull eyes blink slowly, as if striving to pierce the opaque veil which ever hangs between the brain of a sloth and the sights, sounds, and odors of this tropical world. If the orange back-spot was ever of any use in courtship, in arousing any emotion, aesthetic or otherwise, it must have been in ages long past when the ancestors of sloths, contemporaries of their gigantic relatives, the Mylodons, had better eyesight for escaping from saber-toothed tigers than there is need of today.

The climax of a sloth's emotion has nothing to do with the opposite sex or with the young, but is exhibited when two females are confined in a cage together. The result is wholly unexpected. After sniffing at one another for a moment, they engage in a slowed-up moving-picture battle. Before any harm is done, one or the other gives utterance to the usual piercing whistle and surrenders. She lies flat on the cage floor and offers no defense while the second female proceeds to claw her, now and then attempting, usually vainly, to bite. It is so unpleasant that I have always separated them at this stage, but there is no doubt that in every case the unnatural affray would go on until the victim was killed. In fact I have heard of several instances where this actually took place.

A far pleasanter sight is the young sloth, one of the most adorable balls of fuzzy fur imaginable. While the sense of play is all but lacking, his trustfulness and helplessness are most infantile. Every person who takes him up is an accepted substitute for his mother, and he will clamber slowly about one's clothing for hours in supreme contentment. One thing I can never explain is that on the ground the baby is even more helpless than his parents. While they can hitch themselves along, body dragging, limbs outspread, until they reach the nearest tree, a young sloth is wholly without power to move. Placed on a flat bit of ground it rolls and tumbles about, occasionally greatly encouraged by seizing hold of its own foot or leg under the impression that at last it has encountered a branch.

Sloths sleep about twice as much as other mammals, and a baby sloth often gets tired of being confined in the heart of its mother's sleeping sphere, and creeping out under her arm will go on an exploring expedition around and around her. When over two weeks old it has strength to rise on its hind legs and sway back and forth like nothing else in the world. Its eyes are only a little keener than those of the parent, and it peers up at the foliage overhead with the most pitiful interest. It is slowly weaned from a milk diet to the leaves of the Cecropia, which the mother at first chews up for her offspring.

I once watched a young sloth about a month old and saw it leave its mother for the first time. As the old one moved slowly back and forth, pulling down Cecropia leaves and feeding on them, the youngster took firm grip on a leaf stem, mumbling at it with no success whatever. When finally it stretched around and found no soft fur within reach it set up a wail which drew the attention of the mother at once. Still clinging to her perch, she reached out a forearm to an unbelievable distance and gently hooked the great claws about the huddled infant, which at once climbed down the long bridge and tumbled headlong in the hollow awaiting it.

When a very young sloth is gently disentangled from its mother and hooked on to a branch, something of the greatest interest happens. Instead of walking forward, one foot after the other, and upside down as all adult sloths do, it reaches up and tries to get first one arm then the other *over* the support, and to pull itself into an upright position. This would seem to be a reversion to a time — perhaps millions of years ago — when the ancestors of sloths had not yet begun to hang inverted from the branches. After an interval of clumsy reaching and wriggling about, the baby by accident grasps its own body or limb, and, in this case, convinced that it is at last anchored safely again to its mother, it confidently lets go with all its other claws and tumbles ignominiously to the ground.

The moment a baby sloth dies and slips from its grip on the mother's fur, it ceases to exist for her. If it could call out she would reach down an arm and hook it toward her, but simply dropping silently means no more than if a disentangled bur had fallen from her coat. I have watched such a sloth carefully and have never seen any search of her own body or of the surrounding branches, or a moment's distraction from sleep or food. An imitation of the cry of the dead baby will attract her attention, but if not repeated she forgets it at once.

It is interesting to know of the lives of such beings as this — chronic pacifists, normal morons, the superlative of negative natures, yet holding their own amidst the struggle for existence. Nothing else desires to feed on such coarse fodder, no other creature disputes with it the domain of the under side of branches, hence there is no competition. From our human point of view sloths are degenerate; from another angle they are among the most exquisitely adapted of living beings. If we humans, together with our brains, fitted as well into the possibilities of our own lives, we should be infinitely finer and happier — and, besides, I should then be able to interpret more intelligently the life and the philosophy of sloths!

STUDYING THE ESSAY

1. Explain: " No one could prophesy a sloth."
2. Find places where you feel Beebe's eager enthusiasm for the facts of science.
3. What defenses against enemies has the sloth?
4. Describe the " cloaks of invisibility " of other animals.
5. Point out the ways in which the senses of sight, hearing, and smell help to protect the sloth.
6. Point out scientific facts which interested you in this essay.
7. How does the author convince you that the sloth can hold its own in the struggle for existence?
8. Find examples of Beebe's vivid use of language.
9. Words to learn: *savant, arboreal, perpetrated, lichen, stolidly, static, chronic.*

COMPOSITION TOPICS

1. The Classroom Sluggard
2. Describe the habits of an animal you know well — a pet dog, cat, raccoon, bird, or pig, for example. Observe the animal carefully before you write.
3. Write a descriptive paragraph about some wild creature you have seen — a hawk screaming over its nest, a deer bounding off through the woods. Use vivid language in your writing.

CARL SANDBURG, 1878–

Carl Sandburg was born in Galesburg, Illinois, the son of Swedish immigrant parents. His childhood was plagued by poverty; he left school at the age of thirteen and for seven years worked at any job he could get — bricklaying, dishwashing, and house painting. After service in the army during the Spanish-American War, he worked his way through Lombard College, in Galesburg. His degrees do not include an A.B. from Lombard; but he has received ten honorary Litt.D. degrees and two honorary LL.D. degrees for his enormous contribution to the literature of this country.

All of Sandburg's early publications were books of poetry, most of which reflect his early life and his profound belief in the hope and promise of America: *Chicago Poems* (1915), *Smoke and Steel* (1920), and *The People, Yes* (1936). His *Complete Poems* (1950) received the Pulitzer Prize. One other book of poetry deserves special mention — *The American Songbag* (1927), his collection of American folksongs, which he sings to his own accompaniment on the guitar. He has often earned his living and delighted audiences all over America by singing these songs.

But while poetry is in many ways his main concern — even, according to many critics, when he writes prose — the great project of Sandburg's life has been his study of Abraham Lincoln. He has spent the better part of fifty years reading, thinking, and writing about Lincoln, who, like him, came from a poverty-stricken, unproductive background in early Illinois.

When *Abraham Lincoln: The War Years* was published in 1939, the Pulitzer Prize committee was in a quandary. Here was by all odds the best book about Lincoln and the best biography of the year; but according to Joseph Pulitzer's rules, no biography of either Lincoln or Washington can win the prize for biography. So the committee gave Sandburg the Pulitzer Prize for history.

The connection between these facts and the presence in this book of a selection by Carl Sandburg, who is a poet, ballad singer, and biographer rather than an essayist, is this. In 1924, when he had finished *Abraham Lincoln: The Prairie Years*, the first part of his great work, he wrote a preface which "would begin at the death of Lincoln and work back to the day he left Illinois. The reader could then turn to the book and begin with the birth of Lincoln." When Sandburg decided to write *The War Years*, he discarded the early preface, which is reprinted here. This Lincoln preface is a moving, poetic sketch of the last years of a great American. It should inspire you to read further in Sandburg's *Lincoln*, either in the wonderful six-volume biography or in the one-volume life, published in the autumn of 1954.

The poetic style of this preface, the warm human approach to a great man, and the intimate knowledge of the Civil War President are carried on, incredibly, through all of Sandburg's volumes about Lincoln. Those who have not seen any of these books are fortunate to get here a brief glimpse of Sandburg's magical treatment of his great subject.

A LINCOLN PREFACE

In the time of the April lilacs in the year 1865, a man in the City of Washington, D.C., trusted a guard to watch at a door, and the guard was careless, left the door, and the man was shot, lingered a night, passed away, was laid in a box, and carried north and west a thousand miles; bells sobbed; cities wore crepe; people stood with hats off as the railroad burial car came past at midnight, dawn, or noon.

During the four years of time before he gave up the ghost, this man was clothed with despotic power, commanding the most powerful armies till then assembled in modern warfare, enforcing drafts of soldiers, abolishing the right of habeas corpus, directing politically and spiritually the wild, massive forces loosed in civil war.

Four billion dollars' worth of property was taken from those who had been legal owners of it, confiscated, wiped out as by fire, at his instigation and executive direction; a class of chattel property recognized as lawful for two hundred years went to the scrap pile.

When the woman who wrote *Uncle Tom's Cabin* came to see him in the White House, he greeted her, "So you're the little woman who wrote the book that made this great war," and as they seated themselves at a fireplace, "I do love an open fire; I always had one to home." As they were finishing their talk of the days of blood, he said, "I shan't last long after it's over."

An Illinois Congressman looked in on him as he had his face lathered for a shave in the White House, and remarked, "If anybody had told me that in a great crisis like this the people were going out to a little one-horse town and pick out a one-horse lawyer for President, I wouldn't have believed it." The answer was, "Neither would I. But it was a time when a man with a policy would have been fatal to the country. I never had a policy. I have simply tried to do what seemed best each day, as each day came."

"I don't intend precisely to throw the Constitution overboard, but I will stick it in a hole if I can," he told a Cabinet officer. The enemy was violating the Constitution to destroy the Union, he argued, and therefore, "I will violate the Constitution, if necessary, to save the Union." He instructed a messenger to the Secretary of the Treasury, "Tell him not to bother himself about the Constitution. Say that I have that sacred instrument here at the White House, and I am guarding it with great care."

Until late in that campaign of 1864, he expected to lose the November election; military victories brought the tide his way; the vote was 2,200,000 for him and 1,800,000 against him. Among those who bitterly fought him politically, and accused him of blunders or crimes, were Franklin Pierce, a former President of the United States; Horatio Seymour, the governor of New York; Samuel F. B. Morse, inventor of the telegraph; Cyrus H. McCormick, inventor of the farm reaper; General George B. McClellan, a Democrat who had commanded the Army of the Potomac; and the Chicago *Times*, a daily newspaper. In all its essential propositions the Southern Confederacy had the moral support of powerful, respectable elements throughout the North, probably more than a million voters believing in the justice of the cause of the South as compared with the North.

While propagandas raged, and the war winds howled, he sat in the White House, the Stubborn Man of History, writing that the Mississippi was one river and could not belong to two countries, that the plans for railroad connection from coast to coast must be pushed through and the Union Pacific realized.

His life, mind, and heart ran on contrasts. When his white kid gloves broke into tatters while shaking hands at a White House reception, he remarked, "This looks like a general bustification." When he talked with an Ohio friend one day during the 1864 campaign, he mentioned one public man, and murmured, "He's a thistle! I don't see why God lets

him live." Of a devious senator, he said, " He's too crooked
to lie still! " And of a New York editor, " In early life in
the West, we used to make our shoes last a great while with
much mending, and sometimes, when far gone, we found the
leather so rotten the stitches would not hold. Greeley is so
rotten that nothing can be done with him. He is not truthful;
the stitches all tear out." As he sat in the telegraph office of
the War Department, reading cipher dispatches, and came
to the words, Hosanna and Husband, he would chuckle,
" Jeffy D.," and at the words, Hunter and Happy, " Bobby
Lee."

While the luck of war wavered and broke and came again,
as generals failed and campaigns were lost, he held enough
forces of the Union together to raise new armies and supply
them, until generals were found who made war as victorious war has always been made, with terror, frightfulness,
destruction, and valor and sacrifice past words of man to tell.

A slouching, gray-headed poet, haunting the hospitals at
Washington, characterized him as " the grandest figure on
the crowded canvas of the drama of the nineteenth century
— a Hoosier Michelangelo."

His own speeches, letters, telegrams, and official messages
during that war form the most significant and enduring document from any one man on why the war began, why it
went on, and the dangers beyond its end. He mentioned
" the politicians," over and again " the politicians," with
scorn and blame. As the platoons filed before him at a review of an army corps, he asked, " What is to become of
these boys when the war is over? "

He was a chosen spokesman; yet there were times he was
silent; nothing but silence could at those times have fitted a
chosen spokesman; in the mixed shame and blame of the immense wrongs of two crashing civilizations, with nothing

to say, he said nothing, slept not at all, and wept at those times in a way that made weeping appropriate, decent, majestic.

His hat was shot off as he rode alone one night in Washington; a son he loved died as he watched at the bed; his wife was accused of betraying information to the enemy, until denials from him were necessary; his best companion was a fine-hearted and brilliant son with a deformed palate and an impediment of speech; when a Pennsylvania congressman told him the enemy had declared they would break into the city and hang him to a lamp post, he said he had considered " the violent preliminaries " to such a scene; on his left thumb was a scar where an ax had nearly chopped the thumb off when he was a boy; over one eye was a scar where he had been hit with a club in the hands of a Negro trying to steal the cargo off a Mississippi River flatboat; he threw a cashiered officer out of his room in the White House, crying, " I can bear censure, but not insult. I never wish to see your face again."

As he shook hands with the correspondent of the London *Times*, he drawled, " Well, I guess the London *Times* is about the greatest power on earth — unless perhaps it is the Mississippi River." He rebuked with anger a woman who got on her knees to thank him for a pardon that saved her son from being shot at sunrise; and when an Iowa woman said she had journeyed out of her way to Washington just for a look at him, he grinned, " Well, in the matter of looking at one another, I have altogether the advantage."

He asked his Cabinet to vote on the high military command, and after the vote, told them the appointment had already been made; one Cabinet officer, who had been governor of Ohio, came away personally baffled and frustrated from an interview, to exclaim, to a private secretary, " That man is the most cunning person I ever saw in my life "; an Illinois lawyer who had been sent on errands carrying his political secrets, said, " He is a trimmer and such a trimmer as the world has never seen."

He manipulated the admission of Nevada as a state in the Union, when her votes were needed for the Emancipation Proclamation, saying, " It is easier to admit Nevada than to raise another million of soldiers." At the same time he went to the office of a former New York editor, who had become Assistant Secretary of War, and said the votes of three congressmen were wanted for the required three-quarters of votes in the House of Representatives, advising, " There are three that you can deal with better than anybody else. . . . Whatever promise you make to those men, I will perform it." And in the same week, he said to a Massachusetts politician that two votes were lacking, and, " Those two votes must be procured. I leave it to you to determine how it shall be done; but remember that I am President of the United States and clothed with immense power, and I expect you to procure those votes." And while he was thus employing every last resource and device of practical politics to constitutionally abolish slavery, the abolitionist Henry Ward Beecher attacked him with javelins of scorn and detestation in a series of editorials that brought from him the single comment, " Is thy servant a dog? "

When the King of Siam sent him a costly sword of exquisite embellishment, and two elephant tusks, along with letters and a photograph of the King, he acknowledged the gifts in a manner as lavish as the Orientals. Addressing the King of Siam as " Great and Good Friend," he wrote thanks for each of the gifts, including " also two elephants' tusks of length and magnitude such as indicate they could have belonged only to an animal which was a native of Siam." After further thanks for the tokens received, he closed the letter to the King of Siam with strange grace and humor, saying, "I appreciate most highly your Majesty's tender of good offices in forwarding to this Government a stock from which a supply of elephants might be raised on our soil. . . . Our political jurisdiction, however, does not reach a latitude so low as to favor the multiplication of the elephant, and steam on land as well as water has been our best agent of transportation. . . . Meantime, wishing for your Majesty a long and happy life, and, for the generous and emulous people of Siam, the highest possibly prosperity, I commend both to the blessing of Almighty God."

He sent hundreds of telegrams, "Suspend death sentence," or "Suspend execution" of So-and-So, who was to be shot at sunrise. The telegrams varied oddly at times, as in one, "If Thomas Samplogh, of the First Delaware Regiment, has been sentenced to death, and is not yet executed, suspend and report the case to me." And another, "Is it Lieut. Samuel B. Davis whose death sentence is commuted? If not done, let it be done."

While the war drums beat, he liked best of all the stories told of him, one of two Quakeresses heard talking in a railway car. "I think that Jefferson will succeed." "Why does thee think so?" "Because Jefferson is a praying man." "And so is Abraham a praying man." "Yes, but the Lord will think Abraham is joking."

An Indiana man at the White House heard him say, "Voorhees, don't it seem strange to you that I, who could never so much as cut off the head of a chicken, should be elected, or selected, into the midst of all this blood?"

A party of American citizens, standing in the ruins of the Forum in Rome, Italy, heard there the news of the first assassination of the first American dictator, and took it as a sign of the growing up and the aging of the civilization on the North American continent. Far out in Coles County,

Illinois, a beautiful, gaunt old woman in a log cabin said, "I knowed he'd never come back."

Of men taking too fat profits out of the war, he said, "Where the carcass is, there will the eagles be gathered together."

An enemy general, Longstreet, after the war, declared him to have been "the one matchless man in forty millions of people," while one of his private secretaries, Hay, declared his life to have been the most perfect in its relationships and adjustments since that of Christ.

Between the days in which he crawled as a baby on the dirt floor of a Kentucky cabin, and the time when he gave his final breath in Washington, he packed a rich life with work, thought, laughter, tears, hate, love.

With vast reservoirs of the comic and the droll, and notwithstanding a mastery of mirth and nonsense, he delivered a volume of addresses and letters of terrible and serious appeal, with import beyond his own day, shot through here and there with far, thin ironics, with paragraphs having raillery of the quality of the Book of Job, and echoes as subtle as the whispers of wind in prairie grass.

Perhaps no human clay-pot has held more laughter and tears.

The facts and myths of his life are to be an American possession, shared widely over the world, for thousands of years, as the tradition of Knute or Alfred, Lao-tse or Diogenes, Pericles or Caesar, are kept. This because he was not only a genius in the science of neighborly human relationships and an artist in the personal handling of life from day to day, but a strange friend and a friendly stranger to all forms of life that he met.

He lived fifty-six years of which fifty-two were lived in the West — the prairie years.

STUDYING THE ESSAY

1. In what ways does Sandburg show the humanity of Lincoln?

2. Has this essay changed your idea of Lincoln?

3. This essay and " Mary White " are both about the life and death of a loved person. How do Sandburg and William Allen White compare in their approach to their subjects?

4. This essay leads the reader to the beginning of Sandburg's great biography of Lincoln. Find *Abraham Lincoln: The Prairie Years* in your school library and read Chapter 11 — the death of Lincoln's mother — as a companion piece to the essay.

5. Read Walt Whitman's poetic tribute to Lincoln, " When Lilacs Last in the Dooryard Bloomed " and compare the two writers' feelings about Lincoln.

6. Discuss Lincoln's humor.

7. Look up the following words in your dictionary: *elegy, eulogy, dirge, threnody*. Which of these apply to Sandburg's essay?

COMPOSITION TOPICS

1. The Lincoln I Have Come to Know
2. The Personality of the American Hero

E. M. FORSTER, 1879–

        Edward Morgan Forster has had two distinguished careers — the first as a novelist, the second as an essayist. Both careers indicate that he is one of the outstanding men of letters in our time.

After his education at King's College, Cambridge, was completed, Forster moved to Italy. Later he lived in India and Greece. Foreign backgrounds are evident in some of his novels. Between 1905, when *Where Angels Fear to Tread* appeared, until 1924, when *A Passage to India,* his most widely read novel, was published, he was largely a writer of fiction. His use of the " stream-of-consciousness " technique in describing the thoughts rather than the actions of his characters had a notable effect on other writers. Forster's novels, even though they cannot be discussed here, should at least be looked at by the literary-minded student.

Since 1925, Forster has turned more and more to the essay and to the lecture as mediums of expression. *Abinger Harvest* (1936) was his first collection of essays; *Two Cheers for Democracy* (1951), from which the two essays here are taken, is his latest. In his preface to *Two Cheers,* Forster describes the book as follows:

" The opening section, 'The Second Darkness,' concentrates on the war which began for Great Britain in 1939, though earlier elsewhere, and which is still going on. Subjects such as Anti-Semitism, the Nazis, Liberty, the Censorship are here discussed. The climate is political, and the conclusion suggested is that, though we cannot be expected to love one another, we must learn to put up with one another. Otherwise we shall all of us perish." " Tolerance," the first of the two essays in this book, appears in this part of *Two Cheers for Democracy.*

The preface continues: "The second section, 'What I Believe,' covers the same period as the first and sometimes the same subjects, but its climate is ethical and esthetic. . . . I have found by experience that the arts act as an antidote against our present troubles and also as a support to our common humanity, and I am glad to emphasize this at a time when they are being belittled and starved." This second part of a brilliant book includes, besides "Julius Caesar," short essays and speeches mostly about art, music, and literature.

The reader of Forster's essays finds, first of all, a tremendously broad range of interest and a deep sense of the importance of culture. The reader also finds everywhere a strong love of freedom, a deep concern for the sensible building of a world in which human values can be appreciated. Forster's sincerity and his clear thinking are evident on every page. The reader should note that both of these essays were written during World War II — a time when tolerance and primary school dramatics were seldom uppermost in men's minds.

What particularly distinguishes Forster, however, is his style. As a writer Forster is graceful, clear, often humorous. No great effort of mind is required to understand this man. But the reader who is meeting Forster for the first time must note that the simplicity of the style is deceptive: the language may be easy, but the thoughts are often big thoughts. Obviously Forster is not the only writer who has had big thoughts; many others have, and many others have couched their thoughts in "big" — formal — English. The brilliance of writers like Forster and E. B. White is that they are supremely successful in using simple, informal language to express big ideas about man and the world in which he lives.

Students who enjoy these essays are urged to try others. Some very entertaining and rewarding selections are these: "My Wood," "Liberty in England," and "Notes on the English Character," from *Abinger Harvest;* "George Orwell" and "Not Listening to Music," from *Two Cheers for Democracy.* Other students will enjoy a novel like *A Passage to India* or short stories in the volume called *The Celestial Omnibus.*

[*1941*]

TOLERANCE

Everybody is talking about reconstruction. Our enemies have their schemes for a new order in Europe, maintained by their secret police, and we on our side talk of rebuilding London or England, or western civilization, and we make plans how this is to be done. Which is all very well, but when I hear such talk, and see the architects sharpening their pencils and the contractors getting out their estimates, and the statesmen marking out their spheres of influence, and everyone getting down to the job, a very famous text occurs to me: " Except the Lord build the house, they labor in vain who build it." Beneath the poetic imagery of these words lies a hard scientific truth, namely, unless you have a sound attitude of mind, a right psychology, you cannot construct or reconstruct anything that will endure. The text is true, not only for religious people, but for workers whatever their outlook, and it is significant that one of our historians, Dr. Arnold Toynbee, should have chosen it to preface his great study of the growth and decay of civilizations. Surely the only sound foundation for a civilization is a sound state of mind. Architects, contractors, international commissioners, marketing boards, broadcasting corporations will never, by themselves, build a new world. They must be inspired by the proper spirit, and there must be the proper spirit in the people for whom they are working. For instance, we shall never have a beautiful new London until people refuse to live in ugly houses. At present, they don't mind; they demand comfort, but are indifferent to civic beauty; indeed they have no taste. I live myself in a hideous block of flats, but I can't say it worries me, and until we are worried, all schemes for reconstructing London beautifully must automatically fail.

What though is the proper spirit? We agree that the basic problem is psychological, that the Lord must build if the work is to stand, that there must be a sound state of mind before diplomacy or economics or trade-conferences can function. But what state of mind is sound? Here we may differ. Most people, when asked what spiritual quality is needed to rebuild civilization, will reply " Love." Men must love one another, they say; nations must do likewise, and then the series of cataclysms which is threatening to destroy us will be checked.

Respectfully but firmly, I disagree. Love is a great force in private life; it is indeed the greatest of all things: but love in public affairs does not work. It has been tried again and again: by the Christian civilizations of the Middle Ages, and also by the French Revolution, a secular movement which reasserted the Brotherhood of Man. And it has always failed. The idea that nations should love one another, or that business concerns or marketing boards should love one another, or that a man in Portugal should love a man in Peru of whom he has never heard — it is absurd, unreal, dangerous. It leads us into perilous and vague sentimentalism. " Love is what is needed," we chant, and then sit back and the world goes on as before. The fact is we can only love what we know personally. And we cannot know much. In public affairs, in the rebuilding of civilization, something much less dramatic and emotional is needed, namely, tolerance. Tolerance is a very dull virtue. It is boring. Unlike love, it has always had a bad press. It is negative. It merely means putting up with people, being able to stand things. No one has ever written an ode to tolerance, or raised a statue to her. Yet this is the quality which will be most needed after the war. This is the sound state of mind which we are looking for. This is the only force which will enable different races and classes and interests to settle down together to the work of reconstruction.

The world is very full of people — appallingly full; it has never been so full before, and they are all tumbling over each other. Most of these people one doesn't know and some of them one doesn't like; doesn't like the color of their skins, say, or the shapes of their noses, or the way they blow them or don't blow them, or the way they talk, or their smell, or their clothes, or their fondness for jazz or their dislike of jazz, and so on. Well, what is one to do? There are two solutions. One of them is the Nazi solution. If you don't like people, kill them, banish them, segregate them, and then strut up and down proclaiming that you are the salt of the earth. The other way is much less thrilling, but it is on the whole the way of the democracies, and I prefer it. If you don't like people, put up with them as well as you can. Don't try to love them; you can't, you'll only strain yourself. But: try to tolerate them. On the basis of that tolerance a civilized future may be built. Certainly I can see no other foundation for the postwar world.

For what it will most need is the negative virtues: not being huffy, touchy, irritable, revengeful. I have lost all faith in positive militant ideals; they can so seldom be carried out without thousands of human beings getting maimed or imprisoned. Phrases like " I will purge this nation," " I will clean up this city," terrify and disgust me. They might not have mattered when the world was emptier: they are horrifying now, when one nation is mixed up with another, when one city cannot be organically separated from its neighbors. And, another point: reconstruction is unlikely to be rapid. I do not believe that we are psychologically fit for it, plan the architects never so wisely. In the long run, yes, perhaps: the history of our race justifies that hope. But civilization has its mysterious regressions, and it seems to me that we are fated now to be in one of them, and must recognize this and behave accordingly. Tolerance, I believe, will be imperative after the establishment of peace. It's always useful to take a concrete instance: and I have been asking myself how I should behave if, after peace was signed, I met Germans who had been fighting against us. I shouldn't try to love them: I shouldn't feel inclined. They have broken a window in my little ugly flat for one thing. But I shall try to tolerate them, because it is common sense, because in the postwar world we shall have to live with Germans. We can't exterminate them, any more than they have succeeded in exterminating the Jews. We shall have to put up with them, not for any lofty reason, but because it is the next thing that will have to be done.

I don't then regard tolerance as a great eternally established divine principle, though I might perhaps quote " In my Father's house are many mansions " in support of such a view. It is just a makeshift, suitable for an overcrowded and overheated planet. It carries on when love gives out, and love generally gives out as soon as we move away from our home and our friends, and stand among strangers in a queue for potatoes. Tolerance is wanted in the queue; otherwise we think, " Why will people be so slow? "; it is wanted in the tube, or " Why will people be so fat? "; it is wanted at the telephone, or " Why are they so deaf? " or conversely, " Why do they mumble? " It is wanted in the street, in the office, at the factory, and it is wanted above all between classes, races, and nations. It's dull. And yet it entails imagination. For you have all the time to be putting yourself in someone else's place. Which is a desirable spiritual exercise.

This ceaseless effort to put up with other people seems
tame, almost ignoble, so that it sometimes repels generous
natures, and I don't recall many great men who have recommended tolerance. St. Paul certainly did not. Nor did Dante.
However, a few names occur. Going back over two thousand years, and to India, there is the great Buddhist Emperor Asoka, who set up inscriptions recording not his own
exploits but the need for mercy and mutual understanding
and peace. Going back about four hundred years, to Holland, there is the Dutch scholar Erasmus, who stood apart
from the religious fanaticism of the Reformation and was
abused by both parties in consequence. In the same century
there was the Frenchman Montaigne, subtle, intelligent,
witty, who lived in his quiet country house and wrote essays which still delight and confirm the civilized. And England: there was John Locke, the philosopher; there was
Sydney Smith, the Liberal and liberalizing divine; there was
Lowes Dickinson, writer of *A Modern Symposium*, which
might be called the Bible of Tolerance. And Germany —
yes, Germany: there was Goethe. All these men testify to
the creed which I have been trying to express: a negative
creed, but necessary for the salvation of this crowded
jostling modern world.

Two more remarks. First it is very easy to see fanaticism
in other people, but difficult to spot in oneself. Take the
evil of racial prejudice. We can easily detect it in the Nazis;
their conduct has been infamous ever since they rose to
power. But we ourselves — are we guiltless? We are far less
guilty than they are. Yet is there no racial prejudice in the
British Empire? Is there no color question? I ask you to consider that, those of you to whom tolerance is more than a
pious word. My other remark is to forestall a criticism.
Tolerance is not the same as weakness. Putting up with people does not mean giving in to them. This complicates the

problem. But the rebuilding of civilization is bound to be complicated. I only feel certain that unless the Lord builds the house, they will labor in vain who build it. Perhaps, when the house is completed, love will enter it, and the greatest force in our private lives will also rule in public life.

STUDYING THE ESSAY

1. " In my Father's house are many mansions " is found in the fourteenth chapter of the Gospel According to St. John. Can you cite other Biblical quotations or stories which have something to do with the subject of tolerance?

2. According to Forster, why will love not solve the big problems of the world?

3. Discuss issues other than postwar reconstruction to which Forster's ideas about tolerance could be applied.

4. Why is tolerance a " dull " virtue?

5. Look up one or more of the men mentioned in the next-to-last paragraph of the essay and report to the class. (Consult your school librarian about where to look.)

6. Discuss this statement: " It is very easy to see fanaticism in other people, but difficult to spot in oneself."

7. State the central idea of the first paragraph in one sentence. How can this idea be applied to something familiar — life in school or at home, for instance?

8. Find examples of humor in the essay.

9. Compare Forster's point of view with that of Norman Cousins (" The First Citizens of the Atomic Age ").

10. Just what is meant by " Except the Lord build the house, they labor in vain who build it "?

11. Try to locate " Freedom " in *One Man's Meat*, by E. B. White. Read it and compare this essay with " Tolerance."

12. Look up *tolerance* and *toleration* in an unabridged dictionary. Discuss differences in the meanings of these two similar words.

13. Words to learn: *cataclysm, secular, regression, fanaticism.*

COMPOSITION TOPICS

1. Think about a situation with which you are familiar and in which misunderstanding or hard feeling exists. Write a composition discussing the probable effect of tolerance applied to this situation.

2. Retell in your own words the story of the good Samaritan. (See Luke 10: 30–37.) Compare this parable with Forster's essay.

[*1942*]

JULIUS CAESAR

While I was considering what to say about *Julius Caesar*, I happened to go to a school entertainment. It was a large primary school, and the boys mostly came from working class homes; little boys — the eldest couldn't have been fourteen. They acted some scenes out of this very play. They did not act them well — how should they? They had not had the time to rehearse, they forgot their words and said them too fast, also there was not the money to buy properties with: the Roman Senators wore towels and curtains and anything they could scrounge and a solitary garland of green cardboard was handed from Caesar to Brutus and from Brutus to Antony as the occasion required. The audience was more interested in identifying their offspring than in following the plot. Remarks could be heard such as, " There he is, that one's Tom," and there were squeals from babies who were lifted up in their mothers' arms to see better, and seemed critical of what they saw. I was critical myself — yet I had an odd feeling of pleasure and of awe, and certain words of Cassius after the murder came into my mind.

> How many ages hence
> Shall this our lofty scene be acted o'er,
> In states unborn and accents yet unknown!

If Shakespeare had been present with us in that school, he might not have been flattered but he would not have been surprised, for what he expected to occur has occurred: the play lives.

> O Julius Caesar! thou art mighty yet!
> Thy spirit walks abroad.

It was walking with us as well as circumstances permitted: it was part of the civilization of England and of all who read English.

The general immortality of Shakespeare is too vast a subject. Let us keep to this particular play. Why has it caught on? It is about some old Romans who murdered one of their number and were finally defeated by his friends. The incident was chronicled by a Greek historian, Plutarch, and Shakespeare read a translation of it and turned out a play somewhere about 1600. It seems to have been a success from the first. And we today, though we may not rank it with the Great Four — *Hamlet, Othello, Lear, Macbeth* — always hail it as a typical example of his genius, and are excited when the curtain rises.

It is exciting — that is one reason for its popularity. Although it is not carefully constructed like a Greek play or a classical French play, although it is not as cunning in its advance as *Othello* or *Macbeth*, yet it does succeed in startling us and holding us. It effects this by three well-timed explosions. The first of these explosions is of course the murder itself. The preparation for this is masterly — the growth of the conspiracy, omens, storms, apparitions, Portia's forebodings, Calpurnia's dream, the tempting of Caesar to the Senate House, the failure of Artemidorus to save him, the luring away of Antony: and then the deed. And the murder is followed by a second explosion: Antony's funeral speech. The excitement is revived and increased instead of dropping. After that indeed there is a lull and a failure to interest, until we come to the plains of Philippi and the third explosion: the quarrel in the tent between Brutus and Cassius. This is so unexpected, so natural psychologically and so touching that it produces a tremendous effect, and after it, his nerves all exhausted, Brutus beholds Caesar's ghost. I do not mean that these three explosions, these three famous scenes, are the only reason for the play's popularity. But they do provide the excitement, and if a drama does not excite the ordinary man it may satisfy its contemporaries, but it has no chance of being acted " in states unborn and accents yet unknown."

The second reason for popularity is the character drawing, and particularly the character of Brutus. Before I come to it, I am going to risk a generalization about Shakespeare. He was an Elizabethan dramatist, and I do not think the Elizabethans were conscientious over their characters; they would often alter them in the middle in order to get on with the play. Beaumont and Fletcher contain glaring examples of this. Good men become bad and then good again: traitors turn into heroes and vice versa without any internal justification. And Shakespeare sometimes does it too. There is an example — not a glaring one — in this play, in the character of Casca. Casca first appears as extremely polite and indeed servile to Caesar. " Peace ho! Caesar speaks," he cries. Then he shows himself to Brutus and Cassius as a sour blunt contradictious fellow, who snaps them up when they speak and is grumpy when they invite him to supper. You may say this is subtlety on Shakespeare's part, and that he is indicating that Casca is a dark horse. I don't think so. I don't think Shakespeare was bothering about Casca — he is merely concerned to make the action interesting and he alters the character at need. Later on, during the thunderstorm, Casca becomes different again; he walks about with a drawn sword, is deeply moved by the apparitions, and utters exalted poetry. At the murder-scene he wounds Caesar in the neck, and then we hear of him no more. His usefulness is over. Contrast Shakespeare here with a modern writer, like Tolstoy. Tolstoy is conscientious over his characters, he has a personal responsibility to each of them, he has a vital conception of them, and though they are full of contradictions, those contradictions are true to life. Contrast Casca with Dolohov in *War and Peace*. Shakespeare often doesn't mind about his people. And when I am reading him one of my difficulties is to detect when he does mind and when he doesn't. This may be heresy on my part, but it seems to me that a great deal of Shakespearean criticism is invalid because it assumes that his characters are real people, and are never put in just to make the play go. The play's the thing, I suggest.

It is delightful when the characters are real, when Shakespeare does bother about them. Brutus is real, so is Cassius, so is Antony, so perhaps is Caesar himself. Brutus is an intellectual who can do things, who is not (like Hamlet) hampered by doubts. He can do things — but he always does them wrong: his advice is invariably fatal, from the moment of the murder down to the battle of Philippi. He cannot realize that men seek their own interests, for he has never sought his own, he has lived nobly among noble thoughts, wedded to a noble wife. He is kind to his servant. Everything he does is touched with fineness. Yet Brutus is not frigid. He just avoids being a prig. We are able to take him to our hearts. And with him is associated the worldly but far from contemptible Cassius. Those two speak the same language though they sometimes use different words. And against them is opposed Mark Antony — brilliant, sensuous, devoted to Caesar, but heartless otherwise, and treacherous. These three support the play. The character of Caesar is — difficult: Shakespeare does not present him sympathetically. He makes a few fine remarks like

> It seems to me most strange that men should fear;
> Seeing that death, a necessary end,
> Will come when it will come.

But goes on to talk bombast and to assert that he and Danger

> . . . are two lions litter'd in one day,
> And I the elder and more terrible.

Do you detect a contemporary voice here? I do. It is Mussolini's. His infirmities are insisted on: his epilepsy, his deafness. He is pompous, conceited, showing off, dictatorial. Indeed, some modern producers have stressed this and have presented *Julius Caesar* as a study in Fascism. But when Caesar is dead, his spirit is mighty, and haunts Brutus and wins. I don't know what to make of this. If Shakespeare were a modern writer I should be more clear about his conception. I should be certain that he has planned Caesar to be little in life and great in death. But, being an Elizabethan, is it possible that he may be altering Caesar as he alters Casca, for the sake of the play?

Excitement — and enough real people. Here are two of the reasons why *Julius Caesar* lives, and why, after more than three hundred years, it is acted by primary school boys. At the end of the performance to which I have referred, after Brutus, aged twelve, had suicided himself, and fallen with rather a thump, another of the children came forward, in his little brown suit, to speak the epilogue. The epilogue was not by Shakespeare. It ran as follows:

> I come to say our play is done
> We hope you have enjoyed the fun.

The child then retired. He had spoken briefly but justly. Shakespeare is fun. There are murders and ghosts, jealousy, remorse, despair, there is *Othello*, there is *Lear*, there is even *Timon of Athens* — but — how shall I put it? Shakespeare never grumbles. He denounces life but he never complains of it; he presents even its tragedies for our comprehension and enjoyment.

STUDYING THE ESSAY

1. Why would Shakespeare not have been flattered by the performance Forster saw? Why might Shakespeare say of this performance, however, "I told you so"?

2. Why is *Julius Caesar* still popular?

3. If you have read the play, describe in detail the "three well-timed explosions."

4. A member of the class should give a brief report on Mussolini in order to make clear the reasons why Forster compares him with Caesar.

5. What kind of essay is "Julius Caesar"? Refer to the Introduction (pp. ix–xv), if necessary.

6. Words to learn: *properties* (theatrical), *masterly*, *omen*, *apparition*, *foreboding*, *servile*, *subtlety*, *heresy*, *prig*, *sensuous*, *bombast*, *Fascism*.

COMPOSITION TOPICS

1. Amateur Shakespeare Performances I Have Seen
2. The Time I Played Brutus (or Cassius or Caesar or Antony)
3. Audiences, Good and Bad

HELEN KELLER, 1880–

No reader who even pretends to follow current writing is ignorant of the facts concerning the adventurous life of Helen Adams Keller. Left deaf and blind at nineteen months after an illness, she was also dumb, since there seemed no way to teach her to speak. But today she is known everywhere for her achievements, because Miss Anne Sullivan (Mrs. John A. Macy) made her a part of the world of people by teaching her how to communicate with the world about her. Forty-six years of devotion earned Mrs. Macy the title of "the other half of Helen Keller."

A wise aunt of Helen's had said of the little girl who was blind, deaf, and dumb, "This child has more sense than all the Kellers if there is ever any way to reach her mind." In 1887, Miss Sullivan came to Tuscumbia, Alabama, where Helen Keller was born, to take charge of the child's training. How Helen learned the first word, "water," is a thrilling story. Miss Sullivan says: "One day we went to the pump house. I made Helen hold her mug under the spout while I pumped. As the cold water gushed forth, I spelled 'w-a-t-e-r' several times. [Miss Sullivan had worked out a system of spelling words by tracing them on the palm of Helen's hand. As an example, she would pour some water on Helen's hand and then trace out a series of letters on Helen's palm until her pupil realized that the letters represented the substance which she had just felt.] All the way back to the house she was highly excited, and learned the name of every object she touched. In a few hours she had added thirty new words to her vocabulary."

This inspiration of Miss Sullivan lasted until 1936, when the amazing teacher died. During these years Miss Keller received a diploma from Radcliffe College and since then has been awarded honorary degrees by universities all over the world. Since the early thirties she has traveled and lectured widely. After World War II she visited veterans' hospitals throughout the United States and since 1946 has toured Europe, Africa, and the Far East on behalf of the blind. Wherever she has gone, she has been an inspiration to everyone who has had the privilege to see her.

Miss Keller's life and interests may be read in *The Story of My Life* (1902), *The World I Live In* (1908), and the many articles she has contributed to magazines. "Three Days to See" was written for the *Atlantic Monthly*. Certainly one agrees with Mark Twain's statement to her: "You are a wonderful creature — you and your other half together — Miss Sullivan, I mean, for it took the pair of you to make a complete and perfect whole."

THREE DAYS TO SEE

All of us have read thrilling stories in which the hero had only a limited and specified time to live. Sometimes it was as long as a year; sometimes as short as twenty-four hours. But always we were interested in discovering just how the doomed man chose to spend his last days or his last hours. I speak, of course, of free men who have a choice, not condemned criminals whose sphere of activities is strictly delimited.

Such stories set us thinking, wondering what we should do under similar circumstances. What events, what experiences, what associations should we crowd into those last hours as mortal beings? What happiness should we find in reviewing the past, what regrets?

Sometimes I have thought it would be an excellent rule to live each day as if we should die tomorrow. Such an attitude would emphasize sharply the values of life. We should live each day with a gentleness, a vigor, and a keenness of appreciation which are often lost when time stretches before us in the constant panorama of more days and months and years to come. There are those, of course, who would adopt the epicurean motto of "Eat, drink, and be merry," but most people would be chastened by the certainty of impending death.

In stories, the doomed hero is usually saved at the last minute by some stroke of fortune, but almost always his sense of values is changed. He becomes more appreciative of the meaning of life and its permanent spiritual values. It has often been noted that those who live, or have lived, in the shadow of death bring a mellow sweetness to everything they do.

Most of us, however, take life for granted. We know that one day we must die, but usually we picture that day as far in the future. When we are in buoyant health, death is all but unimaginable. We seldom think of it. The days stretch out in an endless vista. So we go about our petty tasks, hardly aware of our listless attitude toward life.

The same lethargy, I am afraid, characterizes the use of all our faculties and senses. Only the deaf appreciate hearing, only the blind realize the manifold blessings that lie in sight. Particularly does this observation apply to those who have lost sight and hearing in adult life. But those who have never suffered impairment of sight or hearing seldom make the fullest use of these blessed faculties. Their eyes and ears take in all sights and sounds hazily, without concentration, and with little appreciation. It is the same old story of not being grateful for what we have until we lose it, of not being conscious of health until we are ill.

I have often thought it would be a blessing if each human being were stricken blind and deaf for a few days at some time during his early adult life. Darkness would make him more appreciative of sight; silence would teach him the joys of sound.

Now and then I have tested my seeing friends to discover what they see. Recently I was visited by a very good friend who had just returned from a long walk in the woods, and I asked her what she had observed. "Nothing in particular," she replied. I might have been incredulous had I not been accustomed to such responses, for long ago I became convinced that the seeing see little.

How was it possible, I asked myself, to walk for an hour through the woods and see nothing worthy of note? I who cannot see find hundreds of things to interest me through mere touch. I feel the delicate symmetry of a leaf. I pass my hands lovingly about the smooth skin of a silver birch, or the rough shaggy bark of a pine. In spring I touch the branches of trees hopefully in search of a bud, the first sign of awakening Nature after her winter's sleep. I feel the delightful, velvety texture of a flower, and discover its remarkable convolutions; and something of the miracle of Nature is revealed to me. Occasionally, if I am very fortunate, I place my hand gently on a small tree and feel the happy quiver of a bird in full song. I am delighted to have the cool waters of a brook rush through my open fingers. To me a lush carpet of pine needles or spongy grass is more welcome than the most luxurious Persian rug. To me the pageant of seasons is a thrilling and unending drama, the action of which streams through my finger tips.

At times my heart cries out with longing to see all these things. If I can get so much pleasure from mere touch, how much more beauty must be revealed by sight. Yet, those who have eyes apparently see little. The panorama of color and action which fills the world is taken for granted. It is human, perhaps, to appreciate little that which we have and to long for that which we have not, but it is a great pity that in the world of light the gift of sight is used only as a mere convenience rather than as a means of adding fullness to life.

If I were the president of a university I should establish a compulsory course in "How to Use Your Eyes." The professor would try to show his pupils how they could add joy to their lives by really seeing what passes unnoticed before them. He would try to awake their dormant and sluggish faculties.

Perhaps I can best illustrate by imagining what I should most like to see if I were given the use of my eyes, say, for just three days. And while I am imagining, suppose you, too, set your mind to work on the problem of how you would use your own eyes if you had only three more days to see. If with the oncoming darkness of the third night you knew that the sun would never rise for you again, how would you spend those three precious intervening days? What would you most want to let your gaze rest upon?

I, naturally, should want most to see the things which have become dear to me through my years of darkness. You, too, would want to let your eyes rest long on the things that have become dear to you so that you could take the memory of them with you into the night that loomed before you.

If, by some miracle, I were granted three seeing days, to be followed by a relapse into darkness, I should divide the period into three parts.

On the first day, I should want to see the people whose kindness and gentleness and companionship have made my life worth living. First I should like to gaze long upon the face of my dear teacher, Mrs. Anne Sullivan Macy, who came to me when I was a child and opened the outer world to me. I should want not merely to see the outline of her face, so that I could cherish it in my memory, but to study that face and find in it the living evidence of the sympathetic tenderness and patience with which she accomplished the difficult task of my education. I should like to see in her eyes that strength of character which has enabled her to stand firm in the face of difficulties, and that compassion for all humanity which she has revealed to me so often.

I do not know what it is to see into the heart of a friend through that " window of the soul," the eye. I can only " see " through my finger tips the outline of a face. I can detect laughter, sorrow, and many other obvious emotions. I know my friends from the feel of their faces. But I cannot really picture their personalities by touch. I know their personalities, of course, through other means, through the thoughts they express to me, through whatever of their actions are revealed to me. But I am denied that deeper understanding of them which I am sure would come through sight of them, through watching their reactions to various expressed thoughts and circumstances, through noting the immediate and fleeting reactions of their eyes and countenance.

Friends who are near to me I know well, because through the months and years they reveal themselves to me in all their phases; but of casual friends I have only an incomplete impression, an impression gained from a handclasp, from spoken words which I take from their lips with my finger tips, or which they tap into the palm of my hand.

How much easier, how much more satisfying it is for you who can see to grasp quickly the essential qualities of another person by watching the subtleties of expression, the quiver of a muscle, the flutter of a hand. But does it ever occur to you to use your sight to see into the inner nature of a friend or acquaintance? Do not most of you seeing people grasp casually the outward features of a face and let it go at that?

For instance, can you describe accurately the faces of five good friends? Some of you can, but many cannot. As an experiment, I have questioned husbands of long standing about the color of their wives' eyes, and often they express embarrassed confusion and admit that they do not know. And, incidentally, it is a chronic complaint of wives that their husbands do not notice new dresses, new hats, and changes in household arrangements.

The eyes of seeing persons soon become accustomed to the routine of their surroundings, and they actually see only the startling and spectacular. But even in viewing the most spectacular sights the eyes are lazy. Court records reveal every day how inaccurately " eyewitnesses " see. A given event will be " seen " in several different ways by as many witnesses. Some see more than others, but few see everything that is within the range of their vision.

Oh, the things that I should see if I had the power of sight for just three days!

The first day would be a busy one. I should call to me all my dear friends and look long into their faces, imprinting upon my mind the outward evidences of the beauty that is within them. I should let my eyes rest, too, on the face of a baby, so that I could catch a vision of the eager, innocent beauty which precedes the individual's consciousness of the conflicts which life develops.

And I should like to look into the loyal, trusting eyes of my dogs — the grave, canny little Scottie, Darkie, and the stalwart, understanding great Dane, Helga, whose warm, tender, and playful friendships are so comforting to me.

On that busy first day I should also view the small simple things of my home. I want to see the warm colors in the rugs under my feet, the pictures on the walls, the intimate trifles that transform a house into home. My eyes would rest respectfully on the books in raised type which I have read, but they would be more eagerly interested in the printed books which seeing people can read, for during the long night of my life the books I have read and those which have been read to me have built themselves into a great shining lighthouse, revealing to me the deepest channels of human life and the human spirit.

In the afternoon of that first seeing day, I should take a long walk in the woods and intoxicate my eyes on the beauties of the world of Nature, trying desperately to absorb in a few hours the vast splendor which is constantly unfolding itself to those who can see. On the way home from my woodland jaunt my path would lie near a farm so that I might see the patient horses plowing in the field (perhaps I should see only a tractor!) and the serene content of men living close to the soil. And I should pray for the glory of a colorful sunset.

When dusk had fallen, I should experience the double delight of being able to see by artificial light, which the genius of man has created to extend the power of his sight when Nature decrees darkness.

In the night of that first day of sight, I should not be able to sleep, so full would be my mind of the memories of the day.

The next day — the second day of sight — I should arise with the dawn and see the thrilling miracle by which night is transformed into day. I should behold with awe the magnificent panorama of light with which the sun awakens the sleeping earth.

This day I should devote to a hasty glimpse of the world,

past and present. I should want to see the pageant of man's progress, the kaleidoscope of the ages. How can so much be compressed into one day? Through the museums, of course. Often I have visited the New York Museum of Natural History to touch with my hands many of the objects there exhibited, but I have longed to see with my eyes the condensed history of the earth and its inhabitants displayed there — animals and the races of men pictured in their native environment; gigantic carcasses of dinosaurs and mastodons which roamed the earth long before man appeared, with his tiny stature and powerful brain, to conquer the animal kingdom; realistic presentations of the processes of evolution in animals, in man, and in the implements which man has used to fashion for himself a secure home on this planet; and a thousand and one other aspects of natural history.

I wonder how many readers of this article have viewed this panorama of the face of living things as pictured in that inspiring museum. Many, of course, have not had the opportunity, but I am sure that many who *have* had the opportunity have not made use of it. There, indeed, is a place to use your eyes. You who see can spend many fruitful days there, but I, with my imaginary three days of sight, could only take a hasty glimpse, and pass on.

My next stop would be the Metropolitan Museum of Art, for just as the Museum of Natural History reveals the material aspects of the world, so does the Metropolitan show the myriad facets of the human spirit. Throughout the history of humanity the urge to artistic expression has been almost as powerful as the urge for food, shelter, and procreation. And here, in the vast chambers of the Metropolitan Museum, is unfolded before me the spirit of Egypt, Greece, and Rome, as expressed in their art. I know well through my hands the sculptured gods and goddesses of the ancient Nile-land. I have felt copies of Parthenon friezes, and I have sensed the rhythmic beauty of charging Athenian warriors. Apollos and Venuses and the Wingèd Victory of Samothrace are friends of my finger tips. The gnarled, bearded features of Homer are dear to me, for he, too, knew blindness.

My hands have lingered upon the living marble of Roman sculpture as well as that of later generations. I have passed my hands over a plaster cast of Michelangelo's inspiring and heroic Moses; I have sensed the power of Rodin; I have been awed by the devoted spirit of Gothic wood carving. These arts which can be touched have meaning for me, but even they were meant to be seen rather than felt, and I can only guess at the beauty which remains hidden from me. I can admire the simple lines of a Greek vase, but its figured decorations are lost to me.

So on this, my second day of sight, I should try to probe into the soul of man through his art. The things I knew through touch I should now see. More splendid still, the whole magnificent world of painting would be opened to me, from the Italian Primitives, with their serene religious devotion, to the Moderns, with their feverish visions. I should look deep into the canvases of Raphael, Leonardo da Vinci, Titian, Rembrandt. I should want to feast my eyes upon the warm colors of Veronese, study the mysteries of El Greco, catch a new vision of Nature from Corot. Oh, there is so much rich meaning and beauty in the art of the ages for you who have eyes to see!

Upon my short visit to this temple of art I should not be able to review a fraction of that great world of art which is open to you. I should be able to get only a superficial impression. Artists tell me that for a deep and true appreciation of art one must educate the eye. One must learn through experience to weigh the merits of line, of composition, of form and color. If I had eyes, how happily would I embark upon so fascinating a study! Yet I am told that, to many of you who have eyes to see, the world of art is a dark night, unexplored and unilluminated.

It would be with extreme reluctance that I should leave the Metropolitan Museum, which contains the key to beauty — a beauty so neglected. Seeing persons, however, do not need a Metropolitan to find this key to beauty. The same key lies waiting in smaller museums, and in books on the shelves of even small libraries. But naturally, in my limited time of imaginary sight, I should choose the place where the key unlocks the greatest treasures in the shortest time.

The evening of my second day of sight I should spend at a theater or at the movies. Even now I often attend theatrical performances of all sorts, but the action of the play must be spelled into my hand by a companion. But how I should like to see with my own eyes the fascinating figure of Hamlet, or the gusty Falstaff amid colorful Elizabethan trappings! How I should like to follow each movement of the graceful Hamlet, each strut of the hearty Falstaff! And since I could see only one play, I should be confronted by a many-horned dilemma, for there are scores of plays I should want to see. You who have eyes can see any you like. How many of you, I wonder, when you gaze at a play, a movie, or any spectacle, realize and give thanks for the miracle of sight which enables you to enjoy its color, grace, and movement?

I cannot enjoy the beauty of rhythmic movement except in a sphere restricted to the touch of my hands. I can vision only dimly the grace of a Pavlova, although I know something of the delight of rhythm, for often I can sense the beat of music as it vibrates through the floor. I can well imagine that cadenced motion must be one of the most pleasing sights in the world. I have been able to gather something of this by tracing with my fingers the lines in sculptured marble; if this static grace can be so lovely, how much more acute must be the thrill of seeing grace in motion.

One of my dearest memories is of the time when Joseph Jefferson allowed me to touch his face and hands as he went through some of the gestures and speeches of his beloved Rip Van Winkle. I was able to catch thus a meager glimpse of the world of drama, and I shall never forget the delight of that moment. But, oh, how much I must miss, and how much pleasure you seeing ones can derive from watching and hearing the interplay of speech and movement in the unfolding of a dramatic performance! If I could see only one play, I should know how to picture in my mind the action of a hundred plays which I have read or had transferred to me through the medium of the manual alphabet.

So, through the evening of my second imaginary day of sight, the great figures of dramatic literature would crowd sleep from my eyes.

The following morning, I should again greet the dawn, anxious to discover new delights, for I am sure that, for those who have eyes which really see, the dawn of each day must be a perpetually new revelation of beauty.

This, according to the terms of my imagined miracle, is to be my third and last day of light. I shall have no time to waste in regrets or longings; there is too much to see. The first day I devoted to my friends, animate and inanimate. The second revealed to me the history of man and Nature. Today I shall spend in the workaday world of the present, amid the haunts of men going about the business of life. And where can one find so many activities and conditions of men as in New York? So the city becomes my destination.

I start from my home in the quiet little suburb of Forest Hills, Long Island. Here, surrounded by green lawns, trees, and flowers, are neat little houses, happy with the voices and movements of wives and children, havens of peaceful rest for men who toil in the city. I drive across the lacy structure of steel which spans the East River, and I get a new and startling vision of the power and ingenuity of the mind of man. Busy boats chug and scurry about the river — racy speed boats, stolid, snorting tugs. If I had long days of sight ahead, I should spend many of them watching the delightful activity upon the river.

I look ahead, and before me rise the fantastic towers of New York, a city that seems to have stepped from the pages of a fairy story. What an awe-inspiring sight, these glittering spires, these vast banks of stone and steel — structures such as the gods might build for themselves! This animated picture is a part of the lives of millions of people every day. How many, I wonder, give it so much as a second glance? Very few, I fear. Their eyes are blind to this magnificent sight because it is so familiar to them.

I hurry to the top of one of those gigantic structures, the Empire State Building, for there, a short time ago, I "saw" the city below through the eyes of my secretary. I am anxious to compare my fancy with reality. I am sure I should not be disappointed in the panorama spread out before me, for to me it would be a vision of another world.

Now I begin my rounds of the city. First, I stand at a busy corner, merely looking at people, trying by sight of them to understand something of their lives. I see smiles, and I am happy. I see serious determination, and I am proud. I see suffering, and I am compassionate.

I stroll down Fifth Avenue. I throw my eyes out of focus so that I see no particular object but only a seething kaleidoscope of color. I am certain that the colors of women's dresses moving in a throng must be a gorgeous spectacle of which I should never tire. But perhaps if I had sight I should be like most other women — too interested in styles and the cut of individual dresses to give much attention to the splendor of color in the mass. And I am convinced, too, that I should become an inveterate window shopper, for it must be a delight to the eye to view the myriad articles of beauty on display.

From Fifth Avenue I make a tour of the city — to Park Avenue, to the slums, to factories, to parks where children play. I take a stay-at-home trip abroad by visiting the foreign quarters. Always my eyes are open wide to all the sights of both happiness and misery so that I may probe deep and add to my understanding of how people work and live. My heart is full of the images of people and things. My eye passes lightly over no single trifle; it strives to touch and hold closely each thing its gaze rests upon. Some sights are pleasant, filling the heart with happiness; but some are miserably pathetic. To these latter I do not shut my eyes, for they, too, are part of life. To close the eye on them is to close the heart and mind.

My third day of sight is drawing to an end. Perhaps there are many serious pursuits to which I should devote the few remaining hours, but I am afraid that on the evening of that last day I should again run away to the theater, to a hilariously funny play, so that I might appreciate the overtones of comedy in the human spirit.

At midnight my temporary respite from blindness would cease, and permanent night would close in on me again. Naturally in those three short days I should not have seen all I wanted to see. Only when darkness had again descended upon me should I realize how much I had left unseen. But my mind would be so crowded with glorious memories that I should have little time for regrets. Thereafter the touch of every object would bring a glowing memory of how that object looked.

Perhaps this short outline of how I should spend three days of sight does not agree with the program you would set for yourself if you knew that you were about to be stricken blind. I am, however, sure that if you actually faced that fate, your eyes would open to things you had never seen before, storing up memories for the long night ahead. You would use your eyes as never before. Everything you saw would become dear to you. Your eyes would touch and embrace every object that came within your range of vision. Then, at last, you would really see, and a new world of beauty would open itself before you.

I who am blind can give one hint to those who see — one admonition to those who would make full use of the gift of sight: Use your eyes as if tomorrow you would be stricken blind. And the same method can be applied to the other senses. Hear the music of voices, the song of a bird, the mighty strains of an orchestra, as if you would be stricken deaf tomorrow. Touch each object you want to touch as if tomorrow your tactile sense would fail. Smell the perfume of flowers, taste with relish each morsel, as if tomorrow you could never smell and taste again. Make the most of every sense; glory in all the facets of pleasure and beauty which the world reveals to you through the several means of contact which Nature provides. But of all the senses, I am sure that sight must be the most delightful.

STUDYING THE ESSAY

1. What does the essay make you think of the author? What sort of person must she be?

2. Compare this essay with Stevenson's " Aes Triplex." How

do the points of view of these two writers differ? How are they alike?

3. Consider these questions: When you look, do you see? When you listen, do you hear? How much have you allowed yourself to use your senses to the utmost?

4. What do you think of the author's plan for her three days of sight? What does she include that you might not include?

5. Have you been to a museum? To a symphony concert, even on television or radio? What do you remember of this experience?

6. Which sense is most valuable to man?

7. Words to learn: *lethargy, lush, subtleties, kaleidoscope.*

COMPOSITION TOPICS

1. The Seeing See Little
2. The Hearing Hear Little
3. Look out your window some day and put down on paper exactly what you see. You should be able to make a long theme out of what you see.
4. Take a familiar object, like a leaf, and try to write about it in such a way that anyone will know what you are describing.
5. Try this game. Put twenty objects on a table. Have several people look at these objects for, say, three minutes and then try to list what they have seen.

ROBERT BENCHLEY, 1887–1945

The foreword to *Inside Benchley* reads as follows: " While thumbing through some old snow which had accumulated in the attic last winter, I came quite by accident upon ten (10) or so volumes of prose works which I had dashed off during my career as a journalist (1915–7:45 P.M.). (Signed) Robert Benchley."

At the end of the same book of short humorous essays there are four appendixes lying in wait for the reader: (1) Glossary of kin, native, and technical terms in the Australian Bushman language, (2) Abbreviations of the books of the Bible, (3) Bibliography of books on psychiatry and sex, and (4) part of the *B* section of the New York City telephone directory.

These ridiculous things give one a partial idea of the kind of man Benchley was. The titles of some of his books also indicate the absurd humor he was capable of: *The Treasurer's Report, and Other Aspects of Community Singing; My Ten Years in a Quandary, and How They Grew; Twenty Thousand Leagues Under the Sea, or, David Copperfield; Benchley Beside Himself.* Incidentally, all of these books are as much fun to read as the titles are ludicrous.

Benchley was born in Worcester, Massachusetts, and was graduated from Harvard in 1912. He then immediately set out on a career in journalism. After an apprenticeship with the Curtis Publishing Company, *Vanity Fair*, the New York *Tribune*, and the New York *World*, he became dramatics editor of *Life*, one of the country's best humor magazines, which disappeared in 1936 when its name was sold to the publishers of the current picture magazine. From 1929 until his death he was a staff writer for the *New Yorker*, in company with Clarence

Day, E. B. White, James Thurber, and other writers represented in this book. For the movies he made about twenty-five "shorts," one of which, "How to Sleep," won an Academy award. He was also a frequent speaker, commentator, and director for radio. It is a pity that he died before the postwar boom in television, because the most delightful part of his readings and his "How to . . ." skits was seeing the man, with his perpetual embarrassed look, his confusion about facts, and his shy smile.

Benchley was an exceedingly modest man who actually considered himself a failure. He was often very vague and awkward in a group of people — characteristics which appear again and again in his essays. But he was immensely kind and generous, even to slight acquaintances. Far from being a failure, he was a brilliant dramatic critic, a humorist whose humor is always kind and usually very wise, a first-class actor, and a brilliant radio personality. In the essay reprinted here you will find both sense and nonsense. The two qualities help to account for his great and continuing popularity as a writer.

THE TOOTH, THE WHOLE TOOTH, AND NOTHING BUT THE TOOTH

Some well-known saying (it doesn't make much difference what) is proved by the fact that everyone likes to talk about his experiences at the dentist's. For years and years little articles like this have been written on the subject, little jokes like some that I shall presently make have been made, and people in general have been telling other people just what emotions they experience when they crawl into the old red plush guillotine.

They like to explain to each other how they feel when the dentist puts " that buzzer thing " against their bicuspids, and, if sufficiently pressed, they will describe their sensations on mouthing a rubber dam.

" I'll tell you what I hate," they will say with great relish, " when he takes that little nut-pick and begins to scrape. Ugh! "

" Oh, I'll tell you what's worse than that," says the friend, not to be outdone, " when he is poking around careless-like and strikes a nerve. Wow! "

And if there are more than two people at the experience-meeting, everyone will chip in and tell what he or she considers to be the worst phase of the dentist's work, all present enjoying the narration hugely and none so much as the narrator who has suffered so.

This sort of thing has been going on ever since the first mammoth gold tooth was hung out as a bait to folks in search of a good time. (By the way, when *did* the present obnoxious system of dentistry begin? It can't be so very long ago that the electric auger was invented, and where would a dentist be without an electric auger? Yet you never hear of Amalgam Filling Day, or any other anniversary in the dental year. There must be a conspiracy of silence on the part of the trade to keep hidden the names of the men who are responsible for all this.)

However many years it may be that dentists have been plying their trade, in all that time people have never tired of talking about their teeth. This is probably due to the inscrutable workings of Nature who is always supplying new teeth to talk about.

As a matter of fact, the actual time and suffering in the

chair is only a fraction of the gross expenditure connected with the affair. The preliminary period, about which nobody talks, is much the worse. This dates from the discovery of the wayward tooth and extends to the moment when the dentist places his foot on the automatic hoist which jacks you up into range. Giving gas for tooth-extraction is all very humane in its way, but the time for anesthetics is when the patient first decides that he must go to the dentist. From then on, until the first excavation is started, should be shrouded in oblivion.

There is probably no moment more appalling than that in which the tongue, running idly over the teeth in a moment of carefree play, comes suddenly upon the ragged edge of a space from which the old familiar filling has disappeared. The world stops and you look meditatively up to the corner of the ceiling. Then quickly you draw your tongue away, and try to laugh the affair off, saying to yourself:

" Stuff and nonsense, my good fellow! There is nothing the matter with your tooth. Your nerves are upset after a hard day's work, that's all."

Having decided this to your satisfaction, you slyly, and with a poor attempt at being casual, slide the tongue back along the line of adjacent teeth, hoping against hope that it will reach the end without mishap.

But there it is! There can be no doubt about it this time. The tooth simply has got to be filled by someone, and the only person who can fill it with anything permanent is a dentist. You wonder if you might not be able to patch it up yourself for the time being — a year or so — perhaps with a little spruce-gum and a coating of new-skin. It is fairly far back, and wouldn't have to be a very sightly job.

But this has an impracticable sound, even to you. You

might want to eat some peanut brittle (you never can tell when someone might offer you peanut brittle these days), and the new-skin, while serviceable enough in the case of cream soups and custards, couldn't be expected to stand up under heavy crunching.

So you admit that, since the thing has got to be filled, it might as well be a dentist who does the job.

This much decided, all that is necessary is to call him up and make an appointment.

Let us say that this resolve is made on Tuesday. That afternoon you start to look up the dentist's number in the telephone book. A great wave of relief sweeps over you when you discover that it isn't there. How can you be expected to make an appointment with a man who hasn't got a telephone? And how can you have a tooth filled without making an appointment? The whole thing is impossible, and that's all there is to it. God knows you did your best.

On Wednesday there is a slightly more insistent twinge, owing to bad management of a sip of ice water. You decide that you simply must get in touch with that dentist when you get back from lunch. But you know how those things are. First one thing and then another came up, and a man came in from Providence who had to be shown around the office, and by the time you had a minute to yourself it was five o'clock. And, anyway, the tooth didn't bother you again. You wouldn't be surprised if, by being careful, you could get along with it as it is until the end of the week when you will have more time. A man has to think of his business, after all, and what is a little personal discomfort in the shape of an unfilled tooth to the satisfaction of work well done in the office?

By Saturday morning you are fairly reconciled to going ahead, but it is only a half day and probably he has no appointments left, anyway. Monday is really the time. You can begin the week afresh. After all, Monday is really the logical day to start in going to the dentist.

Bright and early Monday morning you make another try at the telephone book, and find, to your horror, that some time between now and last Tuesday the dentist's name and number have been inserted into the directory. There it is. There is no getting around it: " Burgess, Jas. Kendal, DDS. . . . Courtland — 2654." There is really nothing left to do but to call him up. Fortunately the line is busy, which gives you a perfectly good excuse for putting it over until Tuesday. But on Tuesday luck is against you and you get a clear connection with the doctor himself. An appointment is arranged for Thursday afternoon at 3:30.

Thursday afternoon, and here it is only Tuesday morning! Almost anything may happen between now and then. We might declare war on Mexico, and off you'd have to go, dentist appointment or no dentist appointment. Surely a man couldn't let a date to have a tooth filled stand in the way of his doing his duty to his country. Or the social revolution might start on Wednesday, and by Thursday the whole town might be in ashes. You can picture yourself standing, Thursday afternoon at 3:30, on the ruins of the City Hall, fighting off marauding bands of reds, and saying to yourself, with a sigh of relief: " Only to think! At this time I was to have been climbing into the dentist's chair! " You never can tell when your luck will turn in a thing like that.

But Wednesday goes by and nothing happens. And Thursday morning dawns without even a word from the dentist saying that he has been called suddenly out of town to lecture before the Incisor Club. Apparently, everything is working against you.

By this time, your tongue has taken up a permanent resting place in the vacant tooth, and is causing you to talk indistinctly and incoherently. Somehow you feel that if the dentist opens your mouth and finds the tip of your tongue in the tooth, he will be deceived and go away without doing anything.

The only thing left is for you to call him up and say that you have just killed a man and are being arrested and can't possibly keep your appointment. But any dentist would see through that. He would laugh right into his transmitter at you. There is probably no excuse which it would be possible to invent which a dentist has not already heard eighty or ninety times. No, you might as well see the thing through now.

Luncheon is a ghastly rite. The whole left side of your jaw has suddenly developed an acute sensitiveness and the disaffection has spread to the four teeth on either side of the original one. You doubt if it will be possible for him to touch it at all. Perhaps all he intends to do this time is to look at it anyway. You might even suggest that to him. You could very easily come in again soon and have him do the actual work.

Three-thirty draws near. A horrible time of day at best. Just when a man's vitality is lowest. Before stepping in out of the sunlight into the building in which the dental parlor is, you take one look about you at the happy people scurrying by in the street. Carefree children that they are! What do they know of Life? Probably that man in the silly-looking hat never had trouble with so much as his baby teeth. There they go, pushing and jostling each other, just as if within ten feet of them there was not a man who stands on the brink of the Great Misadventure. Ah well! Life is like that!

Into the elevator. The last hope is gone. The door clangs and you look hopelessly about you at the stupid faces of your fellow passengers. How can people be so clownish? Of course, there is always the chance that the elevator will fall and that you will all be terribly hurt. But that is too much to expect. You dismiss it from your thoughts as too impractical, too visionary. Things don't work out as happily as that in real life.

You feel a certain glow of heroic pride when you tell the operator the right floor number. You might just as easily have told him a floor too high or too low, and that would, at least, have caused delay. But after all, a man must prove himself a man and the least you can do is to meet Fate with an unflinching eye and give the right floor number.

Too often has the scene in the dentist's waiting room been described for me to try to do it again here. They are all alike. The antiseptic smell, the ominous hum from the operating rooms, the ancient *Digests*, and the silent, sullen group of waiting patients, each trying to look unconcerned and cordially disliking everyone else in the room — all these have been sung by poets of far greater lyric powers than mine. (Not that I really think that they *are* greater than mine, but that's the customary form of excuse for not writing something you haven't got time or space to do. As a matter of fact, I think I could do it much better than it has ever been done before.)

I can only say that, as you sit looking, with unseeing eyes, through a large book entitled *The War in Pictures*, you would gladly change places with the most lowly of God's creatures. It is inconceivable that there should be anyone worse off than you, unless perhaps it is some of the poor wretches who are waiting with you.

That one over in the armchair, nervously tearing to shreds a copy of " The Dental Review and Practical Inlay Worker." She may have something frightful the trouble with her. She couldn't possibly look more worried. Perhaps it is very, very painful. This thought cheers you up considerably. What cowards women are in times like these!

And then there comes the sound of voices from the next room.

" All right, Doctor, and if it gives me any more pain shall I call you up? . . . Do you think that it will bleed much more? . . . Saturday morning, then, at eleven. . . . Good by, Doctor."

And a middle-aged woman emerges (all women are middle-aged when emerging from the dentist's office) looking as if she were playing the big emotional scene in *John Ferguson*. A wisp of hair waves dissolutely across her forehead between her eyes. Her face is pale, except for a slight inflammation at the corners of her mouth, and in her eyes is that faraway look of one who has been face to face with Life. But she is through. She should care how she looks.

The nurse appears, and looks inquiringly at each one in the room. Each one in the room evades the nurse's glance in one last, futile attempt to fool someone and get away without seeing the dentist. But she spots you and nods pleasantly. God, how pleasantly she nods! There ought to be a law against people being as pleasant as that.

" The doctor will see you now," she says.

The English language may hold a more disagreeable combination of words than " The doctor will see you now." I am willing to concede something to the phrase " Have you anything to say before the current is turned on? " That may be worse for the moment, but it doesn't last so long. For continued, unmitigating depression, I know nothing to equal " The doctor will see you now." But I'm not narrow-minded about it. I'm willing to consider other possibilities.

Smiling feebly, you trip over the extended feet of the man next to you, and stagger into the delivery room, where amid a ghastly array of death masks of teeth, blue flames waving eerily from Bunsen burners, and the drowning sound of perpetually running water which chokes and gurgles at intervals, you sink into the chair and close your eyes.

But now let us consider the spiritual exaltation that comes when you are at last let down and turned loose. It is all over, and what did it amount to? Why, nothing at all. A-ha-ha-ha-ha-ha! Nothing at all.

You suddenly develop a particular friendship for the dentist. A splendid fellow, really. You ask him questions about his instruments. What does he use this thing for, for instance? Well, well, to think of a little thing like that making all that trouble. A-ha-ha-ha-ha-ha! . . . And the dentist's family, how are they? Isn't that fine!

Gaily you shake hands with him and straighten your tie. Forgotten is the fact that you have another appointment with him for Monday. There is no such thing as Monday. You are through for today, and all's right with the world.

As you pass out through the waiting room, you leer at the others unpleasantly. The poor fishes! Why can't they take their medicine like grown people and not sit there moping as if they were going to be shot?

Heigh-ho! Here's the elevator man! A charming fellow! You wonder if he knows that you have just had a tooth filled. You feel tempted to tell him and slap him on the back. You feel tempted to tell everyone out in the bright, cheery street. And what a wonderful street it is too! All full of nice black snow and water. After all, Life is sweet!

And then you go and find the first person whom you can accost without being arrested and explain to him just what it was that the dentist did to you, and how you felt, and what you have got to have done next time.

Which brings us right back to where we were in the beginning, and perhaps accounts for everyone's liking to divulge their dental secrets to others. It may be a sort of hysterical relief that, for the time being, it is all over with.

STUDYING THE ESSAY

1. This is a very personal essay, as you must realize. Do you know anyone who reacts to dentistry as Benchley does?

2. "Putting off the evil hour" is a problem in ways other than the one described here. Give examples from your own experience.

3. What are some of Benchley's methods of producing humor?

4. If the essay has a moral, what is it?

5. Discuss this essay with your dentist.

6. This essay is a revelation of a certain weakness in a man's character. What other essays in the book reveal similar weaknesses?

COMPOSITION TOPICS

1. On Not Doing Homework Promptly
2. Dentists Are People
3. I Lose a Tooth

HEYWOOD BROUN, 1888–1939

Matthew Heywood Campbell Broun — he needed only two of this cluster of names — was born in Brooklyn. He attended Harvard with the Class of 1910 but did not graduate because he could not, or did not, pass the French reading examination. This minor error did not seem to hurt his career, however, since from 1908 on he was an extremely prolific newspaper reporter and columnist. He started as a baseball writer for the Morning *Telegraph*, but went to the *Tribune* in 1912, where he started his column called " It Seems to Me." He took the column to the *World* in 1921 and to the *Telegram* in 1928, where it appeared every day until shortly before his death. He was also a contributor to the *Nation* and the *New Republic*, and he had additional time to write eight or ten books of informal essays like " The Fifty-First Dragon." *It Seems to Me* (1935) is a collection of some of the newspaper columns which made him famous.

Broun's life was filled with activity — mental, political, literary. He left the *World* because his publisher disliked his articles in favor of Sacco and Vanzetti. He ran for Congress on the Socialist ticket in 1930 and at one time almost became a Communist. He founded and was president of the American Newspaper Guild, now a C.I.O. union. Besides all this, he was an amateur painter good enough to have several one-man shows in New York galleries.

His life clearly contradicted his appearance. Like Chesterton, he was a very large man, careless of his appearance — " huge, disheveled, like an amiable bear." A friend of his described him as " a large unmade bed." On the surface he was lazy, sociable, a lover of good food and drink, a wit, and an agreeable conver-

273

sationalist. Inside, however, Broun was often unhappy. And although no writer of his time was more admired, he was a very humble person. He could write from the heart about the results of a person's lack of confidence. Broun's concern about the moral fiber, or character, of men is cleverly illustrated in the moral of this story-essay.

THE FIFTY–FIRST DRAGON

Of all the pupils at the knight school Gawaine le Cœur-Hardy was among the least promising. He was tall and sturdy, but his instructors soon discovered that he lacked spirit. He would hide in the woods when the jousting class was called, although his companions and members of the faculty sought to appeal to his better nature by shouting to him to come out and break his neck like a man. Even when they told him that the lances were padded, the horses no more than ponies, and the field unusually soft for late autumn, Gawaine refused to grow enthusiastic. The Headmaster and the Assistant Professor of Pleasaunce were discussing the case one spring afternoon and the Assistant Professor could see no remedy but expulsion.

" No," said the Headmaster, as he looked out at the purple hills which ringed the school, " I think I'll train him to slay dragons."

" He might be killed," objected the Assistant Professor.

" So he might," replied the Headmaster brightly, but he added, more soberly, " we must consider the greater good. We are responsible for the formation of this lad's character."

" Are the dragons particularly bad this year? " interrupted

the Assistant Professor. This was characteristic. He always seemed restive when the head of the school began to talk ethics and the ideals of the institution.

" I've never known them worse," replied the Headmaster. " Up in the hills to the south last week they killed a number of peasants, two cows, and a prize pig. And if this dry spell holds there's no telling when they may start a forest fire simply by breathing around indiscriminately."

" Would any refund on the tuition fee be necessary in case of an accident to young Cœur-Hardy? "

" No," the principal answered, judicially, " that's all covered in the contract. But as a matter of fact he won't be killed. Before I send him up in the hills I'm going to give him a magic word."

" That's a good idea," said the Professor. " Sometimes they work wonders."

From that day on Gawaine specialized in dragons. His course included both theory and practice. In the morning there were long lectures on the history, anatomy, manners and customs of dragons. Gawaine did not distinguish himself in these studies. He had a marvelously versatile gift for forgetting things. In the afternoon he showed to better advantage, for then he would go down to the South Meadow and practice with a battle-ax. In this exercise he was truly impressive, for he had enormous strength as well as speed and grace. He even developed a deceptive display of ferocity. Old alumni say that it was a thrilling sight to see Gawaine charging across the field toward the dummy paper dragon which had been set up for his practice. As he ran he would brandish his ax and shout " A murrain on thee! " or some other vivid bit of campus slang. It never took him more than one stroke to behead the dummy dragon.

Gradually his task was made more difficult. Paper gave way to papier-mâché and finally to wood, but even the

toughest of these dummy dragons had no terrors for Gawaine. One sweep of the ax always did the business. There
were those who said that when the practice was protracted
until dusk and the dragons threw long, fantastic shadows
across the meadow, Gawaine did not charge so impetuously
nor shout so loudly. It is possible there was malice in this
charge. At any rate, the Headmaster decided by the end of
June that it was time for the test. Only the night before a
dragon had come close to the school grounds and had eaten
some of the lettuce from the garden. The faculty decided
that Gawaine was ready. They gave him a diploma and a
new battle-ax and the Headmaster summoned him to a
private conference.

"Sit down," said the Headmaster. "Have a cigarette."

Gawaine hesitated.

"Oh, I know it's against the rules," said the Headmaster.
"But after all, you have received your preliminary degree.
You are no longer a boy. You are a man. Tomorrow you
will go out into the world, the great world of achievement."

Gawaine took a cigarette. The Headmaster offered him a
match, but he produced one of his own and began to puff
away with a dexterity which quite amazed the principal.

"Here you have learned the theories of life," continued
the Headmaster, resuming the thread of his discourse, "but
after all, life is not a matter of theories. Life is a matter of
facts. It calls on the young and the old alike to face these
facts, even though they are hard and sometimes unpleasant.
Your problem, for example, is to slay dragons."

"They say that those dragons down in the south wood are
five hundred feet long," ventured Gawaine, timorously.

"Stuff and nonsense! " said the Headmaster. "The curate
saw one last week from the top of Arthur's Hill. The dragon
was sunning himself down in the valley. The curate didn't
have an opportunity to look at him very long because he felt

it was his duty to hurry back to make a report to me. He
said the monster — or shall I say, the big lizard? — wasn't an
inch over two hundred feet. But the size has nothing at all
to do with it. You'll find the big ones even easier than the
little ones. They're far slower on their feet and less aggressive, I'm told. Besides, before you go I'm going to equip you
in such fashion that you need have no fear of all the dragons
in the world."

" I'd like an enchanted cap," said Gawaine.

" What's that? " answered the Headmaster, testily.

" A cap to make me disappear," explained Gawaine.

The Headmaster laughed indulgently. " You mustn't believe all those old wives' stories," he said. " There isn't any
such thing. A cap to make you disappear, indeed! What
would you do with it? You haven't even appeared yet. Why
my boy, you could walk from here to London, and nobody
would so much as look at you. You're nobody. You couldn't
be more invisible than that."

Gawaine seemed dangerously close to a relapse into his old
habit of whimpering. The Headmaster reassured him:
" Don't worry; I'll give you something much better than an
enchanted cap. I'm going to give you a magic word. All you
have to do is to repeat this magic charm once and no dragon
can possibly harm a hair of your head. You can cut off his
head at your leisure."

He took a heavy book from the shelf behind his desk and
began to run through it. " Sometimes," he said, " the charm
is a whole phrase or even a sentence. I might, for instance,
give you ' To make the ' — No, that might not do. I think a
single word would be best for dragons."

" A short word," suggested Gawaine.

" It can't be too short or it wouldn't be potent. There isn't
so much hurry as all that. Here's a splendid magic word:
' Rumplesnitz.' Do you think you can learn that? "

Gawaine tried and in an hour or so he seemed to have the word well in hand. Again and again he interrupted the lesson to inquire, " And if I say ' Rumplesnitz ' the dragon can't possibly hurt me? " And always the Headmaster replied, " If you only say ' Rumplesnitz,' you are perfectly safe."

Toward morning Gawaine seemed resigned to his career. At daybreak the Headmaster saw him to the edge of the forest and pointed him to the direction in which he should proceed. About a mile away to the southwest a cloud of steam hovered over an open meadow in the woods and the Headmaster assured Gawaine that under the steam he would find a dragon. Gawaine went forward slowly. He wondered whether it would be best to approach the dragon on the run as he did in his practice in the South Meadow or to walk slowly toward him shouting " Rumplesnitz " all the way.

The problem was decided for him. No sooner had he come to the fringe of the meadow than the dragon spied him and began to charge. It was a large dragon and yet it seemed decidedly aggressive in spite of the Headmaster's statement to the contrary. As the dragon charged it released huge clouds of hissing steam through its nostrils. It was almost as if a gigantic teapot had gone mad. The dragon came forward so fast and Gawaine was so frightened that he had time to say " Rumplesnitz " only once. As he said it, he swung his battle-ax and off popped the head of the dragon. Gawaine had to admit that it was even easier to kill a real dragon than a wooden one if only you said " Rumplesnitz."

Gawaine brought the ears home and a small section of the tail. His schoolmates and the faculty made much of him, but the Headmaster wisely kept him from being spoiled by insisting that he go on with his work. Every clear day Gawaine rose at dawn and went out to kill dragons. The Headmaster kept him at home when it rained, because he said the woods were damp and unhealthy at such times and that he didn't want the boy to run needless risks. Few good days passed in which Gawaine failed to get a dragon. On one particularly fortunate day he killed three, a husband and wife and a visiting relative. Gradually he developed a technique. Pupils who sometimes watched him from the hilltops a long way off said that he often allowed the dragon to come within a few feet before he said " Rumplesnitz." He came to say it with a mocking sneer. Occasionally he did stunts. Once when an excursion party from London was watching him he went into action with his right hand tied behind his back. The dragon's head came off just as easily.

As Gawaine's record of killings mounted higher, the Headmaster found it impossible to keep him completely in hand. He fell into the habit of stealing out at night and engaging in long drinking bouts at the village tavern. It was after such a debauch that he rose a little before dawn one fine August morning and started out after his fiftieth dragon. His head was heavy and his mind was sluggish. He was heavy in other respects as well, for he had adopted the somewhat vulgar practice of wearing his medals, ribbons and all, when he went out dragon hunting. The decorations began on his chest and ran all the way down to his abdomen. They must have weighed at least eight pounds.

Gawaine found a dragon in the same meadow where he had killed the first one. It was a fair-sized dragon, but evidently an old one. Its face was wrinkled and Gawaine thought he had never seen so hideous a countenance. Much to the lad's disgust, the monster refused to charge and Gawaine was obliged to walk toward him. He whistled as he went. The dragon regarded him hopelessly, but craftily. Of course he had heard of Gawaine. Even when the lad raised his battle-ax the dragon made no move. It knew that there was no salvation in the quickest thrust of the head, for it had been informed that this hunter was protected by an enchantment. It merely waited, hoping something would turn up. Gawaine raised the battle-ax and suddenly lowered it again. He had grown very pale and he trembled violently. The dragon suspected a trick. " What's the matter? " it asked, with false solicitude.

" I've forgotten the magic word," stammered Gawaine.

" What a pity," said the dragon. " So that was the secret. It doesn't seem quite sporting to me, all this magic stuff, you know. Not cricket, as we used to say when I was a little dragon; but after all, that's a matter of opinion."

Gawaine was so helpless with terror that the dragon's confidence rose immeasurably and it could not resist the temptation to show off a bit.

" Could I possibly be of any assistance? " it asked. " What's the first letter of the magic word? "

" It begins with an ' r,' " said Gawaine weakly.

" Let's see," mused the dragon, " that doesn't tell us much, does it? What sort of a word is this? Is it an epithet, do you think? "

Gawaine could do no more than nod.

" Why, of course," exclaimed the dragon, " reactionary Republican."

Gawaine shook his head.

" Well, then," said the dragon, " we'd better get down to business. Will you surrender? "

With the suggestion of a compromise Gawaine mustered up enough courage to speak.

" What will you do if I surrender? " he asked.

" Why, I'll eat you," said the dragon.

" And if I don't surrender? "

" I'll eat you just the same."

"Then it doesn't make any difference, does it? " moaned Gawaine.

" It does to me," said the dragon with a smile. " I'd rather you didn't surrender. You'd taste much better if you didn't."

The dragon waited for a long time for Gawaine to ask "Why? " but the boy was too frightened to speak. At last the dragon had to give the explanation without his cue line. "You see," he said, "if you don't surrender you'll taste better because you'll die game."

This was an old and ancient trick of the dragon's. By means of some such quip he was accustomed to paralyze his victims with laughter and then to destroy them. Gawaine was sufficiently paralyzed as it was, but laughter had no part in his helplessness. With the last word of the joke the dragon drew back his head and struck. In that second there flashed into the mind of Gawaine the magic word "Rumplesnitz," but there was no time to say it. There was time only to strike and, without a word, Gawaine met the onrush of the dragon with a full swing. He put all his back and shoulders into it. The impact was terrific and the head of the dragon flew away almost a hundred yards and landed in a thicket.

Gawaine did not remain frightened very long after the death of the dragon. His mood was one of wonder. He was enormously puzzled. He cut off the ears of the monster almost in a trance. Again and again he thought to himself, " I didn't say 'Rumplesnitz'! " He was sure of that and yet there was no question that he had killed the dragon. In fact, he had never killed one so utterly. Never before had he driven a head for anything like the same distance. Twenty-five yards was perhaps his best previous record. All the way back to the knight school he kept rumbling about in his mind seeking an explanation for what had occurred. He went to the Headmaster immediately and after closing the door told him what had happened. " I didn't say 'Rumplesnitz,' " he explained with great earnestness.

The Headmaster laughed. " I'm glad you've found out,"

he said. "It makes you ever so much more of a hero. Don't you see that? Now you know that it was you who killed all these dragons and not that foolish little word 'Rumplesnitz.'"

Gawaine frowned. "Then it wasn't a magic word after all?" he asked.

"Of course not," said the Headmaster, "you ought to be too old for such foolishness. There isn't any such thing as a magic word."

"But you told me it was magic," protested Gawaine. "You said it was magic and now you say it isn't."

"It wasn't magic in a literal sense," answered the Headmaster, "but it was much more wonderful than that. The word gave you confidence. It took away your fears. If I hadn't told you that, you might have been killed the very first time. It was your battle-ax did the trick."

Gawaine surprised the Headmaster by his attitude. He was obviously distressed by the explanation. He interrupted a long philosophic and ethical discourse by the Headmaster with, "If I hadn't of hit 'em all mighty hard and fast, any one of 'em might have crushed me like a, like a —" He fumbled for a word.

"Egg shell," suggested the Headmaster.

"Like a egg shell," assented Gawaine, and he said it many times. All through the evening meal people who sat near him heard him muttering, "Like a egg shell, like a egg shell."

The next day was clear, but Gawaine did not get up at dawn. Indeed, it was almost noon when the Headmaster found him cowering in bed, with the clothes pulled over his head. The principal called the Assistant Professor of Pleasaunce, and together they dragged the boy toward the forest.

"He'll be all right as soon as he gets a couple more dragons under his belt," explained the Headmaster.

The Assistant Professor of Pleasaunce agreed. "It would

be a shame to stop such a fine run," he said. " Why, counting that one yesterday, he's killed fifty dragons."

They pushed the boy into a thicket above which hung a meager cloud of steam. It was obviously quite a small dragon. But Gawaine did not come back that night or the next. In fact, he never came back. Some weeks afterward brave spirits from the school explored the thicket, but they could find nothing to remind them of Gawaine except the metal part of his medals. Even the ribbons had been devoured.

The Headmaster and the Assistant Professor of Pleasaunce agreed that it would be just as well not to tell the school how Gawaine had achieved his record and still less how he came to die. They held that it might have a bad effect on school spirit. Accordingly, Gawaine has lived in the memory of the school as its greatest hero. No visitor succeeds in leaving the building today without seeing a great shield which hangs on the wall of the dining hall. Fifty pairs of dragons' ears are mounted upon the shield and underneath in gilt letters is " Gawaine le Cœur-Hardy," followed by the simple inscription, " He killed fifty dragons." The record has never been equaled.

STUDYING THE ESSAY

1. Why did the principal give Gawaine a " magic word "?
2. Why was his conquest greater when he forgot the word?
3. Explain the title.
4. What does Gawaine's whole name mean?

COMPOSITION TOPICS

1. The Meaning of Maturity
2. All of Us Have Many Dragons to Face

WALTER LIPPMANN, 1889–

A native of New York City, Walter Lippmann was a member of the Class of 1910 at Harvard. For two or three years after college he was an active member of the Socialist Party and for a year the secretary to the Socialist mayor of Schenectady. He began his journalistic career as an assistant editor of the *New Republic* (1914–1919). During 1917, as an assistant to the Secretary of War, he was a member of the group sent to Europe to negotiate peace with Germany and to assist in drafting Woodrow Wilson's "Fourteen Points." In 1919, he joined the staff of the New York *World* and became its editor in 1929.

At this point Lippmann, who had for twenty years been a left-wing liberal, reversed his political point of view. Since 1931, as a special writer for the New York *Herald Tribune*, he has been one of the country's most eloquent spokesmen for the intelligent conservative approach to national and world affairs. His many books and magazine articles, as well as his brilliant syndicated column, have established him as one of the few newsmen with a world point of view and a scholarly, philosophical approach to history. His style is a model of clarity, and the organization of his thoughts is invariably clear. Among his most widely read books are *A Preface to Morals* (1929), *The Good Society* (1937), *U.S. Foreign Policy* (1943) and *The Cold War* (1947).

"The Rivalry of Nations" is a Phi Beta Kappa address which Lippmann delivered at the College of William and Mary in 1947. It is a good example of his broad viewpoint, his clear analysis of foreign relations, and his realistic approach to the most serious diplomatic problem of modern times.

284

THE RIVALRY OF NATIONS

If we study the history of American foreign relations during the past forty years, we must be struck by an extraordinary paradox. During this period the United States has emerged from its long isolation. It has become one of the leading powers of the world. Not once but twice during this period the American people have had to face the awful issues of war and peace. Can it be said that during this momentous period we have ever succeeded in forming and agreeing on a foreign policy which foresaw correctly and enabled us to deal successfully with the actual course of events? The record is, I think, clear. We have won both wars. But on the crucial issues our diplomacy has thus far always miscarried. It has been unable to prevent war. It has been unable to avoid war. It has not prepared us for war. It has not been able to settle the wars when they have been fought and won.

At no critical phase in this epoch has the actual outcome conformed with our declarations and our expectations. Never has the country been able to achieve any of the principal objectives to which again and again it has been so solemnly and fervently committed.

Thus from 1914 to 1917 the country believed and hoped that it could avoid participation in the First World War. Yet it was compelled to participate. And when it did participate, it was unprepared because it had believed that it would not have to participate. During that war the country hoped and believed that by a victory it would achieve a lasting and democratic peace. The victory was attained. But the peace which had been promised was not achieved. After the First World War the country again believed that if there were another war, it would be able to remain out of it. Again it did not prepare for war. Once again it was unable to remain out of the war when it came.

During the Second World War the country again believed that with victory over the Germans there would begin an era in which all the victorious powers would agree and be harmonious and become unanimous on the terms and conditions of a just and durable peace. We have had the victory. But we have not been able to attain that peace.

Now, after two victorious world wars we find ourselves discussing the possibility of a third world war. And so we must ask ourselves whether we have become entangled in a degenerating cycle of wars that breed more wars, each more savage and more inconclusive than the last. It is a grim question. We must, however, face it; and I believe that we must answer it by saying that if our present estimates and calculations are no more correct than those on which we acted before, during, and immediately after the First and Second World Wars, then we shall be surprised and disappointed again. Once more we shall not know how to prevent war, or how to prepare for it correctly, or how, assuming we win it, to make peace after it. And if a second world war leads to the third — because we cannot make a settlement of the war we have just won — what ground is there to suppose that we could settle a third world war so that it did not lead to a fourth?

Is it not true that in the twentieth century we have witnessed on the one hand the rise of the United States to pre-eminence among the nations, to a position of great leadership and immense responsibility in shaping the destiny of mankind? And on the other hand, is it not also true that the course of events during the American rise to pre-eminence is strewn with the debris and wreckage of high and hopeful declarations of policy: with Wilson's neutrality, Wilson's Fourteen Points, and the Covenant of the League of Nations; with the Washington treaties of disarmament and the Kellogg pact to outlaw war; with the Dawes Plan, the Young Plan, and the Hoover Moratorium to reconstruct the world after the First World War; with the Stimson doctrine to prevent aggression; with the Neutrality Act before the Second World War; with the quarantine speech of Franklin Roosevelt, and the Four Freedoms, and Hull's Seventeen Points, and the Atlantic Charter, and the Yalta Declaration, and the Truman Doctrine?

When we reflect on this series of declarations and the disappointments which followed them all, we must be struck by the contrast between our capacity as a people to develop national power, and our ability to use it and to manage it successfully. And is it not plain that our failures lie in the field of policy — that is to say, in deciding correctly when, where, how, and to what ends we shall exert the enormous power and influence which we are able to generate?

It cannot be argued that the miscarriages of American diplomacy during the past forty years are due to the weakness of the American nation. Among the powers of the world the United States is the least vulnerable to invasion, to blockade, or, with existing weapons, to decisive assault. The United States has the material resources and it has the productive capacity to develop enormous offensive power in time of war. In time of peace it produces a great export surplus — a surplus above and beyond a high standard of life at home — which renders it economically invulnerable in the outer world. Two great wars have proved the valor of American troops, the fortitude of the American people, and the military competence of American military commanders. Our institutions and our traditions are respected. And on the

whole our participation in world affairs is welcomed by the
great masses of mankind as promising liberty, justice, peace,
and plenty.

We must seek the cause of our diplomatic failures, therefore, in our own minds. We must look for the cause of
trouble not in material circumstances but in our own habits
of thought when we are dealing with foreign affairs and
with the formation of American policy. In the period from
Woodrow Wilson to Harry S. Truman our foreign policy
has miscarried so regularly because there has been interposed
within our own minds, between the outer world and ourselves, a collection of stereotyped prejudices and sacred cows
and wishful conceptions, which misrepresent the nature of
things, which falsify our judgments of events, and which
inhibit the formation of workable policies by which our
available means can be devoted efficiently to realizable ends.

We have brought along with us from our age of innocence, from the nineteenth century when we were isolated
and when we were sheltered from the rivalries of states and
empires, an ideological picture of the world, a philosophical
framework of preconceptions. We think this picture of the
world is real and noble. In fact it is imaginary and false.
And because our philosophy of the nature of international
life is imaginary and false, our efforts to play an effective
part in world affairs are frustrated.

What then is it in our philosophy which, instead of
guiding us, misguides us continually? I think that the question can be answered. The point, as I have already indi-
cated, where our declarations of policy have regularly miscarried is in avoiding war, in preparing for war, and in
settling wars. We must ask ourselves whether there is here
some common factor of error which confuses all of us on the
issues of war and peace. I think there is. I think the error
is a refusal to recognize, to admit, to take as the premise

of our thinking, the fact that rivalry and strife and conflict among states, communities, and factions are the normal condition of mankind. The popular American philosophy of international life refuses to recognize this fact. It denies that in the world as it is, the struggle for existence is fundamental and in the nature of things. This, I believe, is the philosophical error which prevents us from forming an effective foreign policy.

In the American ideology the struggle for existence and the rivalry of nations for advantages are held to be wrong, abnormal, and transitory. Our foreign policy throughout this period has been dominated by the belief that the struggle does not exist, or that it can be avoided, or that it can be abolished. Because of this belief our aim has not been to regulate and to moderate and to compose the conflicts and the issues, to check and to balance the contending forces. Our aim has been either to abstain from the struggle, or to abolish the struggle immediately, or to conduct crusades against those nations that most actively continue the struggle.

Yet in the world as it actually is, the struggle is not abnormal, and it is perpetually renewed. Twice during this period we have sought to abstain from the struggle by declaring our neutrality. We have not been able to stay out of it. Twice we have conducted victorious crusades against the chief troublemaker, believing what was soon disproved by events: that if he could be eliminated, we would then have eliminated all troublemakers. Twice we have sought, by forming universal societies like the League of Nations and the United Nations, to abolish the struggle. They have not abolished the struggle.

Our refusal to recognize the struggle for existence as the normal state of mankind in international affairs has resulted in the repeated miscarriage of American policies. Our efforts to deal with events, as if they conformed or could be made to conform with our ideological picture of what they ought to be, has been rather like using a map of Utopia to find your way around New York City.

The American refusal to recognize the struggle for existence has in this century crystallized in three recognizable patterns of conduct: in a neutrality which assumes that the struggle can be ignored and avoided; in crusades that assume that by defeating the chief troublemaker the struggle for existence will end; in the sponsorship of a universal society which assumes that the struggle can be abolished.

Since 1914 American relations with the outer world have oscillated among these three patterns of conduct. The great debates within this country have turned upon them. But the experience of these forty years shows conclusively, I think, that if we insist on treating the conflict of states, communities, and factions as abnormal, as exceptional, as transitory, we are unable to form an efficient foreign policy. Our American ideology, which we have brought over from a time when we did not have to play a responsible part among the powers of the earth, distorts our judgment when we deal with the problems of power. It distorts our judgment when we have to calculate how a balance can be struck between our aims and our power to realize them.

In practical judgments — and diplomacy, when the stakes are life and death, calls for very practical judgments — the criteria are always relative. There is no such thing as absolute power. Whatever the wealth, the power, and the prestige of a nation may be, its means are always limited. The problem of the maker of policy is to select objectives that are limited — not the best that could be desired but the best that can be realized without committing the whole power and the whole wealth and the very existence of the nation.

But if we examine the issues of foreign policy as they are

presented to our people, we find an overwhelming disposition to regard the choices before us not as relative but as
absolute. We are disposed to think that the issue is either this
or that, either all or nothing, either isolationism or globalism,
either total peace or total war, either one world or no world,
either disarmament or absolute weapons, either pious reso-
lutions or atomic bombs, either disarmament or military su-
premacy, either nonintervention or a crusade, either democracy or tyranny, either the abolition of war or a preventive
war, either appeasement or unconditional surrender, either
nonresistance or a strategy of annihilation.

There is no place in this ideological pattern of the world
for the adoption of limited ends or limited means, for the use
of checks and balances among contending forces, for the
demarcation of spheres of influence and of power and of
interest, for accommodation and compromise and adjustment, for the stabilization of the status quo, for the restoration of an equilibrium. Yet this is the field of diplomacy.
These are the substance and the matter of an efficient
diplomacy.

Our ideologists, however, regard the use of power to
achieve and maintain an equilibrium of power as " power
politics." And they regard the recognition of spheres of
influence as " appeasement." Yet in the absence of a world
state, and except in a world dominated by one supreme
power, there must be an equilibrium among several powers
and a recognition of their spheres of influence. A diplomacy
for the world as it is, which is not to expend itself in verbal
declarations on the one hand, and on crusades of annihilation
on the other, must deal with the balance of power and the
determination of spheres of influence.

But under the spell of our ideological picture of the world,
we exclude from our minds the very subject matter of
diplomacy itself. We would exclude it, we would outlaw

it, and we would excommunicate those who discuss it. We insist on treating the rivalry of nations as something that could not exist among right-thinking men. We do not regulate the rivalries because we hold that the rivalries ought not to exist. And so we are left with our three patterns of policy: to ignore the rivalries by proclaiming our neutrality, or to deny the rivalry and to believe it will disappear if the nations are members of a universal society, or to conduct crusades of annihilation against the lions who do not wish to lie down with the lambs.

How does what I have been saying bear upon the subject which preoccupies us all so anxiously and so profoundly — upon our relations with the Soviet Union, with which we are now engaged in a world-wide diplomatic conflict?

The beginning of wisdom on the Russian question is, I believe, to recognize the historic fact that the division between eastern and western Europe, the rivalry between Russia and the nations of the West, did not begin with Marx, Lenin, and Stalin, nor would it end if the Soviet regime were overthrown or defeated. The cultural and ideological division of Europe is as old as the division of Christendom between Rome and Byzantium. The imperial rivalry with Russia in the Baltic, in eastern and central Europe, in the Danube valley, in the Balkans, in the Middle East, and in the Far East did not begin with the Communists and will not end with Communism. It was one of the great fields of diplomacy under the Czars as it is under the Communists. Rivalry with Russia is a new problem for the United States. But the British Foreign Office has been preoccupied with it for a hundred and fifty years. We had better make up our minds that we shall now be preoccupied with it for a very long time to come.

That being the case, we must give up the notion that the choice is between one world, in which the Russians are our partners, and two worlds, in which we must annihilate the Russians or they must annihilate us. I do not believe that we must either marry the Russians or must fight them, that we must have either a perfect peace or a total war. I believe that the best policy is to recognize that the rivalry will remain, and not to expect it to disappear, and not to think it could be abolished by the United Nations, and not to think it could be abolished by a victorious war; and having recognized that the rivalry is a permanent fact, to use our whole power and influence to regulate it, to keep it within bounds, to establish spheres of influence which limit the rivalry, and a balance of power in the world which checks it.

I do not believe that we can settle the Russian problem once and for all. I do believe we have enough power and influence, if we use them efficiently, to bring about a settlement with Russia in this generation. But it will have to be a settlement which aims not at unanimity, not at ideological harmony, not at the abolition of all our differences and disagreements, but at a truce in the cold war, a *modus vivendi* during which the nations can recover from World War II, at treaties which end in the withdrawal of the armies of occupation in Europe, and the restoration of Europe to the Europeans.

This will not be easy to achieve. It will require the pressure of power — which will offend those among us who do not like power politics. It will require political and economic compromises — which will offend those who regard all compromise as appeasement. But if a truce, and a *modus vivendi*, and a treaty are hard to achieve by power and by compromise, it is certain that without power on the one hand, and compromise on the other, nothing can be achieved.

If we will not or cannot use the classic procedure of diplomacy — which is always a combination of power and compromise — then the best we can look forward to is an era of disintegration in the civilized world, followed perhaps by a war which, once it began, would be savage, universal, and indecisive.

That must not happen. And it need not happen if only our people will abjure their illusions about the nature of the world in which they have so recently become a leading power, and will permit and assist those who must form our policy to go forward on the assumption that our aim is not to marry the Russians and then to live with them happily ever after, nor to fight them and let the whole world be devastated. Our aim is to transact our necessary business with the Russians, at arm's length, coolly, shrewdly, without fear and without extravagant hope, and with as much justice as may be possible where there is as yet no agreement on first principles and where the rivals do not live in the same moral order.

STUDYING THE ESSAY

1. This essay is so well organized that it affords students a good subject for practice in outlining. Try to make a topic or sentence outline, following the original very carefully.

2. Discuss the items mentioned in the sixth paragraph. As an American, you should know something about all of these.

3. What, according to Lippmann, is the principal reason why our foreign policy has failed?

4. What have Americans refused to recognize about the world?

5. What do you know of Russia's history during the last 150 years? Should you know this history?

6. What do you think of Lippmann's conclusion as to a sound policy toward Russia? Try to form this judgment without the "stereotyped prejudices" which Lippmann mentions.

7. Words and phrases to learn: *stereotyped prejudices, sacred cows, preconceptions, ideological, oscillated, criteria.*

COMPOSITION TOPICS

1. The Meaning of the Phrase " Cold War "
2. What can one high school student do to make the world a better place in which to live?
3. How can Lippmann's ideas be applied to less dangerous situations — to rivalry between two schools, for instance?
4. As an exercise in paragraph writing, copy one of Lippmann's topic sentences on a piece of paper. Then close your book and develop this sentence into a paragraph, using *your* own ideas.

ELMER DAVIS, 1890–

Elmer Holmes Davis was born in Aurora, Indiana. After graduation from Franklin College he was awarded a Rhodes scholarship and spent a year at Queens College, Oxford, where he received a degree in 1912. Upon his return to the United States he spent a year on the staff of the magazine *Adventure,* and then took a position on the New York *Times* from 1914 to 1924. For fifteen years after 1924 he turned out a variety of things — short stories for various magazines, six novels, and two or three books of essays.

In 1939 Mr. Davis was called upon to substitute for H. V. Kaltenborn as a news analyst over the Columbia Broadcasting System. He very soon gained a reputation as one of the most objective and least excited of the news broadcasters. He stayed with C.B.S. until 1942, when the government asked him to direct the Office of War Information, a job which he held until 1945. Since then he has been a news analyst for the American Broadcasting Company. It is in this capacity that he is most easily recognized, for his calm and thorough comments on the daily problems of the world have attracted a large audience.

Most of the essays which Elmer Davis writes mantain the same tone that distinguishes his broadcasts. However, much of *But We Were Born Free,* the collection from which this essay is taken, is less full of understatement than most of his works. Here, at least in the first part of the book, he is angry and outspoken about some of the illnesses within the state. " Grandeurs and Miseries of Old Age," however, is the Davis we hear on the radio. The reader can almost hear Davis' voice as he reads the essay, which is a thoughtful discussion of a problem which every man in the world sometime has to face.

GRANDEURS AND MISERIES OF OLD AGE

I am almost sixty-four years old. That is not very old by modern standards, especially in a country whose benevolent government urges on me the advantages of being older still. When I am sixty-five, the Bureau of Internal Revenue assures me, I shall be able to deduct another $600 from my taxable income; and if I have the additional felicity to become blind, I can deduct some more.

I have no ambition to go blind at any age, despite this allurement; for that matter I am not anxious to be sixty-five, though I shall be unless I die pretty soon. My fan mail includes a good many gleeful predictions that I am going to be lynched; but barring that misfortune, I ought to be good for another ten or fifteen years if there is anything in the doctrine of hereditary longevity. But no matter how long I may last I am not persuaded that the best is yet to be, even by Catherine Drinker Bowen's eloquent disquisition in *Harper's* on the magnificence of age. I recognize and applaud her endeavor to reassure us that what is going to happen to all of us, whether we like it or not, is really something pretty good; but I cannot feel that the general public can draw much encouragement from the truly magnificent old age of the various worthies she mentions, notably Mr. Justice Oliver Wendell Holmes.

It is no doubt true, as she says, that " luck being equal, whether a man at eighty finds himself reaping the harvest or the whirlwind depends on how he has spent his forties and thirties and twenties." But luck is not equal; and it may be that to be an Oliver Wendell Holmes or a John Dewey at ninety you had to be a Holmes or a Dewey from the start, both in physical constitution and in potential mental capacity.

I once asked John Dewey how he maintained such intellectual and physical activity at an advanced age, and he said that when you have survived a childhood in Vermont you can take just about anything that happens to you afterward. I have no statistics on the juvenile mortality in Vermont in the 1860's; no doubt all those who survived were tough, but they were not all Deweys. I have a friend aged eighty-four who is better than I am; but to judge from the record she always was, at any age.

To feel that Mrs. Bowen has been overly optimistic is not to accept the dark view of old age held by the author of Ecclesiastes; but that is partly because medical science has made considerable advances since his day. Considerable, but not yet enough. When the grinders cease because they are few, the dentist can replace them; when eyes that look out of the windows be darkened, the oculist can take effective measures. But who can give us back those elastic arteries? (Since writing the foregoing, I have happily discovered that Bourbon retards their ossification.) No doubt in due time the doctors can take care of that and can correct the other deteriorations that now commonly come with advancing years. Some writers have looked forward to the time when men and women will be potentially immortal and will voluntarily retire from life only when they have seen everything and become bored with repetitions. When that happy day comes, Mrs. Bowen's argument will be more persuasive than it is now. In the meantime there is no use kidding ourselves that every man who lives into the late eighties or the nineties can be an Oliver Wendell Holmes, or a John Dewey, or an Arturo Toscanini, no matter how rectitudinously he may have behaved while he was still young enough to have some choice about it. If there be consolations to offset the inevitable physical decay that befalls most of us, they ought to be more generally applicable.

Public life seems to be a pretty good preservative — if not for Presidents, at least for Congressmen, who work about as hard as Presidents, though they have less responsibility. Chairman Robert L. Doughton of the House Ways and Means Committee — one of the most exacting as well as most important committees of the Congress — retired in 1952 at the age of eighty-eight because he was afraid he was getting old and might be not quite so good as he used to be; to everybody else he looked just about as good as ever, which was pretty good. Chairman Adolph J. Sabath of the House Rules Committee was cut off untimely at eighty-six; but he had worn himself out by twenty years of fighting with the beasts at Ephesus — the reactionary majority of his committee. (The successor to his seat in the House is only seventy-eight, which gives him time to mature.) Senator Theodore Francis Green, at eighty-six, is about as lively, mentally and physically, as any man on Capitol Hill, though last year his doctors told him that he would have to stop high-diving. Some people worry because the fate of the world appears to depend in large degree on Winston Churchill, aged seventy-nine, and Konrad Adenauer, aged seventy-eight. But there is a good chance that men who have lasted as long as that may still have some more years of work left in them.

But these men are exceptions, as much as the Franklins and Palmerstons and Gladstones who in past generations kept going long after most men had run down. They offer no great encouragement to the average man.

Perhaps in this matter there is no such thing as the average man. It is common knowledge that some people grow old faster than others, and not till lately has there been official demarcation of the frontier between youth and age. In the fall of 1953 the President said that one reason he appointed Earl Warren as Chief Justice was " his relative youth " — sixty-two. On the same day the Governor of Puerto Rico pardoned a prisoner on account of " his advanced age " — sixty-three. Between those two years, then, must lie the Great Divide, though I seem to have been working so hard that I never noticed it when I passed over it.

But in their relation to old age men differ vastly not only in their abilities and their physical strength, but economically and occupationally. If the insurance companies can be believed, I cannot say much about the average man either; for they tell us, or used to tell us, that 99 per cent of all men of my age are dependent on their children, or pensions, or charity. And even among the one per cent of us who can still make a living there are differences — for instance, whether we are responsible only for ourselves or for organizations and institutions. Most of us in my business, the news business, are responsible only for ourselves; in my particular branch of it there are three men who are ten years older than I am and still going strong; and one of the greatest of editorial writers, the late E. M. Kingsbury, was still at it when he was ninety. But if one of us should go haywire, he could be bounced out with no loss to anybody but himself. The danger that men in responsible executive positions might go haywire is the most serious hazard of old age.

The steady physical deterioration that afflicts most of us is deplorable, but so long as it remains merely physical it is not disastrous. Far worse is the danger that in advanced years a man's mind might go back on him at some unpredictable moment and drive him to make mistakes that would have been unthinkable a year or two earlier. That is why some of our aged statesmen, to all appearance as good as ver, nevertheless find it advisable to retire before that unforeseeable day when all at once they will not be as good as ever, or good at all. Some of them do not retire; Gladstone was beginning to slip, physically at least, in his last ministry, though he saw it and left office before the consequences became too serious. Hindenburg, elected president of the German Reich at seventy-seven, hoped (so Walter Goerlitz tells us) that he would not be left in office till he became senile; " for one never knows one's self when that is happening." He was left in office; it happened, but he did not know it was happening; and that was one of the reasons for the downfall of the German Republic.

The older a man grows, the greater the danger that this will happen to him. Against this and minor miseries of age, what are the offsets? Not all, I am afraid, that have sometimes been recommended. Much has been written about the joys of calm contemplation, in old age, of a long and honorable life. But it is a rare man, unless he has great skill at self-deception, who can review a career, however bespangled with good deeds and glory, without his eye's lighting on something that could have been done otherwise and better, and might have made a considerable difference if it had been done better; but it is too late to do anything about it now. The pleasure in such retrospection seems to me by no means unalloyed.

They tell us too of the joy of seeing long endeavor come to ultimate fruition. Well—— Back in the eighties a young actor named Frank Bacon was playing in California vaudeville with his wife. They had a baby, and like many young couples they needed more money than they had. But then he had an Idea — an idea that might make enough money, and win enough fame, to solve all their problems; an idea for a play about a hotel on the state line, half in Nevada and half in California, and combining (as the late Frank Munsey might have said) the best features of both. He finally got it written — with what effort, and what joy, only the amateur writer knows — and sent it off to a producer (or maybe an agent) in New York. And nothing happened.

It made the rounds of the New York producers, and nothing continued to happen. Meanwhile Bacon and his wife continued to play in vaudeville, and made a living; the baby grew older; with pain, Bacon cut down the play that embodied the Idea into a vaudeville act, which kept them afloat. But it was a long way from California vaudeville to the glories of Broadway; he still hoped for better things, still kept sending the play around — and at last a producer took it. He gave it to the best play doctor of the time for reworking; it was produced on Broadway, with Bacon playing the lead; it ran longer than any play had ever run in New York up to that time, and he made a million dollars out of it — when he was sixty-four.

I heard Frank Bacon tell that story in 1918, and he finished, " Anyway, I can still use the money." He probably used it more wisely at sixty-four than he would have at thirty-four, but he didn't get so much fun out of it; nor was there anything like so much of it, for the income tax was terrific in 1918 and unheard of in the eighties. Nor could any joy that comes to a man with thirty years' more experience approximate the emotion of the beginning author who slips into the mail the manuscript that embodies his Great Idea. After thirty years he may even have come to doubt its greatness.

It has been argued that in old age most of your troubles are behind you. The late Don Marquis once wrote that when you have reached the age of fifty-five, everything has happened to you that can happen; you are no longer in danger of being devastated by something new. He was wrong. Before he was fifty-five he had had about as much bad luck as any man I ever knew, but after that he had some more

— a stroke which laid him flat on his back for the last two years of his life, conscious, but unable to do or even to say anything about it.

There is also mere curiosity. I hope to keep on living for a while to see what happens, but I realize that I may not like it at all. Abraham Lincoln, if he had lived another ten years, would have had a very poor opinion of what the United States had become; but it is always possible that with his tremendous personal prestige and his unequaled political skill he might have prevented it from becoming what it was by 1875. Lesser men can have no such expectation.

There is, however, one offset to the inevitable infirmities, at least for us of the one per cent who have been lucky enough to be able to keep our noses above water; and that is freedom — freedom from the passions of youth. I don't mean what you mean; from that particular passion, I should imagine, few men or women are ever happy to be set free. We read in the pages of history that Sophocles the tragic poet, at the age of eighty-nine, was asked by some impertinent young squirt if he were still able to enjoy the pleasures of love. " My friend," said Sophocles solemnly, " I give thanks to the gods every day that I have been freed from that tyrannous desire." It is, however, the general opinion of men old enough to have an opinion that Sophocles was merely making the best of a bad job — whistling in the graveyard of his capacities.

The dominant passion of most young men — and middleaged men, for that matter — is a lust for Success; they bend most of their efforts toward making a name, or a fortune, or both. But the time comes when they have either made it or not, and it is too late to do much more about it. Accordingly — always provided you have done well enough to keep afloat — ambition fades away; you no longer give a damn, or at any rate not much of a damn.

This too needs qualification, in both directions. A senator who in his eighties is defeated — as several senators have been — for re-election to a seat that he has held for thirty years probably feels even worse about it than he would have felt thirty years earlier; and those unfortunate novelists who under some obscure compulsion still push out a book a year, long after they have nothing left to say, probably hate unfavorable reviews just as much as they did in their youth.

Nor can you ever be quite sure when a man is through. Winston Churchill, at sixty-two, was a failure. He had been, at times, a considerable figure in each party, but now he was out of both parties; he had just tried to organize a King's party to support Edward VIII in the abdication crisis and had failed not only immediately but rather ludicrously; he told his friends that he was done for. Three years later he was called on to save his country, and he did it.

But not many of us are Churchills, any more than we are Lincolns. Nevertheless we of the one per cent can savor the sense of freedom that comes from the disappearance of ambition. When we were younger, getting and spending we laid waste our powers — and sometimes, in the headlong drive for success, some of us were in danger of laying waste something still more important, our conscience. A good many young men have sometimes been confronted with something that they know they ought to do; but if they did it, it might have an unfavorable if not a disastrous effect on their future. They should have done it anyway, no doubt; but it is a good deal easier not to worry about the effect on your future when your future is behind you.

It is quite true that 'tis man's perdition to be safe when for the truth he ought to die — or, as the phrase is more likely to translate itself in these times, when for the truth he ought to lose his job, with small chance of getting another.

But it is, emotionally if not ethically, a somewhat different matter to tell a young man with a wife and children whom he is barely able to support on his salary that for the truth, his wife and children ought to starve too. And that is a situation that increasingly comes up in the present drive, Congressional and local, against freedom of thought — particularly in the schools and colleges where above all freedom of thought must be preserved.

Professors and teachers in schools and colleges are tempted to pull in their horns, to say nothing at all; otherwise their students, or their students' parents, might report them to the American Legion — as has happened — and any deviation from the norm of reactionary thinking will be regarded as subversion. With the result also, as Mrs. Roosevelt reported after her nation-wide travels in the winter of 1953, that the young people who are just coming up and see what is happening begin to be afraid to think and afraid to act, for fear that something they may say or do now will be dug up and thrown at them twenty years later and ruin their careers. (Senator McCarthy has several times damned, or tried to damn, middle-aged men for what they did or said in college and have long since repudiated.) A despotism might be able to stand this loss of heart, though I doubt it; but a republic whose young people are in that state of mind is on its way downhill.

We have got to defeat this attack on the freedom of the mind; and I think we can defeat it if enough of us stand up against it — enough of all kinds of people, rich and poor, young and old. But it takes courage for a young man with a family to stand up to it; all the more obligation on those of us who have nothing left to lose. At any age it is better to be a dead lion than a living dog — though better still, of course, to be a living and victorious lion; but it is easier to run the risk of being killed (or fired) in action if before long you are going to be dead anyway. This freedom seems to me the chief consolation of old age.

STUDYING THE ESSAY

1. What is "the dark view of old age held by the author of Ecclesiastes "?
2. Who is Catherine Drinker Bowen?
3. What do you know about the following old men: Oliver Wendell Holmes, John Dewey, Arturo Toscanini?
4. Find examples of humor in Davis' treatment of old age.
5. According to the author, what is the great danger of old age?
6. Are there any reasons why it might be better not to live too long?
7. What does Davis mean by the freedom of age?
8. Analyze the last three paragraphs of this essay. What is the writer's main theme?

COMPOSITION TOPICS

1. The Complications of Being Young
2. The Problems of Responsibility
3. Describe the oldest person you know. Explain that person's views on life and death and age.

CHRISTOPHER MORLEY, 1890–

Christopher Darlington Morley was born in 1890 in Haverford, Pennsylvania. He was graduated from Haverford College in 1910 and held a Rhodes Scholarship at Oxford from 1910 to 1913. His two brothers — Felix, later a president of Haverford College, and Frank, once editor of the Washington *Post* — were also Rhodes scholars, a record for one family.

During a busy life Morley has written and edited for Doubleday, Page and Company, the *Ladies Home Journal*, the Philadelphia *Evening Public Ledger*, the New York *Post*, and the *Saturday Review*. He is one of the judges of the Book-of-the-Month Club. And he is one of the prime movers in an entirely different kind of club. This is the Baker Street Irregulars, who gather regularly to pay homage to the living spirit of Sherlock Holmes, the greatest of all detectives. In a deer-stalker cap Morley as one of the Irregulars looks completely like the devoted Anglophile that he is. His English parentage, his English education, and his love of English institutions are evident in many of his essays. The titles of some of his books — *Shandygaff*, *Mince Pie*, and *Plum Pudding*, for instance — indicate this love of Britain. And yet, with his Pennsylvania Quaker background and his admiration for Philadelphia and New York, Morley is an entirely American writer. His vocabulary may make the reader think of Lamb, but his idiom is American.

Morley's essays are usually very short. They are more often than not humorous and light in touch. The style is a very careful style. Morley's vocabulary is chosen with meticulous care, and it is very vivid. Like the essays of Lamb, Morley's writings ramble widely, often ignoring the paragraph and other formal

307

methods of organization. Morley's humor is not just the humor of clever lines; it penetrates deeply at times, often unexpectedly. This is especially true of his essay "On Doors," in which the trivial idea of the sound of a closing door leads him to consider all kinds of closing doors, including the closing of the door of life.

"On Unanswering Letters" is an excellent example of his random thinking and of his careful style. The essay is also an excellent example of the compression which the informal essay requires. One of the most delightful things about this essay is the fact that everyone who reads it can see himself not answering a letter and can understand how the essayist feels about the topic.

ON UNANSWERING LETTERS

There are a great many people who really believe in answering letters the day they are received, just as there are people who go to the movies at nine o'clock in the morning; but these people are stunted and queer.

It is a great mistake. Such crass and breathless promptness takes away a great deal of the pleasure of correspondence.

The psychological didoes involved in receiving letters and making up one's mind to answer them are very complex. If the tangled process could be clearly analyzed and its component involutions isolated for inspection, we might reach a clearer comprehension of that curious bag of tricks, the efficient Masculine Mind.

Take Bill F., for instance, a man so delightful that even to contemplate his existence puts us in good humor and makes us think well of a world that can exhibit an individual equally comely in mind, body, and estate. Every now and then we get a letter from Bill, and immediately we pass into a kind of trance, in which our mind rapidly enunciates the ideas, thoughts, surmises, and contradictions that we would like to write to him in reply. We think what fun it would be to sit right down and churn the inkwell, spreading speculation and cynicism over a number of sheets of foolscap to be wafted Billward.

Sternly we repress the impulse for we know that the shock to Bill of getting so immediate a retort would surely unhinge the well-fitted panels of his intellect.

We add his letter to the large delta of unanswered mail on our desk, taking occasion to turn the mass over once or twice and run through it in a brisk, smiling mood, thinking of all the jolly letters we shall write some day.

After Bill's letter has lain on the pile for a fortnight or so, it has been gently silted over by about twenty other pleasantly postponed manuscripts. Coming upon it by chance, we reflect that any specific problems raised by Bill in that manifesto will by this time have settled themselves. And his random speculations upon household management and human destiny will probably have taken a new slant by now, so that to answer his letter in its own tune will not be congruent with his present fevers. We had better bide a wee until we really have something of circumstance to impart.

We wait a week.

By this time a certain sense of shame has begun to invade the privacy of our brain. We feel that to answer that letter now would be an indelicacy. Better to pretend that we never got it. By and by Bill will write again and then we will answer promptly. We put the letter back in the middle of the heap and think what a fine chap Bill is. But he knows we love him, so it doesn't really matter whether we write or not.

Another week passes by, and no further communication from Bill. We wonder whether he does love us as much as we thought. Still — we are too proud to write and ask.

A few days later a new thought strikes us. Perhaps Bill thinks we have died and he is annoyed because he wasn't invited to the funeral. Ought we to wire him? No, because after all we are not dead, and even if he thinks we are, his subsequent relief at hearing the good news of our survival will outweigh his bitterness during the interval. One of these days we will write him a letter that will really express our heart, filled with all the grindings and gear-work of our mind, rich in affection and fallacy. But we had better let it ripen and mellow for a while. Letters, like wines, accumulate bright fumes and bubblings if kept under cork.

Presently we turn over that pile of letters again. We find in the lees of the heap two or three that have gone for six months and can safely be destroyed. Bill is still on our mind, but in a pleasant, dreamy kind of way. He does not ache or twinge us as he did a month ago. It is fine to have old friends like that and keep in touch with them. We wonder how he is and whether he has two children or three. Splendid old Bill!

By this time we have written Bill several letters in imagination and enjoyed doing so, but the matter of sending him an actual letter has begun to pall. The thought no longer has the savor and vivid sparkle it had once. When one feels like that, it is unwise to write. Letters should be spontaneous outpourings: they should never be undertaken merely from a sense of duty. We know that Bill wouldn't want to get a letter that was dictated by a feeling of obligation.

Another fortnight or so elapsing, it occurs to us that we have entirely forgotten what Bill said to us in that letter. We take it out and con it over. Delightful fellow! It is full of his own felicitous kinks of whim, though some of it sounds a little old-fashioned by now. It seems a bit stale, has lost some of its freshness and surprise. Better not answer it just yet, for Christmas will soon be here and we shall have to write then anyway. We wonder, can Bill hold out until Christmas without a letter?

We have been rereading some of those imaginary letters to Bill that have been dancing in our head. They are full of all sorts of fine stuff. If Bill ever gets them, he will know how we love him. To use O. Henry's immortal joke, we have days of Damon and Knights of Pythias writing those uninked letters to Bill. A curious thought has come to us. Perhaps it would be better if we never saw Bill again. It is very difficult to talk to a man when you like him so much. It is much easier to write in the sweet fantastic strain. We are so inarticulate when face to face. If Bill comes to town, we will leave word that we have gone way. Good old Bill! He will always be a precious memory.

A few days later a sudden frenzy sweeps over us, and though we have many pressing matters on hand, we mobilize pen and paper and literary shock troops and prepare to hurl several battalions at Bill. But, strangely enough, our utterance seems stilted and stiff. We have nothing to say. *My dear Bill*, we begin, *it seems a long time since we heard from you. Why don't you write? We still love you, in spite of all your shortcomings.*

That doesn't seem very cordial. We muse over the pen and nothing comes. Bursting with affection, we are unable to say a word.

Just then the phone rings. " Hello? " we say.

It is Bill, come to town unexpectedly.

" Good old fish! " we cry, ecstatic. " Meet you at the corner of Tenth and Chestnut in five minutes."

We tear up the unfinished letter. Bill will never know how much we love him. Perhaps it is just as well. It is very embarrassing to have your friends know how you feel about them. When we meet him, we will be a little bit on our guard. It would not be well to be betrayed into any extravagance of cordiality.

And perhaps a not altogether false little story could be written about a man who never visited those most dear to him, because it panged him so to say good-by when he had to leave.

STUDYING THE ESSAY

1. Find several examples of Morley's careful choice of words.
2. Is Morley describing something which happens to you once in a while? How do your letter-answering habits resemble his?
3. What are the qualities of a good letter?
4. The friendly letter can be a literary masterpiece. In your library look up some letters by Charles Lamb, John Keats, or Elizabeth Barrett Browning. Do you ever try to write a literary letter?
5. Words to learn: *cynicism, speculation, fallacy, felicitous, ecstatic, crass.*

COMPOSITION TOPICS

1. Write a good letter to someone you know and love. Try to avoid the use of slang.
2. On Unpreparing Lessons
3. Write a thank-you letter.
4. If My Desk Could Speak
5. Try writing the letter which the author did not write.

FRANK SULLIVAN, 1892–

Francis John Sullivan — apparently no one knows him by this name — was born in Saratoga Springs, New York, and still lives there. He was graduated from Cornell in 1914 and saw service as an infantry officer in World War I. He had done newspaper work in Saratoga Springs since his 'teens, and after the war he began writing a column for the New York *World*, the paper which had the most brilliant list of special writers ever assembled: Walter Lippmann, Franklin P. Adams (F.P.A.), Alexander Woollcott, Deems Taylor, Robert Benchley, and Heywood Broun. Sullivan has written, thus far, eight books and numerous sketches for various magazines, especially the *New Yorker*. He is also widely known as Mr. Arbuthnot, the cliché expert, in *New Yorker* articles and in radio programs.

His humor, or "slapstick satire," as one reviewer called it, has a wide range, from cliché to wild parodies of opera librettos to burlesque literary criticism like that in "A Garland of Ibids," reprinted below. This essay is taken from a volume neatly called *A Rock in Every Snowball*. Another volume which readers admire also has a ridiculous title: *A Pearl in Every Oyster*. Both titles are significant, for, while much of Sullivan's writing seems merely ridiculous, there is usually a serious or valuable point to it. The footnotes in the essay here reflect a great deal of learning, even though they are in themselves ludicrous. Any one who has ever had to prepare a research paper will understand thoroughly the problems which footnotes cause. *New England: Indian Summer*, which is the object of Sullivan's wit in "A Garland of Ibids," is one volume in a series written by Van Wyck Brooks on the history of American literature. The book is probably in your school library. Have a look at it.

A GARLAND OF IBIDS
FOR VAN WYCK BROOKS

I have just finished reading a book [1] which struck me as being one of the finest books I have read since I read *The Flowering of New England,* by the same author.[2] But there is a fly in the ointment. I have been rendered cockeyed by the footnotes. There seem to be too many of them, even for a book largely about Boston.[3] I do not know why the author had to have so many footnotes. Maybe he had a reason for each one, but I suspect the footnote habit has crept up on him, for I got out his book on Emerson,[4] published in 1932, and he used practically no footnotes in it.

[1] *New England: Indian Summer.*

[2] Van Wyck Brooks, author of *New England: Indian Summer, The Flowering of New England, The Life of Emerson, The Ordeal of Mark Twain,* and other books.

[3] Sometimes referred to as The Hub. Capital and chief city of Massachusetts. Scene of the Boston Tea Party and the arrest of Henry L. Mencken. Bostonians are traditionally noted for their civic pride, or, as an envious New York critic once termed it, their parochial outlook. It is related that on an occasion when Saltonstall Boylston learned that his friend L. Cabot Lowell was leaving for a trip around the world, he inquired of Lowell, "Which route shall you take, L.C.?" "Oh, I shall go by way of Dedham, of course," replied Mr. Lowell. On another occasion, the old Back Bay aristocrat Ralph Waldo Mulcahy said to Oliver Wendell Rooney, "By the way, Rooney, did your ancestors come over on the *Mayflower?*" "Oh, no," replied Mr. Rooney. "They arrived on the next boat. They sent the servants over on the *Mayflower.*"

[4] Ralph Waldo Emerson, Sage of Concord and famous transcendentalist philosopher, not to be confused with Ralph McAllister Ingersoll, editor of *PM.*

You read along in *New England: Indian Summer*, interested to the hilt in what Van Wyck Brooks is telling you
about Longfellow,[5] Thoreau,[6] Phillips,[7] James,[8] Alcott,[9]

[5] Henry Wadsworth Longfellow, Good Gray Poet. Longfellow
was no footnote addict. He preferred foot*prints*. Cf. his "Psalm of
Life":

> And, departing, leave behind us
> Footprints on the sands of time.

[6] Henry David Thoreau, philosopher who lived at Walden Pond
for two years on carrots, twigs, nuts, minnows, creek water, and, as
Margaret Fuller suspected (booming it out at Brook Farm in that full,
rich voice of hers, to the dismay of William Ellery Channing, Henry
Wadsworth Longfellow, Edward Everett Hale, John Lothrop Mot-
ley, Charles Eliot Norton, and William Lloyd Garrison), sirloin
steaks and creamery butter smuggled to him by Emerson. Suffering
as he did from a vitamin deficiency, the result of too much moss in
his diet, Thoreau became somewhat of a misanthrope and would often creep up behind members of the Saturday Club and shout "Boo!"
or, as some authorities maintain, "Pooh!" The matter is not clarified
very much, one must admit, by a letter Mrs. Harriet Beecher Stowe
wrote to her son, Harriet Beecher Stowe, Jr. (not to be confused with
Herbert Bayard Swope), on June 7, 1854, in which she states: "Not
much to write home about, as the saying goes. Dave Thoreau here
for supper last nite [*sic*]. He got into an argument with John Greenleaf Whittier, the Good Gray Poet, as to whether snow is really er-
mine too dear for an earl, and Greenleaf called him a Communist.
Dave then crept up behind Greenleaf and shouted either 'Boo! ' [*sic*]
or 'Pooh! ' [*sic*], I couldn't make out wich [*sic*]. All well here except F. Marion Crawford, Sarah Orne Jewett, Charles Dudley War-
ner, Thomas Wentworth Higginson, and William Dean Howells,
who complain of feeling sic [*sic*]. Your aff. mother, H. B. STOWE, SR."
[7] Wendell Phillips. He was about the only Bostonian of his time
who wore no middle name and he was therefore considered half
naked. Even Mark Twain, when he went to visit Howells in Boston,
registered as Samuel Langhorne Clemens.
[8] Probably not Jesse James. Probably is either William James, de-
viser of Pragmatic Sanctions, or his brother Henry, the novelist. It
was about this time that Henry James was going through his transition period, and could not make up his mind whether he was in England living in America or in America living in England.
[9] Amos Bronson Alcott, educator and bad provider. The Mr. Mi-
cawber of his day. Not to be confused with Novelist Bus Bronson of
Yale or Mrs. Chauncey Olcott.

Lowell,[10] Adams,[11] and other great figures of the Periclean Age of The Hub,[12] when suddenly there is a footnote.

The text is in fine, clear type. The footnotes are in small type. So it is quite a chore to keep focusing up and down the page, especially if you have old eyes or a touch of astigmatism.[13] By and by you say to yourself, "I be damn if I look down at any more footnotes!" but you do, because the book is so interesting you don't want to miss even the footnotes.[14]

When you get to the footnote at the bottom of the page, like as not all you find is *ibid. Ibid* is a great favorite of foot-

[10] James Russell Lowell, poet, essayist, and kinfolk of late rotund, cigar-smoking Back Bay Poetess Amy Lowell, no rhymester she.

[11] Henry Adams, author of *The Education of Henry Adams*, by Henry Adams. Not to be confused with Henry Adams, Samuel Adams, John Adams, John Quincy Adams, Abigail Adams, Charles Edward Adams (not to be confused with Charles Francis Adams, Charles Henry Adams, or Henry Adams), Maude Adams, Franklin Pierce Adams, Samuel Hopkins Adams, Bristow Adams, George Matthew Adams, James Truslow Adams, Adams Express, Adams & Flanagan, Horace Flanagan, or Louis Adamic.

[12] Sometimes referred to as Boston. One is reminded of the famous quatrain:

> Here's to the City of Boston,
> The home of Filene and the Card.,
> Where the Rileys speak only to Cabots
> And the Cabots speak only to God!

[13] In this connection, it is interesting to note that Louisa May Alcott had a touch of astigmatism, if we are to accept the word of Charles Eliot Norton. Edward Everett Hale states in his *Letters*, Vol. XV, Ch. 8, pp. 297 *et seq.*, that William Cullen Bryant told Oliver Wendell Holmes that on one occasion when the fun was running high at Thomas Wentworth Higginson's home and all barriers were down, Thomas Bailey Aldrich had put the question bluntly to Charles Eliot Norton, saying, "Now, listen, has Louisa May Alcott got astigmatism or hasn't she?" Charles Eliot Norton answered, perhaps unwisely, "Yes." Cf. the famous dictum of General William Tecumseh Sherman, sometimes erroneously ascribed to General Ulysses Simpson Grant: "Never bring up a lady's name in the mess."

[14] Ah there, Van Wyck!

note-mad authors.[15] It was a great favorite with Gibbon.[16] How come writers of fiction do not need footnotes? Take Edna Ferber.[17] She doesn't use footnotes. Suppose Edna Herford [18] took to writing her novels in this manner: " Cicely Ticklepaw * sat at her dressing table in a brown study. She had ' a very strange feeling she'd ne'er felt before, a kind of a grind of depression.' † Could it be love? ‡ If so, why had she sent him § away? She sighed, and a soft cry of ' Aye me! ' ¶ escaped her. Seizing a nail file desperately, she commenced hacking away at her fingernails, when a voice behind her said, ' O! that I were a glove upon that hand, that

[15] So is cf.

[16] Edward Gibbon, English historian, not to be confused with Cedric Gibbons, Hollywood art director. Edward Gibbon was a great hand for footnotes, especially if they gave him a chance to show off his Latin. He would come sniffing up to a nice, spicy morsel of scandal about the Romans and then, just as the reader expected him to dish the dirt, he'd go into his Latin routine, somewhat as follows: " In those days vice reached depths not plumbed since the reign of Caligula and it was an open secret that the notorious Empress Theodora *in tres partes divisa erat* and that she was also addicted to the *argumentum ad hominem!* " Gibbon, prissy little fat man that he was, did that just to tease readers who had flunked Caesar.

[17] Edna Cabot Ferber, contemporary New England novelist. It is related of Edna Ferber that she once met Oliver Herford in Gramercy Park and recoiled at the sight of an extremely loud necktie he was wearing. "Heavens above, Oliver Herford! " exclaimed Miss Ferber, never one not to speak her mind. "That is a terrible cravat. Why do you wear it? " " Because it is my wife's whim that I wear it," explained Oliver Herford. "Well, land sakes alive, before I'd wear a tie like that just on account of a wife's whim! " jeered Miss Ferber. "You don't know my wife," said Oliver Herford. "She's got a whim of iron." Miss Ferber later made this incident the basis for the dramatic battle between the husband and wife in her novel *The Cravat*.

[18] No, no, no, not Edna Herford! Edna *Ferber!* Edna Herford is the fellow who had the wife with the iron whim.

* Blonde, lovely, and twenty-one.

† See " I'm Falling in Love with Someone " — Victor Herbert.

‡ Sure.

§ Cleon Bel Murphy, the man she loves.

¶ *Romeo and Juliet*, Act II, Scene 2.

I might touch that cheek! ' ** Cicely reddened, turned. It
was Cleon Bel Murphy! Softly, she told him, 'What man
art thou, that, thus bescreen'd in night, so stumblest on my
counsel! ' " ††

What would Van Wyck Brooks say if Edna Ferber wrote
like that? [19] Yes. Exactly. Now where were we? [20] No, I
was not. I know what I was saying. You keep out of this.
You're a footnote.[21] Yeah? Well, just for that, no more footnotes. Out you go! [22] I am, that's who.[23] See what I mean,
Van Wyck? Give a footnote an inch and it'll take a foot.[24]
I give up. They got me. And they'll get you too in the end,
Van Wyck. You may think you're strong enough to keep
'em under control; you may think you can take a footnote
or leave it. All I say is, remember Dr. Jekyll! Lay off 'em,
Van. I'm telling you for your own good.

— UNEASY BROOKS FAN [25]

** *Ibid.*
†† *Ibid.*
[19] And what would Edna Ferber say if Edna Ferber wrote like
that?
[20] You were saying Louisa May Alcott had astigmatism.
[21] Yeah? And how far would you have got in this article without
footnotes?
[22] Who's gonna put me out?
[23] Yeah? You and who else?
[24] Yoo-hoo! Footnote!
[25] Frank Saltonstall Sullivan.

STUDYING THE ESSAY

1. As literary criticism, compare this essay with Mark Twain's
essay about Cooper's book. How do the writers' points of view
differ? How are they alike? Compare Twain's and Sullivan's essays with a current review in a magazine or newspaper.

2. What are the most ridiculous features of this essay?

3. Sullivan's pages are loaded with references to well-known

people. How many of the individuals listed in footnote 6 or 11 can you identify?

4. What does Sullivan really think of *New England: Indian Summer?*

5. Read some reviews of books, plays, or movies in a good newspaper or magazine. When you find a humorous review, bring it in and read it to the class. Humorous reviews often can be found in the New York *Times* and the *New Yorker.*

COMPOSITION TOPICS

1. Write a review of a poor movie or of a recent book which has little value. Try to entertain the reader, but make sure that the review is accurate.

2. Collect several reviews of the same book. Write a theme in which you analyze reasons for the critics' differences of opinion. (You will, of course, have to have read the book.)

JAMES THURBER, 1894–

      James Thurber is a native of Columbus, Ohio, and a graduate of Ohio State University. Both the city and the university have been immortalized in his writings, notably in *My Life and Hard Times,* one of the great books of American humor, and in other essays about his family and his teachers. The bulk of Thurber's work has appeared in the *New Yorker* magazine. In addition to writing essays, he collaborated with Elliott Nugent on a very successful play, *The Male Animal.* The best of his works may be found in *The Thurber Carnival* (1945) and *Thurber Country* (1953).

Thurber is as important a cartoonist as he is a writer. His drawings are amazingly simple. He does eloquent things with a single line. In the power of his drawing he has even been compared with Matisse, the great French painter whose drawings are masterpieces. Thurber's cartoon world is full of weird animals, ugly women, ineffectual men, and every imaginable variety of misfits. Many of the cartoons are really essays in picture form. A good collection of these cartoons is *Men, Women, and Dogs* (1943).

As a writer, Thurber is difficult to characterize. Being an expert cartoonist, he is a master of caricature, of exaggeration in which the original is still completely real. Grandfather in *My Life and Hard Times* or Aunt Gracie Shoaf in " The Night the Bed Fell " are examples of this kind of writing. While Thurber's cartoons indicate that he is not altogether satisfied with society, only a few of his essays are serious in tone. His satire, as in " The Macbeth Murder Mystery," is usually quiet, penetrating, and clear. And he has a wonderful ear for speech. The things his people say invariably sound right. Behind everything he has done, the reader cannot help seeing Thurber himself — tall, thin, absent-minded, looking with a penetrating, if myopic, eye upon the foibles of the world.

Readers of these essays who have not read *Macbeth* should, of course, repair to the library at once, read the play, and find out who *really* did it. And readers who enjoy " The Night the Bed Fell " will also like Thurber's yarn about the night the ghost got in or his description of himself trying to see something through a microscope.

THE NIGHT THE BED FELL

I suppose that the high-water mark of my youth in Columbus, Ohio, was the night the bed fell on my father. It makes a better recitation (unless, as some friends of mine have said, one has heard it five or six times) than it does a piece of writing, for it is almost necessary to throw furniture around, shake doors, and bark like a dog, to lend the proper atmosphere and verisimilitude to what is admittedly a somewhat incredible tale. Still, it did take place.

It happened, then, that my father had decided to sleep in the attic one night, to be away where he could think. My mother opposed the notion strongly because, she said, the old wooden bed up there was unsafe: it was wobbly and the heavy headboard would crash down on father's head in case the bed fell, and kill him. There was no dissuading him, however, and at a quarter past ten he closed the attic door behind him and went up the narrow twisting stairs. We later heard ominous creakings as he crawled into bed. Grandfather, who usually slept in the attic bed when he was with

us, had disappeared some days before. (On these occasions
he was usually gone six or eight days and returned growling
and out of temper, with the news that the federal Union was
run by a passel of blockheads and that the Army of the Potomac didn't have any more chance than a fiddler's bitch.)

We had visiting us at this time a nervous first cousin of
mine named Briggs Beall, who believed that he was likely to
cease breathing when he was asleep. It was his feeling that
if he were not awakened every hour during the night, he
might die of suffocation. He had been accustomed to setting
an alarm clock to ring at intervals until morning, but I persuaded him to abandon this. He slept in my room and I told
him that I was such a light sleeper that if anybody quit
breathing in the same room with me, I would wake instantly. He tested me the first night — which I had suspected
he would — by holding his breath after my regular breathing had convinced him I was asleep. I was not asleep, however, and called to him. This seemed to allay his fears a little, but he took the precaution of putting a glass of spirits of
camphor on a little table at the head of his bed. In case I
didn't arouse him until he was almost gone, he said, he would
sniff the camphor, a powerful reviver. Briggs was not the
only member of his family who had his crotchets. Old Aunt
Melissa Beall (who could whistle like a man, with two fingers in her mouth) suffered under the premonition that she
was destined to die on South High Street, because she had
been born on South High Street and married on South High
Street. Then there was Aunt Sarah Shoaf, who never went to
bed at night without the fear that a burglar was going to
get in and blow chloroform under her door through a tube.
To avert this calamity — for she was in greater dread of anesthetics than of losing her household goods — she always
piled her money, silverware, and other valuables in a neat
stack just outside her bedroom, with a note reading: " This

is all I have. Please take it and do not use your chloroform, as this is all I have." Aunt Gracie Shoaf also had a burglar phobia, but she met it with more fortitude. She was confident that burglars had been getting into her house every night for forty years. The fact that she never missed anything was to her no proof to the contrary. She always claimed that she scared them off before they could take anything, by throwing shoes down the hallway. When she went to bed she piled, where she could get at them handily, all the shoes there were about her house. Five minutes after she had turned off the light, she would sit up in bed and say "Hark!" Her husband, who had learned to ignore the whole situation as long ago as 1903, would either be sound asleep or pretend to be sound asleep. In either case he would not respond to her tugging and pulling, so that presently she would arise, tiptoe to the door, open it slightly, and heave a shoe down the hall in one direction and its mate down the hall in the other direction. Some nights she threw them all, some nights only a couple of pair.

But I am straying from the remarkable incidents that took place during the night that the bed fell on father. By midnight we were all in bed. The layout of the rooms and the disposition of their occupants is important to an understanding of what later occurred. In the front room upstairs (just under father's attic bedroom) were my mother and my brother Herman, who sometimes sang in his sleep, usually "Marching Through Georgia" or "Onward, Christian Soldiers." Briggs Beall and myself were in a room adjoining this one. My brother Roy was in a room across the hall from ours. Our bull terrier, Rex, slept in the hall.

My bed was an army cot, one of those affairs which are made wide enough to sleep on comfortably only by putting up, flat with the middle section, the two sides which ordinarily hang down like the sideboards of a drop-leaf table.

When these sides are up, it is perilous to roll too far toward
the edge, for then the cot is likely to tip completely over,
bringing the whole bed down on top of one with a tremendous banging crash. This, in fact, is precisely what happened, about two o'clock in the morning. (It was my
mother who, in recalling the scene later, first referred to it
as " the night the bed fell on your father.")

Always a deep sleeper, slow to arouse (I had lied to
Briggs), I was at first unconscious of what had happened
when the iron cot rolled me onto the floor and toppled over
on me. It left me still warmly bundled up and unhurt, for
the bed rested above me like a canopy. Hence I did not
wake up, only reached the edge of consciousness and went
back. The racket, however, instantly awakened my mother,
in the next room, who came to the immediate conclusion
that her worst dread was realized: the big wooden bed upstairs had fallen on father. She therefore screamed, " Let's
go to your poor father! " It was this shout, rather than the
noise of my cot falling, that awakened my brother Herman,
in the same room with her. He thought that mother had become, for no apparent reason, hysterical. " You're all right,
mamma! " he shouted, trying to calm her. They exchanged
shout for shout for perhaps ten seconds: " Let's go to your
poor father! " and " You're all right! " That woke up
Briggs. By this time I was conscious of what was going on,
in a vague way, but did not yet realize that I was under my
bed instead of on it. Briggs, awakening in the midst of loud
shouts of fear and apprehension, came to the quick conclusion that he was suffocating and that we were all trying to
" bring him out." With a low moan, he grasped the glass
of camphor at the head of his bed and instead of sniffing it
poured it over himself. The room reeked of camphor.
" Ugf, ahfg! " choked Briggs, like a drowning man, for he
had almost succeeded in stopping his breath under the del-

uge of pungent spirits. He leaped out of bed and groped toward the open window, but he came up against one that was closed. With his hand, he beat out the glass, and I could hear it crash and tinkle in the alleyway below. It was at this juncture that I, in trying to get up, had the uncanny sensation of feeling my bed above me! Foggy with sleep, I now suspected, in my turn, that the whole uproar was being made in a frantic endeavor to extricate me from what must be an unheard-of and perilous situation. " Get me out of this! " I bawled. " Get me out! " I think I had the nightmarish belief that I was entombed in a mine. " Gugh! " gasped Briggs, floundering in his camphor.

By this time my mother, still shouting, pursued by Herman, still shouting, was trying to open the door to the attic, in order to go up and get my father's body out of the wreckage. The door was stuck, however, and wouldn't yield. Her frantic pulls on it only added to the general banging and confusion. Roy and the dog were now up, the one shouting questions, the other barking.

Father, farthest away and soundest sleeper of all, had by this time been awakened by the battering on the attic door. He decided that the house was on fire. " I'm coming, I'm coming! " he wailed in a slow, sleepy voice — it took him many minutes to regain full consciousness. My mother, still believing he was caught under the bed, detected in his " I'm coming! " the mournful, resigned note of one who is preparing to meet his Maker. " He's dying! " she shouted.

" I'm all right! " Briggs yelled, to reassure her. " I'm all right! " He still believed that it was his own closeness to death that was worrying mother. I found at last the light switch in my room, unlocked the door, and Briggs and I joined the others at the attic door. The dog, who never did like Briggs, jumped for him — assuming that he was the culprit in whatever was going on — and Roy had to throw Rex and hold him. We could hear father crawling out of bed upstairs. Roy pulled the attic door open, with a mighty jerk, and father came down the stairs, sleepy and irritable but safe and sound. My mother began to weep when she saw him. Rex began to howl. " What in the name of God is going on here? " asked father.

The situation was finally put together like a gigantic jig-saw puzzle. Father caught a cold from prowling around in his bare feet but there were no other bad results. " I'm glad," said mother, who always looked on the bright side of things, " that your grandfather wasn't here."

STUDYING THE ESSAY

1. Characterize Father, Briggs Beall, and Aunt Sarah.
2. Could a series of events like this really happen?
3. Discuss the methods by which Thurber produces humor. Consider both exaggeration and understatement. Do you think that the people in the essay are true to life?
4. Read further in *My Life and Hard Times* to learn more about the author and his family.
5. What is meant by a " caricature "? How does it differ from a straightforward description of a person?

COMPOSITION TOPIC

Try to remember the exact details of a curious or humorous episode in your life at home, and write an essay about it. Note that most people find it hard to remember the " little " things from their own lives. Yet these little incidents are often the most interesting material for a writer.

THE MACBETH MURDER MYSTERY

"It was a stupid mistake to make," said the American woman I had met at my hotel in the English lake country, "but it was on the counter with the other Penguin books — the little sixpenny ones, you know, with the paper covers — and I supposed of course it was a detective story. All the others were detective stories. I'd read all the others, so I bought this one without really looking at it carefully. You can imagine how mad I was when I found it was Shakespeare." I murmured something sympathetically. "I don't see why the Penguin-books people had to get out Shakespeare plays in the same size and everything as the detective stories," went on my companion. "I think they have different-colored jackets," I said. "Well, I didn't notice that," she said. "Anyway, I got real comfy in bed that night and all ready to read a good mystery story and here I had *The Tragedy of Macbeth* — a book for high school students. Like *Ivanhoe*." "Or *Lorne Doone*," I said. "Exactly," said the American lady. "And I was just crazy for a good Agatha Christie, or something. Hercule Poirot is my favorite detective." "Is he the rabbity one?" I asked. "Oh, no," said my crimefiction expert. "He's the Belgian one. You're thinking of Mr. Pinkerton, the one that helps Inspector Bull. He's good, too."

Over her second cup of tea my companion began to tell the plot of a detective story that had fooled her completely — it seems it was the old family doctor all the time. But I cut in on her. "Tell me," I said. "Did you read *Macbeth?*" "I *had* to read it," she said. "There wasn't a scrap of anything else to read in the whole room." "Did you like it? " I asked. "No, I did not," she said, decisively. "In the first place, I don't think for a moment that Macbeth did it." I looked at her blankly. "Did what? " I asked. "I don't think for a moment that he killed the King," she said. "I don't think the Macbeth woman was mixed up in it, either. You suspect them the most, of course, but those are the ones that are never guilty — or shouldn't be, anyway." "I'm afraid," I began, "that I — " "But don't you see? " said the American lady. "It would spoil everything if you could figure out right away who did it. Shakespeare was too smart for that. I've read that people never *have* figured out *Hamlet*, so it isn't likely Shakespeare would have made *Macbeth* as simple as it seems." I thought this over while I filled my pipe. "Who do you suspect? " I asked, suddenly. "Macduff," she said, promptly. "Good God! " I whispered softly.

"Oh Macduff did it, all right," said the murder specialist. "Hercule Poirot would have got him easily. "How did you figure it out? " I demanded. "Well," she said, "I didn't right away. At first I suspected Banquo. And then, of course, he was the second person killed. That was good right in there, that part. The person you suspect of the first murder should always be the second victim." "Is that so? " I murmured. "Oh, yes," said my informant. "They have to keep surprising you. Well, after the second murder I didn't know who the killer was for a while." "How about Malcolm and Donalbain, the King's sons? " I asked. "As I remember it, they fled right after the first murder. That looks suspicious." "Too suspicious," said the American lady. "Much too suspicious. When they flee, they're never guilty. You can count on that." "I believe," I said, "I'll have a brandy," and I summoned the waiter. My companion leaned toward me, her eyes bright, her teacup quivering. "Do you know who discovered Duncan's body? " she demanded. I said I was sorry, but I had forgotten. " Macduff discovers it," she said, slipping into the historical present. " Then he comes running downstairs and shouts, ' Confusion has broke open the Lord's anointed temple ' and ' Sacrilegious murder has made his masterpiece ' and on and on like that." The good lady tapped me on the knee. " All that stuff was rehearsed," she said. " You wouldn't say a lot of stuff like that, offhand, would you — if you had found a body? " She fixed me with a glittering eye. " I — " I began. " You're right! " she said. " You wouldn't! Unless you had practiced it in advance. ' My God, there's a body in here! ' is what an innocent man would say." She sat back with a confident glare.

I thought for a while. " But what do you make of the Third Murderer? " I asked. " You know, the Third Murderer has puzzled *Macbeth* scholars for three hundred years." " That's because they never thought of Macduff," said the American lady. " It was Macduff, I'm certain. You couldn't have one of the victims murdered by two ordinary thugs — the murderer always has to be somebody important." " But what about the banquet scene? " I asked, after a moment. " How do you account for Macbeth's guilty actions there, when Banquo's ghost came in and sat in his chair? " The lady leaned forward and tapped me on the knee again. " There wasn't any ghost," she said. " A big, strong man like that doesn't go around seeing ghosts — especially in a brightly lighted banquet hall with dozens of people around. Macbeth was *shielding somebody!* " " Who was he shielding? " I asked. " Mrs. Macbeth, of course," she said. " He thought she did it and he was going to take the rap himself. The husband always does that when the wife is suspected." " But what," I demanded, " about the sleepwalking scene, then? " " The same thing, only the other

way around," said my companion. "That time *she* was
shielding *him*. She wasn't asleep at all. Do you remember
where it says, 'Enter Lady Macbeth with a taper'? "
"Yes," I said. "Well, people who walk in their sleep *never
carry lights!*" said my fellow traveler. "They have a second
sight. Did you ever hear of a sleepwalker carrying a light? "
"No," I said, "I never did." "Well, then, she wasn't asleep.
She was acting guilty to shield Macbeth." "I think," I said,
"I'll have another brandy," and I called the waiter. When
he brought it, I drank it rapidly and rose to go. "I believe,"
I said, "that you have got hold of something. Would you
lend me that *Macbeth?* I'd like to look it over tonight. I
don't feel, somehow, as if I'd ever really read it." "I'll get
it for you," she said. "But you'll find that I am right."

I read the play over carefully that night, and the next
morning, after breakfast, I sought out the American woman.
She was on the putting green, and I came up behind her
silently and took her arm. She gave an exclamation. "Could
I see you alone? " I asked, in a low voice. She nodded cau-
tiously and followed me to a secluded spot. "You've found
out something? " she breathed. "I've found out," I said,
triumphantly, "the name of the murderer! " "You mean it
wasn't Macduff? " she said. "Macduff is as innocent of
those murders," I said, "as Macbeth and the Macbeth
woman." I opened the copy of the play, which I had with
me, and turned to Act II, Scene 2. "Here," I said, "you
will see where Lady Macbeth says, 'I laid their daggers
ready. He could not miss 'em. Had he not resembled my
father as he slept, I had done it.' Do you see? " "No," said
the Amercian woman, bluntly, "I don't." "But it's simple! "
I exclaimed. "I wonder I didn't see it years ago. The reason
Duncan resembled Lady Macbeth's father as he slept is that
it actually was her father!" "Good God! " breathed my
companion, softly. "Lady Macbeth's father killed the

King," I said, " and, hearing someone coming, thrust the body under the bed and crawled into the bed himself." " But," said the lady, " you can't have a murderer who only appears in the story once. You can't have that." " I know that," I said, and I turned to Act II, Scene 4. " It says here, ' Enter Ross with an old Man.' Now, that old man is never identified and it is my contention he was old Mr. Macbeth, whose ambition it was to make his daughter Queen. There you have your motive." " But even then," cried the American lady, " he's still a minor character! " " Not," I said, gleefully, " when you realize that he was also *one of the weird sisters in disguise!* " " You mean one of the three witches? " " Precisely," I said. " Listen to this speech of the old man's. ' On Tuesday last, a falcon towering in her pride of place, was by a mousing owl hawk'd at and kill'd.' Who does that sound like? " " It sounds like the way the three witches talk," said my companion, reluctantly. " Precisely! " I said again. " Well," said the American woman, " maybe you're right, but — " " I'm sure I am," I said. " And do you know what I'm going to do now? " " No," she said. " What? " " Buy a copy of *Hamlet*," I said, " and solve *that!* " My companion's eye brightened. " Then," she said, " you don't think Hamlet did it? " " I am," I said, " absolutely positive he didn't." " But who," she demanded, " do you suspect? " I looked at her cryptically. " Everybody," I said, and disappeared into a small grove of trees as silently as I had come.

STUDYING THE ESSAY

1. If you have studied *Macbeth*, you will fully appreciate the humor of this essay. If you have not read the play, perhaps a member of the class or the teacher will tell you about it.

2. Discuss the American woman's previous reading. How does it match yours?

3. How do you account for her approach to *Macbeth?*

4. In what ways is this essay purely humorous?

5. In what ways does the essay have a serious purpose?

COMPOSITION TOPICS

1. The Comic Book Reader Tackles Literature
2. The Serious Reader Criticizes the Comics
3. What Makes a Good Detective Story?

WILLIAM FAULKNER, 1897–

William Faulkner, the fourth American to win the Nobel Prize for literature (the others were Sinclair Lewis, Eugene O'Neill, and Pearl Buck), is considered by many critics to be America's greatest living novelist. His best work bears out the Nobel citation which praised " his powerful and artistically independent contribution to the new American novel."

Faulkner was born in Mississippi and has lived there all his life. His first novel, *Sartoris,* was published in 1929. Since then he has written more than a dozen novels and many short stories, in most of which the setting is an imaginary county in Mississippi modeled after the area in which he lives. *Intruder in the Dust,* published in 1949, was made into a successful movie, and over a million copies of *Sanctuary* (1931) have been sold. His best short stories are collected in a volume published in 1950.

In his novels and stories, Faulkner is more often than not concerned with the ugliness of life. His characters figure in plots which are full of horror and cruelty. And the style in the novels, while immensely powerful, is often difficult for the reader because of the complicated symbolism and the " stream-of-consciousness " technique which he uses.

None of these characteristics is evident in the short speech which he made in Stockholm when he received the Nobel award. In its six hundred words it has all of the characteristics an essay should have: perfection of style, clarity of thought, and personal quality. In addition to its technical mastery, it is a wonderful statement of faith in a bewildered world. The idea in the speech should be compared carefully with the central thought of " The First Citizens of the Atomic Age " by Norman Cousins, also in this book.

NOBEL PRIZE ACCEPTANCE SPEECH

I feel that this award was not made to me as a man but to my work — a life's work in the agony and sweat of the human spirit, not for glory and least of all for profit, but to create out of the materials of the human spirit something which did not exist before. So this award is only mine in trust. It will not be difficult to find a dedication for the money part of it commensurate with the purpose and significance of its origin. But I would like to do the same with the acclaim too, by using this moment as a pinnacle from which I might be listened to by the young men and women already dedicated to the same anguish and travail, among whom is already that one who will some day stand here where I am standing.

Our tragedy today is a general and universal physical fear so long sustained by now that we can even bear it. There are no longer problems of the spirit. There is only the question: When will I be blown up? Because of this, the young man or woman writing today has forgotten the problems of the human heart in conflict with itself which alone can make good writing because only that is worth writing about, worth the agony and the sweat.

He must learn them again. He must teach himself that the basest of all things is to be afraid; and, teaching himself that, forget it forever, leaving no room in his workshop for anything but the old verities and truths of the heart, the old universal truths lacking which any story is ephemeral and doomed — love and honor and pity and pride and compassion and sacrifice. Until he does so he labors under a curse. He writes not of love but of lust, of defeats in which nobody loses anything of value, of victories without hope and worst of all without pity or compassion. His griefs grieve on no universal bones, leaving no scars. He writes not of the heart but of the glands.

Until he relearns these things he will write as though he stood among and watched the end of man. I decline to accept the end of man. It is easy enough to say that man is immortal simply because he will endure; that when the last ding-dong of doom has clanged and faded from the last worthless rock hanging tideless in the last red and dying evening, that even then there will still be one more sound: that of his puny inexhaustible voice, still talking. I refuse to accept this. I believe that man will not merely endure: he will prevail. He is immortal, not because he alone among creatures has an inexhaustible voice, but because he has a soul, a spirit capable of compassion and sacrifice and endurance. The poet's, the writer's, duty is to write about these things. It is his privilege to help man endure by lifting his heart, by reminding him of the courage and honor and hope and pride and compassion and pity and sacrifice which have been the glory of his past. The poet's voice need not merely be the record of man, it can be one of the props, the pillars to help him endure and prevail.

STUDYING THE ESSAY

1. Study the second paragraph of the speech. Do you agree with the writer?

2. What are the really lasting values on the earth?

3. Compare the theme of the last paragraph with the teachings of the major religions.

4. State the idea of this speech in one sentence.

5. Read this speech aloud. It is worth memorizing.
6. Discuss the history of the Nobel Prize awards.

COMPOSITION TOPICS

1. Try to write a poetic version of the last paragraph of this speech.
2. The Only Thing We Have to Fear Is Fear Itself

DONALD CULROSS PEATTIE, 1898–

It is appropriate that Donald Culross Peattie, whose books are filled with the sweep of American history and the range of America's natural wonders, should be a Middle Westerner who was educated in the East and lives in California. A graduate of Harvard, Peattie is one of the nation's leading naturalists. He is a Fellow of the American Academy of Arts and Sciences, a member of the National Institute of Arts and Letters, and the author of more than thirty books, ranging from technical studies on natural history and botany to *An Almanac for Moderns* (1935). This last is a naturalist's lyric daybook, which won the Limited Editions Club Gold Medal. Among his most popular books are the *Almanac*, now in its fourteenth printing; *Green Laurels* (1936), concerning the work of some of the world's great naturalists; *Audubon's America* (1941); *Journey into America* (1943), a series of essays about little-known episodes in history; and *The Natural History of Trees* (1950), from which "Eastern White Oak" is taken. Mr. Peattie is a roving editor for the *Reader's Digest* and contributes regularly to that magazine.

Like Rachel Carson, Peattie is a scientist who is also a his-torian and a remarkable literary stylist. And like William Beebe, Peattie has the great gift of being able to transmit to his readers his own love of his subject matter. "They are never to be for-gotten," he writes, "that first bird pursued through thicket and over field with serious intent, not to kill but to know it, or that first plant lifted reverently and excitedly from the earth." Peat-tie's love of nature, from the frog's egg and the water spider to the white oak and the Great Plains, makes him spiritually a descendant of Thoreau. Either man would be a wonderful guide on a " nature walk."

"Eastern White Oak " is typical of Peattie's writing. In it there are his broad historical point of view and also his clear scientist's eye for detail. In it there is a sample of the rich, poetic prose which delights the readers of all of Peattie's books. Other exquisite tree portraits in this same book, which is one of the best guides to the trees of America both scientifically and stylistically, are those of the pine, the dogwood, the hemlock, and the sycamore.

EASTERN WHITE OAK

If Oak is the king of trees, as tradition has it, then the White Oak, throughout its range, is the king of kings. The Tuliptree can grow taller, and the Sycamore in the days of the virgin forest had gigantic boles, but no other tree in our silva has so great a spread. The mighty branches, themselves often fifty feet long or more, leave the trunk nearly at right angles and extend their arms benignantly above the generations of men who pass beneath them. Indeed, the fortunate possessor of an old White Oak owns a sort of second home, an outdoor mansion of shade and greenery and leafy music. So deep is the taproot of such a tree, so wide the thrust of the innumerable horizontal roots, that if one could see its whole underground system this would look like a reflection, somewhat foreshortened, of the giant above ground.

Like the detail of a cathedral, the White Oak's minor points are beauty too. When the leaves unfold they clothe

the tree in a veil of vivid red gradually turning pink and then silvery white. In autumn this foliage is a rich winy color, and in its withered final state it tends to cling all winter. The acorns germinate soon after they fall, and before the cold weather their first little roots are in the ground — if they have not been harvested by squirrels or birds with which they are a favorite food. They were a staple of diet, too, with the Indians, for though a little bitter for eating out of hand, they sweeten after boiling.

When the first New England colonists saw White Oak on the shores of Massachusetts Bay, they recognized it gladly as a close relative of the English or Norman Oak (*Quercus robur*), which had for centuries built England's navy and merchant fleet and was a very synonym for staunchness. But that Oak which once covered most of England had been cut and cut; shortages were becoming evident in Queen Elizabeth's day, and increased with alarming rapidity. Cromwell, in sequestrating the Crown lands, and those of the Church and the nobles, saw a ready revenue in leveling the Oaks, and with them he built a great navy. But wooden ships decay faster than Oaks can grow; the proudest ships of the line had a life expectancy of but a few years. So the Cromwellian orgy of Oaken shipbuilding was followed by forest dearth.

This offered a great chance to the American colonies. Our White Oak, however, met with serious opposition from the British shipbuilders and the inspection boards of the Royal Navy. Scornfully they maintained that it was weaker than their own as a structural timber, and that it was far more subject to decay. The truth of this lay simply in the haste of the cutting and carelessness of seasoning. No wood is so troublesome as Oak to season; it must be air-dried, over a long period, yet kept from exposure to sun and rain lest cracks and checks develop.

Indeed, the hastily rushed ships of English Oak were in as bad condition as those of our own Oak. Samuel Pepys describes his inspection of such a vessel in 1677 where he gathered from the boards "toadstools . . . as big as my fist." When Lord Sandwich inspected the ships at Chatham in 1771, it was necessary to shovel away the fungal filth before the timbers could be seen. Often the dry rot never appeared on the surface but, like termites, gnawed away the interior, especially in that most vulnerable place known to sailors as the futtocks or wales — just above the water line, where the heavy guns were carried. The famous disaster of the *Royal George* in 1782 was caused when the whole bottom of the ship dropped out from dry rot.

For all of this, the British loftily shook their heads at American White Oak as far inferior to their own. Well, if the mother country would not take our White Oak, we would build our own ships of it. The immortal frigate *Constitution* had a gun deck of solid White Oak of Massachusetts, her keel was the same wood from New Jersey, while knees of Maryland White Oak framed her keelsons. All-Oak ships became the pride of our shipbuilders; not good enough for the British Navy, they were just good enough to carry the New England sea captains around the world. Nor has White Oak entirely lost its place in the American Navy. The keels of our mine sweepers and patrol boats in World War II were still being laid in White Oak, and some of it came from Franklin D. Roosevelt's estate of "Hyde Park."

On land as on the sea, this great tree gave its strength to our people. Through two centuries the pioneers built their blockhouses of its stout timbers, their bridges, barns, and mills and log cabins. For this is the best all-around hardwood in America. True, White Pine warps and checks less, Hickory is more resilient, Ironwood is stronger, and Locust more durable; but White Oak would stand second to almost all these trees in each property in which they excel and, combining all these good qualities in a single species, it comes out in the end as the incomparable wood for nearly every purpose for which wood can be used. In a great table prepared by the Forest Service on the uses of woods, White Oak almost invariably occupies first, second, or third place under every item, except for wood pulp and plywood, tobacco pipes, artificial limbs, and airplanes. Obviously it is too hard and too valuable for the first two, too heavy for the last two, and since it develops no burls is not made into pipes.

But " pipes," in quite another sense, were some of the first objects made out of White Oak by the colonists, for to them a pipe meant a cask for wine and other liquids. Today we speak of "tight cooperage," meaning barrels that will hold liquids, as contrasted with " slack cooperage " for barrels intended to hold solids. Oak of most sorts is ideal for tight cooperage. So the pioneer people rived their barrel staves out of White Oak by hand, and sent them abroad, especially to France for wine casks and to the West Indies for rum; even from the heart of the Middle West this oaken cargo went floating down the Mississippi to New Orleans for export. For generations, too, the early Americans employed great amounts of the bark in tanning. Unfortunately, the trees stripped for this purpose were taken in spring, the time of year yielding the highest tannin amounts but least favorable for logging operations, which are best performed in winter. So that the peeled logs were left exposed to decay and weathering which, in Oak, is the opposite of seasoning. Always, too, the White Oak has been a fireplace favorite, for as a fuel it is the best all-around wood we have, weight for weight. And it is the heaviest of all our Oaks, as well as marvelously durable in contact with the soil. Indeed, its durability is taken as a standard, other woods being measured in percentages of the durability of White Oak.

As material for furniture, Oak is thus more sturdy than it is graceful. In England it was the favorite during the centuries when solid wood was employed; up to and through the Jacobean period it was uncontested. Thereafter, Walnut and Mahogany came to dispute with it, and their introduction, as well as the use of veneers, gave the cabinetmaker scope for lovelier creations, and Oak began to yield its primacy. Yet it has often returned to favor; in America we still shudder reminiscently over the "golden Oak era." Golden Oak was the name for a high varnish, laid usually on quarter-sawed boards. A quarter-sawed plank of full breadth is one which has one edge at the center of the tree, the other under the bark, and its beauty in White Oak consists in the large size and silvery brilliance of its medullary rays which are properly seen only on this cut of the wood. When an entire room is paneled in quartered Oak, the effect is indeed striking, and it was a great favorite forty and fifty years ago in the houses of the newly rich. The trouble with the "golden Oak era," however, was not with the noble wood, but in the ostentation of the costly display, the machine-made designs of the paneling, and that flashy varnish.

At present Oak as a furniture wood is chiefly used in office desks, though White Oak flooring remains unchallenged, and properly waxed Oak paneling will never cease to hold its high place. But quarter-sawed Oak is not satisfactorily cut from trees under 150 years old and, in general, dimension timbers must come from trees 100 to 300 years of age. So the supply of high-grade White Oak is running out, as the centenarian trees are cut or die.

Yet a hundred years is brief in the life of an old White Oak. There are members of this species still standing that were already tall when Columbus first raised his momentous landfall. In the Friends' Cemetery at Salem, New Jersey, there grows a White Oak that stood out as a landmark when the town was founded in 1675 and Quaker John Fenwick called the Indians together beneath its shade to make with them a treaty that, it is boasted, was never broken on either side. The whole region of the Jersey shore of the Delaware Bay is famous for its great White Oaks that line the streets of ancient towns like Salem, Mantua, Jefferson, and Mullica Hill, and shade the King's Highway which links them all to Philadelphia. The Tatum Oak at Mantua Grove was a giant said to have been 25½ feet in circumference at breast height, 87 feet tall, with a spread of 121 feet across. It is survived by its rival, the Hendrickson Oak of Mantua, which if not so large is not necessarily younger, for size in a tree depends in part upon the amount and closeness to the surface of the ground water. Its base spreads out in mighty buttresses that grip the earth. Half a dozen gigantic boughs sweep out and bend to the ground, with the weight of their years. Six generations of the same family have played here, where two thousand children could probably be gathered in this patriarch's shade. The supply of Indian arrowheads discovered in the soil in which it grows seems never quite exhausted. In the probable life span of this tree have been born, have mightily wrought, and died, William Penn and Benjamin Franklin, George Washington, Thomas Jefferson, Abraham Lincoln, and Woodrow Wilson, Peter the Great, Napoleon, and Beethoven. Thrones have crumbled and new empires arisen; great ideas have been born and great pictures painted, and the world revolutionized by science and invention; and still no man can say how many centuries this Oak will endure or what nations and creeds it may outlive.

Yet there are grander Oaks than this in our country. For reasons not clear, the largest and possibly the oldest are found on the Eastern Shore of Maryland. When, two hundred years and more gone by, the first colonists came to this region of long " necks " of land between the inlet bays and creeks, they built their manor houses in great White Oak forests. And though they long ago cleared, or cut for timber, the forest itself, they were an aristocratic people who appreciated the worth of the noblest old trees, and half a dozen standing today might lay claim to being the largest White Oak in the world.

Judgment on that would depend on one's standard, but the final honors generally go to two titans. The first is the largest of the seven Oaks in the churchyard of ivy-covered St. Paul's at Fairlee, built in 1713. Twenty-four and a half feet in girth, this tree is 118 feet tall and has a spread of 127 feet. Its rival, the great Oak at Wye Mills, is a monarch of superbly symmetrical beauty with a spread of 148 feet — a dimension unequaled by any other Oak in our silva. The Wye Oak's appearance of utmost antiquity is enhanced by great " knees " three or four feet high that surround its base.

With trees such as these, it is no wonder that Maryland has adopted the White Oak as its state tree, or that it was to the Eastern Shore that naval architects turned when the frigate *Constitution* was to be remodeled. There they would find White Oak timbers great enough to replace the original keelsons and futtocks and compass-timber that had been selected in the days of our forest abundance. Today the visitor who walks the decks of *Old Ironsides*, where she rests in honored peace in Boston Harbor, can feel an oaken-hearted strength, still sound, that is part of our American heritage.

STUDYING THE ESSAY

1. What are the characteristics of a large White Oak?
2. What is the connection between this tree and American history?
3. What are the uses of its wood?
4. What are the dimensions of some of the great White Oaks?
5. What have you read about the frigate *Constitution?*

COMPOSITION TOPICS

1. My Favorite Tree
2. America before the Forests Were Cut
3. Conservation of Forests
4. Tree Farming

E. B. WHITE, 1899–

In a review of Elwyn Brooks White's latest book, *The Second Tree from the Corner*, Irwin Edman had this to say: " It is high time to declare roundly that E. B. White is the finest essayist in the United States." These are strong words, but reading the essays bears out the judgment.

E. B. White was born in Mount Vernon, New York, and educated at Cornell. After service in the army during World War I, he went west, worked for the Seattle *Times,* saw Alaska, and then returned to New York, where he finally became a contributing editor of the *New Yorker* – a very fortunate association which has made critics ask which is the more important: the man or the magazine. In any case, some of the best writing in the magazine has come from White's pen.

In 1937 White and his family moved to a farm in Maine. For the next five years he wrote a monthly column for *Harper's* magazine called " One Man's Meat," although he never stopped contributing, at the same time, to the *New Yorker*. The essays written for *Harper's,* including the two in this volume, were published in book form in 1944. They show White at the top of his form and are, according to Clifton Fadiman, the best American essays since Thoreau. *One Man's Meat* contains many things: intimate glimpses of the problems of the farmer; character sketches of Maine neighbors; commentaries on war, politics, religion, children, and animals. It is a unique book, worth reading, rereading, and pondering.

For a number of years critics have been trying, often in vain, to explain why White's essays are so good. One quality is invariably present: a style so clear, so economical, so forceful that the reader always thinks, " This couldn't be said better."

James Thurber, for many years a colleague of White on the *New Yorker*, referred to "those silver and crystal sentences which have a ring like nobody else's sentences in the world."

Another vivid characteristic of White's writing is his point of view. His defense of freedom, of truth, and of world order has been absolutely consistent throughout his career as a writer. While there is some justification for calling White a humorist because of one or two early books and because of the many shafts of humor in his essays, there is far more justification for calling him one of the outstanding political philosophers of the day. The essays in *One Man's Meat* that were written after the outbreak of World War II and those in *The Wild Flag* and in many pages of the *New Yorker* are among the most eloquent statements of faith in freedom that have appeared in our time. And yet White never preaches. The depth and force of his ideas are more often than not disguised in an easy, colloquial language which may for a time belie the truths which he is expressing.

White's books are of several kinds. *The Second Tree from the Corner* (1954), like *One Man's Meat*, is a collection of essays and other writings, chiefly from the *New Yorker*. *Stuart Little* (1945) and *Charlotte's Web* (1952) are children's books, the first about a mouse, the other about a spider and her farm friends. These two delightful yarns are probably read more widely by adults than by children because the stories have meanings deeper than the easy style would suggest. *The Wild Flag* (1946) is a collection of *New Yorker* pieces about world government. There are other books in the list, but these five are perhaps the best introduction to White's writing.

WALDEN

Miss Nims, take a letter to Henry David Thoreau. Dear Henry: I thought of you the other afternoon as I was approaching Concord doing fifty on Route 62. That is a high speed at which to hold a philosopher in one's mind, but in this century we are a nimble bunch.

On one of the lawns in the outskirts of the village a woman was cutting the grass with a motorized lawn mower. What made me think of you was that the machine had rather got away from her, although she was game enough, and in the brief glimpse I had of the scene it appeared to me that the lawn was mowing the lady. She kept a tight grip on the handles, which throbbed violently with every explosion of the one-cylinder motor, and as she steered around bushes and lurched along at a reluctant trot behind her impetuous servant, she looked like a puppy who had grabbed something that was too much for him. Concord hasn't changed much, Henry; the farm implements and the animals still have the upper hand.

I may as well admit that I was journeying to Concord with the deliberate intention of visiting your woods; for although I have never knelt at the grave of a philosopher nor placed wreaths on moldy poets, and have often gone a mile out of my way to avoid some place of historical interest, I have always wanted to see Walden Pond. The account which you left of your sojourn there is, you will be amused to learn, a document of increasing pertinence; each year it seems to gain a little headway, as the world loses ground. We may all be transcendental yet, whether we like it or not. As our common complexities increase, any tale of individual simplicity (and yours is the best written and the

cockiest) acquires a new fascination; as our goods accumulate, but not our well-being, your report of an existence
without material adornment takes on a certain awkward
credibility.

My purpose in going to Walden Pond, like yours, was
not to live cheaply or to live dearly there, but to transact
some private business with the fewest obstacles. Approaching Concord, doing forty, doing forty-five, doing fifty, the
steering wheel held snug in my palms, the highway held
grimly in my vision, the crown of the road now serving
me (on the righthand curves), now defeating me (on the
lefthand curves), I began to rouse myself from the stupe-
faction which a day's motor journey induces. It was a delicious evening, Henry, when the whole body is one sense,
and imbibes delight through every pore, if I may coin a
phrase. Fields were richly brown where the harrow, drawn
by the stripped Ford, had lately sunk its teeth; pastures
were green; and overhead the sky had that same everlasting
great look which you will find on page 144 of the Oxford
pocket edition. I could feel the road entering me, through
tire, wheel, spring, and cushion; shall I not have intelligence with earth too? Am I not partly leaves and vegetable
mold myself? — a man of infinite horsepower, yet partly
leaves.

Stay with me on 62 and it will take you into Concord.
As I say, it was a delicious evening. The snake had come
forth to die in a bloody S on the highway, the wheel upon
its head, its bowels flat now and exposed. The turtle had
come up too to cross the road and die in the attempt, its
hard shell smashed under the rubber blow, its intestinal
yearning (for the other side of the road) forever squashed.
There was a sign by the wayside which announced that
the road had a " cotton surface." You wouldn't know what
that is, but neither, for that matter, did I. There is a cryptic

ingredient in many of our modern improvements — we are awed and pleased without knowing quite what we are enjoying. It is something to be traveling on a road with a cotton surface.

The civilization round Concord today is an odd distillation of city, village, farm, and manor. The houses, yards, fields look not quite suburban, not quite rural. Under the bronze beech and the blue spruce of the departed baron grazes the milch goat of the heirs. Under the porte-cochère stands the reconditioned station wagon; under the grape arbor sit the puppies for sale. (But why do men degenerate ever? What makes families run out?)

It was June and everywhere June was publishing her immemorial stanza; in the lilacs, in the syringa, in the freshly edged paths and the sweetness of moist beloved gardens, and the little wire wickets that preserve the tulips' front. Farmers were already moving the fruits of their toil into their yards, arranging the rhubarb, the asparagus, the strictly fresh eggs on the painted stands under the little shed roofs with the patent shingles. And though it was almost a hundred years since you had taken your ax and started cutting out your home on Walden Pond, I was interested to observe that the philosophical spirit was still alive in Massachusetts: in the center of a vacant lot some boys were assembling the framework of the rude shelter, their whole mind and skill concentrated in the rather inauspicious helter-skeleton of studs and rafters. They too were escaping from town, to live naturally, in a rich blend of savagery and philosophy.

That evening, after supper at the inn, I strolled out into the twilight to dream my shapeless transcendental dreams and see that the car was locked up for the night (first open the right front door, then reach over, straining, and pull up the handles of the left rear and the left front till you hear the click, then the handle of the right rear, then shut the right front but open it again, remembering that the key is still in the ignition switch, remove the key, shut the right front again with a bang, push the tiny keyhole cover to one side, insert key, turn, and withdraw). It is what we all do, Henry. It is called locking the car. It is said to confuse thieves and keep them from making off with the laprobe. Four doors to lock behind one robe. The driver himself never uses a laprobe, the free movement of his legs being vital to the operation of the vehicle; so that when he locks the car it is a pure and unselfish act. I have in my life gained very little essential heat from laprobes, yet I have ever been at pains to lock them up.

The evening was full of sounds, some of which would have stirred your memory. The robins still love the elms of New England villages at sundown. There is enough of the thrush in them to make song inevitable at the end of day, and enough of the tramp to make them hang round the dwellings of men. A robin, like many another American, dearly loves a white house with green blinds. Concord is still full of them.

Your fellow-townsmen were stirring abroad — not many afoot, most of them in their cars; and the sound which they made in Concord at evening was a rustling and a whispering. The sound lacks steadfastness and is wholly unlike that of a train. A train, as you know who lived so near the Fitchburg line, whistles once or twice sadly and is gone, trailing a memory in smoke, soothing to ear and mind. Automobiles, skirting a village green, are like flies that have gained the inner ear — they buzz, cease, pause, start, shift, stop, halt, brake, and the whole effect is a nervous polytone curiously disturbing.

As I wandered along, the toc toc of ping pong balls drifted from an attic window. In front of the Reuben Brown house a Buick was drawn up. At the wheel, motion-

less, his hat upon his head, a man sat, listening to Amos and
Andy on the radio (it is a drama of many scenes and without an end). The deep voice of Andrew Brown, emerging
from the car, although it originated more than two hundred miles away, was unstrained by distance. When you
used to sit on the shore of your pond on Sunday morning,
listening to the church bells of Acton and Concord, you
were aware of the excellent filter of the intervening atmosphere. Science has attended to that, and sound now main-
tains its intensity without regard for distance. Properly
sponsored, it goes on forever.

A fire engine, out for a trial spin, roared past Emerson's
house, hot with readiness for public duty. Over the barn
roofs the martins dipped and chittered. A swarthy daughter
of an asparagus grower, in culottes, shirt, and bandanna,
pedaled past on her bicycle. It was indeed a delicious evening, and I returned to the inn (I believe it was your
house once) to rock with the old ladies on the concrete
veranda.

Next morning early I started afoot for Walden, out Main
Street and down Thoreau, past the depot and the Minute-
man Chevrolet Company. The morning was fresh, and in
a bean field along the way I flushed an agriculturalist,
quietly studying his beans. Thoreau Street soon joined
Number 126, an artery of the State. We number our high-
ways nowadays, our speed being so great we can remember
little of their quality or character and are lucky to remember their number. (Men have an indistinct notion that if
they keep up this activity long enough all will at length
ride somewhere, in next to no time.) Your pond is on 126.

I knew I must be nearing your woodland retreat when
the Golden Pheasant lunchroom came into view — Sealtest
ice cream, toasted sandwiches, hot frankfurters, waffles,
tonics, and lunches. Were I the proprietor, I should add

rice, Indian meal, and molasses — just for old time's sake. The Pheasant, incidentally, is for sale: a chance for some nature lover who wishes to set himself up beside a pond in the Concord atmosphere and live deliberately, fronting only the essential facts of life on Number 126. Beyond the Pheasant was a place called Walden Breezes, an oasis whose porch pillars were made of old green shutters sawed into lengths. On the porch was a distorting mirror, to give the traveler a comical image of himself, who had miraculously learned to gaze in an ordinary glass without smiling. Behind the Breezes, in a sun-parched clearing, dwelt your philosophical descendants in their trailers, each trailer the size of your hut, but all grouped together for the sake of congeniality. Trailer people leave the city, as you did, to discover solitude and in any weather, at any hour of the day or night, to improve the nick of time; but they soon collect in villages and get bogged deeper in the mud than ever. The camp behind Walden Breezes was just rousing itself to the morning. The ground was packed hard under the heel, and the sun came through the clearing to bake the soil and enlarge the wry smell of cramped housekeeping. Cushman's bakery truck had stopped to deliver an early basket of rolls. A camp dog, seeing me in the road, barked petulantly. A man emerged from one of the trailers and set forth with a bucket to draw water from some forest tap.

Leaving the highway I turned off into the woods toward the pond, which was apparent through the foliage. The floor of the forest was strewn with dried old oak leaves and *Transcripts*. From beneath the flattened popcorn wrapper (*granum explosum*) peeped the frail violet. I followed a footpath and descended to the water's edge. The pond lay clear and blue in the morning light, as you have seen it so many times. In the shallows a man's waterlogged shirt undulated gently. A few flies came out to greet me and convoy

me to your cove, past the No Bathing signs on which the
fellows and the girls had scrawled their names. I felt
strangely excited suddenly to be snooping around your
premises, tiptoeing along watchfully, as though not to tread
by mistake upon the intervening century. Before I got to
the cove I heard something which seemed to me quite wonderful: I heard your frog, a full, clear *troonk*, guiding me,
still hoarse and solemn, bridging the years as the robins had
bridged them in the sweetness of the village evening. But
he soon quit, and I came on a couple of young boys throwing stones at him.

Your front yard is marked by a bronze tablet set in a
stone. Four small granite posts, a few feet away, show where
the house was. On top of the tablet was a pair of faded blue
bathing trunks with a white stripe. Back of it is a pile of
stones, a sort of cairn, left by your visitors as a tribute, I
suppose. It is a rather ugly little heap of stones, Henry. In
fact the hillside itself seems faded, browbeaten; a few tall
skinny pines, bare of lower limbs, a smattering of young
maples in suitable green, some birches and oaks, and a number of trees felled by the last big wind. It was from the
bole of one of these fallen pines, torn up by the roots, that I
extracted the stone which I added to the cairn — a sentimental act in which I was interrupted by a small terrier
from a nearby picnic group, who confronted me and wanted
to know about the stone.

I sat down for a while on one of the posts of your house
to listen to the bluebottles and the dragonflies. The invaded
glade sprawled shabby and mean at my feet, but the flies
were tuned to the old vibration. There were the remains of
a fire in your ruins, but I doubt that it was yours; also two
beer bottles trodden into the soil and become part of earth.
A young oak had taken root in your house, and two or
three ferns, unrolling like the ticklers at a banquet. The only

other furnishings were a DuBarry pattern sheet, a page torn from a picture magazine, and some crusts in wax paper.

Before I quit I walked clear round the pond and found the place where you used to sit on the northeast side to get the sun in the fall, and the beach where you got sand for scrubbing your floor. On the eastern side of the pond, where the highway borders it, the State has built dressing rooms for swimmers, a float with diving towers, drinking fountains of porcelain, and rowboats for hire. The pond is in fact a State Preserve, and carries a twenty-dollar fine for picking wild flowers, a decree signed in all solemnity by your fellow-citizens Walter C. Wardwell, Erson B. Barlow, and Nathaniel I. Bowditch. There was a smell of creosote where they had been building a wide wooden stairway to the road and the parking area. Swimmers and boaters were arriving; bodies plunged vigorously into the water and emerged wet and beautiful in the bright air. As I left, a boatload of town boys were splashing about in mid-pond, kidding and fooling, the young fellows singing at the tops of their lungs in a wild chorus:

> Amer-ica, Amer-ica, God shed his grace on thee,
> And crown thy good with brotherhood
> From sea to shi-ning sea!

I walked back to town along the railroad, following your custom. The rails were expanding noisily in the hot sun, and on the slope of the roadbed the wild grape and the blackberry sent up their creepers to the track.

The expense of my brief sojourn in Concord was:

Canvas shoes	$1.95	
Baseball bat	.25	} gifts to take back
Left-handed fielder's glove	1.25	to a boy
Hotel and meals	4.25	
In all	$7.70	

As you see, this amount was almost what you spent for food for eight months. I cannot defend the shoes or the expenditure for shelter and food: they reveal a meanness and grossness in my nature which you would find contemptible. The baseball equipment, however, is the kind of impediment with which you were never on even terms. You must remember that the house where you practiced the sort of economy which I respect was haunted only by mice and squirrels. You never had to cope with a shortstop.

STUDYING THE ESSAY

1. One of the joys of reading is comparing the ideas of different writers. Having read both Thoreau and E. B. White on the subject of Walden, find ways in which the two writers resemble each other and ways in which they differ.

2. Find examples of White's effective use of colloquial English.

3. How is White's world different from Thoreau's? Are any details unchanged since Thoreau lived at Walden Pond?

4. Find examples of poetic writing in this essay.

5. Do you think that White would change his times for those of Thoreau? Be ready to defend your answer.

6. In what respects is the ending of this essay brilliant?

7. Try reading the essay aloud.

COMPOSITION TOPICS

1. Have you ever gone back to a place you have not seen since you were very young? If you have, try to describe your feelings about this place as you looked at it with older eyes.

2. Signboards on the Landscape

[*1942*]

GETTING READY FOR A COW

This month an event is scheduled to take place here which is the culmination of four years of preparation. I am going to get a cow. Perhaps I should put it the other way round — a cow is going to get me. (I suspect I am regarded hereabouts as something of a catch.)

To establish a herd, even to establish a herd of one, is a responsibility which I do not lightly assume. For me this is a solemn moment, tinged with pure eagerness. I have waited a long time for this cow, this fateful female whom I have yet to meet. Mine has been a novitiate in which I have groomed myself faithfully and well for the duties of a husbandryman; I feel that now, at the end of these years, I have something to offer a cow.

Of course I could have got a cow immediately on arriving here in the country. There is no law against a man getting a cow before he, or she, is ready. I see by *Life* magazine that Chic Johnson, the Hellzapoppin farmer of Putnam County, N. Y., established his herd by " buying the World's Fair Borden Exhibit." This struck me as a rather clearcut case of a man who was perhaps not ready for his cows. He probably had not even had himself tested for Bangs. " At the dairy," said the article, describing a party the actor was throwing, " cows were milked and ridden bareback." Mr. Johnson was photographed in the act of trying to strike up an acquaintance with one of his own cows, but I noticed she had averted her gaze. He was wearing shorts and a jockey cap. From the photograph I judged that the cows were in clean, modern quarters, and there seemed to be a great many of them (I counted forty cows and ten milkmaids — enough to keep an actor in cream); but I think probably it will suit me better to have one cow with whom I am well acquainted than a barnful of comparative strangers in all stages of lactation.

I knew from the very first that some day there would be a cow here. One of the first things that turned up when we bought the place was a milking stool, an old one, handmade, smooth with the wax finish which only the seat of an honest man's breeches can give to wood. A piece of equipment like that kicking around the barn is impossible to put out of one's mind completely. I never mentioned the name " cow " in those early days, but I knew that the ownership of a milking stool was like any other infection — there would be the period of incubation and then the trouble itself. The stool made me feel almost wholly equipped — all I needed was the new plank floor under the cow, the new stanchion, the platform, the curb, the gutter, the toprail, the litter alley, the sawdust, the manger, the barn broom, the halter, the watering pail, the milk pail, the milk cans, the brushes, the separator, the churn, the cow, and the ability to milk the cow.

And there was the barn itself, egging me on. There it stood, with the old tie-ups intact. Every morning the sun rose, climbed, and shone through the south windows into the deserted stalls, scarred and pitted from bygone hooves. I tried not to look. But every time I walked past I admired the ingenious construction of the homemade stanchions, set in a solid wooden curb and locked with pegs and tumblers, everything handhewn by a man who had fashioned, with ax and chisel, whatever he had needed for himself and his creatures. Men familiar with the habits and desires of cows have advised me to take those old stanchions out because of their rigidity, which is too confining for a cow, and I have already begun the work, but not without many misgivings and a feeling of guilt. The urge to remodel, the spirit of demolition, are in the blood of all city people who move to the country, and must be constantly guarded against. I have seen too many cases of farmhouses being torn limb from limb by a newly arrived owner, as though in fright or in anger.

There is something bumptious in the common assumption that an old house or an old barn must be hacked to pieces before it is a fit place in which to settle. The city man coming suddenly to the country customarily begins his new life by insulting someone else's old one; he knocks blazes out of his dwelling house, despite its having served former owners well for a hundred years or more. My own house is about a hundred and forty years old — three times my age — yet I, a mere upstart, approached it as though it didn't know its business and weren't quite fit for me the way it was, when the truth, as I now see it, was that I was not quite fit for *it*. Quite aside from the expense and inconvenience of razing one's newly acquired home, there is a subtle insult in the maneuver, the unmistakable implication that the former inhabitants lived either in squalor or in innocence, and that one's neighbors, in houses of similar design and appointments, are also living in squalor or innocence. Neither is true. But the demolition goes right ahead. The place of a newly arriving city man always looks more like a battleground than a home: earthworks are thrown up around the foundation wall, chimneys are reduced to rubble, and on the front lawn a cement mixer appears, with its little wheels and big round abdomen. It would be a comical sight if it were not so dispiriting.

I don't know why people act in this panicky way. I do

know for a fact that a man can't know the quality of his home until he has lived in it a year or two; and until he knows its good and bad qualities how can he presume to go about remodeling it? In the frenzy of resettlement one often does queer things and lives to regret his mistakes. When I go into my neighbors' "unimproved" houses in the dead of winter and feel how comfortable they are and cheerful, the sills banked with spruce boughs, the little heating stoves standing in candid warmth in the middle of the room, the geraniums and flowering maples blazing away in tin cans on the sunny shelf above the sink, with no pipes to freeze under the floors and no furnace around which huddle full ash cans like gloomy children, I always chuckle over the commotion city people make in their determination that their farmhouse shall be "livable." They have no idea how livable a farmhouse can be if you let it alone. We have too many preconceptions, anyway, about life and living. There is nothing so expensive, really, as a big, well-developed, full-bodied preconception.

But as far as my cow was concerned, it was not so much any hesitancy at ripping things up and changing things around, not so much a matter of equipment and housing; it was simply that I felt the need of a personal probationary period. If a man expects his cow to have freshened before he gets her, she has a right to expect that some important change will have been worked in him too. I didn't want a cow until I could meet her on her own ground, until I was ready, until I knew almost as much about the country as she did — otherwise it would embarrass me to be in her presence. I began this probation in 1938. For more than a year I kept my cow in the hindmost region of my thoughts. It was almost two years before I even allowed myself to dwell on her form and face. Then I began to lay the groundwork of my herd.

My first move was to purchase fifteen sheep and a case of dynamite. The sheep, I figured, would improve my pasture, and the dynamite would keep me out of mischief in the meantime. Before they were done, the sheep managed to serve another useful purpose: I had no desire to have a cow on the place until I had learned how an udder worked, and my first lambing time taught me a lot about that. The way to learn to sail a big boat is first to sail a little one, because the little one is so much harder to manage. The same is true of udders. I can milk a sheep now, with her small cleverly concealed udder, and so I have no hesitancy about going on to a larger and more forthright bag. The dynamite also turned out to have a second purpose — it had the advantage of letting people know something was going on around here.

That fall when we dynamited for my cow was a great time. I set out to revive a run-out hayfield, and while I was at it I thought I would remove the rocks. I hadn't the slightest notion of what I was getting into, except that I knew I was establishing a cow, and, true to form, thought first of demolition. The rocks didn't look like much when I made my preliminary survey, but I discovered as time went on that a rock is much like an iceberg — most of it is downunder. A very great deal of spadework had to be done around the horse-size rocks before you could hook on to them with the team, and of course the others had to be drilled before they could be exploded. Hand drilling is tedious business, but I didn't have sense enough to charter an air-drill, which I learned later I could have done. The cow receded. There were days when I almost forgot her, so engrossed did I become in the amazing turn which my probation had taken. It was the end of summer; the days were hot and bright. Across the broad field, newly plowed, would come the exultant warning cry of "Fie-ah!" Then the breathless pause, then the blast, and the dunnage and rock fragments flying into the sun, then another pause and the sound of falling wreckage.

Although the field had been turned over by the plow, the fragmentation from the blasting left it looking more like a gravel pit than a seedbed. There was a tremendous lot of work to be done just hauling away the debris after the bombing was over. The plowman hooked his team to the drag and I borrowed a tractor and another drag from a neighbor, and together we went at it. Day after day we loaded the drags, hauled them to the edge of the woods, and tossed the rocks off, creating a kind of hit and miss stone wall. I learned to throw the chain over a big rock with a " rolling holt," back the tractor up to it, and ease the rock on to the drag by giving it a nudge of power. The cow seemed a long way off, but I held her firmly in my thoughts, as a soldier holds the vision of home and peace through a long campaign in a foreign land. Rivers of sweat flowed into the dry, chewed-up soil; mountains of granite slogged along the dragways, all to achieve, in some remote time, the blade of new grass, the tiny jet of yellow milk. The whole thing seemed like a strangely tangential episode, as if I had wandered off on an idiot's holiday.

And after the rocks had been torn from the earth and removed, then there was the matter of dressing the field. Having no cow, I had no dressing, except a small amount of sheep manure and hen manure which would be needed for the gardens. The field would need thirty or forty spreader loads. After much exploring, some dressing was located in a barn cellar within reasonable trucking distance, and for some days I lived close to a dung fork. This phase of the work had a cow smell and seemed somehow closer to the main issue.

All winter the land and I lay waiting. In spring the frost

opened cracks and seams in the field to receive the seed. I marked out courses with guide stakes and sowed the long lanes, working on a windless morning. The rains of spring never descended that year, and summer ushered in one of the most blistering droughts on record. The new grass drooped, the weeds jumped up and sang. The result of a year's labor seemed meager, doubtful. But it turned out that there was established in spite of the dry season what a farmer calls a good bottom. As soon as it got half a chance the field picked up miraculously. This summer, under benign rains, it has become a sweetly rolling green, like something Grant Wood might have sent me.

Meantime the sheep had been at work in the pasture, quietly, with no dynamite. Their golden hooves had channeled among the rocks and ferns, and they had fertilized easily as they went. The time was approaching when I might take unto myself a cow. I began to see her as a living being who was growing closer to me, whose path and mine were soon to cross. I began having the sort of daydreams I used to have at fifteen: somewhere in the world (I would think) is the girl who is some day to be my wife. What is she doing? Where is she? What is she like?

Of course there was still the matter of the barn — a fit place for this dream creature to spend her winter nights. The thought of a concrete floor flashed through my mind, and was quickly gone. I had invested in one concrete floor when I built my henhouse, and one concrete floor is enough for any man's lifetime. The sensible thing would be to lay a good smooth plank floor, with a six-inch platform, and perhaps a gutter. I turned, as one always does turn in any critical time, to the mail order catalogue and began a study of floor plans — stalls and gutters and curbs and stanchions and rails and partitions. I learned about stanchions, stanchion anchors, alignment devices; I began to pit the high curb against the low curb, the single post stall against the double. One evening after dark I went to the barn with a two-foot rule and a flashlight and measured up the job, working carefully and late, in pitch black except for the concentrated beam of the flash — an odd tryst, as I think back on it, but part of my beautiful romance. When I returned to the house I made a plan, drawn to scale, showing a maternity pen, three stalls, a raised platform, an eleven-inch curb hollowed out to six inches at the anchor point, and a gate, everything worked out to the inch. The platform is to be cut on the bias — a long stall (4 foot 10) at one end, in case my lovely girl turns out to be an Amazon, a medium-size stall (4 foot 4) for a medium-size bride, and a short stall (3 foot 8) for the heifer which will inevitably bless this marriage.

There have been setbacks and reverses. Priorities worked against me and I soon found out that barn furnishings were almost unobtainable. I sent to Sears for their Russet Cow Halter, 32D449, the one with the adjustable crown and the brown hardware to match her eyes and hair, but they returned the money, with a grim note, Form Number 7, rubber stamped. Where they got the rubber for the stamp I have no idea.

Tomorrow the carpenter arrives to start tearing out the old floor. When the last stanchion is anchored and the last brushful of whitewash has been applied to wall and rafter, I shall anoint myself and go forth to seek my love. This much I know, when the great day comes and she and I come marching home and pause for a moment in the barnyard before the freshly whitened door, *she's* got to carry *me* across the threshold. I'm tired.

STUDYING THE ESSAY

1. During your English course you have learned that a composition should have unity — a beginning, a middle, and an end. Analyze this essay in terms of unity.

2. Outline the things White did to get ready for the cow. Are all of these things logical?

3. Why are the two opening paragraphs effective?

4. "My first move was to purchase fifteen sheep and a case of dynamite." What would Thoreau think of this move?

5. This is an intensely personal essay. How does it reveal elements of White's character?

6. Can you find examples of "those silver and crystal sentences which have a ring like nobody else's sentences"?

7. In style and in method White shows many similarities to Lamb and Stevenson. Can you find these similarities?

COMPOSITION TOPIC

All of you have looked forward to a new possession — if not a cow, then a fishing rod, a car, an evening dress, a new desk, or something else. Write a theme about the preparations you made for this new possession. Try to show the kind of person you are by frankly describing your feelings.

RACHEL CARSON, 1907–

The youngest of the scientist-essayists represented in this book is Rachel Louise Carson. Her love of both
science and writing started early. She says that her mother first
introduced her to nature when they were living in Springdale,
Pennsylvania. When she attended The Pennsylvania College for
Women, in Pittsburgh, her intention was to study literature, but
she soon shifted to biology. She took her degree in science, got
her master's degree at Johns Hopkins University, and later studied at the Marine Biological Laboratory at Woods Hole, Massachusetts. After teaching for some years at Johns Hopkins and at
the University of Maryland, she became, in 1936, a biologist for
the United States Bureau of Fisheries. She is now Editor-in-
Chief of the United States Fish and Wildlife Service, for which
she has written many bulletins, including a most attractive pam-
phlet called "Guarding Our Wildlife Resources" (1948).

Miss Carson has written articles for the *Atlantic, Colliers,* the
Yale Review, Science Digest, and the *New Yorker.* Parts of *The
Sea Around Us,* from which this essay is taken, were printed as
a most unusual "Profile" in the last-named magazine. Her first
book, about life in the sea, was *Under the Sea Wind* (1941).
This had a number of good reviews, but not a great many readers until after *The Sea Around Us* (1951) became a Book-of-
the-Month Club selection and a best seller. In 1951 Miss Carson
received a Guggenheim Fellowship for work on an as yet un-
published book.

In Miss Carson's writing, as in Peattie's, there is a great deal of
poetry. Her smooth, lyric style and her contagious enthusiasm
about the wonder and the magic of the sea are the most vivid
characteristics of this essay. It is worth noting that she herself

says that her absorption in the mystery and meaning of the sea was stimulated by the friendship and encouragement of William Beebe. Her love of her subject, her technical knowledge, and her beautiful style make " The Long Snowfall " and the rest of the book a distinguished addition to the American literature of science.

THE LONG SNOWFALL

A deep and tremulous earth-poetry.
— LLEWELYN POWYS

Every part of earth or air or sea has an atmosphere peculiarly its own, a quality or characteristic that sets it apart from all others. When I think of the floor of the deep sea, the single, overwhelming fact that possesses my imagination is the accumulation of sediments. I see always the steady, unremitting, downward drift of materials from above, flake upon flake, layer upon layer — a drift that has continued for hundreds of millions of years, that will go on as long as there are seas and continents.

For the sediments are the materials of the most stupendous " snowfall " the earth has ever seen. It began when the first rains fell on the barren rocks and set in motion the forces of erosion. It was accelerated when living creatures developed in the surface waters and the discarded little shells of lime or silica that had encased them in life began to drift downward to the bottom. Silently, endlessly, with the deliberation of earth processes that can afford to be slow because they have so much time for completion, the accumulation of the sediments has proceeded. So little in a year, or in a human lifetime, but so enormous an amount in the life of earth and sea.

The rains, the eroding away of the earth, the rush of sediment-laden waters have continued, with varying pulse and tempo, throughout all of geologic time. In addition to the silt load of every river that finds its way to the sea, there are other materials that compose the sediments. Volcanic dust, blown perhaps half way around the earth in the upper atmosphere, comes eventually to rest on the ocean, drifts in the currents, becomes waterlogged, and sinks. Sands from coastal deserts are carried seaward on offshore winds, fall to the sea, and sink. Gravel, pebbles, small boulders, and shells are carried by icebergs and drift ice, to be released to the water when the ice melts. Fragments of iron, nickel and other meteoric debris that enter the earth's atmosphere over the sea — these, too, become flakes of the great snowfall. But most widely distributed of all are the billions upon billions of tiny shells and skeletons, the limy or silicious remains of all the minute creatures that once lived in the upper waters.

The sediments are a sort of epic poem of the earth. When we are wise enough, perhaps we can read in them all of past history. For all is written here. In the nature of the materials that compose them and in the arrangement of their successive layers the sediments reflect all that has happened in the waters above them and on the surrounding lands. The dramatic and the catastrophic in earth history have left their trace in the sediments — the outpourings of volcanoes, the advance and retreat of the ice, the searing aridity of desert lands, the sweeping destruction of floods.

The book of the sediments has been opened only within the lifetime of the present generation of scientists, with the most exciting progress in collecting and deciphering samples made since 1945. Early oceanographers could scrape up surface layers of sediment from the sea bottom with dredges. But what was needed was an instrument, operated on the principle of an apple corer, that could be driven vertically into the bottom to remove a long sample or " core " in which the order of the different layers was undisturbed. Such an instrument was invented by Dr. C. S. Piggot in 1935, and with the aid of this " gun " he obtained a series of cores across the deep Atlantic from Newfoundland to Ireland. These cores averaged about 10 feet long. A piston core sampler, developed by the Swedish oceanographer Kullenberg about 10 years later, now takes undisturbed cores 70 feet long. The rate of sedimentation in the different parts of the ocean is not definitely known, but it is very slow; certainly such a sample represents millions of years of geologic history.

Another ingenious method for studying the sediments has been used by Professor W. Maurice Ewing of Columbia University and the Woods Hole Oceanographic Institution. Professor Ewing found that he could measure the thickness of the carpeting layer of sediments that overlies the rock of the ocean floor by exploding depth charges and recording their echoes; one echo is received from the top of the sediment layer (the apparent bottom of the sea), another from the " bottom below the bottom " or the true rock floor. The carrying and use of explosives at sea is hazardous and cannot be attempted by all vessels, but this method was used by the Swedish *Albatross* as well as by the *Atlantis* in its exploration of the Atlantic Ridge. Ewing on the *Atlantis* also used a seismic refraction technique by which sound waves are made to travel horizontally through the rock layers of the ocean floor, providing information about the nature of the rock.

Before these techniques were developed, we could only guess at the thickness of the sediment blanket over the floor of the sea. We might have expected the amount to be vast, if we thought back through the ages of gentle, unending fall — one sand grain at a time, one fragile shell after another, here a shark's tooth, there a meteorite fragment — but the whole continuing persistently, relentlessly, endlessly. It is, of course, a process similar to that which has built up the layers of rock that help to make our mountains, for they, too, were once soft sediments under the shallow seas that have overflowed the continents from time to time. The sediments eventually became consolidated and cemented and, as the seas retreated again, gave the continents their thick, covering layers of sedimentary rocks — layers which we can see uplifted, tilted, compressed, and broken by the vast earth movements. And we know that in places the sedimentary rocks are many thousands of feet thick. Yet most people felt a shock of surprise and wonder when Hans Pettersson, leader of the Swedish Deep Sea Expedition, announced that the *Albatross* measurements taken in the open Atlantic basin showed sediment layers as much as 12,000 feet thick.

If more than two miles of sediments have been deposited on the floor of the Atlantic, an interesting question arises: has the rocky floor sagged a corresponding distance under the terrific weight of the sediments? Geologists hold conflicting opinions. The recently discovered Pacific sea mounts may offer one piece of evidence that it has. If they are, as their discoverer called them, " drowned ancient islands," then they may have reached their present stand a mile or so below sea level through the sinking of the ocean floor. Hess believed the islands had been formed so long ago that coral animals had not yet evolved; otherwise the corals would presumably have settled on the flat, planed surfaces of the sea mounts and built them up as fast as their bases sank. In any event, it is hard to see how they could have been worn down so far below " wave base " unless the crust of the earth sagged under its load.

One thing seems probable — the sediments have been unevenly distributed both in place and time. In contrast to the 12,000-foot thickness found in parts of the Atlantic, the Swedish oceanographers never found sediments thicker than 1000 feet in the Pacific or in the Indian Ocean. Perhaps a deep layer of lava, from ancient submarine eruptions on a stupendous scale, underlies the upper layers of the sediments in these places and intercepts the sound waves.

Interesting variations in the thickness of the sediment layer on the Atlantic Ridge and the approaches to the Ridge from the American side were reported by Ewing. As the bottom contours became less even and began to slope up into the foothills of the Ridge, the sediments thickened, as though piling up into mammoth drifts 1000 to 2000 feet deep against the slopes of the hills. Farther up in the mountains of the Ridge, where there are many level terraces from a few to a score of miles wide, the sediments were even deeper, measuring up to 3000 feet. But along the backbone of the Ridge, on the steep slopes and peaks and pinnacles, the bare rock emerged, swept clean of sediments.

Reflecting on these differences in thickness and distribution, our minds return inevitably to the simile of the long snowfall. We may think of the abyssal snowstorm in terms of a bleak and blizzard-ridden arctic tundra. Long days of storm visit this place, when driving snow fills the air; then a lull comes in the blizzard, and the snowfall is light. In the snowfall of the sediments, also, there is an alternation of light and heavy falls. The heavy falls correspond to the periods of mountain building on the continents, when the lands are lifted high and the rain rushes down their slopes, carrying mud and rock fragments to the sea; the light falls mark the lulls between the mountain-building periods, when the continents are flat and erosion is slowed. And again, on our imaginary tundra, the winds blow the snow into deep drifts, filling in all the valleys between the ridges, piling the snow up and up until the contours of the land are obliterated, but scouring the ridges clear. In the drifting sediments on the floor of the ocean we see the work of the " winds," which may be the deep ocean currents, distributing the sediments according to laws of their own, not as yet grasped by human minds.

We have known the general pattern of the sediment carpet, however, for a good many years. Around the foundations of the continents, in the deep waters off the borders of the continental slopes, are the muds of terrestrial origin. There are muds of many colors — blue, green, red, black, and white — apparently varying with climatic changes as well as with the dominant soils and rocks of the lands of their origin. Farther at sea are the oozes of predominantly marine origin — the remains of the trillions of tiny sea creatures. Over great areas of the temperate oceans the sea floor is largely covered with the remains of unicellular creatures known as foraminifera, of which the most abundant genus is Globigerina. The shells of Globigerina may be recognized in very ancient sediments as well as in modern ones, but over the ages the species have varied. Knowing this, we can date approximately the deposits in which they occur. But always they have been simple animals, living in an intricately sculptured shell of carbonate of lime, the whole so small you would need a microscope to see its details. After the fashion of unicellular beings, the individual Globigerina normally did not die, but by the division of its substance became two. At each division, the old shell was abandoned, and two new ones were formed. In warm, lime-rich seas these tiny creatures have always multiplied prodigiously, and so, although each is so minute, their innumerable shells blanket millions of square miles of ocean bottom, and to a depth of thousands of feet.

In the great depths of the ocean, however, the immense pressures and the high carbon-dioxide content of deep water dissolve much of the lime long before it reaches the bottom and return it to the great chemical reservoir of the sea. Silica is more resistant to solution. It is one of the curious paradoxes of the ocean that the bulk of the organic remains that reach the great depths intact belong to unicellular creatures seemingly of the most delicate construction. The radiolarians remind us irresistibly of snow flakes, as infinitely varied in pattern, as lacy, and as intricately made. Yet because their shells are fashioned of silica instead of carbonate of lime, they can descend unchanged into the abyssal depths. So there are broad bands of radiolarian ooze in the deep tropical waters of the North Pacific, underlying the surface zones where the living radiolarians occur most numerously.

Two other kinds of organic sediments are named for the creatures whose remains compose them. Diatoms, the microscopic plant life of the sea, flourish most abundantly in cold waters. There is a broad belt of diatom ooze on the floor of the Antarctic Ocean, outside the zone of glacial debris dropped by the ice pack. There is another across the North Pacific, along the chain of great deeps that run from Alaska to Japan. Both are zones where nutrient-laden water wells up from the depths, sustaining a rich growth of plants. The diatoms, like the radiolaria, are encased in silicious coverings — small, boxlike cases of varied shape and meticulously etched design.

Then, in relatively shallow parts of the open Atlantic, there are patches of ooze composed of the remains of deli-

cate swimming snails, called pteropods. These winged mol-
lusks, possessing transparent shells of great beauty, are here
and there incredibly abundant. Pteropod ooze is the characteristic bottom deposit in the vicinity of Bermuda, and a
large patch occurs in the South Atlantic.

Mysterious and eerie are the immense areas, especially in
the North Pacific, carpeted with a soft, red sediment in
which there are no organic remains except sharks' teeth and
the ear bones of whales. This red clay occurs at great depths.
Perhaps all the materials of the other sediments are dissolved
before they can reach this zone of immense pressures and
glacial cold.

The reading of the story contained in the sediments has
only begun. When more cores are collected and examined
we shall certainly decipher many exciting chapters. Geologists have pointed out that a series of cores from the Mediterranean might settle several controversial problems concerning the history of the ocean and of the lands around
the Mediterranean basin. For example, somewhere in the
layers of sediment under this sea there must be evidence, in
a sharply defined layer of sand, of the time when the deserts
of the Sahara were formed and the hot, dry winds began to
skim off the shifting surface layers and carry them seaward.
Long cores recently obtained in the western Mediterranean
off Algeria have given a record of volcanic activity extend-
ing back through thousands of years, and including great
prehistoric eruptions of which we know nothing.

The Atlantic cores taken more than a decade ago by Piggot from the cable ship *Lord Kelvin* have been thoroughly
studied by geologists. From their analysis it is possible to
look back into the past 10,000 years or so and to sense the
pulse of the earth's climatic rhythms; for the cores were
composed of layers of cold-water globigerina faunas (and
hence glacial stage sediments), alternating with globigerina

ooze characteristic of warmer waters. From the clues furnished by these cores we can visualize interglacial stages when there were periods of mild climates, with warm water overlying the sea bottom and warmth-loving creatures living in the ocean. Between these periods the sea grew chill. Clouds gathered, the snows fell, and on the North American continent the great ice sheets grew and the ice mountains moved out to the coast. The glaciers reached the sea along a wide front; there they produced icebergs by the thousand. The slow-moving, majestic processions of the bergs passed out to sea, and because of the coldness of much of the earth they penetrated farther south than any but stray bergs do today. When finally they melted, they relinquished their loads of silt and sand and gravel and rock fragments that had become frozen into their under surfaces as they made their grinding way over the land. And so a layer of glacial sediment came to overlie the normal globigerina ooze, and the record of an Ice Age was inscribed.

Then the sea grew warmer again, the glaciers melted and retreated, and once more the warmer-water species of Globigerina lived in the sea — lived and died and drifted down to build another layer of globigerina ooze, this time over the clays and gravels from the glaciers. And the record of warmth and mildness was again written in the sediments. From the Piggot cores it has been possible to reconstruct four different periods of the advance of the ice, separated by periods of warm climate.

It is interesting to think that even now, in our own lifetime, the flakes of a new snow storm are falling, falling, one by one, out there on the ocean floor. The billions of Globigerina are drifting down, writing their unequivocal record that this, our present world, is on the whole a world of mild and temperate climate. Who will read their record, ten thousand years from now?

STUDYING THE ESSAY

1. Of what are the "snowflakes" in "The Long Snowfall" composed?

2. What does Miss Carson mean by saying that "the sediments are a sort of epic poem of the earth"?

3. Why do people study the sediments on ocean floors?

4. Find examples of especially descriptive writing.

5. Find examples of the excitement which scientific research can give a person.

6. Discuss the background which a writer must have in order to write an essay like this.

7. Compare Miss Carson's approach to science with that of William Beebe and of Donald Peattie.

8. Words to learn: *silica, tempo, seismic, meteorite, tundra.*

COMPOSITION TOPICS

1. A Drop of Water under a Microscope
2. Snowflakes
3. Sharks' Teeth and the Ear Bones of Whales

ALISTAIR COOKE, 1908–

Many readers of this book have probably seen
Alistair Cooke on television as the master of ceremonies who
has given " Omnibus " a great deal of its value. But Cooke is
much more than a TV star. He is a brilliant cosmopolite who,
born in Europe, has had much to say about America.

Cooke was born in Manchester, England, and received his
A.B. degree in 1930 from Cambridge University, where, as a
TV viewer might guess, his favorite activity was dramatics. He
came to this country in 1932 for a year of study at Yale and another year at Harvard, during which time, he says, he fell in
love with the United States. From 1934 to 1937 he was a movie
critic for the British Broadcasting Company. Beginning in 1936
he became the London correspondent for N.B.C., covering
events ranging from the abdication of Edward VIII to the Davis
Cup tennis matches.

At the beginning of World War II Cooke came to the United
States and in 1941 became a citizen. Here he has been a correspondent for British papers, especially the Manchester *Guardian*. His reporting of the trial of Alger Hiss resulted in the pub-
lication of his book, *Generation on Trial*. A more recent book,
One Man's America (1952), reflects his deep feeling for the
United States which is found in the magazine article printed
here.

Cooke is primarily a journalist, a reporter. Unlike many reporters, however, he looks at people and places as a man of deep
culture, of wide travel, and of sophistication. His writing does
not rank him as a great stylist, but his enthusiasm for his adopted
country and his suave, scholarly approach make " On Discovering the United States " an outstanding article.

ON DISCOVERING THE UNITED STATES

The " art of travel " is a phrase bandied cheerfully between travel agents, publishers, and fashion experts, but I can't, after deep thought, recall a single classic book devoted to the art of discovering the United States.

The closest thing that comes to mind is something like Andrew Child's *Overland Route to California*, which begins at Traders' Point on the Missouri River and goes on through fifty-five bald and humorless pages with such entries as: " Ford of Wood River, where it is one rod wide, and easily forded in ordinary stages of water. Grass good. Some timber on the river. The road is excellent and runs near the Platte River for twenty-one miles, to Prairie Dog Town and Swamp, on south of road." Mr. Child's aim, however, was not to discover the art of anything, except possibly of survival. He was writing a guide for those who came after, and from his day to Temple Fielding's, the practical guidebook (" Don't leave valuables in any hotel room in Egypt ") has been the most satisfying item of travel literature. Once you leave the guidebooks you soar off into the heady altitudes with Doughty and D. H. Lawrence and Lafcadio Hearn. You are in the presence of men who use a landscape as a mirror of their immortal souls. It is often a moving experience — I mean for the reader, too — but it does not help the intending traveler to enlarge or refine his own experience of the same good ground. I like to hear what the Grand Canyon did to the psyche of J. B. Priestley, but if I had never been there before, I should be grateful for the information that you don't have to go up from Williams and have the Canyon hit you with the finality of a heart attack. You can go north at Flagstaff to Cameron and from there west see the marvel build level by level and gorge by gorge.

Twenty years ago I would have been greatly indebted to any man who passed on to me the simple rule that I learned from nothing and nobody but repeated frustration and many headaches at the end of day: namely, when you are driving west, start early in the morning and end early in the afternoon; when you are driving east, start near noontime and drive until sunset. This way you have the long light behind you most of the day and a minimum of sun head-on. This is not just a rule of comfort. It is an invitation to see the American landscape in three dimensions and in its accurate shifting color. With the long morning light behind you on one journey, and the horizontal afternoon sun on the other, you can feel the texture of the land, see the rivers run like mercury but in their proper dimension; the mountains are rounded and palpable, every clump of sage and mesquite breaks and recomposes the middle distance, and the vistas are infinite.

This is the sort of information I suspect a lot of people would like to have, for it is halfway between the earthy warnings of the guidebooks (about how to cure vapor lock in the Rockies, or when to check in at a motel) and the bland stratosphere of the traveling philosopher, whose object is to discover himself through the stimulus of a new environment rather than to help you to the knowledge of it.

If any reader thinks I am complaining about this gap before leaping in to fill it, I had better say at once that I am not your man. It could be done for the United States only by a lifelong traveler who had no ax to grind and who was an artist of great range. A man who would never talk with Vermonters as he would with Texans. A connoisseur of many kinds of rivers. A natural detective in the folkways of the regions. A lover of American trees who knew where and why they compose such different landscapes. An expert in the problems of real estate in five climates. An Audubon of the back country. A man who grasped the separate economies of Detroit, Los Angeles County, and Atlantic City. A man who could guess by a glance at the map and the immigration statistics why Half Moon Bay, California, grows artichokes, and what national group inhabits the Sand Country of Wisconsin or eastern Long Island. A man who had been moved by MacLeish's " Light on the Long Ohio " before he read about it; who, blindfold, could taste the steel particles in the air and know he was in Pittsburgh; who could look at a fence in Iowa and guess at the farmers' preoccupations thereabouts and make a decent estimate of their income; who was as sensitive as De Tocqueville to the " simple but grand arrangement of this continent into two vast regions," and as alert as DeVoto to the steady decline of the milkshake from Nevada all the way east to New York.

I wonder if such a man, when he appears, will be a native American. There is good precedent to suppose he will not. For the native is the best guide to his region but seldom to his whole country, and especially when it is, like this, a continent. Indeed, this has been a consoling thought to me on many journeys. Often after some excursion with a local expert — whether it was into the mysteries of oil drilling, or goat raising, or the wildflowers of the Pacific Coast — I have marveled at my own audacious optimism in ever hoping to get the elementary hang of this country in one lifetime. Happily, if you push on, this mood does not last. You leave a cigar manufacturer, say in Tampa, and move on a few miles to Tarpon Springs. You ask the sponge fishers there about Ybor City and the elements of the cigar business. And they look at you with the wild surmise of a New Yorker, whose preconceptions about the manufacture of cigars they most likely share. After twenty years of mooching around this land, I have come to fall back on a simple rule, which I now pass on as the first of several intended to help the adventurous American discover his country. Don't trust a native about his state, unless he is the " state editor " of a newspaper in the capital city. Trust the native about his immediate region, and trust your observation about the " simple, grand arrangement " of the whole country. After many pitfalls, I would add the afterthought: never think you know. I made a hobby for years of a couple of periods of California history. I thought I was pretty well acquainted with the progress of the Gold Rush anytime after Mr. James Marshall of New Jersey turned up those pealike particles by the American River. A single day in Coloma taught me many surprising things.

All this is by way of spreading out my negative credentials. But there are some advantages in having been what the Bible calls a stranger within the gates, and the Immigration Department more succinctly a " resident alien." Not being bred to the local mores, you are less bound by them. If you haven't all your life done the usual thing on the Fourth of July, you might stumble into something unusual; my first Fourth was spent comparing the sports outfits and guessing the social status of spectators at a boat race in Vancouver, Washington. Whereas there are suburbanites who wouldn't care to spend a vacation away from the lake where their ambitious neighbors go, and Bostonians who would expire if they had no Cape to summer on, a foreigner possessing similar strains of conservatism and snobbery has little status to lose in a foreign land. He looks at a map and stabs a pin. Or he likes the sound of an Indian place name. Or he attributes high romance to some place he had heard about in school. And he goes there. When I was a boy there was a song — written, I have since learned, by an Englishman who never left home:

Ho-ome in Pas-a-deea-eea-eena,
There when grass is greea-eea-eener,
I wanna go.

I now know that for an Englishman to seek greener grass than England's anywhere outside the Willamette Valley is an idiot's quest. But it sounded like a heavenly prospect. And, in time, I went.

So I will not try to write about the three classical American vacations: the trip to the mountains, to the ocean, to the lake. Like everybody else, I have my favorites among these sober perennials. But I should like to hope that more and more sound and sober citizens will learn to break the family habit and join the restless hordes who annually restore De Tocqueville's original image of the American of one hundred and twenty years ago: "If at the end of a year of unremitting labor he finds he has a few days' vacation, his eager curiosity whirls him over the vast extent of the United States, and he will travel fifteen hundred miles in a few days. . . . Death at length overtakes him, but it is before he is weary of his bootless chase of that complete felicity which is forever on the wing."

This, then, is a personal anthology of the greatest experiences of traveling in America. Some of them coincide with what the travel folders say; the Grand Canyon is a miracle, though a million visitors have said so. But many do not. I don't wish to bully you into sharing my favorite places. You, too, have your ego — a fact any travel guide sooner or later learns to face. There are people who, once they have a tour laid out for them by somebody else, develop the conviction that forbidden pastures must be greener. Some of the Argonauts contracted this itch and took many a short cut to starvation.

It is my own experience that I wasted the first couple of

trips by accepting without question the European belief
that the American landscape changes very slowly over vast
stretches, and that one part of any region is much the same
as another. This preconception is deeply shared by most
Americans when they think of an unfamiliar part of their
land. A Westerner comes east to friends in Waterbury or
Bridgeport and has seen "New England." An Easterner
drives west expecting great things of Utah and later shudders to remember it as the gaping wilderness between
Salt Lake City and Wendover that he streaked across by
night.

I have before me the map on which I marked my first
tour of the United States. It was planned, if that is the word,
according to some rough guidebook prejudices and some
interested parties I happened to come across. Minnesota, a
Minnesotan told me, had ten thousand lakes. Yellowstone
had to be seen to be believed (so it has). Crater Lake was
supposed to be bottomless. Hollywood was known to be
Babylon, and any student — even of divinity — hankers for
one taste of the temptations he is determined to renounce.
Then there was the Grand Canyon, and those famous Indians at Taos. Dallas exerted an irresistible pull, because it has
been immortalized in England by our beloved Louis Arm-
strong as "that Texas town that never seen ice or snow."
New Orleans I put down because it was vaguely described
to me as being something like Paris during the Second Empire (it is not). Memphis was mandatory because of the
blues.

Since it was the first trip, of course it was wonderful.
But not wonderful enough. It took several more for me to
realize, with much groaning, how close I had been to incomparable sights, how often I had skirted a type of country which achieves its true magnificence thirty miles south
or so. I had been through El Paso three separate times be-

fore I learned what I was missing up at Carlsbad. The fourth time, I bullied an Englishman along to make the detour. He protested that a cave was a cave in any land. When the grand tour was over he declared that the Carlsbad Caverns, those Grand Canyons upside down, were the single most impressive sight on this continent.

For the second rule: try to suit the place to the season. Much of the enjoyment of our country depends disproportionately on the time of year you see it. Few countries are so uniformly blighted by the northern winter. And few great natural regions swing so dramatically from boredom to glory as California does in the spring and New England in the fall. You may visit California a hundred times, but if you have never gone down the San Simeon Highway at the end of April and seen the lupines drenching over the mountains, or smelled the lilac in the sea breeze at many a turn in Marin County, you have not been there. The same may be said of Southern Arizona a month or more earlier. For the desert in midsummer or winter and the desert in flower is the difference between hell and heaven. You may boast of your Arkansas hawthorns in the fall, or your wealth of oaks anywhere between Pennsylvania and the Dakotas; but the fall in Vermont and New Hampshire and Southern Massachusetts is the thing itself: anywhere, in fact, in New England west of the glacial coastal shelf and at any altitude that has enough evergreens to show off the surrounding deciduous blaze. By the same caution, I would say that Yosemite should be seen either in midwinter or midsummer. In August, especially, the waterfalls may have slowed to a foaming tinkle but the grass in the valleys is golden, which marvelously improves the rising immensities of green tree and gray rock.

A third hint I would like to press on anybody about to try a cross-country tour is to make a resolve to explore some back country, no matter how rigidly planned your route or how exacting your time schedule. (As a matter of horse sense, if you are a rigid planner you are probably murder as a companion, and if you have a demanding time schedule you have no business driving across the country in the first place.)

"Back country" is a big and comparatively ancient American word and embraces everything from the Gullah strip of the South Carolina coast and the inner recesses of the Ozarks to the Robbers' Roost country of Utah and almost anywhere fifty miles inland from California's Coast Range. To a traveling American, somebody else's back country is the country not mentioned in the travel folder. I would urge anyone who habitually dashes down the Florida coast line to weave inland occasionally and look at the lake country. And if sometime you are leaving the sublime military prospect of Lookout Mountain, overlooking Chattanooga, and are on your way to Nashville and the Hermitage, make a big loop to the northest off U.S. 41. Take in Rome and Carthage, Defeated and Difficult, and meet the people and the tough soil that bred Cordell Hull.

When you get out West, and if you are a stranger there, the back country could well mean the broad cement highway that does not happen to span the shortest distance between two of California's well-advertised clichés. I am not egging anybody on to get lost in the Wasatch Mountains or choke up in the Owens Valley. The sort of thing I suggest is this: going west from Salt Lake City, for example, resist the impulse to line up behind the impatient cavalcade that swishes off to Reno via the "short" route of U.S. 40, via Elko and the Carson Sink. Go due south to Ely (the copper pit at Ruth is worth a detour in itself), and then flatten out across the three hundred-some miles of sage and juniper and salt flats and rippling hills that lie between Ely and Carson City. This is one of the easiest and loveliest drives in America.

I end, as all knowing travelers do, with the absolute, confidential, hard-earned low-down: with the memories of the places that have stirred me most, the private discoveries that you must be *mad* not to want to make your own.

My favorite day's drive, anywhere in the United States, is east from Spokane to Missoula. This takes you through the Spokane Valley and up into the little Swiss lakes of the Coeur d'Alene country, then through the blue shaggy canyons of the incomparable Bitterroot Mountains, through battling rain and sun, through emerald valleys gleaming under black skies; then for eighty or a hundred miles you plunge and wind with the Clark Fork River, the bluebirds and the larch above you, and above them always the noble battalions of Douglas fir, and above that the cold moving upper air of Montana which produces towering ramparts of cloud and a sky of the purest blue this side of eternity.

If I had to choose one of all the natural phenomena of America to see before I died, it would be Bryce Canyon. Southern Utah, anyway, is a region that every American should visit periodically, if only to humble him in his new pride of world leadership. Here a tree is a Johnny-come-lately, and the land is almost as old as God. If you fear the Russians, if you are in an indecent hurry or chronically mad at any human, go and pause for a day at Bryce, roam the vast horseshoe all day long as the sun turns over, and consider how these thousands of cathedrals came to be built. They are massed in an amphitheater as stupendous as the Grand Canyon. Yet they are as exquisite as English Gothic. These domes and temples and shimmering spires run from scarlet through the whole Max Factor palette to the waxiest white. They burn at your feet in blinding gold and faint into purple on the horizon. Bryce is one of the great spectacles of this earth. And the lesson for Americans is that it took fifty million years to make and was done with nothing but drops of water.

Bryce apart, there is no point in saying much else about the National Parks. Most of them are known and none of them ought to be passed by. But now I think of many far-apart places, most of them revered with a proprietary air by the people who live close by but not much talked about by tourists. I recall, with a pleasure I should like to pass on, the fine Gulf drive from St. Petersburg up through Clearwater, past the Greek fishing fleet at Tarpon Springs, round to Tallahassee, down to Apalachicola past miles of dunes swimming with rosemary, and then along the hundred-mile gypsum beach which stretches from Panama City to Pensacola.

There is, to a stranger, the surprise of the lush rolling country of Southern Indiana. The first delighted discovery of the Finger Lakes in New York. The noblest vista in the East — that from French Asylum, Pennsylvania, overlooking the Susquehanna. The bare charm of the Davis Mountains around Alpine and Marfa in West Texas. The fertile high meadows of the (misnamed) Rockies in July. The first shock of the beautiful suburbs of Kansas City. The privilege of a journey down on an ore freighter from Duluth to the tip of Lake Michigan. A night in Natchez. The discovery of a village in Western Kansas with no doors on the main street: it was named Victoria, after their Queen, by a group of flighty and lazy Englishmen, who retired without a shot before the invading Russians who are there today growing the Turkey red wheat they introduced.

And, in California — but that would be another three thousand words. For here is most of the splendor of the American landscape and of many other lands besides: of Egypt and Spain and Yorkshire and Switzerland. Much of it is inland, away from " the Coast " to which the business-

man, the tourist, and the Hollywood ten-percenter are magnetized. The salt flats east of the Sierras. The lovely Sespe
country. The breathless prospect of the Channel Islands
floating above the clouds as you see them from the top of the
La Cumbre lookout. The one-day lesson in the life zones
painlessly provided by a trip over the Pines-to-Palms Highway. The great transition from the reptilian landscape of
Maricopa and Taft over the mountains and into the twentieth century at Santa Barbara. The glacial loneliness of
Shasta. The hot interior places where Father Serra thought
it worth while to bless a bell and a live oak and make a
church for a few gauping Indians looking on. The haunted
Spanish square of San Juan Bautista. The grave of Doña
Maria Concepción. The long descent through bristling canyons by the furious Shasta River, a million miles from sun-
tan oil and pismo clams and Marilyn Monroe. Please don't
get me started on California.

This is not a record filched from old notebooks or dispatches. It is the green memory of one man's wanderings
through this vast land, which will always remain unknown
till it is known each time to one beholder. If some of these
admirations seem eccentric, and others too lavish, remember
they are the fruit of the morning innocence which dawned
on me at the end, not at the beginning, of my first tour of
the country. I started out with all my preconceptions filed
in place, imagining vile cities (of which there are many)
spaced by dreary plains (of which there are some) before
you arrived at the approved high spots — the Canyon, Crater
Lake, Yellowstone, The Dalles, and so on. This is not a
frame of mind restricted to Europeans. Americans, too,
need to discard the ads and follow their interests, explore
the despised sticks, and be modest before the unknown. If
you do this, the chances are you will come to marvel at
your discovery of what you had thought most familiar.

The felicity of being " ever on the wing " will not be complete this side of the grave. But three hundred years after
John Donne, you will say with him: " O my America! my
new-found land."

STUDYING THE ESSAY

1. " Trust the native about his immediate region." How broad,
or how narrow, is your idea of the United States? Whether or
not you have traveled widely, have you a general idea of what
your country looks like?

2. What are Cooke's main rules about getting the most out of
travel?

3. Here are some well-known writers listed in this article:
D. H. Lawrence, Lafcadio Hearn, Bernard De Voto, J. B. Priestley. Who are they?

4. Do you own an atlas? If you do, or if you can borrow one,
look up some of the places Cooke mentions.

5. Many of you live near places mentioned in the essay. Can
you defend them as Cooke does?

6. What is there to be said for knowing a lot about one's own
country?

7. Do you think it is true that a foreigner can learn more
about this country than an American can?

8. Alistair Cooke *looks* at things and also *sees them*. What is
the difference between *looking* and *seeing?*

COMPOSITION TOPICS

1. Try to describe, for an outsider, the best things about the
county, the township, or the city in which you live.

2. Choose a single feature of your surroundings — a hill, a
tree, a valley, a building — and write a description of it. Make
the description vivid enough to interest another person. Try to
see as well as look.

JOSEPHINE JOHNSON, 1910–

Josephine Winslow Johnson is a native of Missouri. During her college years her interest was almost evenly divided between art and literature. She was educated at both Washington University, in St. Louis, and the St. Louis Art School. She wrote short stories for various magazines; she also painted murals for two elementary schools in St. Louis and had her water colors exhibited. She has taught at the People's Art Center in St. Louis and at the Breadloaf School of English at Middlebury College, Vermont.

Miss Johnson has had a deep love for the country ever since her family moved to a farm during her childhood. Her appreciation of the country is reflected in her Pulitzer Prize-winning novel, *Now in November* (1934), concerning farm life in the Middle West, and in poetry, short stories, and essays like "Tenants of the House," which is one of a series of articles about the trials which the author and her family suffered when they moved into an old house in Newtown, Ohio. She says that she is interested in books, particularly poetry; in cooking, walking, the making of puppets; in all forms of art; in animals (pigs, hedgehogs, hawks, bats, sheep, and all the others, too); in her husband and her children; and in beautiful writing.

"Tenants of the House" is unusual. How many families have ever had an attic full of bats? But this is not an essay in natural science. What matters is not so much what is done with the bats as what goes on in the writer's mind as she thinks about the problem. Thus the writing has the strong personal tone of the informal essay. Her prose — "quiet and beautiful," Louis Untermeyer calls it — has depth and poetry and the care of the literary craftsman.

TENANTS OF THE HOUSE

Like the night, an old house has a thousand eyes. Small shapes and forms have inhabited it from generation to generation. When one comes, as we did last year, to live in such a house, one must expect small unwinking eyes in the darkness; the cracks in the floor, the knotholes in the wood, the ancient beams of the cellar, have a life of their own. There is the loud tick of the wood beetle, the soundless scurry of the centipede like a furry shadow, and the sudden appearance of black ant borings around the kitchen sink.

But there were also certain tenants that no one told us about at all.

The enormous house was beautiful and its cost was reasonable, much more reasonable than that of a house of normal size — a rare and capricious combination. In addition there were three acres around it, and at the back door a tall and crumbling brick structure, big as another house, which had been used as the servants' quarters long ago. We bought all this and moved in at Christmas time. Not until April were we aware that we were no longer alone, and that, added to all the registered members of the family and the migratory assorted insect life, up from their southern wintering spa had come the tenants of over a hundred years, the enormous summer colony of the *Fledermäuse,* the *chauves-souris* — in the colder English, bats.

The extent of this home-coming was not apparent to us all at once. We began to be aware of bats drifting out from under the eaves at twilight, swooping to and fro under the southern porch, and then scattering high over the cornfields, weaving long swinging patterns until they were lost, invisible in the night.

"The bat is an insect eater," I said. "Bats help keep the balance of nature, and therefore are very good things to have around." The balance-of-nature had a comforting sound, but one evening when standing in peace, admiring the magnificent silhouette of our great brick mansion against the sky, we became aware that the cometlike streak of bat after bat from the narrow eaves had been going on for a long, long time.

"You sit on this side of the house and count," my husband said. "I'll take the other side." His voice had a curious, strained sound.

For a little while I sat in silence and counted. Fifty bats went by. Fifty more. I got tired of counting and just watched the streakings and swoopings, undiminished in number or timing, go on and on.

After a while Grant came back with a look that seemed clearly dark and thoughtful, even in the dim twilight gloom. "And how many did *you* count? " he asked. His voice was that of one who graciously withholds his news, knowing its nature can never be topped or spoiled.

I said I'd only counted a hundred but that they'd kept coming on and on.

"I counted one thousand three hundred and seventy-three! " he said. "Good God! Why do you suppose nobody ever *told* us? "

Bats were still flowing out from under the eaves.

As June warmed into July a mousy smell like musky mignonette became a palpable presence. It filled the upper rooms thick as a furry fog and started to creep softly and smotheringly down the stair. And then the bats themselves, a few of the finally estimated four thousand, began coming *inside* the house. Their small restless shapes would appear suddenly, swooping across a lighted room. From the cracks around sills, from supposedly sealed fireplaces, and from God knows where, they crept forth, and a long, curiously unforgettable summer had begun.

In the wonderful, illustrated *Natural History* by S. G. Goodrich, which I referred to in this trying time, published in 1859 and full of amazing lore and truly horrendous etchings of the Bat Megaderm and the Bat Rhinolophus Nobilis (size of life), there appear these memorable sentences: " In a rude age, the imagination needs little encouragement to convert objects so really curious and strange as these we have been describing, into hideous monsters, endowed with supernatural powers. It is the province of education and enlightened reason to reduce these horrid creations of fancy to the comparatively simple and innocent dimensions of truth."

Now my husband, educated and enlightened though he be, may be described as a brave man who abhors bats. With the exception of his four years in the army, his bravery and his abhorrence herein reached all the climax of their conflicting powers — beyond which man neither can nor is expected to go. As twilight of each evening drew on, he would fetch the kitchen broom, place it close at hand, and with his back against the wall relax nervously and begin to read. By the front door we kept an empty wastebasket and a flat cookie tin. We did not often have long to wait. A soundless shadow would speed across the light, casting its signature athwart the page; Grant would leap up with the broom and the evening was begun.

The radar mechanism of the bat is such that he avoids all obstacles in *front* with unerring accuracy. On the wing he is not likely to touch anything he does not wish to devour. (This is hard to believe, of course, and it is next to impossible to convince the white-faced guest that the low slicing dive which fans his cheek and lifts his hair is a deliberate miss, and not a deliberate attack that failed.) After some trial and error and considerable sweat, Grant learned to out-wit the radar warning by swinging at the bat from *behind*, fouling its control mechanisms, as he put it, and speeding it into the nearest wall, where it bumped, folded, and fell to the floor. Then the wastebasket would be inverted over it, the cookie tin slipped under the wastebasket, and the whole borne hastily out the front door. One evening I released the lid too soon; the bat turned around and scuttled back into the house on its elbows, and had to be swept out again.

Several times I was awakened at night by the sense of a presence in the room, and once, stumbling to find the light, I stepped on a soft-furred thing that squirmed under my bare foot. Other furred things with wings swept back and forth across the room an inch or two above Grant's inno-cent sleeping face. He is a sound sleeper and did not wake while I furiously beat the air with his shirt and finally drove them into the darkness of the upper hall and quietly shut the door. In the morning I found them snuggled between the curtain folds and upside down on the shades.

It is almost impossible to convey the largeness, the oldness, the vulnerability of an ancient house, the smallness, the craft-iness, the dexterity of a bat. Convinced that they were com-ing inside through the window sills of an upper room (dur-ing the day we could hear them talking to each other inside the hollow wood), we hired a carpenter who came unhap-pily, removed the window frame and sill, announced it had been impossible for bats to get in from the outside and re-placed the boards, sealed it all up — and the bats continued to enter.

Reports of our unusual number of what Mr. Goodrich de-scribes as " one of the most remarkable groups in the whole circle of animated nature " began to circulate in Cincinnati, and two naturalist friends expressed what seemed to us a somewhat unnatural eagerness to go up under the roof, look around for themselves, and study the Vespertilionidae *in situ*. Bearing a tremendous amount of camera equipment, a stout cotton bag, and dressed nonchalantly in shorts and T shirts, Karl and Woody arrived one humid Saturday morning and disappeared cheerfully up the small trap door in the ceiling. They ranged about in the hot fragrant darkness for some time. For quite a long time in fact, and sometimes they were very quiet. Another fragment from Mr. Goodrich's book began to haunt me with its gentle incisiveness. " In India," he wrote, " the megaderms may be heard on quiet evenings crunching the heads and bones of frogs." But eventually the men returned with about sixty bats in the bag and the heartening report that the old manse probably contained the largest concentration of bats in the world outside of Dante's Inferno and the Carlsbad Caverns. We sat awhile meditatively on the front porch, drank iced coffee, and watched the bag undulate and nearly walk off by itself.

As a naturalist Karl took only a calm, detached view of the situation. Woody, who had worked for exterminating companies, remarked that no company would guarantee a bat job, but that they might try — for a price. The thought of actually exterminating four thousand bats, not just driving them away, was truly appalling to me.

On the other hand, if we merely drove them out, there was always the great brick servants' quarters for their refuge, open to sun and wind, impossible to seal, too expensive to demolish, and but a few paces from the back door, where the gentlest breeze could bring the musky presence right back into the house again. Karl and Woody were sympathetic about our unusual problem; told us to be of good cheer, that the bats would leave with the first frost sometime in October; and after a while swung the bag in the car and went home to stuff bats and develop some excellent pictures of the attic.

A few weeks passed. Friends who used to drop in began quietly staying away. Then one sweltering summer day, impelled by a curious mixture of duty and what is sometimes referred to as the death wish, Grant determined to carry this fragmentary battle to the very stronghold under the roof itself, drive out the bats once and for all, and sell the guano to connoisseurs in the garden clubs. His plan was simple and based on close, if not loving, observation of the creatures' nocturnal habits. At ten in the evening, long after the working hours of the bats had started, he would go up with a bright light. This would drive away any of the more home-loving type who might have expected to spend the evening in.

12 P.M. Go up and light two sulphur candles.

4.30 to 5 A.M. Bats return, smell sulphur, and go — elsewhere.

4 P.M. Grant to go up into dark attic (now to be free of sulphur fumes and all bats), plug up holes with aid of light shining in from outside, and problem is solved.

The plan began on schedule at ten o'clock. Grant dressed himself carefully in his old army clothes, tucked the pants legs into combat boots, put on a pair of beekeeper's gloves that came up over his shirt sleeves, and then carefully placed over his head a paper bag in which he had cut two eye-holes sealed with clear cellophane. He then buttoned on another shirt (to keep the mammals from coming up under the bag), took a last look at the known and loved, and climbed the ladder up to the trap door, beyond which lay, Mr. Goodrich had assured us, only " the simple and innocent dimensions of truth." The opening of the trap door let down a staggeringly warm wave of truth, but Grant silently struggled through and stood up with his light.

It was at this point that that plan began to disintegrate. In the first place, more bats like to stay in at night than you would imagine — if you care to think about bats staying in at night. Disturbed by the glare and sound, dozens of furry bodies let go of the beams and started swirling insanely around and around in the narrow space. Some opened their mouths and snarled and the pinkness showed up quite clearly, outlined by their little pointed teeth. The bat has a peculiar cry which can only be described as a chitter or at times a horrendous smacking kiss. Chittering and kissing, the bats swirled about with no apparent intention of being driven forth to feed in the cool starlight outside.

Nevertheless, Grant decided to go ahead, step up the procedure by lighting the sulphur candles now, and drive them all out at once. This he did, placing them in pans of water to keep the whole house from burning up, and descended the ladder, a seriously disturbed man, if not positively paranoiac. The most shattering experiences of life do not all occur at the age of four but may well crop up in a 101° attic surrounded by antagonistic bats as one approaches the age of forty. It is, I think, of vast importance to know that there are men today who can emerge from an experience of this nature with only a slight tic and a tendency to shudder at a loud and aggressive kissing sound. Also those who can, go back up again.

In the gray dawn I went out expecting to find the outside of the house a mass of fluttering wings and frustrated *Fledermäuse*. But there was not a bat in sight. At 4 P.M. (we at least kept to *our* part of the plan) we discovered that the sulphur had neither driven them away entirely nor kept them entirely from returning. It had in fact suffocated a certain selected number.

The smell of dead bats, live bats, and sulphur descended heavily throughout the house. Two days later, for the last time, a grim, tight-lipped man dressed in his airtight suit ascended the ladder bearing a bucket, twenty pounds of naphtha flakes to further discourage and repel the bats, and a bottle of pine oil deodorant to drown the smell. Fighting his way among swirling and snarling little shapes, he collected all the bodies he could find, spread out the naphtha flakes — mainly by throwing balls of them at the bats — splashed pine oil over the rafters, and lowered the bucket of dead ones down through the door. (I buried them in the potato patch and was amazed at how light is even a whole bucketful of bats.) Then Grant came down, sealed up the trap door, and removed the ladder to the tool house. Something in his kindly open nature had hardened, and his eyes had the withdrawn and distant look of those who have known some experience not communicable to mortal men.

The summing up of that summer's efforts was an unpleasant old house, redolent with naphtha, pine oil, sulphur, live bats, and dead bats. Bats were distributed about uncomfortably behind shutters; bats in hollow pillars of the porch; and most of the bats up under the roof where they had always been.

This was in August. We sat down in exhaustion and waited for the first sharp breath of frost to send them south.

The whole winter passed, in which we spoke sporadically of " doing something " about them. We thought of having a carpenter come who would go up and stop up every hole inside and out, a task of microscopic research and patience. But we did not know what the spring would then bring forth. Perhaps a house *completely* decorated with fur-lined shutters, or a brick bat-roost at the back door, or — knowing the nature of the bat, a nightmare thought occurred to me. They would find one hole — one infinitesimal hole up under the eaves, and all four thousand would enter in the spring, and every night all four thousand would line up in a long, sinuous queue from beam to beam and, chittering and shoving, make their exit from that one hole, and in the gray dawn similarly return.

Thus April was upon us and the mass immigration took place again and nothing had been done to keep them out — and nothing could have been — and all that was left was the chance of a professional mass extermination. It is difficult to explain, wholly apart from the costliness of such a thing, the moral scruples involved. Four thousand bats is a lot of life, and for a long time I could not bring myself to sanction such a sweeping and drastic destruction. They were just too many to be killed. For two months I temporized, delayed, hoped that this year would be different, better; but by June things were obviously the same — and worse. The walls might as well have been completely porous as far as bats were concerned. We came to dread the gathering darkness, and not a single evening passed without at least two and sometimes four swooping shadows moving from room to room. Sometimes they held off until eleven, giving us false hopes of a peaceful night, but always and invariably before the stroke of midnight they were there.

We could not stand it any longer and we hardened our hearts and opened our bank account. We called an exterminating company and had them make an estimate, but this was only the beginning.

The exterminator estimator said that the old end plates should be torn from the roof and replaced with new snug end plates — replaced after the brickwork had been pointed up to seal the place. We called a carpenter, an enormous fellow, who came, looked, and said that there was no sense mending the end plates until the gutters were repaired; so he called a tinsmith. The tinsmith said that he could not repair the gutters until the carpenter had torn off the molding.

At this point, the carpenter revealed that he had grown too fat for ladder work and called in a subcarpenter who climbed up on the roof and reported that the molding was the gutter and the gutter was a solid, hand-carved beam made from a single cedar and forty-five feet long without a break other than the rotten spot objected to by the tinsmith. The larger carpenter — who turned out to be more in the nature of a broker or procurer — said to chop it down anyway. And on a hot June morning the sub-and-smaller carpenter actually began to saw and chop, and the last and final ousting of the tenants began.

The great rotting gutter came down in sections, the carpenter reported there was a hell of a lot of bats up there, but they did not come out by daylight, and the tinsmith returned, put in a new gutter, and the carpenter sealed up all the holes that he could find.

I took the children and in a somewhat cowardly fashion fled the state, and my husband went to stay with friends. The fire chief was informed, a large warning poison sign was posted on the door (reported later by a neighbor child as " that skiliton on your house "), and the exterminators set the cyanide gas cans up inside the attic. For a week the house was uninhabitable. Thousands of bats were killed and had to be shoveled out by hand and lowered down the trap door in buckets. A few hundred escaped and went behind the shutters, from which the exterminator drove them with a mouse powder, and these died outside.

Well, it was done, and successfully, and gradually the incomparable smell of dead bats faded from the hot summer air. Friends looked upon us again with something besides horror; our relatives, convinced we had been the center of a potential plague, communicated kindly with us again; those humorists who had delighted in saying the Cannons *really* have bats in their belfry were desolate; and we now sleep peacefully at night without the soundless intrusion of little swooping wings.

But I am not wholly happy about it all, for bats on such a grand scale as ours seemed an extraordinary phenomenon, a hundred years' accumulation of life, and an act of God not to be tampered with too much. Will not nature take her revenge in some unknown and probably terrifying form? Sometimes at midnight I listen for the sound of monstrous insect wings, of mosquitoes hungry and humming in the dark, armed with the knowledge of their enemies' mass death, and come at last into their own. And beyond the sinister hum I hear the laughter of little bat ghosts, sneering in the night.

STUDYING THE ESSAY

1. Explain the last paragraph of the essay.
2. Find examples of Miss Johnson's effective style. Here is a sample: " It (the mousy smell) filled the upper rooms thick as a furry fog." There are many such poetic uses of figures of speech in this essay.
3. In what ways is the author's point of view unusual?
4. Words to learn: *capricious, migratory, appalling, sporadically, queue.*

COMPOSITION TOPICS

1. Describe any extermination problem you or your family have had.
2. Write a scientific description of the common bat — the " little brown bat " — which plagued the author.
3. Besides bats, what other problems often face the new owners of old houses?

NORMAN COUSINS, 1912–

Norman Cousins, the youngest writer represented in this book, is one of America's most distinguished editors and an important philosopher. He is a man whose concern about the survival of freedom and the integrity of the human race has produced some of the most cogent editorial essays of our times.

A native of Union, New Jersey, Cousins graduated from Teachers' College, Columbia University, but has never taught in the classroom. His classes are large ones, however — the audiences who hear him lecture and the readers of his books and editorials. Cousins's career in journalism began with a year on the New York *Post* and five years as an editor of *Current History*. In 1940 he went to the *Saturday Review of Literature* (now simply the *Saturday Review*); in 1942 he became its editor. He is a consultant on international relations for N.B.C. During the war he was chairman of the editorial board for the Overseas Bureau of the Office of War Information. He has been President of the World Federalists. Among his books, the two best are probably *Modern Man Is Obsolete* (1945) and *Who Speaks for Man?* (1953), from which this essay was taken. These books are among the strongest pleas yet written for world order, world law, and the dignity of man.

Cousins' deeply-felt conviction is that man is doomed if he continues to develop atomic power without considering moral values and the freedom of the human spirit. His approach to world problems is realistic, and he has never, like so many liberal thinkers, changed his mind about the significance of that original, horrible sunburst over Hiroshima. No ivory-tower thinker, he saw the Bikini test bomb, and he has been to Hiroshima. When he writes of world problems, as he does regularly in the *Saturday Review*, what strikes the reader immediately is the deep sincerity of what he says.

His prose has the force, the depth, and the incisiveness to be the perfect medium for his clear thinking. Although Cousins is profoundly disturbed by the course of recent history, he is by no means a pessimist, as the essay here shows. (Whether the 1954 hydrogen bomb which "surprised" its creators will change his point of view is not yet evident.) Like E. B. White, whose thinking resembles that of Cousins, his hope for the world lies in man himself. "The First Citizens of the Atomic Age" is one of the most eloquent statements of faith in mankind that has appeared. This essay, and the entire book from which it comes, should make young Americans pause to organize some mature thoughts about the world.

THE FIRST CITIZENS OF
THE ATOMIC AGE

Only at quite rare moments have I felt really good to be alive. I could not but feel with a sympathy full of regret all the pain that I saw around me, not only that of men but that of the whole creation. From this community of suffering I have never tried to withdraw myself. It seemed to me a matter of course that we should all take our share of the burden of pain which lies upon the world. — ALBERT SCHWEITZER

It can hardly be a matter for surprise that our race has not succeeded in solving any large part of its most difficult problems in the first millionth part of its existence. Perhaps life would be a duller affair if it had, for to many it is not knowledge but the quest for knowledge that gives the greatest interest to thought — to travel hopefully is better than to arrive. — SIR JAMES JEANS

The dogmas of the quiet past are inadequate to the stormy present. The occasion is piled high with difficulty, and we must rise with the occasion. As our case is new, so we must think anew and act anew. We must disenthrall ourselves.

— ABRAHAM LINCOLN

Mankind is now in one of its rare moods of shifting its outlook. The mere compulsion of tradition has lost its force. It is our business — philosophers, students, and practical men — to re-create and re-enact a vision of the world, including those elements of reverence and order without which society lapses into riot, and penetrated through and through with unflinching rationality. Such a vision is the knowledge which Plato identified with virtue. Epochs for which, within the limits of their development, this vision has been widespread are the epochs unfading in the memory of mankind. — ALFRED NORTH WHITEHEAD

Hiroshima wasn't what I expected. I expected resignation; I found rehabilitation. I expected desolation; I found rejuvenation.

In Hiroshima I found people who, having survived atomic catastrophe, restored their lives, and, even more important, restored their faith in the human race and their faith in themselves. The citizens planned to make their city one of the most beautiful in the world.

From the back yard of the small inn where I stayed, I had a fairly good vantage point for viewing the city, with its many rivers and levees. In front of me, across the river, I could see perhaps six square miles of the city, stretching along the banks of the river and sprawling out beyond. The city itself is fairly flat, built at sea level. Hiroshima is a seaport, though from this vantage point it seemed completely surrounded by a ring of mountains.

The hurry-up, improvised quality of the wooden buildings on the other side of the river gave the city something of the appearance of an American mining town in the West a century ago. The resemblance was even stronger because of the mountains in the background.

From where I stood, I could see the general area hit hardest by the atomic bomb; I could see what is now the most famous landmark of the atomic explosion — the dome, or what used to be a dome, of the old Industrial Exhibition Hall. Just enough of the curved steelwork was left so that you could tell it was a dome. Another four- or five-story structure, off to the left a few hundred yards away, showed evidence of considerable damage.

Apart from these two buildings, Hiroshima was completely rebuilt — rebuilt, that is, on a sort of overnight basis. The homes, the stores, the industrial buildings were thrown up very hastily. But the greatest difficulty hasn't been putting up the new buildings and shacks. The greatest difficulty has been clearing away the rubble.

The river in front of me was at low tide; you could walk across its full width of about five hundred feet without getting your ankles wet. I looked out across the river and could see the streets clearly marked — electric and telephone poles, very little open area, and no rubble or evidence of the bomb whatsover, except for the old dome skeleton.

Of course, when I actually walked through the streets I could see many wounds still open. There were the gutted foundations of the concrete buildings, even though four years of weeds and grass do a great deal to smooth over and conceal the old ruins.

Right next to the small inn where I stayed was the wreckage of what was once a fairly large two-story stone home. All that was left was part of a wall, the large concrete gateposts, and the iron gate itself — most of it twisted out ot shape. I went poking around behind the wall and came across a family of five living under a piece of canvas propped up by boards, with the stone wall as the principal inside wall surface. Directly in front of their home, if you want to call it that, which measures about seven feet by seven feet, the family had cleared away the rubble and planted a vegetable garden.

On the fourth anniversary of the atomic bombing, I stood at the spot which is believed to mark the center of the atomic explosion. Directly in front of me were two fairly thick and round stucco columns or gateposts on a very small plot raised about one foot off the ground level as a marker and memorial.

These columns were all that was left of Dr. Shima's hospital, which was directly under the atomic burst. A new hospital had been built right in back of the old gateposts. It was a two-story affair, painted white. Patients waved from the windows.

As you stand at the spot marking the center of the atomic explosion, it's difficult to describe the things you feel. Here, four years ago, there was a flash of heat which at the split second of fission was many times the surface temperature of the sun. And suddenly, even before a stop watch could register it, the heart of a city was laid open with a hot knife. I talked to dozens of people who were in it — dozens who were crippled and burned and suffering from diseases of radioactivity — and their stories were very much the same.

The sudden flash of light brighter than the morning sun — much shorter, much more intense than lightning, much more intense than any light ever seen before on this earth. If you lived through that second, you found that your clothes were on fire, and your arms and legs and face were on fire, and you rushed out into the street and ran, for everyone else was running — no one knew where. And everything was now blazing, and you were inside the fire, trying to run somewhere. Then someone yelled, "Run for the river!" and you threw yourself into the river, and thousands of others did the same thing, and you wondered what happened to your family, to your children or your parents. No one knew where anyone was, but there were people all around you, and other people were jumping from the bridges into the river, and the dead bodies were all around you in the river; but you could hardly hear the people crying because the blaze was like rolling thunder sweeping over you. And all day and night the fire ate your city and burned your dead, and all night you stayed in the river to cool your burns; but the tide ran out and you buried yourself as deeply in the mud as you could and prayed for the tide to come back in again with the water from the sea to cool your fevered body, even though it was salt water and it cut into your burns, but at least it was cool. The hours passed slowly, and you searched the sky for the light of morning, but the city was a torch and it was difficult to see the sky. But then morning came, and you joined the thousands of others running through the black smoke, stumbling over the wreckage of the buildings, the sounds of the dying all around you. You were too much in a hurry to notice you had no clothes; it was hard to see that others had no clothes either, for their bodies were like charcoal.

This, then, was Hiroshima in the first hours of the Atomic Age. It was something new in the solar system — getting at the heart of matter and ripping it apart, and causing the smallest units of nature to smash each other and set off a flash as though a piece of the sun itself had broken away, and sending out strange rays that went through the bones and did things to the composition of human blood that had not been done before or dreamed of before. This was the triumph of mind over matter in the ultimate and most frightening sense.

As you stood in front of the large stone columns from the old hospital gateposts, and you reached over and felt the rough, raised surface of the stone, its composition altered because the surface had been melted by the explosion, you wondered why people would ever come back to the city again — not merely Hiroshima but any city — any city that man ever built, for by this bomb he had placed a curse on every city everywhere. You wondered what the lure could be that could bring people out from the hills and back to this place of compressed agony. You wondered, but you didn't have very far to look for the answer, for the answer was all around you. You could see it in the faces of the people who passed on the street. You could see it in the brisk life-loving walk of the young people. You could hear it in the full laughter of children. You could see it in the eagerness of young boys and young men playing ball with each other wherever there was a place to play ball. The answer you found was that there are deeper resources of courage and regeneration in human beings than any of the philosophers had dared to dream. The answer you found was that the greatest force on this earth — greater than any device yet conjured up in the laboratories — is the will to live and the will to hope.

As you looked around you in Hiroshima, you saw a young woman of about twenty-four or -five with a baby strapped to her back. She was wearing Western dress, though she had on Japanese wooden shoes. There was nothing defeatist about the girl. She was starting out to raise a family; she was going to do it in Hiroshima, and nowhere else; she believed in life, and nothing could change it. And as she passed you, and you looked at the back of her neck and down her left arm, you saw the seared and discolored flesh that is the badge of citizenship in Hiroshima today. The girl stepped to one side to allow a modern bus to pass — it was a bus filled with Japanese baseball players in uniform, for baseball has become the national pastime in Japan to an extent not approached even in America. The baseball players were singing, some of them, and you thought you saw, but couldn't be quite sure — you thought you saw the familiar atomic burns on one or two arms and faces.

Another thing you wondered about was what the people themselves thought about the bomb and America. You spoke to them about it, and it was hard to believe that what they said was the way people can or should feel after having lived through an atomic explosion.

There was no bitterness, except in one or two cases. They said, most of them, that if it hadn't been Hiroshima it would have been another city and that they had no right to ask exemption at the expense of their fellows.

They said, most of them, that they had taken part in something that would save the lives of millions, for they believed, most of them, that Hiroshima, in the words of the mayor, Shinzo Hamai, was an exhibit for peace, a laboratory that had demonstrated the nature of the new warfare so dramatically that it would destroy war itself.

They believed that two years of blinding, grinding warfare were squeezed into a single bomb and that the smashing of Hiroshima made it possible for many millions of Japanese to stay alive, for they then knew by this bomb that the war was forever lost to them.

Some of them, of course, said things they thought you wanted to hear, but their voices and their eyes would frequently give them away.

And then, as counter-balance perhaps, you would find a woman — a woman barber who took over the shop after her husband died in the explosion — who would turn her head and say that she never wanted to look at any American, for she was afraid he would see the hate she had in her heart for the people who could stain their honor as Americans did by dropping such a bomb. She lost her husband and two children, and when it pained her heart to think about it she would think of America and know that such evil could come only from evil people.

Then there were some who blamed it on the Japanese government, who said that when Japan first bombed China they were certain that God would visit the crime on the Japanese a thousandfold. Some blamed it on the Japanese government because it had converted Hiroshima into a military base and shipping point, and they were certain that America would find this out and destroy the city.

This was the first I had heard about Hiroshima as a city of military importance. As I spoke to people and questioned them, the picture began to take shape. When a girl of nineteen told me about her experience in the bombing, she spoke of all the soldiers running past her house on the way from the barracks near the old castle. When the photographer who took films for me told about his experience in the bombing, he spoke of his sensation while riding a train two miles away from Hiroshima on his way to work. He said that when he heard the explosion he thought the large ammunition supply center near the old Parade Grounds had been blown up, for the explosion was too loud for even the largest bomb. Others on the outskirts of the city spoke of the same feeling. I spoke to one man who operated a bus to the ammunition dump; he gave me some idea of its size and said that many thousands worked there during the war.

It was freely admitted, once you referred to it, that Japan was divided into two military zones: the headquarters for the North in Tokyo, and the headquarters for the South in Hiroshima.

Later that evening I discussed with Mayor Hamai the military importance of Hiroshima during the war. He spoke freely and fully. Hiroshima had been Japan's chief port for sending soldiers overseas. It had housed large ammunition supply depots.

I asked the mayor whether it was true, as I had heard in some of my conversations, that as many as 60,000 soldiers had been stationed in Hiroshima at the time of the bombing. He was familiar with the reports but believed that the number may have been closer to 40,000. Then I learned for the first time something I had seen in no report about Hiroshima since the end of the war. I learned that 30,000 soldiers had died in the atomic bombing of Hiroshima and that this figure had been suppressed by the Japanese police, then under orders from the Japanese government to conceal the military death toll and the military importance of Hiroshima as well as to minimize the general damage and civilian death toll. Japan had been taken completely by surprise, and didn't want the United States to know how effective the weapon had been, so that what little bargaining power she had at the peace table might not have been further reduced; and that, once having announced false figures, Japan was reluctant to embarrass herself by giving out the true ones.

I learned that the only figures since used by the American government about Hiroshima have been supplied by Japanese sources and that the original figures supplied by the Japanese police had never been corrected. I further learned from Mayor Hamai, who was in charge of rationing in Hiroshima during the war and who was given the responsibility for issuing new certificates after the bombing, that the population of Hiroshima had decreased 110,000 when a check was made three months after the bombing — and that this figure did not include 30,000 military personnel or the many thousands of volunteers from outside the city brought in to construct fire-retention barriers, or the thousands who have died since. The city's own estimate today, said Mayor Hamai, is 210,000 to 240,000, which includes all those who have died since. The highest previous figure made public was 100,000.

The following day Mayor Hamai took me on a tour of Hiroshima's hospitals. It was an experience difficult to put out of your mind, and you tried hard to put it out of your mind because you saw things that whatever sanity you might have had cried out against. You saw beds held together with slabs of wood; nowhere did you see sheets or pillows; you saw dirty bandages and littered floors and rooms not much larger than closets with four or five patients huddled together. You thought back to what you saw in the D.P. camps in Germany, and you knew that nothing you had seen in Germany or anywhere else put human pride to such a strain.

You looked in on an operating room that seemed little better than a crude abattoir. You saw rooms where whole families had moved in with the patient. You saw all this with unbelieving eyes, and then you had some idea of what Mayor Hamai meant when he said that Hiroshima needed America's help to take care of the sick. For all the hospitals in Hiroshima were destroyed or gutted or severely damaged by the bomb, and hospital facilities in Japan are not easy to come by. People can throw up shacks to live in inside a week or two, but a hospital is nothing to be thrown together. Everything is needed that makes a hospital a hospital, Mayor Hamai said: surgical equipment and rubber gloves for operations and sterilizers and X-ray equipment and beds and pots and pans.

As he spoke, I thought of the millions of dollars being spent by the United States in Hiroshima in the work of the

Atomic Bomb Casualty Commission — excellent work and important work, for it can tell what happens to people in atomic warfare. Nothing of those millions goes to treat the victims of the atomic bomb. The Casualty Commission only examines patients; it doesn't treat them. And you had the strange spectacle of a man suffering from radioactive sickness getting thousands of dollars' worth of analysis but not one cent of treatment from the Commission.

On the second floor of the Memorial Hospital in Hiroshima, near crowded rooms of children who are serious tuberculosis cases, a woman rushed out to me and fell at my feet, sobbing as I have heard few people sob. Dr. Akio Asano, the tall, scholarly, youthful head of the hospital, told me that she had heard an American had come to Hiroshima and that she had just been praying to Kami for the American to come to the hospital so that he might be able to see how sick her little girl was and how badly she needed certain medicine they didn't have in Hiroshima. She had been praying when I walked in. The little girl was seven years old. Her father had been killed in the atomic explosion. Her name was Nobuko Takeuchi. She had been ill of tuberculosis for several months, complicated by a series of mastoid infections, for which there had been several operations. But now she had what Dr. Anso described as the worst case of tuberculosis he had ever seen in a child of her age, and she might not live for more than a few weeks unless she was able to get large doses of streptomycin. But nowhere in Hiroshima could you get streptomycin.

That night I became a black marketeer. We established contact with what are called sources in Japan, and a few grams of streptomycin were rushed over to the hospital. But little Nobuko needed forty to fifty grams, and we sent wires to Tokyo and even to the United States to get the medicine in time. The Church World Service in the United

States heard about the appeal and rushed a fairly substantial package of streptomycin by air mail. (The medicines kept Nobuko alive for almost a year; then her frail body succumbed to an attack of meningitis.)

After we left the hospital, Mayor Hamai told me of his dream for a modern hospital in Hiroshima that would become part of the Hiroshima Peace Center, for which the Reverend Kiyoshi Tanimoto, of the Nakaregawa Church of Christ in Hiroshima, had gone to the United States in search of support. I had been working with Mr. Tanimoto in the United States, getting groups together to advance the idea of a Hiroshima Peace Center, but not until now did I realize how important were the units that were to go into it. The Peace Center would have, in addition to the hospital, an orphanage, a home for the aged, a civic recreation center, a peace institute study center, and a medical research center.

The next tour was of the orphanages for children whose parents were killed in the atomic explosion. I should like to report on one of them in particular — the Yamashita Orphanage, located about eight miles outside the city on a hillside. It is operated by Mr. and Mrs. Yamashita as a public service with whatever help and support they can get from the city and its people, and from the outside world. It is the largest of the four orphanages for Hiroshima children, providing care for almost one hundred youngsters ranging in age from four years to seventeen years. The youngest was born just a few hours before the bombing.

Mr. and Mrs. Yamashita were able to survive the bombing despite severe burns. Mrs. Yamashita, who had been close to the center of the explosion, said that suddenly there was a bright light and her body was on fire. She was carrying her two-year-old baby at the time, and the first thing she did was to smother the flames that enveloped the child. Then she picked up the baby and ran until she reached the fields outside the city, where she lived for three days on the ground before word came that people were returning to the city.

On her return with the child she found Mr. Yamashita, already under treatment. Recovery was slow for both of them, but after six months they were able to resume their lives, and they decided to dedicate themselves to the care of orphans. They got land and homes outside Hiroshima and built their little colony.

Mr. and Mrs. Yamashita were now completely recovered, except that the old wounds burn and itch in extremely warm or cold weather. Mrs. Yamashita said that she had been unable to have a successful pregnancy since the bombing, having experienced four miscarriages. She spoke of other women in Hiroshima in like circumstances.

The Yamashita Orphanage was, I think, the high spot of my visit to Hiroshima. Living conditions were better and brighter than I had seen almost anywhere else in the city. The children there were more alert, more responsive, and seemed quicker and happier than I had seen almost anywhere in Japan. The food was adequate and well prepared; there was ample play space; and, what was more important, the children were not starved for want of affection. Dozens of the younger ones hung on to Mrs. Yamashita like kids hanging on to an American mother's skirts in a department store. The quality of the teaching in the orphanage was as high as you would find anywhere in Japan. There was only one thing wrong with the Yamashita Orphanage. There was not enough of it. It ought to be five times as large, and would be, if outside help were forthcoming.

Before coming to Japan, several people told me that they would like to adopt Japanese children orphaned by the bombing. Under the Oriental Exclusion Act, however, these adoptions were not possible. It occurred to me that the next best thing might be *moral* adoptions. By moral adoptions I was thinking of Hiroshima children who would be adopted by American families and who would carry the names of the people adopting them. The children would continue to live in Japan — perhaps in some place such as Yamashita's — but the American families would be responsible for their care and upbringing. Then, later, if Congress passed a law permitting Japanese children to come to America, these morally adopted children could become legally adopted as well.

The next morning Mayor Hamai took me to the site of the old castle that had been destroyed by the bomb. Here, on an artificial hillside, you could overlook the city with its seven rivers and its many bridges. You could see the many homes and stores going up. The sound of the city, with its old trolleys, and the sounds of the pile drivers and the hammers and saws blended into a drone, as it sometimes does high up in a skyscraper.

There on the hillside that morning, a small group of citizens broke ground for the Hiroshima Peace Center, and re-dedicated their city to the cause of peace by renaming it the Peace City. Mayor Hamai, in introducing me, spoke of his hope that within a few years there might rise on this site an institute for the study of world peace, as part of the Peace Center project.

I said I came to Hiroshima expecting to see the end of the world. Instead, I found the beginning of a better one. I expected to find that Hiroshima, like many of the cities I saw in Germany the previous year, would be flattened out, its only heights those of rubble. True, there were few stone or concrete buildings in Hiroshima by contrast with such cities as Cologne, Aachen, or Berlin, but the wounds here went as deep as, or deeper than, any city in any war had ever suffered. Yet what was most important about Hiroshima, I said, was not that the debris and the remains of the old city have been cleared away and that a new city is in the process of being rebuilt. What was most important was what has happened inside people. I was not referring to the lack of bitterness, for even if it were bitterness it is doubtful that history would completely withhold sanction. I referred to the proof of personal regeneration, the rediscovery and re-inforcement of personal purpose, the capacity for personal rededication.

I tried to make the point that hope cannot exist, either in the individual or society, without the prospect of regeneration. And yet the power of regeneration is undervalued by modern man. The idea of regeneration in too many cases has been tied to the idea of immortality, identifying it as the principal means of achieving ends beyond life, rather than as an end in life itself, essential and attainable.

The sense of personal regeneration in Hiroshima was discernible and unmistakable. There was not only proof of the power of life over death, but of the individual discovery of fathomless physical, emotional, and spiritual resources. This regeneration soared far beyond personal rehabilitation to a restoration of vital faith in human destiny. There was in the making there, I said, a larger definition of the purposes of man than it seemed within our ken to imagine only a few years ago. In the days following the bombing many people in Hiroshima must have believed that they were witnesses to the death both of a city and of an age — and in a sense they were right. But that feeling had changed color and composition with the passing of the months. Today there was a new vision in Hiroshima. The city had a mission to explain itself to the world, to offer itself as a laboratory specimen in the making of world peace.

Such a vision was important and good, for personal recovery must be part of a larger pattern. However impressed we may be with man's capacity for regeneration, we must ask ourselves: regeneration for what? So that man may be afforded an even larger test of his capacity to survive atomic catastrophe? Hiroshima was an ideal classroom for history, but little will have been learned if the only lesson is that survival and regeneration are possible. Regeneration was possible in Hiroshima because it had the rest of the world to draw on. But what will the rest of the world draw upon?

Not survival but the condition of man is the problem. Not whether he can endure atomic fire but whether he can avert it. And in dedicating itself to this purpose the city of Hiroshima defined a mission as urgent as it was noble.

Even as we broke ground for a new Peace Center, we were aware that peace in the world was less a fact than it was a word and that while the will to peace was deep inside peoples everywhere, there was as yet no adequate means by which this will could be translated into effective reality. There existed nowhere on a world level an agency responsible to mankind as a whole, an agency which could listen and act to the end that human life may be protected and developed. To say that such an agency is more easily imagined than achieved, and is therefore to be avoided, is to condemn the history of progress.

Certainly true peace will be difficult to achieve. Life itself is difficult. But an honest effort is required before we can be sure that what is difficult may not also be possible. And such an effort — a supreme, common effort in the name of the world's peoples — has yet to be called for, let alone attempted. The problem confronting us is neither interplanetary nor supernatural. It is a man-made problem, one well within our reach to examine and solve.

When I returned to the United States, I had in my pocket a message that Mayor Hamai asked me to convey to Ameri-

cans. It was written in his own hand. It was appended to
four large bound volumes containing the signatures of
106,000 citizens of Hiroshima sending their greetings to the
American people. This was the Mayor's message:

"There is much I would like to say to America. First of
all, I would like to thank those Americans who have helped
us to bring a dead city back to life.

"It is not my place or purpose to try to tell Americans
what ought to be done. But what I can do is to tell them
about what will happen to the world's cities if something is
not done to stop war. The people of Hiroshima ask nothing
of the world except that we be allowed to offer ourselves as
an exhibit for peace. We ask only that enough peoples know
what happened here and how it happened and why it happened, and that they work hard to see that it never happens
anywhere again.

"We the people of Hiroshima are sick at heart as we look
out at the world and see that nations are already fighting the
initial skirmishes that can grow into a full war. We know
that stopping war is not a simple thing and that there are
grave questions that have to be solved before the world can
have true peace. We know, too, that peace is not to be had
just for the asking; all nations must agree to it.

"But we also know that some nation must take leadership
in building the type of peace that will last. And we are looking to America for that leadership. America can call for
world law, and all the world will listen. Leaders of a few
nations may not want to listen, but their people will hear.
Let the call go out from America for a federation of the nations strong enough to prevent war, and a thrill will be
known in the hearts of millions of people everywhere. This
is the best hope of averting a war which would see thousands of Hiroshimas. And this is the message the people of
Hiroshima ask that you take back to America."

STUDYING THE ESSAY

1. For an outside reading assignment, try *Hiroshima*, by John Hersey. This short book is the story of what happened when the bomb fell. Then, in the light of this extra reading, discuss the value of Norman Cousins' essay.

2. How does Cousins suggest the awful effect of the bomb?

3. What details does the author give of what actually happened to Hiroshima? Why does he choose these details?

4. How is Hiroshima an " exhibit for peace "?

5. Why does Cousins find in Hiroshima the beginning of a better world?

6. Discuss Mayor Hamai's message to Americans. What, according to Cousins and the Mayor, is the best hope for averting future war?

7. Alexander Pope said, " The proper study of mankind is man." In the light of this essay, do you think Pope was right?

8. How does this essay qualify as a " personal " essay?

9. Compare this essay with Lippmann's " The Rivalry of Nations." Do the two essays have any similar ideas?

COMPOSITION TOPIC

You have heard and read thousands of words about A-bombs, H-bombs, C-bombs and other agents of mass destruction. How do you think the human race can avoid destruction? Comparison of themes, a class forum, or a debate on this topic may crystallize your thinking about this very important point.

CLASSIFICATION
ACCORDING TO TYPES

Because some essays will fit more than one type, no classification can be rigid. A grouping like the following, however, may be helpful in the study of this book.

INFORMAL ESSAYS

FORMAL ESSAYS

DESCRIPTIVE ESSAYS

CHARACTER SKETCHES

CLASSIFICATION
ACCORDING TO THEMES

There are innumerable ways in which to group the essays in any collection. In the following arrangement, the essays are listed under five headings of major ideas.

HUMAN VALUES

SUGGESTIONS
FOR FURTHER READING

MAGAZINES

Four magazines which regularly carry essays by our best writers are *Harper's*, the *Atlantic*, the *New Yorker*, and the *Saturday Review*. Essays in these magazines are on a wide variety of subjects, from education and manners to business and politics. " Profiles " in the *New Yorker* are often first-rate biographical writing. All four of these magazines also contain excellent reviews of plays, movies, concerts, television programs, books, and records.

The Sunday Magazine Section of the New York *Times* often features an essay of quality. And the Sunday Book Review of the same newspaper can be depended upon for at least one excellent critical essay, usually the article starting on the first page.

Less widely-circulated periodicals which feature the essay are the quarterlies like the *American Scholar*, the *Yale Review*, and *Foreign Affairs*. Many libraries subscribe to these quarterlies, in which the writing is usually distinguished.

Such magazines as *Life*, the *Saturday Evening Post, Holiday*, and *Colliers* are good sources for the " article " — the objective, impersonal journalistic essay.

Readers of the essay should be alert to recognize good writing wherever it appears. Sometimes a really brilliant essay will appear in an unexpected place, like a farm magazine or a fashion magazine. The reader of this book may perhaps be discriminating enough to recognize the value of such accidental " finds."

BOOKS

Books described in the introductions throughout this volume are not included below, even though those books are the best " extra " reading list that could be recommended. Each year brings new publications to augment a list like this one. Check your school library carefully to find the new volumes as they come in. Your librarian will help you.

COLLECTIONS OF ESSAYS BY VARIOUS WRITERS

Adams, J. D., *The New Treasure Chest: An Anthology of Reflective Prose* (Dutton, 1953). A good book to pick up and read during stray moments of leisure. Most of the great writers are represented.

Bader and Wells, *Essays for Our Times* (Harper, 1947). Many types of writing by many kinds of writers.

Eaton, H. T., *Panorama* (Harcourt, Brace, 1940). A high school text of average difficulty. Nearly all the selections are modern.

Gehlmann, John, *The Challenge of Ideas* (Odyssey, 1950). A textbook. Many of these up-to-date selections cannot properly be called essays, but much of the writing is thought-provoking.

Lester, John A., *Essays of Yesterday and Today* (Harcourt, Brace, 1937). Good selections from the work of many of the writers represented in this book, and others.

Walter, E. A., ed., *Essay Annual* (Scott). The year's best magazine essays.

White, E. B. and K., *A Subtreasury of American Humor* (Coward-McCann, 1945). Many excellent humorous essays, in addition to poetry, stories, etc.

BOOKS BY INDIVIDUAL WRITERS

Some of these books are groups of short essays. Others are reflective volumes in which a chapter can often be termed an essay. In all of these volumes the reader can find interesting and valuable points of view as well as good writing.

Andrews, Roy Chapman, *Heart of Asia* (Duell, 1951). Adventures in the Far East. Exciting, easy reading.

Beebe, Lucius, *Mixed Train Daily* (Dutton, 1947). Entertaining essays about the little one-train-a-day railroads of the United States.

Beerbohm, Max, *Observations* (Doubleday, 1925). Beerbohm was a close friend of Chesterton and a gifted satirist. Pleasant, stimulating reading.

Bemelmans, Ludwig, *Father, Dear Father* (Viking, 1953). A delightful tour of Europe by the writer, his daughter, and her poodle. Very entertaining reading.

Bowen, Catherine Drinker, *Friends and Fiddlers* (Little, Brown, 1938). The amateur musician will enjoy these sketches of string players good, bad, and indifferent. By the well-known biographer of Oliver Wendell Holmes and John Adams.

Bowen, Elizabeth, *Collected Impressions* (Knopf, 1950). Essays and reviews by one of the best stylists of our time. Not easy reading.

Brooks, Charles S., *Chimney-Pot Papers* (Yale, 1919). Literary essays — informal, genial, highly personal.

Brooks, Van Wyck, *Writer in America* (Dutton, 1953). Seven essays about life and letters. Not very easy reading, but rewarding.

Brown, Rollo Walter, *I Travel by Train* (Appleton, 1939). Very penetrating, well-written essays about the United States during the depression. Interesting contrast to Alistair Cooke's essay in this book.

Buck, Pearl S., *Tell the People* (Day, 1945). Essays about mass education in China by the Nobel Prize-winning novelist.

Burroughs, John, *Birds and Bees* (Houghton, n.d.). The great American classic in the field of natural science.

Bush, Vannevar, *Modern Arms and Free Men* (Simon and Schuster, 1949). Hard-hitting discussions of the United States in an atom-bomb world, by a leading physicist. Not easy reading.

Carlyle, Thomas, *Heroes and Hero-Worship* (Everyman, 1934). Scholarly work on history by one of England's great prose writers.

Ceram, C. W., *Gods, Graves and Scholars* (Knopf, 1951). Fascinating accounts of the great archaeologists, their guesses, and their discoveries.

Chase, Mary Ellen, *The Goodly Heritage* (Holt, 1932). Essays on education, by a gifted novelist and teacher.

Chesterton, G. K., *A Handful of Authors* (Sheed and Ward, 1953). A new collection of critical essays.

Conant, James B., *Education and Liberty* (Harvard, 1953). Essays about the place of schools in a democracy, by the former president of Harvard.

Conrad, Joseph, *The Mirror of the Sea* (Doubleday, 1906). Essays about ships and the men who sailed them, by a sailor who became one of England's great novelists.

De Quincey, Thomas, *Confessions of an English Opium Eater* (Everyman, 1930). De Quincey, a contemporary of Lamb, is one of the best prose stylists of the nineteenth century. "The Opium Eater" and "The English Mail Coach" are among the best.

Douglas, William O., *Strange Lands and Friendly People* (Harper, 1951). Travels in the Near East. Mr. Douglas, a distinguished American statesman, writes sympathetically of many kinds of people. Other books by this writer are equally good.

Gallico, Paul, *Farewell to Sport* (Knopf, 1938). Essays by a sports writer who became so disgusted with some of the unpleasant aspects of professional sports that he quit sports and became a novelist. Acid, well-written comments.

Gibbings, Robert, *Coming down the Seine* (Dutton, 1953). Brilliantly written, clever travel book. Compare with Stevenson's *An Inland Voyage*.

Goldsmith, Oliver, *The Citizen of the World* (Everyman, n.d.). Delightful informal essays in which a fictional Chinese gentleman comments upon English manners and customs in the eighteenth century.

Hand, Learned, *The Spirit of Liberty* (Knopf, 1953). An inspiring book on the meaning of America's freedom. Every high school senior should read it.

Hayakawa, S. I., *Language in Thought and Action* (Harcourt, Brace, 1949). The book is a brilliant, often humorous study of human thought as revealed in language.

Hazlitt, William, *Essays* (Oxford, 1904, and other editions).

Hazlitt is one of the great nineteenth-century English essayists and perhaps England's greatest critic. His work is not easy reading, but many students will enjoy such things as "Table Talk."

Hearn, Lafcadio, *Out of the East* (Houghton, 1895).

——, *Two Years in the French West Indies* (Houghton, 1890). The descriptive essay at its best, by a sensitive writer of Greek-Irish and Japanese background.

Hemingway, Ernest, *Death in the Afternoon* (Scribner, 1932). Essays about bull fighting, fascinating in detail and beautifully written. For the mature reader.

Highet, Gilbert, *People, Places, and Books* (Oxford, 1953). Radio essays on many subjects by a professor of Latin at Columbia University. Point of view and style are original.

Holbrook, Stewart, *The Age of the Moguls* (Doubleday, 1953). Entertaining essays about America's tycoons.

Holmes, Oliver Wendell, *The Autocrat of the Breakfast Table* (Houghton, n.d.). Conversational essays on a variety of subjects. The conversation goes every which way and is often disconnected, but reveals an original and humorous mind.

Huxley, T. H., *On a Piece of Chalk, and Other Essays* (Macmillan, 1929). The title essay is amazing, in both scope and style. A good companion-piece to "The Long Snowfall."

Kazin, Alfred, *A Walker in the City* (Harcourt, Brace, 1951). A boyhood in the New York slums. Brilliant writing.

Liebling, A. J., *The Wayward Pressman* (Doubleday, 1947). Miscellaneous essays, mostly from the *New Yorker*. Very pleasant, satiric writing.

Lindbergh, Charles A., *The Spirit of St. Louis* (Scribner, 1953). A brilliant autobiography of a great aviator. One of the best books of its kind.

Lucas, E. V., *Selected Essays* (Methuen, 1933). Humorous, personal essays by an English writer who has been called the most successful essayist since Stevenson.

Macaulay, T. B., *Critical and Historical Essays* (Everyman, n.d.). Another of the great Victorian writers — historian, poet, essayist. His essay on Johnson, in the *Encyclopedia Britannica*, is famous. Other essays are equally good, in spite of a somewhat ponderous style.

Mencken, H. L., *A Mencken Chrestomathy* (Knopf, 1949). This collection by Mencken of his own favorite writings is delightful reading. Subjects range from sports to morals, to the theater, to the essayist's pet hates. Brilliant style.

Newton, A. E., *The Amenities of Book-Collecting* (Little, 1918). Essays about great books by a collector who loved every page of every rare volume he owned — and he owned a lot of them.

O'Casey, Sean, *I Knock at the Door* (Macmillan, 1939). The first volume of one of the most wonderful autobiographies ever written. Much humor and much bitterness appear as the author describes his childhood in the slums of Dublin.

Orwell, George, *Shooting an Elephant* (Harcourt, Brace, 1950).

———, *Such, Such Were the Joys* (Harcourt, Brace, 1953). Two volumes by the author of *1984*. Orwell's essays reveal a style better than that in his novels. A profound point of view makes these books ideal for the mature reader. All sorts of subjects are treated.

Perelman, S. J., *The Best of S. J. Perelman* (Modern Library, 1946). Zany humor. Sophisticated, very funny essays on many topics.

Perry, Bliss, *Pools and Ripples* (Little, 1927). Three completely delightful essays about fishing for trout and salmon by a Harvard professor of English.

Phelps, William Lyon, *What I Like* (Scribner, 1933). Light critical essays by a great teacher, a professor for many years at Yale.

Plato, *Dialogues* (many editions). Try first the "Apology," an eloquent description of the death of Socrates.

Poe, E. A., *Selected Prose and Poetry* (Rinehart, 1950). This volume includes some of Poe's essays on the art of writing. Important in the history of our literature; brilliant, biased, hard reading.

Ruskin, John, *Selections and Essays* (Scribner, 1916). Brilliant, somewhat difficult essays about art and allied subjects.

Santayana, George, *Soliloquies in England* (Scribner, 1922). Essays on many subjects by the great Spanish-born American philosopher. Much wisdom and beauty are here.

Schweitzer, Albert, *Out of My Life and Thought* (Holt, 1949). An autobiographical essay almost without peer in modern literature. Schweitzer — doctor, musician, writer, missionary — has been called the greatest man in the world.

Skinner, Cornelia Otis, *Excuse It, Please* (Dodd, 1936). Humorous sketches about many subjects, from horse shows to hiring a maid. Other books by this writer are equally entertaining.

Smith, Logan P., *All Trivia* (Harcourt, Brace, 1934). Short essays, many in a light vein, by a Philadelphia Quaker who became editor of the Manchester *Guardian*. These sketches are worth thoughtful reading.

Saint-Exupéry, Antoine De, *Wind, Sand, and Stars* (Reynal, 1939).

———, *Flight to Arras* (Reynal, 1942). Perhaps the best books ever written about flying. *Flight to Arras* is a wonderful book about the modern pilot's emotions concerning war and the death of his country. Poetic, beautiful prose.

Strunsky, Simeon, *No Mean City* (Dutton, 1944). Essays about New York City by a *Times* man who knew the city well and who could write eloquently about the New York miracle. People who do not live in New York will enjoy the book too.

Thoreau, Henry D., *The Portable Thoreau* (Viking, 1947). This book is included here because it is a good collection of Thoreau's writings, not easily found in any other single volume.

Tomlinson, H. M., *The Sea and the Jungle* (Everyman, 1928). Sketches of life in Brazil and on a British tramp steamer. The poetic style of these essays is almost indescribable.

van Dyke, Henry, *Fisherman's Luck* (Scribner, 1910). Graceful essays on fishing and many related topics.

Walton, Isaac, *The Compleat Angler* (Modern Library, 1936). The most famous essays about fishing. No sportsman should be without it: it has lasted well for about three hundred years.

Wechsler, James A., *The Age of Suspicion* (Random, 1953). Thoughtful autobiography of a newspaperman who speaks out strongly for freedom. Good for comparison with Cousins, Lippmann, and others.

White, Stewart Edward, *The Cabin* (Doubleday, 1911).

———, *The Forest* (Doubleday, 1922). Two books of readable essays about the outdoors by an expert.

Woollcott, Alexander, *While Rome Burns* (Grosset, 1934). Entertaining essays on many topics, from drama to murder. Original point of view; easy reading.